Learning and Memory

For my wife, Debbie, and my sons, Oliver and Linus,
and my parents, Jerry and Bari

Sara Miller McCune founded SAGE Publishing in 1965 to support the dissemination of usable knowledge and educate a global community. SAGE publishes more than 1000 journals and over 800 new books each year, spanning a wide range of subject areas. Our growing selection of library products includes archives, data, case studies and video. SAGE remains majority owned by our founder and after her lifetime will become owned by a charitable trust that secures the company's continued independence.

Los Angeles | London | New Delhi | Singapore | Washington DC | Melbourne

Learning and Memory

Darrell Rudmann
Shawnee State University

Los Angeles | London | New Delhi
Singapore | Washington DC | Melbourne

FOR INFORMATION:

SAGE Publications, Inc.
2455 Teller Road
Thousand Oaks, California 91320
E-mail: order@sagepub.com

SAGE Publications Ltd.
1 Oliver's Yard
55 City Road
London EC1Y 1SP
United Kingdom

SAGE Publications India Pvt. Ltd.
B 1/I 1 Mohan Cooperative Industrial Area
Mathura Road, New Delhi 110 044
India

SAGE Publications Asia-Pacific Pte. Ltd.
3 Church Street
#10–04 Samsung Hub
Singapore 049483

Acquisitions Editor: Abbie Rickard
Editorial Assistant: Jennifer Cline
Marketing Manager: Katherine Hepburn
Production Editor: Veronica Stapleton Hooper
Copy Editor: Ellen Howard
Typesetter: C&M Digitals (P) Ltd.
Proofreader: Dennis W. Webb
Indexer: Karen Wiley
Cover Designer: Anupama Krishnan

Printed in the United States of America

Library of Congress Cataloging-in-Publication Data

Names: Rudmann, Darrell S., author.

Title: Learning and memory / Darrell Rudmann, Shawnee State University.

Description: First Edition. | Thousand Oaks : SAGE Publications, [2017] | Includes bibliographical references and index.

Identifiers: LCCN 2017026480 | ISBN 9781483374833 (pbk. : alk. paper)

Subjects: LCSH: Learning, Psychology of. | Memory. | Neuropsychology.

Classification: LCC BF318 .R73 2017 | DDC 153.1/5—dc23
LC record available at https://lccn.loc.gov/2017026480

This book is printed on acid-free paper.

17 18 19 20 21 10 9 8 7 6 5 4 3 2 1

Contents

PART I: LEARNING 73

4 Behavioral Learning 75

5 Social Learning 107

6 Affect and Motivation in Learning 131

7 Cognitive Learning 157

PART II: MEMORY 187

8 Retrieval 189

9 Episodic and Autobiographical Memories 217

10 Semantic Memory 245

11   Forgetting   271

PART III: ADVANCED TOPICS   303

12   Learning and Memory in the Real World   305

Preface

The study of human learning and memory is a remarkably complex area of study. It lies at the intersection of nearly all human activity, both those actions we are consciously aware of as well as those we are not. Experimental psychologists have investigated human learning for the past one hundred years and, over time, have developed a number of theoretical approaches to try to capture the complexities of human learning. Some of the theoretical approaches resulted in radical changes within the field itself, altering how psychologists explain milestones in child development, what managerial techniques work best, whether we should trust our confidence in our own memories, and how to train your dog. Now, modern brain imaging brings another perspective to both back up and refute those theories that had been based primarily on behavioral research. My purpose in writing this textbook is to provide the reader with an understanding of the core concepts that are foundational to the study of human learning and memory.

This textbook is for students who are relatively new to psychological science, and it provides a broad survey of the major theoretical perspectives of learning and memory. Instead of focusing solely on older learning theory or only on contemporary memory research, this text includes classic behaviorist theories of learning, social learning theories, theories of emotion and motivation in learning, modern cognitive theories of learning and memory, and the neurological underpinnings of these perspectives. I have developed an approach that I believe clearly juxtaposes the different theoretical approaches in a modern way.

This textbook is most appropriate for courses that bridge learning and memory, such as "Psychology of Learning and Memory," and is the textbook I have been trying to find for my own learning and memory course. It is written primarily for students who have had perhaps one introductory course in psychology. The text could be used as a core or supplementary text for graduate courses in education (educational leadership, school psychology, curriculum and instruction programs), or for graduate health sciences courses with a need for a resource on psychological theories on learning and memory in development.

To help the student and the instructor with the myriad of important concepts and theories to cover, each chapter includes an outline, a short set of learning objectives, overview and summary sections, review questions, related resources, and references. Whenever possible, I provide descriptions of classic and modern research mixed with real-life stories that illustrate applications of the concepts and theories. For instructors, I have prepared a set of slides with artwork from the book, a test bank of multiple-choice questions to pull from, and suggested activities and lecture extenders for each chapter.

> "Memory is not what is recorded but what we remember."
>
> —Octavio Paz

Acknowledgments

I must acknowledge the help and encouragement I have received from editors Reid Hester, Abbie Rickard, and Veronica Stapleton Hooper of SAGE Publications and copy editor Ellen Howard. Several years of work resulted from a fairly innocent question

I had asked Reid about an out-of-print text, and not once have I felt their support for this project waiver. I would also like to thank the following undergraduates for helping me develop supplemental material and activities:

Lauren Beam

Jessica Hilterbrand

Trever Jacks

Jade Lightle

Victoria McDowell

L. Catherine Smith

Jordan Zweigart

I am thankful for Tess Collier, a Shawnee State University librarian and my article wrassler. I'm also thankful for the anonymous reviewers who provided feedback on what were some pretty awful drafts. I attempted to incorporate every comment that I could, and the improvement overall was substantial.

I would also like to thank the following reviewers for their feedback and contributions to the manuscript:

Vivian C. Hsu, PhD, Penn State University Abington

Jennifer A. Joy-Gaba, Virginia Commonwealth University

Any errors remaining in the text are mine alone. You're more than welcome to let me know what improvements you would like to see in future editions at drudmann@shawnee.edu.

About the Author

Darrell Rudmann earned his PhD in 2005 from the University of Illinois in Educational Psychology with a concentration in Learning and Instruction. Since 1996, he has taught undergraduate psychology courses at several open-access institutions (Parkland Community College, Champaign, Illinois; Indiana University East in Richmond, Indiana; Shawnee State University, Portsmouth, Ohio). He is currently an Associate Professor at Shawnee State University and Chair of the Social Sciences Department.

History of Learning and Memory

Chapter Outline

Learning Objectives

1. Identify the contributions of philosophers to the early study of learning and memory.
2. Understand the basic assumptions of behaviorism.
3. Summarize the major contemporary approaches to the study of learning and memory.
4. Describe the six themes of the textbook.

Overview

Our ability to learn and store what we have learned is a remarkably important capability, pervasive to nearly every aspect of our lives. Consider the following "thought experiment": imagine you had the opportunity to have the vacation of your dreams but would never remember it, or you could have the memory of the vacation but would not have taken the trip at all. Which would you select? Most of us are initially pulled in the direction of wanting the trip but having no memory of it—but, of course, you can see the problem. Having no memory of the trip means the trip will have no influence on us afterwards. No happy memories, no feeling of satisfaction, no photos or videos to share. In fact, we'd probably still be pining to take that trip—the very one we had already had—because we would've forgotten we'd already taken it! It may be counter-intuitive now, but having a memory of the trip, even if a false one, could likely have a larger impact on us than a forgotten journey.

"Buddy O'Dell"

As a young man, my grandfather Delor "Bud" Benoit was a professional boxer who went by the show name "Buddy O'Dell," although he was not Irish (see Fig. 1.1). He credited the violin lessons he was made to take as a child for his early boxing experience—he had to fight off bullies as he was walking to and from lessons while protecting his violin. He fought Jake La Motta in 1942 and lost in a close decision. His boxing experience left him with occasional vision problems, but he was otherwise in very good health. While serving as Seaman Specialist in the US Navy in World War II, his ship, the USS Princeton, was hit by a 500-pound bomb from a Japanese dive bomber. Despite his dislocated shoulder from the blast, he was able to tie a lifeline around a wounded crewmate and lower his body down a stairwell before a lieutenant encouraged Bud to jump off the deck into the ocean. The Princeton continued to burn and secondary explosions began, taking more lives, until rescuing destroyers had to sink it.

Bud was a serious poker player, and (as the family legend goes) he would sometimes travel to Las Vegas and gamble until he had enough money to pay the rent. He was always a smooth, easygoing talker who seemed to be able to hold a conversation with anyone; maybe it was the result of his blue-collar upbringing plus his university experience at Michigan State University on a boxing scholarship. He eventually earned a JD, and spent his career doing administrative work for State Farm Insurance.

Today he is 91 years old and living in a monitored group home for seniors. His health has always been exceptionally good, but gradual

FIGURE 1.1   **Bud's boxing days**

changes to his memory had started to occur. The loss of his memory meant not keeping up with basic home cleanliness. He kept firing the cleaning service his adult daughter (my mother) would hire for him, telling them he could take care of it himself. His dogs would eliminate about anywhere, and he would not remember to clean up after them. His stove had to be replaced after the family found a nest of rats living in the back of it. He came to believe he didn't have enough money to get by, even though he was fairly well off. But he didn't remember. Eventually, scam artists and occasionally his bank would take advantage of his inability to remember his money situation. At one point, family members had to camp outside his house to scare off a woman coming to collect a large sum of money he had promised her as down payment for some future return investment (similar to that Nigerian prince email scam, except that criminals were physically at your home!).

The decision to move Bud from his long-term home was not an easy one for my mother. Even though he adapted to his new surroundings fairly well, he repeatedly asked to return to his old home, since that's what he remembered as his. He once talked a hospital shuttle driver into taking him there instead of his group home. It had been emptied months earlier, and he had no key to get in. By now, despite his acumen for talking people into doing what he wanted, he no longer remembered or recognized family members, including my mother. It's been this way for some time. The loss of memory begins to take away who one was, after a while, and adjusting to new circumstances is difficult.

Recently, my mother arrived at the group home, and Bud met her at the door. He knew her name, and asked her to come in and sit. Once seated, he turned to her and said, "All right. What am I doing here?" In the conversation that followed, my mother and her father had a very lucid conversation about what had been happening to him over the past few years and the decisions that had been made to that point. She explained. He apologized for the trouble he had caused.

It was not to last. By the next visit, he was back to not remembering. He has adjusted to his new home and seems happy, but he remembers little. It is as if, somewhere under the memory loss and likely brain decay, the person I know as my grandfather is still there, unable to get out (see Fig. 1.2).

FIGURE 1.2   A recent photo of Bud

This has become a common story. Many families, particularly those with long-living parents, are running into events like these. While the physical form of the person is still present, and often their habits and even personality remain intact, the loss of memory is catastrophic for individual functioning. The "remembering power" of the brain is so beneficial that its loss is extremely noticeable.

In this book, we will explore what it means to learn and to know. We will explore the vast amount of research on learning and the kinds of memory, the amazing diversity of activities that memory supports, and what happens when memory fails us. My goal is to convince you that, ultimately, we are what we learn and remember. Much of who we are and who we believe ourselves to be is determined not by what precisely has happened to us, but by what we remember of what has happened to us and the stories we believe those remembrances tell. To start our in-depth study of memory, let's examine where the field of study on learning and memory has been and where it is today. We'll start with classic philosophical approaches and then move to more recent, contemporary approaches.

Early Philosophical Approaches

It's understandable to question whether it is worth looking back to earlier centuries to understand what we do today. It doesn't always feel relevant, and instead is like rehashing the past. In this situation though, questions about learning, memory, and the nature of knowledge reach back a long ways. Prior to psychological science, the nature of mind and memory were exclusively in the domain of philosophy and theology. In many cases, the general ideas that philosophers had about learning and memory are still represented in modern theories. So, while delving so far into the past can seem like a detour, what you will find in this section are ideas and relationships that are prescientific, but are around to this day. Having a basic understanding of these ideas will prepare you for the modern research and theory we'll encounter in the next chapters.

Socrates's Early Functionalism

The Greek philosopher Socrates (469–388 BCE) noted that many objects could be grouped together as "instances" of the same idea even if they do not look alike, such as different chairs. The physical, surface features were not always what mattered. He suggested that objects in our memory are based on their functions. That is, objects in memory are stored by the potential function that they may serve. For example, the diversity in what people consider to be "cars" is rather large, but it doesn't seem to take us long to add new models we encounter into a "car" category. Socrates's idea about this conceptualization of how memory for objects works allows that what we remember and know about the world isn't constrained by the physical or material aspects of the real-world objects. Thus, whether a coffee mug is made of ceramic or plastic or steel is irrelevant to our being able to remember what a coffee mug is and to recognize one. Using Socrates's conceptualization of knowledge, one can also recognize a coffee mug as a mug even if it is cracked or chipped. This "functional" approach to explaining how we know what objects are is an approach that is still around today.

Aristotle's Associationism

The Greek philosopher Aristotle (364–323 BCE; see Fig. 1.3) intuited a number of the issues and approaches that were later developed by other philosophers and psychologists.

FIGURE 1.3 Aristotle

© Marie-Lan Nguyen/Wikimedia Commons

He based at least some of his intuitions on the theories of his teacher, Plato (427–347 BCE), who had used various metaphors to try to capture the nature of human memory. Plato had described memory as being like wax, on which impressions could be made. He noted that some people were better at recording memories than others. For some people, it was as if their wax was less pliable. This is an observation that psychologists now often call a matter of "individual differences."

Likewise, Aristotle noted that memory is not particularly static or frozen, but could move; it has a relatively fluid nature. Thinking of one thing can cause one to think of or remember something else. Aristotle proposed that this fluid process of thinking and remembering obeyed a set of rules such as similarity, contiguity, and causal properties. For instance, remembering one event can remind us of another similar event, hence the term "similarity." We encounter this often in daily life. Thinking of one embarrassing moment makes other related moments seem to come to mind quite readily. Our memories appear to be highly interconnected based on similarity.

Aristotle noted that we tend to associate those events or objects that occur together frequently, which he called his rule of contiguity. Experiencing two events together enough, and we form a connection between them in memory. We associate applause with acknowledgement of a stellar performance. All of marketing is based on this rule: I might like eating cheeseburgers, but with lots of exposure to marketing through billboards and commercials, I have come to associate a large yellow "M" with cheeseburgers.

When we experience an event that reliably produces a certain outcome, we will recall that outcome. This is Aristotle's rule of causal properties. Instead of learning a simple association between two events, we can decide that one event is causing the other. An infant in a high chair playing with toy keys might be delighted by the sound of dropping the toy keys on the floor (and watching family scurry to pick the toy up). After a while, the infant will become less interested. At that point, the infant presumably can recall the outcome and is less surprised or interested in it.

Aristotle also intuited that memory is similar to searching for information—much like clicking around on web pages from the Internet, following from one site to another, following a path between memories. He also believed that concepts were arranged mentally in a hierarchy. That is, there are classes of concepts arranged in levels: some concepts embody a great many other objects, like "furniture," whereas others are of a lower level and are more specific, like "side-table drawer."

In summary, Socrates and Aristotle posited ideas that are foundational to the field today. These include Socrates's idea that the function of what objects do might be what constitutes our knowledge of them, and Aristotle's claim that there are different mechanisms for learning.

Descartes's Dualism

The French philosopher Rene Descartes (1596–1650; see Fig. 1.4) believed that at least some knowledge was innate, that is, with us from birth. In particular, he believed certain abstract concepts could not be sensed directly. For instance, he believed that there is an innate idea of "perfection," and that a supernatural being, "God," embodies all aspects of perfection. He also believed that other abstract concepts we possess—such as time, hope, and infinity—could not be experienced through the senses and, as a result, were most likely innate. Some of these ideas may have been simply capitulations to the powerful Catholic Church system that was present at the time; but other concepts that Descartes believed could not be experienced through the senses, so they had to be internally based.

FIGURE 1.4   **Rene Descartes**

©iStockphoto.com/GeorgiosArt

Hence, he believed that what we sense of the world around us is largely accurate, since our minds have a sense of what perfection is, as well as an understanding of the perfection of the God who created the world.

Descartes famously posited that one could make a distinction between the "mind" and the "body," the physical support for mental activity. He concluded that the human body interacted with an immaterial soul somewhere in the brain. Neuropsychology, the study of the workings of the brain and nervous system, is commonly based on prior damage from disease or injury and has a long history that began during this time.

Descartes was a pioneer in his understanding of the mechanical nature of physiology that human and animal bodies function like a kind of machine. During Descartes's time, theory and research into the anatomy began in earnest, mostly through the dissection of animals. The belief that some element of God was embodied in humans did not extend to animals, who were thought not to possess a soul or a consciousness. As a result, animals were primarily thought of as "automata," or machines. This belief was not uncommon in that time. This led to a rise in animal research, primarily to understand the mechanics of physiology and anatomy. Unfortunately, this does mean that little thought or concern was given to the animals that were dissected and cut open, often while awake, during a time when there were no anesthetics.

Locke's *Tabula Rasa*

John Locke, a British philosopher, disagreed with multiple aspects of Descartes's stance on the innateness of ideas (see Fig. 1.5). In contrast to Descartes, Locke (1632–1704) believed all human knowledge comes from experience with the world around us. At birth, we are devoid of ideas—a *tabula rasa*, or blank slate. The mind has two kinds of experiences of the world: sensations of objects and those reflections we have upon our own ideas. We have these impressions immediately in the conscious mind and can recall them later as memories. Locke believed that the same mechanistic approach used to explain

FIGURE 1.5   John Locke

©iStockphoto.com/denisk0

how the human body functions could also be used to explain human thought. In other words, basic or simple ideas could be had by experiencing the world around us—how the sun feels on our skin, or how peanut butter tastes. These simple ideas are like images, are highly sensory in nature, and could not be reduced to any smaller unit of thought since they were just sensory impressions.

If we combine many of these simple ideas or images, they can give rise to more complex ideas, Locke suggested. Experiencing a "book" is the result of a combination of simpler sensory experiences that might involve shape, texture, weight, and temperature. All mental content he believed to be the result of adding different sensory units. The basic view Locke advocated is not terribly different from how a child might build a fairly complex house or space ship from toy building blocks. The simple ideas combined together form more advanced, complex ones. In every instance, however, the idea is made up of sensory elements and is not an abstraction. Locke was not specific about how these ideas were combined or associated, although he clearly believed contiguity and similarity played large roles, as Aristotle had proposed.

So, from Locke's perspective, memories are a copy of earlier sensations. Normal memories, therefore, are fairly accurate since they are a replication of what was experienced. There is an interesting theoretical consequence to this view: If memories are exact copies of direct sensations, then no change or distortion can occur. There can be no misconceptions if memory is simply a copy of a sensory event, like a photocopy made from a copier machine. It is also unclear if memories can have gaps—missing pieces of information—under Locke's approach.

Locke's ideas were extremely influential inside of philosophy. Locke was considered to be an empiricist, meaning one who relies on observation and experimentation to support his or her ideas. His beliefs on empiricism drove much of the developing science of the day. Locke's ideas and approach had an impact on psychology as well. His brand of philosophy, associationism, that learned connections between different ideas and events are the basis for all thought and meaning, was the foundation for a movement in psychology known as "behaviorism" in early 20th century America. We'll discuss behaviorism as a movement in the next major section (p. 11), and Chapter 4 is devoted to a major theory of the movement.

In summary, Descartes and Locke exist in a kind of philosophical chokehold. Descartes proposed the existence of innate knowledge for understanding the world and distinguished between the functions of mental activity and the structure of the physical body. Locke, however, took a hard-line, sensory-only approach to learning and memory.

Kant's Interactionism

German philosopher Immanuel Kant (1724–1804; see Fig. 1.6) provided a compromise between Descartes's and Locke's views, seeing both approaches as partially right and partially wrong. A child doesn't have innate, genetic concepts like "car," or "bottle," or "ball" at birth, Kant reasoned; but the child certainly has the biological underpinnings to form those concepts at the right time. The biological structure may include unconscious reasoning skills (like understanding time and space) that allow the child to form these concepts when he or she is ready to understand and learn them. In what is known as Kant's *interactionism,* mind and body interact and influence each other. In modern terms, this is like having the computer hardware and an operating system to allow software and apps to run on it.

From Kant's perspective, we have the biological capacity to interpret the world around us (e.g., eyes, ears, touch, the nervous system). This means the biological system that

FIGURE 1.6   Immanuel Kant

©iStockphoto.com/ZU_09

makes up the human body grants the ability to form abstract ideas like "ball" when the human is ready. Of course, if people can interpret stimuli in the environment, then that also means people can misinterpret what goes on around them. I'm reminded of my oldest son, who, as a toddler, refused to eat vegetables. I tried to introduce him to vegetable juice through a colored sippy cup. When I handed the cup to him, he saw the dark-colored liquid in the transparent cup. He announced "Chocolate milk!" and—before I could correct him—proceeded to drink. He was immediately disgusted, and I could never get him to try vegetable juice again. Our interpretations of the external world are, on the whole, quite accurate, but not always perfect. This is a distinct advantage to Kant's ideas over Locke's, which didn't permit distortions based on expectations or misunderstandings.

What one knows of the world, according to Kant, is what one can perceive of it. Our knowledge of the world is constructed in a generally accurate way, but it is not a perfect copy. Kant's view also tolerates those gaps in knowledge that develop from time to time, perhaps when someone is distracted or too fatigued. Additionally, Kant expected that when there are gaps in what is learned and remembered, people could make inferences about what should be there. These ideas are still popular within the field today. Kant used the term schema for the abstract knowledge that we mentally form of the external world, and a considerable number of theories have been developed to try to explain the mental structure of the abstract knowledge of the world.

William James's Functionalism

Our last philosopher is, in many ways, at the transition point between philosophy and psychology. Considered to be the founder of American psychology, William James (1842–1910; see Fig. 1.7) wrote one of the most popular textbooks on psychology in his day, although he himself did not like to think of himself as a psychologist. Many of his

FIGURE 1.7   William James

https://commons.wikimedia.org/wiki/File:Wm_james.jpg, {{PD-US}}

topic choices for chapters were prescient of modern topics in psychology despite the coming wave of behaviorism in America. He had a particular view of how people learn that incorporated biological change with development, much like psychologists attempt to do today.

James believed that the nervous system is adaptable and can be modified by experience. Particular motor skills become associated within the nervous system over time as a sequence is learned, so practice is important for learning a particular skill or habit. While he believed the nervous system was flexible, it was so only until age 30. After that, habits become rigid (he was not correct in this regard). Therefore, he believed it was necessary to teach all young people good habits at an early age. He believed that learning the right set of habits could eliminate many social ills, including war, famine, and ugliness. He encouraged all youth to be drafted into the military to develop the necessary habits for later. The idea that learning a particular set of habits will instill a better life is a value many parents encourage in their children, and it is the basis of many self-help books and websites on productivity and happiness.

James was able to clearly define what he meant by a "memory": "knowledge of an event, or a fact which is out of conscious awareness currently," and the awareness "that we have thought or experienced it before" (James, 1890, p. 648). We use memory, according to James, to reproduce those earlier events and facts. These events and facts leave paths or traces between nerve centers in the brain. Experience adds to the traces of a memory and strengthens it.

In summary, Kant and James began the process of modernizing conceptualizations of the act of learning and language around the phenomenon of memory. Kant proposed that the biological structure of the human body gives rise to our mental activities, and that we perceive our world around us and build what we know. James successfully promoted the field through a popular textbook on psychology, which included and defined modern topics such as learning through experience and memory.

For the remainder of this chapter, we'll examine the major movements that have contributed to our understanding of how learning and memory work, beginning with the movement that was inspired by Locke's theories, behaviorism.

A Twentieth-Century Approach: Behaviorism

Locke's ideas had an impact on psychology some time later. The behaviorist movement in psychology began in the early part of the 20th century, lasted well into the 1960s, and primarily occurred in the United States. The name behaviorism was applied to the movement precisely for how it sounds: the study of how people and animals changed their behaviors due to interactions with their environment. It was strictly focused on observable behaviors as part of a desire to make psychology as a field more of a true science. If a behavior was unobservable, it was unmeasurable, and therefore not worth pursuing. This meant that highly popular topics today, such as consciousness, motivation, dreams, personality, thought, and memory, were not considered to be topics that could be successfully researched.

The behaviorists used Locke's ideas of a blank slate and of associations as the bases of thought and reframed them as stimulus-response associations. People form a connection between an event in the environment, like seeing a plate of cooked food, and a response such as hunger. Often the responses of interest were negative emotions: fear, disgust, or anxiety. Behaviorists would not have studied emotions directly, however. Rather, they would have considered them to be merely the words we use to anthropomorphize those situations, at worst, or phenomena that couldn't be studied, at best.

For a major part of the 20th century, research into the mental aspects of the human experience were set aside as American psychologists focused primarily on systems of stimulus-response associations through reinforcements and punishments, with a heavy focus on refining research methodology (primarily through experimentation). While many of the findings that came out of this period have been abandoned as psychology moved on, the techniques for rigorous research design have not been left behind. Behaviorist theories are still applied in a variety of situations, including advertising and marketing, animal training, classroom management, and in therapeutic settings. We'll take a closer look at behaviorists and their approach to learning in Chapter 4.

Contemporary Approaches

Besides the behaviorist tradition, there are three main approaches to the study of learning and memory today. By the 1970s, a renewed interest within American psychology on mental activities meant a shift in focus away from strict behaviorism. First, psychologists took a greater concern for how the social situation affects how we learn. Social learning theory (sometimes referred to as social cognitive theory) was developed to describe how people learn by watching what happens to others and by imitating the successes others have. The expectations people form for themselves became of interest, since they affect how much effort people will put into an activity.

Second, psychologists began to reconsider whether abstract, unobservable human activities like thought, memory, and attention could be systematically studied after all. Cognitive psychology is the study of higher mental activities, such as attention, memory, and thinking.

Finally, technological advances to enable imaging the brain and its functions have led to a greater understanding of the physical basis underlying learning and memory, or cognitive neuroscience. Cognitive neuroscience has the benefit of not necessarily requiring subjects who have suffered brain injury in order to be studied, as neuropsychology often does. For just the practical implications of being able to use healthy subjects alone, cognitive neuroscience has generated a lot of excitement for its scientific potential. Because it's important to be able to see where the distinctions between each approach lie, let's take a closer look at each approach.

Social Learning

Social theories of learning advanced past behaviorism by including those aspects of learning that involve the presence of other people, whether real or imagined. For example, social comparison is the act of comparing how we performed to the performance of others. From a strict behaviorist perspective, how others perform shouldn't affect our learning, but often it does. When the first exam scores of a class are handed out, people will, sometimes quite surreptitiously, find a way to see how they did in relation to other students. The comparison shouldn't really matter, but it often does. If everyone received a high score, then your score isn't as revealing about your mastery of the material or your capabilities in that area—it just shows that as a whole, everyone understands the material similarly. On the other hand, if you were the highest or lowest scorer in the class, that tells you something about your situation as well.

A sense of fairness or equity can be quite important in situations in which we are evaluated too. Did the students who put in a lot of time and effort on an assignment tend to earn higher scores than those students who did not? Or do the results appear to be independent of the effort people put in? Both situations send a message about the class.

Expectations also play a large role in motivation to learn and remember. When a parent promises a reward to a child for earning high grades and then reneges on the arrangement later, claiming to have forgotten, this broken promise is remembered. How will the child respond to the next promise? How about a younger sibling, who has watched this exchange play out? When people form expectations about the time and effort involved in doing a task, they examine the outcome with a critical eye to see if it matched what they were hoping for.

One major barrier to learning is the learner's belief about whether or not material can be learned at all. Our self-efficacy for the activity, the belief we have about our own ability to perform a task, is highly predictive of whether we will attempt the task, how hard we will persist, and how creative we are at completing it (Pajares & Urdan, 2006). If someone does not believe he or she can accomplish a particular task, then why bother trying?

In sum, social learning theories are those that try to explain human behavior by incorporating not just the component of thought but the social component as well.

Cognitive Psychology

Cognitive psychology is the study of higher mental activities. Cognitive psychology encompasses all psychological research that involves the study of language, attention, acquiring and representing knowledge in the mind, judgment, and decision making. The overarching question of cognitive psychology might be, "How does the mind use information?"

Cognitive psychologists often approach human learning and memory from the perspective of how people process information, information-processing theories, or how people think about their own thinking, called "metacognition." Of particular interest for us is how people try to control their own learning and assess their own memory abilities, a subfield known as *metamemory*.

Information-Processing Theories

A long-standing, fundamental assumption in cognitive psychology is that we can approach the human mind as a high-powered computer, examining its capacity, speed, and abilities in a fairly similar way to how one might talk about technical specification of some hardware for sale in a store. How much can we remember? What helps us to store more information? What helps us to remember, and what gets in our way when we can't? In the past, the information-processing approach was the only option for studying memory in people with normal functioning, since the brain imaging technology simply wasn't developed enough to answer the questions people had. Nowadays this approach often works in tandem with the cognitive neuroscience approach.

Hermann Ebbinghaus (1850–1909) was a pioneer in this approach to mental activity. He took the study of learning and memory from the realm of philosophers and moved it into the realm of psychological science. Adopting an attitude that remains prevalent in psychology today, he explored learning and memory by collecting data on how well people can perform a task, instead of solely theorizing about it. Ebbinghaus's methods are fairly simple by today's standards, but his approach was thorough enough that his results provided insights that are still talked about today. Briefly, Ebbinghaus used lists of "nonsense syllables" in a consonant-vowel-consonant pattern as the stimuli to memorize and try to recall later, such as CEG, TIB, and PAH (Ebbinghaus, 1885/1964). He would monitor how many tries it took to learn a list of nonsense syllables and quiz himself over a period of days to track his forgetting. We'll return to Ebbinghaus and his work in Chapter 7.

Today, modern memory researchers often rely on three key functions or processes to describe aspects of human memory (see Fig. 1.8). Encoding is the act of sensing some stimuli in our environment, like light or sound, and extracting the meaning from it in your mind. An example is sensing the shape, color, and texture of an object in a parking lot and then realizing that it is a car that is moving toward you too quickly to be safe. Encoding is a critical process if we are encountering something for the first time. Storing is the act of retaining information for a period of time. The information can come in many forms, including images, knowledge, impressions, and feelings. The duration of time can be relatively short, such as a second or two, or it could be a lifetime. As we move forward through this book, we will encounter many instances of memory researchers attempting to study what kinds of information we store, where in the brain, and how the information is organized in the mind. Retrieval is the act of attempting to remember some information. Often researchers are interested in trying to understand why some memories are easily recalled, whereas other memories are not. Often researchers will use the word *cues* for those hints that we use to try to retrieve a particular memory, like the search term we might enter into a search engine to find a website.

FIGURE 1.8   The three key processes

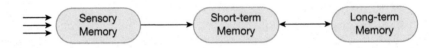

FIGURE 1.9   Diagram of basic Atkinson-Shiffrin model

So, when watching a movie for the first time, we can expect a fair amount of encoding the characters and the plot of the movie, and storing the parts that really caught our attention. Later, we can retrieve some of that information when a friend asks what the movie was like. If these three processes sound like using a computer—that is, entering information, saving a document, and later, opening the file again—that's by design. This analogy of the mind as a computer has been a tremendous benefit to memory research and has stimulated much work and theory over the past few decades.

One particular model of how human memory works emerged from verbal learning research in the 1960's and became so well known that it has been called the "modal" model of memory, meaning the most commonly talked about and referenced. While it is not an active focus of research today, the terms used in this model are now a part of our cultural vernacular. The *Atkinson-Shiffrin model* (Atkinson & Shiffrin, 1968; see Fig. 1.9), named after the people who described it, claims that memory for some stimulus or information will reside in one of three states: a sensory buffer, a short-term memory store, or long-term memory. The sensory buffer is essentially the beginning of the encoding process as a person registers some stimulus within his or her sense systems, such as a voice, and the information is briefly held. Should attention be given to that particular sensation, it will move into what was called short-term memory, where it can be kept mentally active for as long as desired by continually thinking about it. Finally, with enough continual thinking, it could end up being stored for a long period of time, in long-term memory.

Besides its general popularity, the Atkinson-Shiffrin model is a good example of many information-processing theories. First, information is assumed to pass through stages, sequentially. Additionally, these theories may not necessarily be expected or required to have direct mapping onto parts of the brain. These kinds of models are meant to be diagrams of abstract functioning that people seem to do when they think. Of primary interest to cognitive psychologists is what information a person uses when he or she wrestles with an important decision. The mechanics of brain functioning are usually of secondary interest.

The Atkinson-Shiffrin model is still a useful framework for talking about human memory in broad terms. Most, if not all, modern research today targets particular memory phenomena more specifically than this model. Essentially, the field has incorporated it and moved beyond it.

Metamemory Awareness and Strategies

Metamemory is part of an area in cognitive psychology called metacognition, or thinking about one's own thinking. Metamemory includes the acts of knowing what our strengths are for learning and remembering and strategies we might use to help us study. It includes knowing when to stop studying material because we have learned something well enough, as well as when to stop because of frustration. It is an activity we do all the time, yet we may not realize it. Mental activities such as deciding whether we are better at spelling than grammar, or that to study for a history quiz you need to make flashcards, or that you might have to email the professor to ask for more time on your paper are all examples of thinking about your own thinking in order to decide what to do next. Whenever we are making judgments about different strategies we could use for handling a situation or problem, we are thinking metacognitively.

Miller, Galanter, and Pribram's (1960) test-operate-test-exit model (TOTE) was the model of metacognition that broke cleanly away from behaviorist approaches to learning and remembering. Behaviorists had assumed that learning was primarily a matter of learning a particular response to some external stimulus; little or no evaluation or thought was required on the part of the individual at all. The TOTE model claims that what people do when engaging in an activity is to see whether the situation is currently what we want (a "test"), then make a change ("operate"), check again to see if we have arrived at the goal state (another "test"), and if so, leave this process ("exit"). This is repeated as long as necessary. For example, when using an automatic car wash, the act of driving the car to the right spot within the facility (where the front tires stop at the bumper and the electric signs change to a red "STOP") requires some monitoring: "Am I there yet? How about now?" TOTE models metacognitive activity. It's easy to imagine how the TOTE model might be used while learning. "Do I understand this chapter?" or "How much of this to I need to memorize?" or "What really are the main points of this section?" are all metacognitive questions relating to memory and are metamemory questions.

Flavell, Friedrichs, and Hoyt coined the term "metamemory" in 1970. Research questions for metamemory studies include investigating people's confidence for learning material. Are we ever too confident? What strategies, if any, do people use to remember important information? How does our ability to judge our memories change from childhood, to adulthood, to old age? Any time you talk to other students about strategies for succeeding in a particular class or for a particular assignment, metamemory is involved.

Cognitive Neuroscience

Research into the mechanics of the brain and nervous system, essentially the hardware that "runs" the human mind, has continued well past the techniques Descartes used. Instead of exclusively relying on patients or animals who had suffered injuries, researchers can now take images of the brain in action. Neuroscientists study the brain at the cellular and molecular levels in order to describe theoretical, metabolic structures of the brain that give rise to different brain functions. Neuroscientists focus on (1) neurons, the primary building blocks of the central nervous system; (2) the gaps between the neurons; and (3) the chemicals that are used to facilitate communication between neurons.

Neuroscientists use a variety of techniques. The use of neuroimaging to see the brain as it operates is relatively new, but it has much potential for altering the course of study for learning and memory research. Sometimes neuroscientists will activate single neurons to study how they behave, a technique called single-cell recording—although usually their focus is on how groups of neurons work together. In some studies, mind-altering drugs are used to study how neurons communicate across synapses.

Integrating the Approaches

A major challenge for psychologists and neuroscientists has been attempting to integrate across fields. Social learning and cognitive psychology research have been mutually reinforcing, since both use behavioral assessments for data, and researchers in each area have similar training. Neuroscience and cognitive psychology have been more challenging to integrate, for philosophical and practical reasons, which are discussed next.

Descartes's theorizing about the mind-body problem has had one unexpected ramification. By conceptually splitting the functions of the "mind" from the actions of the "body" and hence the brain, psychologists have pursued describing the mind in their own fashion while cognitive neuroscientists have pursued documenting brain activity in theirs. One major issue stemming from these two focal areas is that cognitive psychologists and neuroscientists tend to have different educational backgrounds and training. This is a broad generalization, but neuroscientists approach the study of the brain from a metabolic "systems" perspective. They are looking to see what the neural underpinnings of mental activities are by identifying where they are housed and how those mental activities are supported. Cognitive psychologists, while interested in the neural basis for their theories, tend to take a "process" approach—looking for theories that focus on how the mind allows people to function. Today, with the ability to image the brain, there is a greater desire to map or connect cognitive models of learning and memory to an underlying neural structure. This has presented new challenges in the incongruence between how the two camps study and theorize about their ideas.

Consider the Atkinson-Shiffrin model of memory stores, described above. This model of cognitive processes behind memory has similarities with other cognitive models (Weldon, 1999). The flow of information through the model is sequential. That is, information works in a stepwise fashion. Information is stored in one stage at a time, and not spread out across different stages simultaneously. Information is transferred from one stage to the next, computationally, as a computer might be programmed to do. This model is primarily constructed to describe at an abstract level the functioning that should be going on in the mind based on behavioral data. No assumptions about the biology underneath the model are claimed.

For a period of time, cognitive neuroscientists were hoping to find one-to-one connections between the models that cognitive psychologists were creating and their own findings. But our understanding of the brain has evolved in the past several decades quickly. While the psychological functioning of the brain can be described in sequential models like the Atkinson-Shiffrin model, the mechanical functioning of the brain itself isn't sequential or as easily compartmentalized as cognitive models tend to be. The brain is a fairly dynamic and interconnected processing machine, which makes finding a neural basis for sequential, stage-like cognitive theories difficult, if not completely impossible.

So, the role that neuroscience plays in psychological science and the relationship between it and cognitive psychology are still being clarified. Perhaps the cognitive psychologists are best at identifying *what* the mind does, and the neuroscientists uncover *how* the brain affords what the mind can do. Some cognitive psychologists believe that the behavioral research that they do must come first, with the neuroscience following it later (Toth & Hunt, 1999).

Overall, neuroscience techniques are contributing to psychological science in three major ways. First, human abilities to learn and remember can be mapped to specific parts of the brain, documenting the mechanisms behind existing theories. Second, neuroscience techniques can provide constraints or limits to existing theories. Using behavioral research, such as experiments, psychologists are relatively free to propose whatever brain functioning they might imagine is operating behind a particular theory. With neuroscience evidence, it's possible to find that a theory is either physically impossible or that the brain is not activating in accordance to the theory, which is fairly strong evidence that

FIGURE 1.10   The four primary approaches to learning, with a biological basis underneath

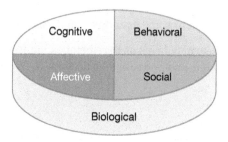

the theory is flawed. Third, neuroscience techniques can be used to generate new theories of human functioning based on patterns of brain activity that existing theory may not have accounted for.

This simple diagram may help clarify matters when thinking about the state of psychological science. There have been four general approaches or "frames" to the study of human and animal behavior in psychology. Psychologists approach human behavior from either behavioral, cognitive, social, or affective perspectives (see Fig. 1.10). Each of these approaches dictates the pertinent variables of interest and occasionally the most preferred kinds of research. There are no firm boundaries between them; each acts as a kind of shorthand for grouping related theories and concepts.

Behavioral approaches to learning focus solely on the actual movements of a learner. Social learning takes into account the presence of others and to whom we give the credit for our learning (ourselves or the situation). Cognitive theories of learning focus entirely on the mental processing that occurs to encode, retain, and retrieve information. Emotions and our motivations play a clear role in learning as well. Underlying each of these approaches, of course, are the biological structures that support the organism's capabilities.

Ultimately, each approach has strengths and limitations to what it can bring to describe and explain the range of activities that make up what we call "learning." In fact, it's not uncommon to see modern theories try to bridge more than one approach, and they will often be called "social-cognitive" or "cognitive-behavioral" theories.

Themes in the Book

These themes will be reoccurring throughout the textbook, and they give an indication of what we will find as we take a closer look at the immense amount of research on learning and memory.

1. There are different kinds of learning (cognitive, behavioral, social), and our emotions and motivations play a role in what we learn and store.

2. We are constantly learning, even when we are not aware of doing so. That is, learning occurs at multiple levels of awareness.

3. The brain is the basis of and gives us several separate memory systems.

4. Complex memories are stored all over the brain, across layers as well, not in any one spot, or even in one system.

5. The human memory system's best trait—learning the gist or "take away" message of an event or some material—can be its biggest weakness.

6. The context of learning helps us to remember, but it can limit our ability to recognize when our knowledge will be useful.

CHAPTER SUMMARY

Philosophers posited a number of ideas that are still with us today. One is the distinction between memories of sensory experiences and abstract ideas. Some philosophers proposed that the purpose or meaning of a particular object, its function, is what defines an object, more than its actual structure. Ideas may be formed through the association or connection of several events or ideas to each other. Descartes was responsible for making the distinction between the mind and the body, a distinction between mental function and physical structure; but it was Kant who reconnected them by explaining how the physical form gives rise to the capabilities for mental abilities and understanding. Locke believed that all knowledge was a combination of sensory experiences in some form; but Kant asserted that we construct our understanding of the

world instead, which means it is an interpretation and can be inaccurate. William James defined memory as knowledge of an event that we currently do not have in conscious awareness, and he used the term "traces" to describe the paths of memories across centers of the brain.

The approaches that will be the focus of this book are: behavioral theories of learning (Chapter 4), social learning theories that examine the role of others (Chapter 5), cognitive learning theories that take either an information-processing approach or metamemory approach (Chapter 7), emotional and motivational influences on learning and memory (Chapter 6), and cognitive neuroscience attempts to account for the biological underpinnings of human learning and memory (Chapter 3).

REVIEW QUESTIONS

1. Of the following philosophers, which do you think were the most far apart in their views about memory? Aristotle, Descartes, Locke.

2. Which of the philosophers seemed to represent the most contemporary view of what you know about learning and memory so far?

3. What is the single defining idea behind "behaviorism" and its approach to learning and memory?

4. How are social learning theories an advance from behaviorism?

5. What is the single defining idea behind an "information-processing" approach to learning and memory?

KEY TERMS

FURTHER RESOURCES

- Weblink: A large collection of materials about and by William James

  o http://www.uky.edu/~eushe2/Pajares/james.html

- Weblink: The William James Society

  o http://society.wjsociety.org

- Weblink: B. F. Skinner, Interviews on YouTube

  o https://www.youtube.com/watch?=xjiXX418MMk&
     list=PL19011A6D1D5C7638&index=8

REFERENCES

Atkinson, R. C., & Shiffrin, R. M. (1968). Human memory: A proposed system and its control processes. In K. W. Spence & J. T. Spence (Eds.), *The psychology of learning and motivation* (Vol. 2, pp. 89–195). Oxford, England: Academic Press. Retrieved from https://doi.org/10.1016/S0079-7421(08)60422-3

Ebbinghaus, H. (1964). *On memory.* New York, NY: Dover. (Original work published 1885)

Flavell, J. H., Friedrichs, A. G., & Hoyt, J. D. (1970). Developmental changes in memorization processes. *Cognitive Psychology, 1,* 324–340.

James, W. (1890). *The principles of psychology* (Vol. 1). New York, NY: Holt.

Miller, G. A., Galanter, E., & Pribram, K. H. (1960). The unit of analysis. In *Plans and the structure of behavior* (pp. 21–39). New York, NY: Holt.

Pajares, F., & Urdan, T. C. (Eds.). (2006). *Self-efficacy beliefs of adolescents.* Information Age Publishing. Retrieved from https://www.amazon.com/Self-Efficacy-Beliefs-Adolescents-Adolescence-Education/dp/1593113668#reader_1593113668

Toth, J. P., & Hunt, R. R. (1999). Not one versus many, but zero versus any: Structure and function in the context of the multiple memory systems debate. In J. K. Foster & M. Jelicic, *Memory: Systems, process, or function?* (pp. 232–272). New York, NY: Oxford University Press.

Weldon, M. S. (1999). The memory chop shop: Issues in the search for memory systems. In J. K. Foster & M. Jelicic, Memory: Systems, process, or function? (pp. 162–204). New York, NY: Oxford University Press.

©iStock.com/andresr

Common Research Methods in Learning and Memory

Chapter Outline

Learning Objectives

1. Identify the common features of learning and memory studies (e.g., performance tasks and performance measurements).

2. Define and distinguish between the three common approaches to the empirical study of learning and memory.

3. Describe the characteristics that can be used to evaluate the quality of a study.

Overview

Today, psychological researchers collect evidence to support their ideas. It's no longer enough to have a belief about how some phenomenon works; the researcher has to conduct some kind of study that carefully examines the acts of learning and memory. In addition, how a researcher goes about collecting data, as well as how the data can be interpreted, are held to high levels of scrutiny. The manner in which a researcher conducted a study should be documented and reported well enough for someone else to replicate. Outside factors that may have altered the data should be either eliminated or controlled, or at least documented. Researchers are expected to interpret the trends in the data they collect quite conservatively, and not to use the data to allege results for which they did not truly have support.

But what is the relevance for looking specifically at research methodology for a student of the field? First, knowing the methodology a field uses tells us a lot about that field itself. Fields are not defined just by their chosen topics of interest, but by the accepted techniques, the tools of the trade. What do the professionals in this field study? How do they usually collect evidence to support their ideas? How do they analyze what they find?

Second, it is wise in our modern society to have some idea of what high quality research in the social sciences should be like. We are bombarded with supposed research "findings," such as "Oreos May Be as Addictive as Cocaine" (Locker, 2013). If true, these study results are a big deal, and might cause people to change how they conduct their lives. For most of our adult lives, we don't have experts on hand who have spent time studying the field and watching trends to put new findings into context. We are largely left on our own to reflect on scientific news reports that will be written by people who may have extensive, minimal, or no research training at all. With easy access to content on the Internet, our exposure to research of variable quality and questionable expert opinion is higher than ever before. It's not unheard of for established media outlets to favor some results over others, or alternatively, for an outlet to favor results that sound outrageous over the normal, routine progress that scientists usually make. So, it's important to know something about what constitutes good social science research just to help us all become more critical of the various "findings" we'll be exposed to by the media, as well as those shared by our friends and colleagues.

Finally, you may find that you need to conduct a study yourself, whether for a class, your program, or for an employer. Many of the kinds of studies we will be discussing in this textbook are relatively inexpensive to conduct. Often it's a matter of carefully thinking through how to go about it. Many classic studies in memory and cognitive psychology are remarkably inexpensive and do not require expensive equipment, but they are important in terms of findings.

In fact, you may find that you need to examine yourself and your own habits at some point: A self-study is never a bad idea. For example, take a moment to consider this question: How many hours (or minutes) a week do you spend studying for your classes? Be honest: Is the number you arrived at an intuition, or can you document it? Which days of the week, typically? Do you distribute your time equally across all subjects? People often vastly overestimate the amount of time they spend on a project. It happens to all of us: Boice (1990) found college professors believe they work an average of 60 hours a week, but their own logs showed it to be an average of 29 hours a week. Self-studies such as keeping a log or diary can be very informative about our real habits and patterns, and can be the first step to improving our lives. They are a kind of research study, one that is conducted with one subject—you.

In this chapter, we'll look at features that are common to virtually all social science studies, and then take a look at some research methods that are unique to learning and memory studies.

Common Features

Nearly every study will involve the participants performing some task and will collect some data about their performances. Let's look at each in turn.

Performance Tasks

The performance task is exactly what it sounds like. The participants are observed doing what they are expected to do, such as reading an essay, studying a list of words, or solving a puzzle. The performance task in a study is usually easy to spot because it is what each participant was asked to do. In the field of learning and memory, often the performance task is to encourage people to learn and remember some action or material so the researcher can test a hypothesis. The performance task will nearly always involve being exposed to some stimulus of interest, perhaps a list of words. The words will have been chosen for a particular reason, such as their differences in length, or how they vary in their emotionality (e.g., "COTTON" vs. "VOMIT"). Perhaps the expectation is that the participants will have stronger memories of them later, or perhaps they will bypass them more readily and forget them.

To get some idea of what happens with memorization over time, the participants might have to repeat the task several times, perhaps with different lists of words. Alternatively, they might have to look at some pictures and arrive at a quick judgment about them in order to give an answer. The time it takes to respond tells the researcher something about how difficult the task was to perform. To repeat, the performance task in a study is usually easy to locate because it is what each participant was asked to do.

There are a wide variety of performance tasks that are used in learning and memory research. Just to familiarize you with a few, some common performance tasks that assess memory for knowledge are word lists, cue-target word lists, and implicit learning tasks. When participants are asked to memorize word lists, the participants are usually well aware of the task at hand and know they are to try their hardest. The lists are usually constructed primarily to answer questions about the raw power of human memory as well as where difficulties might lie. Do people have more or less trouble memorizing words that are concrete versus abstract ("APPLE" vs. "JUSTICE")? Does the length of the word matter for how easy it is to memorize? How many words can the average adult memorize correctly? Some tests for Alzheimer's patients will use a learning list task consisting of only three words. To have memory difficulties with a list of only three items is considered to be quite severe.

Hermann Ebbinghaus was the first to develop lists of verbal stimuli for the purpose of examining how people learn and how much they can memorize. Using fake syllabi, three letters in length, all in a consonant-vowel-consonant format, he found that the more time he spent studying a particular list, the better he was able to recall it later. His total time hypothesis claims that how well one can remember information depends primarily on how long one has spent studying it.

Ebbinghaus also was able to track the decline of memory. That is, by studying a fixed list of nonsense syllables and testing himself on it repeatedly, he could monitor his rate of forgetting. He found that once he had fully memorized a list, he forgot most of it within an hour. What information did remain after the initial period of forgetting tended to last for quite a long time, up to a month. Ebbinghaus' graph of his results, or forgetting curve, indicates that what we learn is either forgotten quickly, or it lasts quite a while (see Fig. 2.1).

Mary Whiton Calkins (1863–1930), the first woman to complete the work for a PhD in psychology at Harvard (but not the first woman to be awarded a doctorate there) and the first woman president of the American Psychological Association, provided a novel approach to the use of memorized lists of words to study learning and memory. Calkins (1898) pioneered the paired-associate technique to examine the associations between stimuli. In this technique, participants study pairs of stimuli, such as numbers and colors. When being tested, one stimuli from each pair is given as a hint or "cue" for the "target" stimuli to be recalled later. When used with verbal stimuli, the participants memorize a list of cue and target words they will be tested on later. In other words, instead of just memorizing "BEACH TABLE BLOCKS," participants will cue words for each, such as "sun-BEACH fable-TABLE water-BLOCKS." Then, when being quizzed, the participant will be given the cue words only (sun, fable, and water).

Why was this an important development? The cue words meant it was now possible to test the kinds of connections people made when studying the material. For example, seeing "sun" and trying to remember "BEACH" is a kind of conceptual connection: the two are commonly experienced together. For "TABLE," the cue word "fable" is not generally associated with it, but they do rhyme. In the last case, there is no normal association between "water" and "BLOCKS." A list of cue-target words of this kind would allow for a comparison between using hints that rhyme versus hints to the meaning of a word. Calkins's invented technique allowed

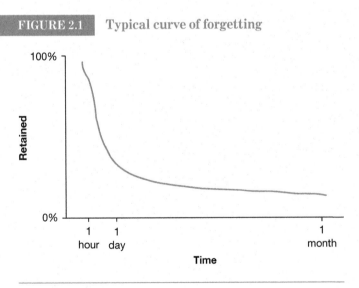

FIGURE 2.1   **Typical curve of forgetting**

100%

Retained

0%

1 hour   1 day   1 month

Time

for a new kind of experimental manipulation—using the relationship (or lack thereof) between the cue and target words to see which kinds of relationships are beneficial for memory. The assumption underlying this technique is that the stronger the association, the more important that kind of learning is for the human memory system.

Selective Interference Tasks

A variant on tests of the raw power of memory and its limitations is when the researcher wants to try to selectively interfere with some part of memory performance. The idea behind attempting to interfere with performance is to find out what the mental processes that support memory are. An analogy would be trying to find out why the car stopped running. A number of actions might be tried to figure out what is going on "inside" the engine, such as turning the key in the ignition and listening for a click, checking the electricity, and looking at the fuel gauge.

The memory researcher attempts to interfere with a select part of the memory process by including a dual task, a secondary task that the participants have to complete at the same time. The researcher would be examining whether or not the dual task slowed down or interfered with the primary performance task. For example, to find out the extent to which language and speech sounds make up memories when studying a list of words, a researcher could either play audio of a speech in native language while participants are trying to study or play an instrumental song instead. The dual task may be to simply ignore the additional audio as much as possible. The extent to which the speech interfered with the activity of memorizing would give some idea of what extent the act of memorizing words relied on speech sounds. If the to-be-ignored speech made memorizing a list of words difficult, then the act of memorizing words must be very phonetic in nature; if the additional speech had little or no effect on memorizing words, then memorizing words might be more visual in nature, or rely on some other kind of encoding.

Implicit learning tasks are memory tasks that expose the participant to some stimulus without being explicitly told to study it. Implicit tasks are used when the researcher wants to know to what extent people can learn a pattern or pick up a skill with little or no awareness. The participant might be exposed to words flashed on a screen too briefly to notice consciously and then quizzed on them later. Or, stimuli might be arranged in a particular order to see if the participant can learn the sequence without knowing. These tasks test for implicit learning, meaning information that is presented without conscious awareness on the part of the participant. Much research has been conducted on the intentional kinds of memory tasks that people choose to engage in during normal life: actively trying to remember phone numbers, passwords, postal codes, routes, and grocery items. But people learn information incidentally as well. Simply by living out our day we encounter a large amount of stimuli that we may remember, if even weakly. Certainly a lot of advertisers believe this kind of spurious exposure to information about products is helpful. (Essentially, implicit memory tasks are a kind of secondary task of which the participant is not aware.)

Performance Measurement

If participants are being asked to perform some task, then some aspect of the performance will need to be measured. Like performance tasks, measurements of performance can vary widely. Here are four general kinds that we will encounter repeatedly in this text: rates of correct/incorrect answers, reaction times, metamemory judgments, and brain activity. Let's look at each of these in turn.

Accuracy

If a goal of the human memory system is to store information for retrieval later, then looking at how well participants learned information under various conditions will likely require calculating the number of correct answers, usually calculated as a percent correct. While the percent correct is certainly an important measure, a parallel but not identical measure is the number of errors, usually calculated as a percent incorrect. Some conditions might cause people to remember information incorrectly, such as situations in which all of the answers provided on a multiple-choice question look generally familiar, or when a lot of time has passed since learning some material. A researcher can find that a particular recall technique designed to boost recall creates more correct answers and more incorrect answers as well. This means that the memory boost was coming at a cost of remembering false information too, which is not usually desired.

In some cases, they will be asked to recall the information, and in other cases, they will be asked to recognize the information. In a recall test, the participants have to generate their answer completely, like an essay exam or fill-in-the-blanks test question. Hints or cues may or may not be provided, and participants may be asked to recall them in the order they were learned, or in any order. Imagine, as in Nickerson and Adams (1979), being handed a page with two circles on it and being asked to draw the front and back sides of a penny from memory as completely and accurately as possible. In a *recognition test,* participants can pick from a display of options. The order of the options may be jumbled or randomized, but usually the correct answer is provided in the display. Multiple-choice questions are a recognition test; a line of mug shots (a photo array) also tests for recognition. This difference of recall tests being more difficult than recognition tests is interpreted as recall tests assessing memory strength more accurately, since the correct answer is not provided as a cue. There are many research findings that appear to apply only to recall tests, and not to recognition tests. This indicates that the effect being studied is going to present itself under one circumstance: when the correct answer is not provided but must be generated. Consider how you have to study for an essay exam versus a multiple-choice exam.

Efficiency

Another common dependent variable is how long the participants took to complete the task, or reaction time (sometimes referred to as response latency). The basic assumption is that the faster a correct response is, then the more efficient the processing must be. It's a metric to measure cognitive effort and was initially known as "mental chronometry." F. C. Donders (1868), a Dutch psychologist, created a system for measuring mental events in the late nineteenth century. A researcher compares the reaction time of a simple stimulus, like a light, to different tasks and makes comparisons about the mental workload involved with each mental event.

Reaction time measurements are common with implicit memory tasks, since the researcher cannot ask a direct question about something the participant was exposed to without her awareness. The goal is to evaluate the participant's performance in familiar situations, even though the participant doesn't remember being exposed to the situation before.

In some cases, reaction time measurements are used to evaluate what people have learned about issues that are politically and culturally sensitive, topics that are difficult to directly question people about. Essentially, these techniques assess prior learning that occurred outside of a formal research environment. In the late 1970s and 1980s, public awareness of sexual violence against women increased, with planned marches such as "Take Back the Night" and other organized activities. Public discourse over what constituted sexual aggression, sexual harassment, or just poor social skills continued for over a decade. The discourse included mainstream movies such as *The Accused* starring Jodi Foster (Jaffe & Lansing, 1988) that depicted a gang rape at a bar. Public attention reached a crescendo with the infamous "Tailhook Scandal," in which a large group of Navy airmen were accused of sexually assaulting women and some men at a convention in Las Vegas in 1991 (Winerip, 2013). Many Navy personnel were formally disciplined.

With this background in mind, some psychologists used an implicit task and reaction times to better understand the thinking of people who are sexually aggressive. Bargh, Raymond, Pryor, and Strack (1995) evaluated the role of power in the minds of sexually aggressive men. As you might guess, it's not satisfactory to simply interview them and ask about a behavior that is clearly controversial in society, so an implicit task is used— one that the participants won't normally notice. In the first experiment reported in this study, male undergraduates were seated at a computer screen and were asked to read a word aloud as soon as they saw it. These words were selected for being generally—but not specifically—sex-related, such as "bed" or "motel." How long it took them to see the word and start speaking the word was timed, making their dependent variable a reaction time measure. The participants were not aware that another word was being presented extremely rapidly beforehand and was being covered up or "masked" so they could not consciously tell what it was. Some of the words were about physical power ("strong," "macho") or authoritative power ("boss," "control"). The researchers found that those males who had been screened as high risk for sexual aggression and sexual harassment would read the words out loud more quickly than did males who were not high risk, when they had been unknowingly presented with power words. This difference was interpreted as evidence that some men find the concept of "power" to be naturally associated with the concept of "sex," mentally. A second study found that only the sexual aggressors were likely to rate a female confederate as more attractive as a result of the power word priming.

Metamemory Judgments

Another kind of dependent variable is a metamemory judgment, that is, measurements of the metamemory of the participants. Participants may be asked how how confident they are in their answers, a confidence rating metamemory judgment. Confidence ratings can be used to evaluate how accurate participants are in their own awareness of their learning.

A researcher might ask the participant to consider how easy it will be to learn some material in what is called an ease-of-learning (EOL) judgment. You may be aware of making this judgment when you start reading a new chapter in a book. How difficult to study does it appear to be? After studying for a while, participants might be asked how certain they are that they know the material, a judgment-of-learning (JOL) estimate. You probably make this judgment when you have decided that you have studied for a particular chapter enough to move on to other things. Participants might be asked whether they could come up with the answer to a question before taking the trouble of answering it, a feeling-of-knowing (FOK) judgment. As a student, you engage in these judgments all the time; you may have found that these metamemory judgments are what have enabled you to get this far in your studies. Imagine when you turn to some reading that you are required to do for a class. Initially you will make a snap judgment as to how difficult it looks and how ready you feel to take it on, an EOL judgment. After reading for a while, you will occasionally stop and consider whether you comprehend the material enough that you can proceed, a JOL judgment. Later, when the instructor asks the class a question about the material, you will have a sense of "does the answer seem familiar, and can I retrieve it if I try?"—a FOK judgment. Research on metamemory has examined how accurate we are in these judgments; as you might guess, we are not always 100 percent correct.

Brain Functioning

Several techniques have become fairly popular for examining the role of the brain and central nervous system in supporting psychological phenomena. Since neuroscience can be said to be concerned primarily with the systems of the brain, and cellular and molecular activity, two general approaches have evolved for brain study: documenting brain structures and tracking brain activity. Documenting structural or anatomical forms of the brain has been done using X-rays (computed tomography, or CT scans) and sensing structures through magnetic fields and radio waves (magnetic resonance imaging, or MRIs).

However, many disparate parts of the brain may be involved in higher-order functioning like most forms of learning and memory. It's of greater interest to see how the brain functions metabolically to support these activities rather than the anatomical brain structures themselves, so other techniques are necessary.

One way to monitor brain activity is to track the tiny waves of electricity that emanate from the outer shell of the brain and can be sensed outside the skull, a technique called electroencephalography or EEG. These electrical waves can be measured in millivolts and plotted on a graph as a study participant engages in some activity, such as reading or looking at pictures. Electrodes are placed on the participant's head in order to take these readings. As a measurement, the researcher can see which tasks provoke more or less activity and roughly where the surges in brain waves occurred. EEG readings (electroencephalograms) can be used to identify general areas of the brain where activity is occurring. EEG readings are considered excellent for measuring brain activity in real time.

Other approaches take advantage of the fact that the cellular activity behind thought and thinking requires oxygen. Blood flows through the brain to the areas that require the oxygen the blood brings with it, about 4 to 6 seconds after brain activity in a particular region has started. Monitoring the blood flow in the brain gives an indication of where brain activity is occurring in the brain. To evaluate the change in blood levels over time, researchers generate two images of a participant: one image during a basic activity and another during the performance task. The difference in brain activity between those states is subtracted, pixel by pixel, to create a difference image. This difference image shows the areas of the brain where new brain activity took place as the result of the participant's engaging in the performance task.

The two most common methods for making a difference image are positron emission tomography, or PET, and functional magnetic resonance imaging, or fMRI. In both cases, blood levels in the brain are monitored before and during a performance task to record where new brain activity occurs. With PET, the participant ingests a small amount of a low-level radioactive substance that integrates into the blood stream. This radioactive substance is monitored as it courses through the brain during the performance task.

The fMRI is generally preferred over the PET because it doesn't require ingesting any kind of substance. Instead of monitoring for the presence of a radioactive substance, fMRI monitors the change in oxygen levels in the brain and hence the presence of blood, which is an indirect measure of brain activity.

To sum up, usually the dependent (measured) variable will be a percent correct, a percent incorrect, or reaction times. Other studies will use metamemory judgments to see how people evaluate their own learning and memories. Modern brain imaging has led to another kind of dependent variable, letting neuroscientists understand more about the system underlying the experience of learning and memory. In many modern studies, there are several dependent variables used together to create a more precise "profile" of the performance of the participants.

Let's look at the three major research designs used in learning and memory next.

Surveys and Interviews

One way to find out how people learn and about their memories is simply to ask them. This is often done using questionnaires or surveys and, sometimes, with interviews. Regardless of the format, simply asking people has a number of advantages. It is relatively inexpensive to do, particularly online, and can be a very quick way to gather data. A researcher can ask people what tricks they use to try to use to help their memory, and why they think they remember better in some occasions than in others.

Probably the first published report using an interview to evaluate memory was by James M. Cattell (1895). He asked students questions about historical events, what they remembered from a lecture a week before, and the previous week's weather. Often the students added new information to the lecture that had not been presented. He found that of fifty-six students, only seven remembered having had snow the week before. Cattell took these results as a bad sign for how reliable memory really was.

The major strengths of the survey and interview method are that they are fast and inexpensive. In some situations, surveying people about what they remember is the only option. For example, to study the vivid memories people form after a catastrophic event like a natural disaster, a memory researcher may whip together a set of questions about the disaster that can be delivered to students the next time class meets. This has been done numerous times to study "flashbulb memories" (Brown & Kulik, 1977), those vivid, emotional memories of major events in our lives. It's not in the researcher's power to create a natural disaster. There is no manipulation, and groups of people cannot be randomly assigned. So this approach is nonexperimental in nature. The researcher has to wait for something highly newsworthy and monumental to occur, such as an assassination of a national figure or an earthquake, before creating a survey. After some period of time, for example, three months or perhaps three years, the researchers will contact as many of the survey respondents as possible for a follow-up interview to see if they still remember the event in the same way. Neisser and colleagues (1996) surveyed groups of college students after an earthquake near San Francisco in 1989. Some of the students experienced the earthquake personally, others lived nearby, and others only heard about it on the news. The researchers conducted follow-up interviews a year and a half later to see if the accuracy changed depending on proximity to the event.

It's critical that surveys of what people remember attempt to validate the truthfulness, or veracity, of what is recalled. What people remember does not always correspond to what actually occurred. Bahrick, Hall, and Berger (1996) asked roughly 100 undergraduates what their grades were in each of their core high school classes for all four years. With the students' permission, Bahrick and colleagues checked the 3,220 recalled grades with their high school transcripts and found about 29 percent of the remembered grades were incorrect. Usually the inaccurate grades were inflated.

The convenience and low-cost benefits of simply asking people about their memories is balanced by a number of disadvantages. First, people don't necessarily answer questions honestly, particularly if they know that their answers will not be verified. They may feel pressure to respond a certain way even when the interviewer doesn't mean to apply any.

What are the ways in which someone's report about their own learning and memory be inaccurate? In some cases, people may misremember because of their own internal expectations. Conway and Ross (1984) demonstrated this by asking a set of randomly selected college students interested in a study skills course to evaluate their study skills before the course began. After the several-week course was over, the students who took the class were asked how their study skills were at that time and to recall what their study skills had been like before taking the class. All of the participants reported that their study skills had improved, but in reality, they were reporting the same level of study skills as they had before the course began. They were, after the class, misremembering their study skills before the class. They downgraded their own earlier impressions of themselves in order to see the class as beneficial! Even without external pressure to please others, we may presumably seek to please ourselves and to help ourselves feel like the activities we engage in are good uses of our time.

A second problem for surveys of learning and memory is that people may not know how good or bad their memories truly are relative to those of other people. Our attitudes toward our own memory may not be very accurate. Someone who is actually quite forgetful may feel she has a strong memory, since she doesn't remember all the times she forgets. Preschoolers are remarkably confident about their memories, even when they are aware that they are not perfect at a memorization task (Flavell, Friedrichs, & Hoyt, 1970). Conversely, older adults often feel sensitive to memory decline with age and will take steps to help themselves. Ironically, for healthy older adults, their true rate of forgetting is often about the same as other adults (Herrmann, 1982). In a review of the literature, Herrmann found that while people's beliefs about their own memories are stable over time, they are not necessarily accurate. Most studies found only a weak relationship between people's beliefs about their memories and their actual ability to remember. When we survey people for their memory performance, we are most likely assessing their attitudes about their own memory, rather than how effective their memory is.

Finally, some functions of the human learning system are not entirely within our awareness. We can do some activities so quickly that not much conscious awareness, if any, is required. Looking around and taking in what we see happens so quickly that most of us can't report the psychological processing going on at the same time. I personally was once interviewed about my choice of detergent as I was leaving a grocery store. The activity of picking it out had been so quick—it was such a minor decision to me—I had no real memory of how I had made the decision. While I may know the outcome of a decision, the process to arrive there may not be consciously available enough for me to verbalize it. In many ways, it's easier to consider the result or product of our thinking rather than the process it took to get that result (White, 1988).

For a more powerful argument about the nature of learning and memory, it may be necessary to go beyond diaries and surveys to manipulate some factor in order to see what the consequences for learning are. In other words, an experiment is needed.

Memory Diaries

Some researchers have taken it upon themselves to study their own memories. This involves keeping a diary, recording various events from their lives, and later on quizzing themselves in some fashion.

This approach to memory is a little like a combination of field research and a case study. No variables are intentionally manipulated, as the researcher simply records a little about each day. Memory diaries are typically case studies, and often the researcher is the only participant in the study. They are longitudinal studies, meaning that these studies take place over long periods of time. Researchers will keep the memory diary active for years. Linton (1982) collected six years' worth of her own memories by writing down two memories a day. She reread two of them each month, at random. She would try to remember the events described, estimate their date, and try to put them in chronological order. She rated each memory for how important it was as well as how emotional it was, both when she wrote down the memory and when she recalled it. She experienced two kinds of forgetting: in one, from repeating an event; in another, memories were simply lost. Repeating an event, such as trips to the same town to attend a conference, generated a series of memories that became indistinguishable from each other over time. She was left with a generic, composite memory (e.g., "events that happened on my trips to this town") rather than specific event memories. She simply forgot about 30 percent of the memories overall. For memories that were older than two years, it seemed easier for her to try to remember them using a themed search (e.g., "parties I went to," "sporting events") instead of a chronological search. She couldn't find any relationship between how important she had thought the memory was at the time or how emotional it was and her ability to recall it later.

Diary studies have the particular advantage of being fairly lengthy, comprehensive, and well within the control of the memory researcher. Of course, like any case study, it's hard to make broad conclusions from studies with only one subject. What if a memory researcher happens to have an excellent memory, or is more interested in the task simply because this is his or her area of study? Also, the participant is free to select the memories he or she chooses to record, so there is a potential for selection bias (a process for selecting items that is not truly random) in terms of which data are collected.

Memory researchers have refined Linton's techniques. Wagenaar (1986) kept a record of one memory a day for six years. He categorized parts of each memory by who was present, the time of day, where he was, and what the activity was. To evaluate the issue of the diarist getting to select which memories to preserve, Brewer (1988) asked college students to wear pagers that the research team would trigger by paging them at random times. When the pagers went off, the students were to record what they were doing, and thinking, and where they were. They also recorded a special memory from each day, similar to what Linton and Wagenaar had done in their memory diary studies. Weeks and months later, the participants were then quizzed to see what they remembered of these incidental moments. As you might guess, the college students did not remember nearly as many of these incidental memories as those they were allowed to select out as important and to record.

Experiments

Experiments are by far the most common research design used in learning and memory research. Experiments stand out from other general research techniques by their power to provide explanations for *why* participants act a certain way. These causal explanations are due to a unique feature of experimental research design—a controlled environment with one or more factors that the researcher intentionally manipulates.

All studies, whether surveys, diary studies, experiments, or any other method, will include some form of data collection or measurement. In an experiment, this measured variable is called the dependent variable. The power of experiments comes from the use of an additional kind of variable that sets it apart—an independent variable. An independent variable is a factor that is intentionally manipulated by the researcher. It is a factor that the researcher suspects may cause a change in the performance of the participants, so it will be used as a way to test for that connection or for a way to control for it. Sometimes the researcher has a hypothesis and wants to see if she can successfully demonstrate a connection between an independent variable and performance on the dependent variable; or it could be that there is a known connection already, so the researcher uses the manipulation as a way to incorporate previous research and control the effects of that variable.

Sometimes an independent variable may be quite subtle, and the participants won't even be aware of it. For example, a list of words that participants are required to memorize and recall may contain concrete nouns (e.g., "house," "book," "couch") and abstract nouns ("justice," "anger," "smooth"). In some studies, a word is presented onscreen for such a brief time (perhaps 80 milliseconds) that the participants don't consciously see the word; and the words used will vary on some dimension, such as calming versus upsetting words (e.g., "quiet" and "slow" in contrast to "mold" and "vomit").

Other times, independent variables are fairly obvious and clear, such as a memory study involving some sort of psychoactive substance or medication. A number of studies have attempted to determine whether taking ginkgo biloba is useful for remembering (for a recent meta-analysis, see Laws, Sweetnam, and Kondel, 2012). Typically this will involve having one set of participants take the medication for some period of time and another set of participants who do not, the independent variable. Then, both sets are given a memory task, and measurements are made. Often the participants who are not taking the substance will be given a placebo, some substance that is not psychologically active, like a sugar pill. In drug trials such as these, the participants and the researcher will not know which participant is in which condition until the end of the study. The independent variable creates different "conditions" for the performance task, and different participants are placed into these different conditions, usually randomly.

Winograd and Soloway (1986) wanted to evaluate whether it was wise to store important or valuable objects, like jewelry or cash, in unusual places. People going on a trip may attempt to hide something important in case their home is broken into during the trip. From the perspective of remembering, is this wise to do? In the first experiment reported, Winograd and Soloway formed three groups of undergraduates. The three groups studied a set of objects and their locations in different ways. One group examined a set of sentences, such as "The jewelry is in the oven," and "The lottery ticket is in the sugar bowl"; and they rated each one for how memorable that location would be. Another group of students rated each sentence for how likely it would be to store an object in that unusual location. A third group was asked to mentally imagine storing those objects in those locations. All three groups were asked to recall where each item was in a surprise test. Winograd and Soloway found that the more unusual or unlikely a location was, the less likely the participants would correctly recall the location. The researchers interpret their findings as being unsupportive of the idea of hiding valuables in unusual places—they are too easy to forget!

In this study, the independent variable is fairly easy to locate. There is one clear manipulation, and the researchers created three groups of participants by asking each group to study the material differently. "Study Method" would be an appropriate name for this variable. In contrast to an independent (manipulated) variable, a dependent variable does not split the participants into groups. Everyone in this study will be measured along the same dimension—recall of location.

Experiments that split the participants into competing groups as Winograd and Soloway (1986) did are called between-groups studies. The researcher is looking for changes in the dependent variable(s) across the groups of participants that the independent variable created. Other studies incorporate the independent variable differently: The same set of participants will be asked to experience the performance task in each of the different conditions of the independent variable. Experiments that use the participants in all conditions created by the independent variable are called within-subjects studies. To see whether it mattered when students took notes by typing or handwriting, Rudmann (2013) asked students to write down a list of words, take a test on those words, then type a list of words, and receive a test on those words. This was then repeated once. How many words they could remember whether they were handwriting or typing were compared. (They were statistically the same: handwriting or typing individual words didn't matter, according to this study.) In Rudmann's study, the participants are essentially competing against themselves under different circumstances. Their ability to remember words was compared across the two conditions. Typically, within-subjects studies require fewer participants, since the participants do the task repeatedly. Within-subjects studies have an additional feature: Their findings can be viewed as more powerful because any differences were found for one set of individuals, instead of for different groups of individuals, who may vary from each other naturally, as with between-groups designs.

Despite the greater efficiency, not all hypotheses can be investigated using within-subjects designs. Recall that before brain imaging techniques were as developed as they are today, researchers studying the brain's role in learning and memory had to use brain damage as the primary method of uncovering what functions were associated with what parts of the brain. This means either stimulating the brains of animals to create lesions, a practice that dates back to Rene Descartes's time, or finding people with pre-existing brain damage for study, such as victims of car accidents. If a researcher is using brain damaged patients as participants, then she will be using a between-groups design, since it's not possible to have the patients alternate from one group to the other (brain damaged vs. non-brain damaged). This is a common issue for many variables that are important in the social sciences, such as age, race, and sex. The researcher can use only between-groups designs for those variables, despite the better efficiency of the within-subjects designs.

Of course, some independent variables do not permit the random assignment that would allow us to call them true independent variables. A researcher cannot randomly assign people to a brain damaged group, or to one gender or the other, or to a particular age group. As a result, those kinds of independent variables are often called quasi-independent variables, simply to denote to others that true random assignment was not possible.

Ultimately, the true power of experimentation is the potential to produce a finding that is a causal statement, such as "Talking on a cell phone while driving appears to worsen a driver's ability to see obstacles on the road" (Strayer, Drews, & Johnston, 2003; Strayer & Johnston, 2001). The use of an independent variable sets it apart from all other forms of research; and, for this reason, it is heavily favored by many researchers.

To sum up, we have reviewed three common research designs in learning and memory research: surveys and interviews, diary studies, and experiments. Each has its individual strengths and weaknesses. Surveys and interviews are inexpensive and quick to perform but tend to reflect attitudes about learning and memory rather than actual learning. Diary studies often have a good element of authentic realism, but are usually conducted with only one person, the researcher, and can include only those memories that a person consciously chooses to include. Experiments are the most powerful approach to providing explanations for how learning and memory work, but they require a high amount of careful control and design in order to produce findings that others in the field can take seriously.

Issues of Quality

Whenever we are presented with the results of a study, there are a number of possible questions to consider when trying to address the quality of the study. No one study can answer every question about a particular phenomenon. Ultimately, for any study, the primary question is: Was the study convincing? To what extent were the researchers able to support or debunk the hypothesis?

Here's a recent example of a well-designed series of studies that is very relevant for today's students. Mueller and Oppenheimer (2014) asked college students to take notes by hand or on a laptop while listening to some relatively unknown lectures from the popular online series *TED Talks*. Afterward, the students engaged in about a half-hour of other, unrelated tasks. To see what they had retained from the lectures, they answered factual questions, such as names and dates, and conceptual questions about broader issues in the lectures. The students who had taken notes by hand provided better answers to the conceptual questions than those who had taken the notes on a laptop. Looking at their notes, the researchers found that students using laptops tended to write down the lectures nearly verbatim. Perhaps handwriting means forcing oneself to focus on the meaning rather than transcription? This effect for better results from handwritten notes continued even when the laptop users were told to avoid writing down their notes verbatim. In a third study, the researchers found the performance of the handwriting group well above that of the laptop group again when both groups were given the opportunity to study their notes.

Generally speaking, research studies can be evaluated from two perspectives: (a) for their methodology, or internal validity, and (b) for their generalizability to other situations, or external validity. For internal validity, concerns involve the design and execution of the study itself. For example, were there enough subjects in the study to draw any conclusions? Mueller and Oppenheimer (2014) used several hundred students. How many participants is enough is widely debated, but usually 20 per level of the independent variable is considered a necessary minimum (Simmons, Nelson, & Simonsohn, 2011). Mueller and Oppenheimer's methods are reported clearly and could readily be replicated by someone else. In terms of external validity, Mueller and Oppenheimer appeared to have selected an excellent population to use for comparison to environments with adult learners by using college students. It is a great concern for the field that the majority of studies are conducted using college undergraduates, who are not terribly representative of the global population as a whole (Henrich, Heine, & Norenzayan, 2010); but to use college students for a study on how to study in college seems reasonable. Can we extrapolate the findings to children, however? That would probably be unwise, until such a study has been completed.

All of these issues over the quality of using surveys to study human learning and memory are questions about their validity, a concept that can be applied to any research study. For a study to be valid, it should accomplish what the researchers claim it does. Surveys for memory research may be particularly prone to problems about validity unless they are designed very carefully. If someone were to claim, for example, that older people become more forgetful with age because they reported being more forgetful on a survey, a reader could correctly question the validity of that conclusion. It's quite likely that older people believe they are more forgetful, but are they really?

One issue that tends to affect experimentation more so than other approaches is the extent to which the experiment mirrors real-life situations and behaviors, called ecological validity. Does the study seem to capture real-life behavior and situations well, or does it seem completely artificial? The expectation is that a study should provide some amount of mundane realism, or aspects of normal life, in order to provide findings that are directly applicable to people and their lives. It's possible for well-controlled studies in contrived settings to produce behaviors from people that they may not normally do.

Of course, the power to explain the causes of some phenomena with experimentation can come at a kind of cost: In order to conduct a well-designed, convincing experiment, it may be necessary to create a highly controlled environment in which to conduct it. This could include a sound-proofed room perhaps, or the use of eye-tracking equipment, or a task that is simply unusual or very odd. A well-designed experiment can be so removed from the experience of daily life that its findings, while stable and large (or "robust"), may also be removed from the experience of daily life. This level of rigor may be needed when conducting highly exploratory, basic kinds of research; but before drawing conclusions about the normal "real-world" experiences of humans, it may be best to conduct studies that at least attempt to mirror normal daily life, in setting and in task.

CHAPTER SUMMARY

Virtually all studies feature some task that the participants do or are observed doing. In this field, it will typically involve some form of learning and retrieval later on. Common tasks include studying lists of words, paired-associate tasks, dual tasks, or implicit learning tasks that the participants aren't aware of. Typical ways to measure participants' performance include accuracy (usually percent correct and incorrect), efficiency in processing (reaction time), judgments about their own accuracy, and brain imaging.

Common research designs involve surveys and interviews, memory diaries, and experiments. Surveys can be built relatively quickly and are an inexpensive way to collect data, but it's not clear that people are always fully aware of how well they learn and remember. Also, people can be particularly motivated to sway their presentation of themselves based on what they think they should say. Memory diaries are intensive, longitudinal records of personal events that researchers can quiz themselves over later on. While powerful, they do take a long time; and they usually involve the memories of only one person, who can fall prey to bias in selecting what to record. Experiments can make causal connections between variables, because they include an independent variable, some factor that is intentionally manipulated by the researcher to evaluate its effect on the measured or dependent variables. Experiments are the most powerful technique for understanding human psychology; but they require careful planning to execute well, and may not resemble real life if too highly controlled (a problem of lacking ecological validity).

All studies can be evaluated for their internal validity—how well the study was constructed and can be replicated—and external validity—to what extent the results can be generalized or applied to other groups of people.

In the next chapter, we'll take a look at the biological basis underlying the human learning and memory systems, and examine some of the models and research on simpler (less complex) forms of learning.

REVIEW QUESTIONS

1. What are the common kinds of performance tasks in learning and memory research?

2. What are the common kinds of performance measures taken in learning and memory studies?

3. How are surveys, memory diary studies, and experiments different from each other?

4. What advantages and disadvantages do memory diaries, surveys, and experiments provide for the study of learning and memory?

5. What are the key issues in evaluating the quality of research?

KEY TERMS

Attitudes   30
Between-groups   33
Case studies   31
Causal explanations   32
Confidence rating   27
Correct answers   26
Dependent variable   32
Difference image   28
Dual task   25
Ease-of-learning   27
Ecological validity   35
Electroencephalograms   28
Electroencephalography   28
Errors   26

External validity   34
Feeling-of-knowing   28
Forgetting curve   24
Functional magnetic
   resonance imaging   28
Implicit learning   25
Implicit learning tasks   25
Independent variable   32
Internal validity   34
Judgment-of-learning   27
Longitudinal   31
Metamemory judgment   27
Paired-associate technique   24
Percent correct   26

Percent incorrect   26
Positron emission tomography   28
Quasi-independent variables   33
Reaction time   26
Recall test   26
Response latency   26
Selection bias   31
Selectively interfere   25
Total time hypothesis   24
Validity   35
Within-subjects   33
Word lists   23

FURTHER RESOURCES

1. Weblink: A video explanation of how PET scanning works:

   o https://www.youtube.com/watch?v= GHLBcCv4rqk

2. Weblink: Explanation and demonstration of MRIs from Oxford:

   o http://www.oxfordsparks.ox.ac.uk/mri

3. Weblink: One application of memory diaries isn't research-based, but it is an application of the technique to help foster children. "Lifebooks" are memory diaries created by a guardian or social worker for a foster child in order to help create a narrative for the child's journey to adulthood:

   o https://www.childwelfare.gov/topics/adoption/ postplacement/lifebooks/

REFERENCES

Bahrick, H. P., Hall, L. K., & Berger, S. A. (1990). Accuracy and distortion in memory for high school grades. *Psychological Science, 7*(5), 265–271.

Bargh, J. A., Raymond, P., Pryor, J. B., & Strack, F. (1995). Attractiveness of the underling: An automatic power → sex association and its consequences for sexual harassment and aggression. *Journal of Personality and Social Psychology, 68*(5), 768–781.

Boice, R. (1990). *Professors as writers: A self-help guide to productive writing.* Stillwater, OK: New Forums Press.

Brewer, W. F. (1988). Memory for randomly sampled autobiographical events. Retrieved from http://doi.apa.org/psycinfo/ 1988-98127-002

Brown, R., & Kulik, J. (1977). Flashbulb memories. *Cognition, 5*(1), 73–99.

Calkins, M. W. (1898). Short studies in memory and in association from the Wellesly College Psychological Laboratory. *Psychological Review, 5*(5), 451–462. https://doi.org/10.1037/ h0071176

Cattell, J. M. (1895). Measurements of the accuracy of recollection. *Science, 2*(49), 761–766.

Conway, M., & Ross, M. (1984). Getting what you want by revising what you had. *Journal of Personality and Social Psychology, 47*(4), 738.

Donders, F. C. (1868). Over de snelheid van psychische processen. Onderzoekingen Gedaan in Het Physiologisch Laboratorium Der Utrechtsche Hoogeschool (1968–1869), 2, 92–120.

Ebbinghaus, H. (1885/2013). Memory: a contribution to experimental psychology. *Annals of Neurosciences, 20*(4), 155–156.

Flavell, J. H., Friedrichs, A. G., & Hoyt, J. D. (1970). Developmental changes in memorization processes. *Cognitive Psychology, 1*(4), 324–340.

Henrich, J., Heine, S. J., & Norenzayan, A. (2010). The weirdest people in the world? *Behavioral and Brain Sciences, 33*(2–3), 61–83.

Herrmann, D. J. (1982). Know thy memory: The use of questionnaires to assess and study memory. *Psychological Bulletin, 92*(2), 434.

Jaffe, S., & Lansing, S. (Producers), & Kaplan, J. (Director). (1988). *The accused.* United States: Paramount Pictures.

Laws, K. R., Sweetnam, H., & Kondel, T. K. (2012). Is ginkgo biloba a cognitive enhancer in healthy individuals? A meta-analysis. *Human Psychopharmacology: Clinical and Experimental, 27*(6), 527–533. https://doi.org/10.1002/ hup.2259

Linton, M. (1982). Transformations of memory in everyday life. In U. Neisser (Ed.), *Memory observed: Remembering in natural contexts,* 77–91. New York, NY: Freeman.

Locker, M. (2013, October 16). Oreos may be just as addicting as cocaine. *Time.* Retrieved from http://newsfeed.time .com/2013/10/16/oreos-may-be-as-addictive-as-cocaine/

Mueller, P. A., & Oppenheimer, D. M. (2014). The pen is mightier than the keyboard: Advantages of longhand over laptop note taking. *Psychological Science,* 0956797 614524581.

Neisser, U., Winograd, E., Bergman, E. T., Schreiber, C. A., Palmer, S. E., & Weldon, M. S. (1996). Remembering the earthquake: Direct experience vs. hearing the news. *Memory, 4*(4), 337–358. https://doi.org/10.1080/0965821963 88898

Nickerson, R. S., & Adams, M. J. (1979). Long-term memory for a common object. *Cognitive Psychology, 11*(3), 287–307. https://doi.org/10.1016/0010–0285(79)90013–6

Rudmann, D. S. (2013). *Memory for typed versus handwritten words.* Presented at the meeting of the Midwestern Psychological Association, Chicago, IL.

Simmons, J. P., Nelson, L. D., & Simonsohn, U. (2011). False-positive psychology undisclosed flexibility in data collection and analysis allows presenting anything as significant. *Psychological Science,* 0956797611417632. https://doi .org/10.1177/0956797611417632

Strayer, D. L., Drews, F. A., & Johnston, W. A. (2003). Cell phone-induced failures of visual attention during simulated driving. *Journal of Experimental Psychology: Applied, 9*(1), 23.

Strayer, D. L., & Johnston, W. A. (2001). Driven to distraction: Dual-task studies of simulated driving and conversing on a cellular telephone. *Psychological Science, 12*(6), 462–466.

Wagenaar, W. A. (1986). My memory: A study of autobiographical memory over six years. *Cognitive Psychology, 18*(2), 225–252.

White, P. A. (1988). Knowing more about what we can tell: "Introspective access" and causal report accuracy 10 years later. *British Journal of Psychology, 79*(1), 13.

Winerip, M. (2013, May 13). Revisiting the military's Tailhook Scandal. *The New York Times.* Retrieved from http://www.nytimes.com/2013/05/13/booming/revisiting-the-militarys-tailhook-scandal-video.html

Winograd, E., & Soloway, R. M. (1986). On forgetting the locations of things stored in special places. *Journal of Experimental Psychology: General, 115*(4), 366.

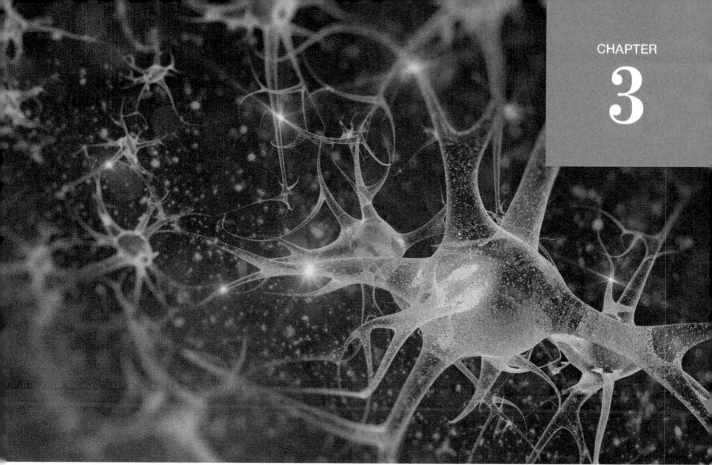

Neurological Basis of Learning

Chapter Outline

Learning Objectives

1. Describe how neurons communicate information.
2. Explain how learning may occur at the cellular level.
3. Describe how classical conditioning theory explains basic associative learning.
4. Define skill learning, and identify the optimal forms of practice and feedback for learning.
5. Define implicit learning, and describe what is learned in implicit learning.

Overview

Underlying all learning and the act of storing information for later retrieval are the biological structures that support those activities. The dramatic importance of the biological support for learning and memory can be seen in cases where the biological functioning stopped, or was curtailed, such as in the following famous case.

The Case of H.M.

Prior to the 1950s, it was commonly assumed that the memories we store are distributed across the brain and that no single area in the brain was responsible for memories. Henry G. Molaison, in 1953 at the age of twenty-seven, had an operation on his brain to attempt to relieve the blackouts and convulsions from seizures that he had been experiencing since about the age of nine. At this age, the seizures were incapacitating, and he was unable to perform his job as a mechanic. (The seizures might have begun due to a head injury stemming from a collision with a bicycle rider, but the ability to evaluate the brain for damage at that time was relatively poor by today's standards.) Mr. Molaison's neurosurgeon, having tried everything else, proposed an experimental surgery to remove two small slivers from his brain, both cuts primarily from the hippocampus, a part of the brain shaped like a small curved horn about level with the ears.

Mr. Molaison's personality remained intact, but he lost the ability to form new memories. Surprising researchers of the day, he retained all prior knowledge about his earlier life before the surgery, but he was unable to form any new memories. So each time he met with someone, read a story, or engaged in an activity, it was like the first time. Conscious learning stopped. He was able to store information for about twenty seconds, and then it was gone. The fact that a relatively small amount of brain damage had had such a major impact on his memory was surprising at the time.

This sparked an intense amount of research and study on both Mr. Molaison and other amnesiacs—people who suffered some form of permanent memory loss. Despite initial skepticism, by the 1970s, it was clear that amnesiacs had trouble retaining new memories (Roediger & Craik, 2014). "H.M.," as he was known in the scientific literature to protect his privacy, was believed to be one of the most "pure" amnesiacs, and he participated in about five decades of research before his death in 2008. More clinical data has been gathered about him than any other man in history (Dittrich, n.d.). After his death, his brain was exhaustively scanned to get more information on how his memory characteristics related to his brain.

So, let's turn to what we know today about the underpinnings of how we learn, at a cellular level. How do the cells in our nervous system function, and how do they adapt to new circumstances in order to help us learn, or to make basic associations between events and ideas?

In this chapter, we will review the fundamentals of how cells in the nervous system communicate ("neurotransmission") before looking at some hypothesized ways our nervous system may adapt to support learning. Then, we'll examine three areas of research on simple, noncomplex forms of learning.

How Neurons Communicate: Neurotransmission

The basis of all learning is, at some point, represented by cellular activity within the central nervous system, the brain, and the spinal cord. The cells that appear to be primarily responsible for information flow throughout the central nervous system are called neurons. Let's review how they communicate with each other, so that we can conceptually understand how they are likely to adapt to changes in our environment.

Neurons are uniquely equipped for communication, relative to other cells in the body. Besides a cell body, mitochondria, and an outer membrane like other cells have, neurons have dendrites and at least one axon (see Fig. 3.1).

Like branches on a tree, any one neuron can have many dendrites. These dendrites play the role of accepting incoming information; they support the sites on the neuron where information can be received. These receptor sites, like landing pads, wait for molecules to land on them and chemically bind to them. Not every receptor site will accept every kind of transmitted molecule that they are exposed to. Usually they specialize in particular molecules, the way different keys fit into different locks.

In contrast, axons send information to other cells. When a neuron fires, a process that starts at the neuron's cell body, a chemical and electrical wave runs down the length of the axon. This wave, called an action potential or "neural impulse," moves down the axon at a set, fixed rate. This action potential is what readies the neuron to send information to other cells.

This process is entirely chemical and electrical. Neurons, when resting, are negatively charged at between –50 and–80 millivolts. This is because of the presence of negatively charged ions and/or molecules in the axon. A neuron fires when its overall polarity reaches to a specific threshold (the precise threshold required varies across neurons). When a neuron fires, the "wave" of energy that rolls down the axon is the result of the negatively charged molecules being pushed out of gates along the axon and permitting positively charged molecules to be drawn into the axon. This process runs down the axon and, at the end, the action potential causes chemicals to be released.

FIGURE 3.1 Diagram of a basic neuron

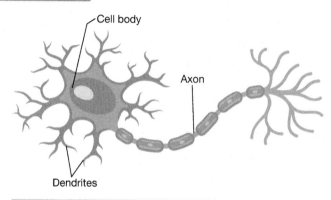

Source: Garrett (2015, Figure 2.3, p. 25).

Neurons generate their own chemicals to be used in the act of communicating with other cells. These chemicals, molecules called neurotransmitters, are made at the cell body. When a neuron fires, the action potential pushes collections of the neurotransmitters down the axon in synaptic vesicles, tiny sacks made of membrane. These vesicles ride the wave down the axon. At the end of the axon, these vesicles attach or dock to the ends of the axon, open, and release the neuron's neurotransmitters.

Neurons do not touch each other. They come microscopically close—within 30 mm—but they do not connect. When these neurotransmitters are released, they float into a gap or synapse between the neuron and other cells. Some, but not necessarily all, of these neurotransmitters will float across the gap and find receptor sites on the next neuron and bind to them, continuing the path of information. These receptor sites are supported by dendritic spines, like mushrooms or tiny branches, that extend from the shaft of the dendrite itself. Some will not find a receptor site that will accept them, and they may decay in the gap. Others may be reabsorbed by the original neuron in a process called reuptake.

What causes a neuron to change polarity enough to meet the firing threshold? Neurotransmitters are themselves molecules with positive or negative charges. As they cross the synapse from the first, presynaptic, neuron to bind with dendrites on the next, postsynaptic, neuron, they alter the polarity of that second neuron. Some neurotransmitters bring the neuron closer to the threshold; other neurotransmitters discourage the neuron from meeting the threshold. Neurotransmitters that make the postsynaptic neuron less polarized (closer to the "threshold" for firing) are called excitatory. Likewise, those neurotransmitters that decrease the polarity of the postsynaptic neuron, making it less likely to fire, are called inhibitory.

Any one neuron might be on the receiving end of numerous axons of different neurons and neurotransmitters with positive or negative charges. These charges may cancel each other out. The polarity of the cell body of a neuron then will bob until it reaches the firing threshold, which triggers the action potential that will distribute its neurotransmitters into the synapse, possibly to reach other cells. This overall process is remarkable for the kind of flexibility it provides to living organisms for learning and adapting to experiences.

Neurons produce a number of different chemicals we refer to as neurotransmitters; there are more than one hundred. About thirty are known to be important for psychological functioning, and nine have been the focus of most research. Neurons may focus primarily on sending or receiving one particular neurotransmitter or may handle several; the end result is that different neurons can become chemical "pathways" through the brain. It's tempting to think of the pathways as chains of neurons, sequentially processing information, but this is not the case. Clusters of neurons will specialize in particular neurotransmitters and route information to different parts of the brain in more of a web-like fashion than single, sequential neurons strung together.

Given this description of how neurotransmission works, how do neurons accommodate new experiences to support the act of learning?

How Neurons Adapt to Support Learning

Having an understanding of how neurotransmission works helps to explain the possible ways that "learning" happens at a physiological level. Research with rats in different kinds of environments led to the realization that neurons adapt to the experiences of the organism (Rosenzweig, 1984). This adaptation can continue for the entire lifespan. Neurobiologists have found that the structure of neurons and their chemistry can change due to exposure to different environments, a phenomenon often referred to as plasticity. Plasticity can occur in one of several ways.

Chemical Changes Across Existing Synapses

First, there can be changes to the chemical aspect of the neurotransmission process, as opposed to changes to the structure of interacting neurons. Possibly, the presynaptic neuron will generate and release more of a neurotransmitter. Studying neurons up close to see whether this kind of change is possible has been challenging. The brain is a complex organ, and monitoring for learning of a new concept at a neural level as it occurs in someone's mind is extremely difficult.

One strategy for trying to learn and test learning at the neural level is to find a simpler organism that is easier to study than humans. Kandel (1976) focused on a large sea slug named *Aplysia californica* to reduce the complexity of the brain being studied to find out more about how neurons adapt when learning occurs. The Aplysia is about the size of a fist. From an anatomical perspective, it has a number of advantages for research. First, the sea slug has a relatively simple brain, making it easier to study. Second, its neurons are considered to be the largest in the animal kingdom, so they can be seen without high-powered imaging techniques. Also, it's possible to move the sea slug's brain, which normally resides in its gut, away from its body for study while leaving it neurally connected, allowing for easier observation (see Fig. 3.2).

From a behavioral perspective, the sea slug provides a particular advantage as well. It has a reflex that can be modified with experience. The sea slug defensively withdraws its gill when its siphon—a tube that ingests and expels water—is stimulated, called the gill withdrawal reflex. This choice for learning research turned out to be extremely

FIGURE 3.2   Photo of a sea slug

Source: Aplysia californica emitting ink cloud, Genny Anderson, https://commons.wikimedia.org/wiki/File:Aplysia_californica .jpg, CC BY-SA 4.0.

beneficial. Given a simpler life-form with reflexive behavior that can change depending on how it is stimulated, research on the neural level of learning was possible without advanced equipment.

The Aplysia is capable of some basic forms of learning that are nonassociative (Kandel, 1976). Nonassociative learning, originally proposed by Ivan Pavlov (1927/2015), includes the forms of learning in which only one stimulus is involved. Learning comes from the mere exposure to that specific stimulus. For instance, the sea slug's gill withdrawal reflex weakens if the siphon is touched repeatedly, a kind of simple learning called habituation. Habituation is the decrease of a behavioral response to a stimulus after repeated stimulation. With exposure, the response decreases with familiarity. Imagine cheerleaders at a game asking people in the stands to clap and cheer. With the initial encouragement, the fans will respond; but if the cheerleaders ask continuously for too long, eventually people tire and start to ignore the requests.

The Aplysia shows other kinds of learning phenomena. If there is a long delay between taps on the Aplysia's siphon, however, the original strength of the reflex returns, a learning phenomenon called spontaneous recovery. Spontaneous recovery is when a response reappears after a delay. Staggered stimulation can work best to initiate a strong response. This may be why cheerleaders time their requests to the crowd. Other animals and people learn these basic reflexive responses as well. Also, the sea slug can reflexively react strongly to a *weak* stimulus to its siphon if its tail has just received a strong shock. This stronger response is because of being overly ready due to an earlier stimulus is called sensitization. This similar to hearing a door slam loudly and becoming "on edge," ready for it to happen again.

With further research, Kandel and his associates were able to locate where, neurologically, habituation was occurring in sea slugs. The change in the communication between the neurons that sensed the touch and the neurons that issued the command to withdraw the gill was happening in the synapse between these cells. The synaptic connection was being weakened; essentially, less excitatory information is sent from the presynaptic, sensory neuron to the postsynaptic, motor neuron (Kandel, 2001).

The term "habituation" is a general term for decreases in responding to a stimulus, and can be applied to a wide range of learning situations (see Thompson & Spencer, 1966, for an overview). The specific neurobiological term for the decrease in neural responding at a synapse is known as long-term depression (LTD). The opposite of LTD can happen as well. Repeatedly stimulating a neuron that triggers the stimulation of the next postsynaptic cell can also cause improved long-lasting efficiencies in the neurotransmission between two cells. This process, known as long-term potentiation (LTP), strengthens the neural connection. Such a relationship between neurons was predicted by Donald Hebb in 1949. He expected that when the axon of one neuron repeatedly stimulates the dendrites of another neuron, eventually those neurons were going to develop ways of becoming more efficient with their communication. The idea that "neurons that fire together, wire together" became known as Hebbian learning and led researchers to explore the possibility of "Hebb synapses." LTP appears to be one form of Hebbian learning.

In laboratory conditions, slices of areas of the brain known to be involved in memory can be "trained" using electrical stimulation to respond less frequently for about an hour (see, e.g., Bear, 2003). LTD and LTP have been most extensively studied in the tissue that makes up the hippocampus, the area of the brain that was part of the surgery that Henry Molaison underwent (see, e.g., Davies, Lester, Reymann, & Collingridge, 1989).

To measure learning with infants, child psychologists use highly creative techniques to get a sense of what an infant is used to. Renée Baillargeon developed a novel approach for measuring what infants are capable of learning on the idea of habituation (1995). She measured how long infants look at stimuli, or gaze time. The assumption is that infants look away from stimuli they have habituated to and, thus, have learned; but they will continue to look at stimuli that are surprising or novel to them. Baillargeon assessed whether infants have a sense of intuitive physical reasoning by showing them physically possible scenes, such as a ball rolling behind a screen to be stopped by a block, and physically impossible scenes, such as a ball rolling behind a screen and somehow passing through the block that should have stopped it. Baillargeon found that infants stare longer at the physically impossible task, concluding that infants have the ability to reason about physics on an elementary level (see Fig. 3.3).

Kibbe and Leslie (2011) evaluated whether infants can remember the features of objects that have been hidden from view. They placed two objects on a platform in front of infants and hid them both behind screens. When the screen in front of one or the other was removed, infants saw either the correct object, the incorrect object, or nothing. Kibbe and Leslie found that the six-month-olds were not surprised to find the wrong object, but they were surprised if the object didn't return when the screen was lifted (see Fig. 3.4). Apparently six-month-olds can habituate to the idea of an object being present, but not necessarily to the visual features of that object.

The basic assumption of child psychologists' use of gaze time to evaluate learning is conceptually similar to neural patterns of habituation, as Kandel (2001) described. However, we cannot assume at this time that infant studies like those explained earlier are in fact producing the exact same neural adaptations as neuroscientists describe.

FIGURE 3.3 Physical situations that are impossible (a ball traveling through a wall) trigger a longer gaze time from infants.

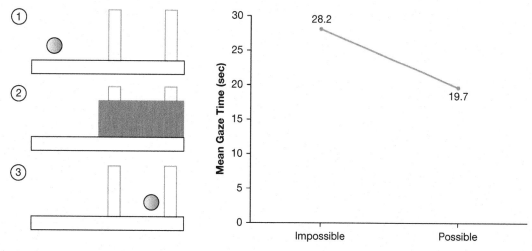

Source: Adapted from Baillargeon, R. (1995).

FIGURE 3.4   A longer average gaze time when an object is missing implies surprise.

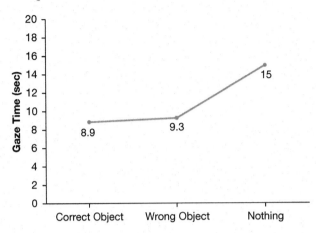

Source: Adapted from Kibbe, M. M., & Leslie, A. M. (2011).

They may be, but the imaging techniques haven't yet been developed to allow this level of data collection.

Changes to the Dendrites

Another way that neurons could change in order to accommodate new experiences is with changes to the dendrites of the postsynaptic neuron. Possibly, the dendrites on the post-synaptic neuron will become more sensitive to a particular transmitter, either through more receptor sites or thicker dendrites, so that the electrical conduction is greater for the same amount of neurotransmitter.

The ability to track changes at the level of dendrites is a relatively recent development. To do this, neuroscientists will generally use simpler life-forms than humans, and they will alter the environments of the animals they use in order to spark the neurological adaptation for learning. With humans, we might be concerned with more specific issues such as when a child can grasp a certain concept, like "verbs" as opposed to "nouns," but researchers use a different scale of learning when working with nonhuman animals.

Gelfo, De Bartolo, Giovine, Petrosini, and Leggio (2009) found evidence of several kinds of changes to the dendrites when learning occurs. Male Wistar rats were housed in different kinds of environments for three and a half months. Some of the rats were housed in environments that were considered to be "enriched"—meaning that they provided additional opportunities for the rats to learn—while some were not. This meant more social interaction, more room to explore, more objects to play with, and more physical activity (Gelfo et al., 2009). More than three months later, neuron samples from prefrontal and parietal cortices of the rats in the enriched and the standard, nonenriched environments were taken for study. Examining the samples for how many dendrites were present, their density, and their length, the researchers found that some of the dendrites were longer for the rats in the enriched conditions (see Fig. 3.5). Often they were greater in number. Sometimes they had more "nodes," surface areas that receive neurotransmitters. The environment did appear to stimulate substantial change in the dendrites of rats in an enriched environment. However, these changes did not happen in

FIGURE 3.5   Neurons in enriched environments show more dendritic branching.

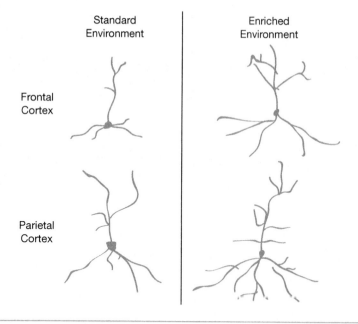

Standard Environment

Enriched Environment

Frontal Cortex

Parietal Cortex

Source: Adapted from Gelfo, F., et al., (2009).

every area of the cortex from which they had samples from, and one type of dendrite was often more affected by the enrichment than the other!

Although this is generally hypothetical at the moment, some neuroscientists have proposed that larger, mushroom-shaped receptor sites or spines on the shaft of dendrites tend to be resistant to change (Hayashi & Majewska, 2005; for an overview, see Bhatt, Zhang, & Gan, 2009). Those larger parts of dendrites might indicate where learning has become relatively fixed and permanent. Some change is still possible; changes at the synapse could still occur. Smaller, thinner receptor sites can be generated that are more flexible for forming weaker connections with other neurons. Possibly, the larger sites on a dendrite have become part of the pathways for well-learned memories, whereas the thinner tendrils are still being shaped by learning (Rudy, 2013).

Additional Neurons

Another way to learn is by the creation of new neurons entirely, called neurogenesis, creating new synapses along the way. This clearly happens just prior to birth and in the first year of life (Leuner & Gould, 2010), and it appears to continue for the duration of life for all mammals (Gould, 2007). At a young age, it could be primarily driven by physical maturation, but some adapting to the environment will be happening during this time as well. In human infants, the number of neurons and synapses tends to peak for the entire lifespan at the age of two! Often there are "extra" neurons making redundant synaptic connections with the same muscle tissue, for example. This rapid production of many synaptic connections, synaptogenesis, permits human infants to be as adaptable as possible to their new surroundings. As the infant develops the abilities to see, hear, and move better, the unnecessary neural connections in the central nervous system are discarded in a process called pruning.

Rats and other mammals in enriched environments tend to have heavier brains because of more brain tissue, a sign of greater neural growth (Rosenzweig, 1984). However, the evidence is not clear on whether neurons are always necessarily the result of learning in adulthood (Leuner, Gould, & Shors, 2006). This is because of the correlational nature of the research at this time.

In sum, there are a variety of ways that neurological changes can occur to adapt to experience. These can involve changes at the synapses, the dendrites, or with wholly new neurons. The methods of adapting are constantly being researched and documented now, but knowing which method is used for any organism more complex than Aplysia is less clear. At this time, it is difficult to pinpoint which specific method is occurring, for example, when someone learns the name of a new coworker.

Having reviewed neurotransmission and how neurons are believed to adapt to environmental change, we are now ready to take a look at an area of learning theory that shares many conceptual similarities with that of the Aplysia. Classical conditioning involves associative learning between two events, instead of just one.

Classical Conditioning

Classical conditioning, also known as Pavlovian conditioning, is a model of how people and animals can make a simple association or connection between events, or an event and an emotional reaction, or an event and a memory (Pavlov, 1927/2015). It has been broadly tested for different settings and a wide variety of animals, as well as people of different ages. One of the remarkable aspects of this particular theory is how ubiquitous it is.

At its most basic, classical conditioning explains how we learn to use a cue as a signal for what is about to happen (see, e.g., Hollis, 1997; Mineka & Zinbarg, 2006; Rescorla, 1988). It has generally been thought to occur involuntarily (Skinner, 1938). Some researchers will refer to the process of classical conditioning as "signaling," describing the way animals learn from their environments, and from each other, how to detect rivals and predators (Hollis, 1997). It's an advantage for animals if they can quickly detect those cues that will let them know about important events for their survival. Of course, animals do not teach each other these cues though a formal education process like we humans do. It's been an evolutionary advantage for all kinds of animal life-forms to develop a biological system that can support rapid learning of important environmental signals. These signals may involve territory marking, predator-prey interactions, courtship, and reproduction.

Most modern researchers today see classical conditioning as describing how ideas can become connected (e.g., Bouton, 1994; Jara, Vila, & Maldonado, 2006), but Pavlov's original framework for his theory of learning was modeled after physiological reflexes. Ivan Petrovich Pavlov (1849–1936), a Russian scientist who won a Nobel Prize in 1904 for his work on digestion, was well-known for his systematic and careful approach to his work. He was highly organized and ran a laboratory that required new workers to replicate work that had already been done. So, besides introducing new students to the field, all prior work in the lab was verified for its results. (If the replication failed, another lab worker would be brought in to replicate the original.) In this manner, the amount and quality of the research he produced was impressive.

Pavlov's primary interest was in how the digestive system worked. At the time, this area of physiology was considered difficult to study due to the nature of the digestive organs—they were too hard to observe through normal surgery. Pavlov developed new and cleaner methods for operating on animals (dogs) that allowed for observation of the digestive tract by creating fistulas, openings, in parts of the dogs' digestive systems. To his credit, most of his animal subjects survived his surgeries because of his surgical skill and focus on extreme cleanliness when operating (apparently, he disliked the sight of blood).

Naturally, Pavlov's research on the digestive system would mean accounting for the kinds of innate secretions that are made in the digestive system, including salivation. These secretions are reflexive and untrained. He found that a small amount of diluted acid on a dog's tongue produced a strong response of salivation. After a while he noticed that the dogs became used to the routine of having the splash on their tongues as he carried out his studies, and the dogs would salivate too early—before the acid had been placed on their tongues. This could happen when they saw a bowl that contained food because of their consistent feeding schedule, or when they heard the lab workers who were going to feed them. Initially this was seen as a problem for accurate recording of the properties of the digestive system. Given that the nature of the digestive system is to help break down food to absorb nutrients for survival, the "premature" salivation seemed to be mental in nature, and Pavlov called them "psychic secretions."

As a physiologist foremost, describing this finding presented a problem. Pavlov had questioned whether psychology could be considered a true science, and this finding was clearly the result of the dog's mental activities. Pavlov resolved this by adopting the view that a concept of "reflexes" could be used to describe the functioning of the brain, such as connections between sensations and motor responses—a view another Russian physiologist had recently proposed (Sechenov, 1863, reprinted 1965). In this way, he reframed his findings of mental associations as a matter of learned reflexes, using terminology that sounded more like what a physiologist would use. This background should explain Pavlov's reasoning for his terminology that does not sound terribly like psychology.

As Pavlov introduced in his 1904 Nobel Prize address, "A neutral stimulus can be associated or paired with an existing stimulus and response repeatedly, until the neutral stimulus becomes a learned cue for the response on its own." This conditional reflex (sometimes the past tense is used, as in conditioned reflex) can act as a predictor or trigger to an existing reflex.

Before a conditional reflex can be learned, an innate reflex must already exist between two events, such as between the presentation of food on the tongue and the salivation response. Pavlov termed these the unconditional stimulus (UCS) and unconditional response (UCR). (Most introductory textbooks use the past tense of these terms, which stems from a mistranslation of Pavlov's original terms.) They are "unconditional" because together they make up an innate, physiological reflex and, as such, are not learned. No one had to actively teach the dog to salivate when presented with food.

Next, during learning, some new stimulus that previously had no direct association with the unconditional stimulus and response is introduced. This could be the sight of lab workers carrying a bowl of food, or the sound of their feet as they approach, or even the time of day. Essentially, this new stimulus is being paired repeatedly with the already-existing unconditional reflex as the lab worker then feeds the dog. After a while, the visual stimulus of the lab worker or any other relevant cue triggers the response of salivation, before the food has been placed on the tongue. After learning, what had been a neutral stimulus is now a conditional stimulus (CS) that can trigger the response, now called a conditional response (see Fig. 3.6).

FIGURE 3.6   **Flowchart of the stages of learning in classical conditioning**

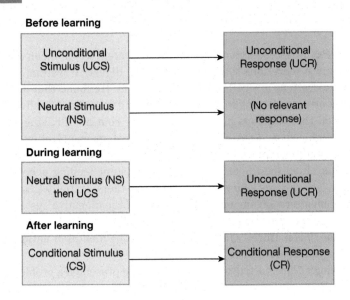

Source: Adapted from Gelfo, F., et al., (2009).

To study conditional reflexes, Pavlov and his assistants began to experiment with different kinds of stimuli, how many pairings were necessary, when the learning or conditioning occurred, and how strong the salivary response was (see Fig. 3.7). Pavlov was well-suited for pursuing this line of work with his large staff and systematic approach. It is not clear whether he ever used a bell as the conditional stimulus, as many textbooks report, but he did appear to use whistles, metronomes, buzzers, and other auditory stimuli. Just to control the presence of sound around the dogs when running his experiments, he had a laboratory space built for the dogs with two feet of dirt in the walls for insulation (his "Tower of Silence").

FIGURE 3.7   **Response times decrease with more pairings.**

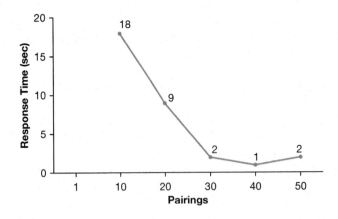

Classical conditioning has a dramatically broad number of applications, which is surprising given the rather restricted and unconventional line of research that inspired the theory. Yet classical conditioning captures the learning to associate an environmental cue to another situation or our own responses very well. One dramatic example comes from combat veterans who have returned home from serving overseas in the past decade. Some of them have found that the sounds of fireworks around holidays trigger memories and emotions from combat ("Veteran asks for courtesy with holiday fireworks," 2014). In combat areas, there is exposure to bombs, small-arms fights, as well as rocket attacks. The physical and mental impact of explosions—even assuming no injury—is likely to be reflexively unconditional to many negative emotions, such as fear and anxiety. The accompanying sounds then are quickly conditioned as stimuli that accompany those explosions and become cued reminders of past trauma. Some of these veterans have begun encouraging their local community to set off fireworks with some consideration, since unexpected fireworks can trigger days of sleepless nights and an increase in post-traumatic stress disorder symptoms.

A less dramatic but common form of classical conditioning is involved in test anxiety. Test anxiety is used to describe situations where a test taker's anxiety causes a drop in performance on the exam (Sarason, 1961). Most research on test anxiety supports the idea that it can cause test takers with normal skills to underperform and do worse than they are capable of. Research has looked at the role of the instructions for a test, and what the nature and source of the "anxiety" in test anxiety might be. Highly anxious test takers tend to perform worse on tasks that are complex and timed (Siegman, 1956) and when they are told that the test is an important one (Sarason, 1961). What appear to be happening are not only the symptoms of physiological arousal, but the negative thinking that comes from a fear of being evaluated (Paulman & Kennelly, 1984; Sarason, 1984).

However, one cause of test anxiety appears to be a history of poor test results. Highly anxious test takers have been found to have poor organizational skills when studying that then sets them up for difficulty (Naveh-Benjamin, McKeachie, & Lin, 1987). Over time, they develop a history of frustration and disappointment with testing. It's possible that this anxiety leads to becoming a conditional response to test taking as well as to education in general.

To review, an organism learns to associate what had been a neutral stimulus with a preexisting stimulus and response during learning. Afterward, the now-conditional stimulus can trigger the response (or something similar to it) on its own.

Pavlov and later researchers spent a great amount of time and effort on examining the process of acquiring a conditional reflex. Timing of the presentation of the neutral stimulus during learning has been found to matter greatly. Let's use the end of a class period as an example. Most teachers have one or more "tells" when they are nearing the end of the material they have for the class period and when they anticipate winding down. Perhaps it is looking at their watch quickly, or turning off the projector. It could be verbal, such as saying, "Do we have any questions?" While they may or may not realize it, students learn to read these cues after a while and start packing up before the end of class is announced. So, what makes for the most effective presentation timing for learning the conditional reflex? Presenting the neutral stimulus after the unconditional stimulus has appeared rarely turns the neutral stimulus into a conditional stimulus (Miller & Barnet, 1993). If the professor announces the end of class and then looks at her watch, students are not likely to make a connection. If the neutral stimulus is presented at exactly the same time as the unconditional stimulus, there can be a weak association with the unconditional response. So if the professor announces the end of class while glancing at her watch, a weak conditional reflex might be learned. Perhaps during the term, she will look at her watch during lecture one day and some students in class will wonder, "Is it time to leave already?"

The strongest conditional reflex is built when the neutral stimulus occurs just before the unconditional stimulus. If a professor always looks at her watch and then a second or two later announces the end of the class, the neutral stimulus becomes a conditional "cue" that acts as a signal. That the unconditional stimulus and response are *contingent up* the neutral stimulus creates a learned association that is rapidly acquired and strong. Predictability is key (Rescorla, 1988). This is why cats so quickly develop a learned response to hearing a can opened in the kitchen, why people will start to wince if they see someone about to drag their nails along a chalkboard, and why they may salivate when they smell someone making microwavable popcorn.

Can any stimulus become a conditional stimulus? Some stimuli appear to be more apparent, or salient, to the learning organism and will become associated more quickly (Forsyth & Eifert, 1998; Maltzman & Boyd, 1984). Our hypothetical professor who checks her watch at the end of the lecture is providing an action that probably can be fairly easily associated with the end of class, since her action alludes to "time," and classes usually have a fixed end time. Another action, like adjusting a shirt collar, may not be learned as quickly. The relationship between her checking the watch and the end of class gives the impression of a cause-and-effect relationship to the students in her classes. Note this cause-and-effect relationship only has to be apparent to the students and might not be true in reality; it's possible that the professor has some other unknown reason for glancing down at her watch, but it won't matter to the students.

Is a learned, conditional reflex permanent? No, but then again, it can return quickly after being unlearned. The connection between the conditional stimulus and conditional response can end, particularly if the organism finds that the conditional stimulus no longer predicts the unconditional stimulus that provokes the response. For example, perhaps a professor usually ends an evening class about ten minutes early. After a while, the students become conditioned to the ten-minute early time as signaling the end of the class. But alas, at about midterm, he begins to lecture all the way through and sometimes goes overtime. The significance of the ten-minute early time fades.

And this is what has been found (Bouton, 1994; Pavlov, 1927/2015). The learned connection can weaken in a process called extinction. By repeatedly presenting the conditional stimulus without the unconditional stimulus, the response to later presentations of the conditional stimulus alone fades. The CS as a cue is no longer as predictive. Another example of this could be the tension one would feel driving past the scene of a car accident he or she had been in previously. A new accident doesn't happen (hopefully) each time that section of road is driven on, and after a while, the scene becomes decoupled from having had the accident (UCS) that provokes an emotional response (CS) of fear and pain.

The idea that emotional responses to a situation or thought can be learned is powerful, since the emotional response should be able to be unlearned. Mental health professionals are typically most concerned with those emotional responses that are negative and can interfere with daily functioning and obligations such as anxiety and depression. Hence, one entire approach to psychotherapy has been based on the idea of extinction from classical conditioning theory. "Behavioral theories," those that approach change in a client by asking him or her to alter their actions, often have a component that is based on the concept of extinction, called exposure. In exposure therapies, the client is

FIGURE 3.8   Responsiveness to a CS can generalize to other similar stimuli, but it will be weaker.

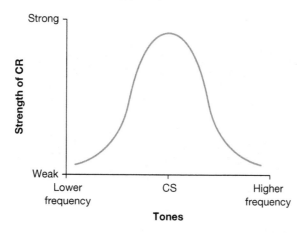

presented with stimuli that has been connected to a situation that provoked a negative emotional response, whether an assault, a traumatic car accident, or combat experience. The stimuli can be real or imagined. Then the client has to wait out the emotional response. Essentially the cue that has been predicting something traumatic becomes disassociated by repeating this kind of activity. The client finds that the thought of spiders or germs or the sound of fireworks no longer implies the actual traumatic event that was feared. This kind of approach has had success with treating phobias as well as obsessive-compulsive disorders, both of which have anxiety as a fundamental, emotional conditioned response (for an overview, see Mineka & Zinbarg, 2006). One challenge with this approach to therapy is that the process of extinction, as a learning mechanism, can take much longer than the original conditional reflex took to learn. The therapist and client have to commit to working on the extinction procedure.

But after extinction, the connection is not completely gone. Extinction itself can end very quickly if the UCS is reintroduced after extinction, or spontaneous recovery, just as can happen to Aplysia. When spontaneous recovery occurs, the initial strength of the conditional reflex is weaker than before, but it recovers at a much higher rate than in the initial trials of learning.

Likewise, the extinction of a connection that had been spontaneously recovered is faster as well. Although the connection remains, it is weaker all around. So if the professor begins to end class ten minutes early again, relearning will happen much more quickly than before but the strength of the connection will not be as great. If the following week, as the professor goes overtime again, then extinction happens again all the more rapidly (see Fig. 3.8).

Pavlov found other properties of this kind of learning to make associations. Once a conditional stimulus had been learned, the organism will respond to other stimuli that are similar in nature but not exactly the same, a property called generalization. Pavlov's dogs would respond to a tone that was similar in pitch to the learned CS, but it could be a little higher or lower. Typically, however, the strength of the response (in salivation) would decrease the more dissimilar the CS was from the stimulus (see Fig. 3.9).

FIGURE 3.9   Discrimination for a specific stimulus can be learned as well.

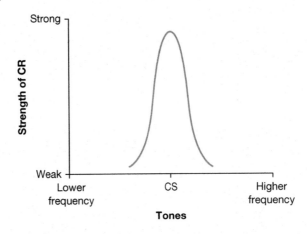

Source: Adapted from Fancher, R. E., & Rutherford, A. (2011).

Hence it is quite likely that fireworks do not actually have the fully physical or auditory impact of a rocket, gunfire, or a land mine, but their sound may be similar enough to create a resurgence of emotional responses.

Pavlov also found he could teach the dogs to discriminate between two or more stimuli, a process called differentiation. He could teach them to salivate at one symbol but not another that was similar. The presentation of a tone at one pitch might be followed by food, but not a tone at another pitch. The dogs would then learn to respond only to the conditional stimulus and ignore (even fall asleep) when presented with the other. Using this technique, Pavlov found that dogs didn't distinguish between colors very well and concluded they were colorblind.

Computer user interface design impacts millions of consumers and office workers daily. When working with a device, a primary issue is properly identifying which keys perform which functions. This is additionally difficult when the same key may do more than one task or have an "off/on" state, as the SHIFT key does. The digital keyboard that is used on a popular model of cellular phone presents a shift key as "on" when the up arrow is dark and contrasts with a white background, matching other letter keys on the keyboard, so the keyboard will produce capital letters. When the shift key is shown as "off," the up arrow is bright white. In both cases the letters on the keyboard are displayed in all caps. A website has been created to act as a reminder (http://ismyshift-keyonornot.com). This presents difficulties in distinguishing the proper role and wastes time; an earlier version of the keyboard had the shift key turn blue when enabled. While this example is mostly humorous, the implementation of confusing controls and signs can have life-or-death consequences in the medical, construction, and aerospace fields (Norman, 2013; Proctor & Van Zandt, 1994).

Besides associating a neutral stimulus to the unconditional stimulus to create a conditional reflex, classical conditioning can be extended to explain how another neutral stimulus, like a flash of light, can be associated with the original conditional stimulus (CS1). This new conditional stimulus (CS2) can then trigger the response too, in what is called second-order conditioning (or "higher-order conditioning"). The CS2 is presented with the CS1 and, after some trials, can generate the UCR even though the CS2 was never paired with the UCS. It's possible that higher-order conditioning underlies our ability to form "mental models" of situations and events by enabling us to perceive causal connections between the events, even when they do not necessarily occur together (Jara et al., 2006).

Attitudes, or our evaluations of objects, ideas, or people, appear to develop from classical conditioning. Olson and Fazio (2001) demonstrated how a classical-conditioning paradigm can create an attitude toward a novel object without conscious awareness of the association by pairing different Pokemon with positive or negative words as part of a larger task for the participants. Without any awareness, the pairings altered the participants' pleasantness ratings of the Pokemon. Similarly, Baccus, Baldwin, and Packer (2004) used a classical conditioning paradigm to increase the self-esteem of computer users by showing them a smiling face while they completed a word task.

One particularly troubling consequence of second-order classical conditioning is the development and maintenance of negative social attitudes that are derived from exposure to media reporting of the news. Just the exposure to the people presented as criminals on the nightly news means conditioning viewers to associate characteristics of gender, race, religion, age, and geographic location with "criminality." These implicit attitudes are viewed as involuntary, uncontrollable, and often unconscious evaluations of groups of people (Gawronski & Bodenhausen, 2006). While much of the news after the attacks on September 11, 2001, attempted to remain neutral to the nationality and apparent religion of the plane hijackers, the repeated presentations of "Arab," "Muslim," and "terrorist" within news stories should have, according to Pavlovian conditioning, conditioned people to make connections between those terms and the bombings (see, e.g., Das, Bushman, Bezemer, Kerkhof, & Vermeulen, 2009). These associations might be unconsciously learned and do not rise to the level of media framing or bias by themselves, but they still could exert an influence if unchecked by more controlled, consciously aware thinking. It's completely possible for someone, without awareness, to espouse one set of values or political views while behaving contrarily. Relatedly, Galdi, Arcuri, and Gawronski (2008) found that most of the voters in their sample who stated that they were undecided about a political event (like an election) already had implicit attitudes that predicted their eventual explicit attitude.

Implicit attitudes may be formed from childhood experiences. Implicit attitudes toward obesity was predicted better by the participants' own childhood weight and the weight of their mothers, but explicit attitudes toward obesity were predicted best by the participants' current weight (Rudman, Phelan, & Heppen, 2007). If findings like these hold true for most implicit attitudes, then they may be resistant to change since they tend to be outside of voluntary control and current experiences.

Further Applications

Since classical conditioning theory describes such a fundamental form of learning, the applications of it extend well past the examples we have looked at so far. This section looks at the role of classical conditioning in three surprisingly connected areas: sleep habits, drug overdoses, and education.

Virtually everyone struggles with insomnia at some point in their lives. The inability to get to sleep and stay asleep affects our waking lives in several ways, including weaker concentration, irritability, and poorer memory formation. In the worst cases, it can create a mental fatigue that is symptomatically similar to drunkenness. These situations create a problem for driving, operating machinery, or simply sticking to a good routine of diet and exercise. In some cases, insomnia can result from prescribed medications, stress from school or work, or a sleep disorder such as sleep apnea. But for many, insomnia is tied to the poor sleep habits that people develop (Lacks & Morin, 1992).

The bedroom, particularly the bed itself, is a stimulus that can trigger associations with the activities that commonly take place there; and for some, these include studying, watching television, checking social media, playing video games, eating, or hanging with friends, in addition to sleep and sex. From a classical conditioning perspective, the "bed" does not form a strongly conditioned cue to the activity of sleep, since it's associated with so many other activities. Part of maintaining good sleep hygiene is to use the bed primarily for sleep, so the body becomes conditioned to that activity in that space. When wanting to rest, getting into bed at night signals the proper activity, and the body relaxes (Smith & Haythornthwaite, 2004; Stepanski & Wyatt, 2003). If the sleeper wakes up too soon, sleep hygienists recommend quietly getting something to drink, mostly in the dark, and returning to bed.

While combating insomnia may involve training the body to do a desired activity in a particular spot, educators face a different problem: encouraging the activation of knowledge in places other than the classroom. *Transfer* involves being able to correctly identify real-world situations outside the classroom where some learned information or skill is applicable (Mayer & Wittrock, 1996), such as algebra or physics (Bassok, 1990). Unfortunately, most formal learning occurs in a staid classroom environment well removed from daily life, and (as you might have guessed) this means what is learned in that space can become conditioned to that environment. Hence, foreign language skills become easier to retrieve in Spanish class than at a Mexican restaurant. This means educators may find they need to schedule field trips to rehearse these skills outside the school building and encourage parents to practice learned skills at home (Bransford, Sherwood, Vye, & Rieser, 1986). Here the goal is to dilute the conditioned stimulus of the classroom. (In a later chapter, we will take a closer look at research on learning that is dependent on the context in which it was learned.)

While students may struggle with retrieving knowledge in contexts other than where they learned them, the role classical conditioning plays in uncontrolled, illicit drug use can be deadly. The public is more aware of drug use and the corresponding physiological impact on the body—terms like "tolerance" and "withdrawal" are now part of the common lexicon. To review, tolerance describes the effect of a drug losing its effectiveness with repeated use as the body's immune system adapts to the foreign substance. Withdrawal describes the effect of the immune system continuing to counteract the foreign substance if a person stops taking it as often as before. The body's attempt to adapt to the drug use now works against the individual, sometimes severely.

The counteractions of the body's immune system appear to be somewhat conditioned to the environment. That is, when the individual repeatedly uses a drug at home, the immune system starts to trigger the counteractions whenever the person is at home; the home environment has become a conditioned stimulus for self-administration of the drug (Siegel, Baptista, Kim, McDonald, & Weise-Kelly, 2000). Most likely, the thoughts and awareness of the person spontaneously trigger the body to prepare for possible usage of the drug in the same way that someone who has been experiencing stress at work begins to tense up involuntarily around the office. Unfortunately, these counteractions will not engage when the person decides to get high with a friend at his or her home. The body hasn't been conditioned to this new environment. So, the experienced drug user who now ingests the same amount of a drug that he or she has taken before finds the learned tolerance for the drug does not kick in and a "normal" amount of the drug creates a stronger reaction and can cause an overdose (Siegel, 1984; Siegel, Hinson, Krank, & McCully, 1982; Siegel & MacRae, 1984). This has become a commonly accepted explanation for why people tend to overdose in new environments rather than the usual ones.

Now let's turn to how skills are learned, particularly repetitive motor tasks. Like classical conditioning, the development of motor skills involves associating the correct movements with cues in the environment. Like classical conditioning, much of skill learning can be involuntary.

Skill Learning

Skills provide the ability to function in a wide range of contexts, including educational, recreational, and work settings. Starkes, Deakin, Allard, Hodges, and Hayes (1996) interviewed professional golfer Moe Norman who, by his 60s, had won over fifty tournaments and set over twenty-four course records. He is viewed now as one of the most accurate ball hitters ever in the sport (Neuman, 2014). When asked what made him such a good golfer, he would show "his left hand, the surface of which is so black and calloused that it looks like the tire of a race car" (p. 103). Extended practice is critical for extremely high levels of performance. At the age of 16, Moe Norman began hitting 800 balls a day to practice.

The study of how people acquire skills is often different from other areas of learning because the procedural skills themselves are of interest, not the language and knowledge needed to talk about them (Lee & Schmidt, 2008). How actions are made is the focus. Motor skills are those specific behaviors involved in the procedure necessary for tracing a line, shooting a basketball, using a tool, or dancing. The ability to move is a critical part of life—for feeding, survival, and reproduction. The issue is not usually which behavior to make so much as making the needed behavior when necessary. Some motor skills are seen as "closed-loop" skills, meaning that the execution of the behavior gives immediate feedback on what is next step for continuous motion, such as tracing a line. The environment for the activity is predictable and not likely to change: the task for the performer is to pick the correct action and to execute it. Table air hockey is an example—the nature of play is straightforward and contained. In contrast, "open-loop" skills may be necessary in more dynamic, complex environments where the precise action necessary may not be clear, such as a team sport like hockey or soccer.

There is evidence that learning a new motor skill appears to make structural changes to the brain, beyond just changes to the neurons themselves. Draganski and colleagues (2004) made brain scans of people both before and after spending three months learning to juggle, and found that structural changes to the temporal and parietal lobes had occurred. These areas are known for their relationship to movement, spatial thinking, and visual attention. These changes started to reverse themselves after three months of not juggling.

While we are generally aware of the activities that we do to improve ourselves, it appears the conscious memory of having done the activity for practice is not necessary for learning motor skills. We might be familiar with the general task but be unable to verbalize the rules behind the task or when we might have experienced the activity last. Amnesiacs such as Henry Molaison may do well with learning new motor skills, but they will not remember having practiced (Corkin, 1968; Milner, Corkin, & Teuber, 1968).

During the past one hundred years of research into motor skill learning, researchers develop tasks that their participants have not learned before, such as using Morse code, typing, or unusual drawing tasks such as tracing a mirror image (Snoddy, 1926, is an early example). As with any learning, motor skill learning will require gathering information about the procedure and what needs to be done, retaining that information over time, and successfully transferring those skills to similar or new environments.

Fitts (1964) proposed three stages for motor skill learning. First, the individual works to understand the requirements of the task and what is involved. This is primarily a cognitive stage, and the person is likely to need instructions to follow. Next, there is a motor stage, in which the typical movement patterns are gradually strengthened through repetition and with the help of sensory feedback. Usually the instructions are no longer necessary at this stage. Finally, the movements become automatic, and those behavior patterns are integrated into longer sequences that don't require much attention. It's possible at this point to engage in some secondary activity simultaneously while doing this primary one.

Another approach to the study of skill learning has been to observe experts in a range of fields, including physics, sports, music, and chess, and see how they acquire *expertise*. These researchers try to find skilled behaviors and decisions that can be recreated in laboratory conditions and tracked over time to see how those skills are developed. For many intense sports, performance may peak when the athlete is in his or her twenties (Ericsson, 1996). For more cognitive skills, such as physics and chess, peak age is highly variable and centers around the thirties. Long-term study of world-class experts in a domain has found that after starting practice, the experts-to-be transition to full-time at a critical point in their careers. At that point, they begin trying to set achievements for themselves, such as breaking records. The cost involved in the transition to full-time is often an issue for many (Ericsson, 1996).

Researchers have primarily investigated both the role of practice and the role that knowledge of the results (typically in the form of feedback) have on skill learning.

Role of Practice

The aspect of skill learning most commonly researched is, perhaps unsurprisingly, the role of practice. The default conception of practice is that more is better, and this is mostly true. The power law of practice describes the finding that simply repeating a task in practice trials tends to speed up performance, but the rate of improvement varies over time. The improvement in performance happens in a logarithmic (curved) function. There are great improvements to be made in the beginning of learning, but after a while, the improvements in performance become smaller despite many more trials.

Chase and Simon (1973), comparing length of time most internationally recognized performers had spent in training to reach that status, found it took about ten years for someone to reach that level of performance. This period of time seems to be a constant across many domains (Anders & Charness, 1994; Anders, Krampe, & Tesch-Römer, 1993; Charness, Krampe, & Mayr, 1996). This does not mean that participating in an activity for ten years will automatically make one an expert, so much as that dedicated focus for about a decade seems to be a commonly necessary prerequisite for national-grade expertise (see Fig. 3.10).

Ericsson, Krampe, and Tesch-Römer (1993) also claim that it is not a matter of simply repeating a task to reach a peak level of performance. Ericsson and his colleagues have proposed that to truly advance beyond one's peers, a specific kind of practice is needed—essentially, practice with the goal of removing errors. Deliberate practice involves working on a clear task of appropriate difficulty, with feedback and repetitions to correct mistakes. The purpose of deliberate practice is to become able to create an optimal performance reliably. Enjoyment of the activity itself is secondary.

Ericsson's focus on deliberate practice is not likely to be the entire story. Many people who engage in some activity wishing to excel at a national or international level drop

FIGURE 3.10   Hours of estimated practice by age for good violinists. The ranges show the variance in reported practice from low performing to expert and professional violinists.

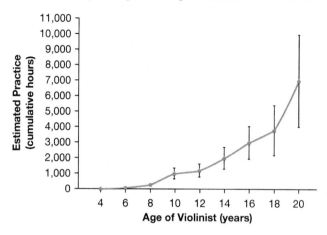

out at some point, due to many possible factors, including financial strain, lack of motivation, or a lack of innate talent (Sternberg, 1996). The combination of those factors may be simply impossible to study empirically over the lifetimes of randomly selected individuals who might attempt to excel at a task.

To what extent should a specific motor skill be studied in isolation from or in combination with other skills? In other words, does practicing switching from one skill to a related one create a contextual interference in learning those skills? Most complex activities, such as playing soccer, require mastery of a number of movements that are not reproduced one at a time in a predictable sequence—instead, the player is expected to have mastered a range of movements that can be produced as the situation demands.

Shea and Morgan (1979) reported on a classic test of this sort of situation. Participants had to complete either blocked schedules of movements—that is, one movement executed repeatedly—or schedules of random moves. In the blocked schedule, the participant would be able to execute a move, get feedback in the form of seeing the result, and repeat it. In the random schedule of moves, it would not be clear from one moment to the next which move would be next. Nothing would be repeated more than once. It's possible to imagine the blocked schedule as being similar to a soccer coach who asks the team to work on a particular skill, such as an outside-of-the-foot pass, repeatedly. The random block would be more like calling out random skills or scrimmage.

The blocked schedule produced faster learning in the participants in the Shea and Morgan study (1979). However, when participants returned ten days later and repeated the schedules from before, the participants who had experienced the random schedule showed greater improvement. Possibly, the interference of other skills may be worse for learning a new skill but has a benefit with retention. Learning an isolated task is a problem for incorporating into a context of numerous moves; learning in a context can help to retain the skill by providing more variety (Battig, 1979). So, blocked practice means that the movement prepares the individual only to repeat the movement—it cues itself—whereas random practice means having to learn to be ready for something else. This random practice might help for retaining and transferring skills since the wider range of behaviors cues any one movement. An example of this might be a fifth grader who is struggling with timed multiplication tests. Initially it might be best to focus on just one set of multiplication factors, but eventually the range of possible combinations should become more flexible so the child is best prepared for whatever sequence of quiz prompts are presented in class.

The benefit of randomized practice might be because the varied movements present an opportunity for the learner to discern contrasts between the different movements; the entire experience might be more memorable (Lee & Schmidt, 2008). Wright and Shea (1991) found that with increasingly complex tasks, the learners became more dependent on the situation for contextual cues to improve performance. This could be a problem for, say, baseball players who begin to forget their skills in ball parks that are not where the team typically practices. Additionally, for each movement, there will be a space in time between when it is practiced and when it is called for again. This means that the learner has to recall and reconstruct the movement, practicing the retrieval of that movement in addition to the action itself (Lee & Magill, 1983).

Of course, these principles assume that a coach or teacher is picking the training schedule for the learner. What if the learner picks the schedule? Some evidence indicates that the schedules the learner picks out individually are what are best for him or her (Keetch & Lee, 2007). But in some cases, knowing the best overall schedule appears to be a challenge, particularly if the results are counterintuitive. Is it better to have long, infrequent practice sessions? Or short ones that are repeated frequently? Often, because of busy schedules and procrastination, we are left to put all of the effort into a task near a deadline. Working at the last minute for long hours often feels like we are shouldering the burden of effort simply because we can feel the strain. But is that the best way to learn a skill?

Role of Feedback

Another factor heavily researched in motor skill learning is the role of feedback, or being presented with knowledge of results of a performance. Outside of research environments, feedback often has a social element, and can come from a variety of other people beyond ourselves, including coaches and teachers (Glaser, 1996). For example, figure skaters are usually under a very high level of monitoring from a team of coaches (Starkes, Deakin, Allard, Hodges, & Hayes, 1996). Other people may structure the tasks to be performed so they gradually increase in difficulty and choose those tasks more likely to provide growth and feedback. Ideally the instructor can remove support over time as the learner masters the necessary skills and becomes more self-regulated and reliant on self-study (Charness, Krampe, & Mayr, 1996). For example, figure skaters are usually under a very high level of monitoring from a team of coaches (Starkes et al., 1996).

Is having knowledge of the results while learning helpful? Feedback has been found to be good for learning a motor skill, generally, but it can be overdone. If too much feedback was given, the learning process was disrupted (Salmoni, Schmidt, & Walter, 1984; Winstein & Schmidt, 1990). Feedback may primarily act as guidance, and it doesn't necessarily cause learning to occur.

If providing feedback helps with learning, when should it be given—while the learner is performing the task, or after? Wulf and Schmidt (1989) found providing feedback during the task itself was helpful when learning the task, but reducing the amount of feedback over all helped to improve memory for the skill. In one condition, participants who did not receive any feedback during the learning phase retained the information longer than those who did. Possibly the presence of guiding feedback, while helpful to learn a skill, can become a crutch if the learner begins to expect it. Wulf and Schmidt suggest starting training with guiding feedback but reducing it over time.

Encouraging self-analysis appears to help retention as well. Swinnen, Schmidt, Nicholson, and Shapiro (1990) found the timing of feedback was best for retention when the participants were asked to describe how well they did after a trial performance, encouraging some open reflection, before providing any feedback. Providing instantaneous feedback after a performance didn't allow the participants to develop their own ability to detect the mistakes they were making.

Should feedback be given on every trial, or only occasionally? Providing feedback during every trial, such as a video display showing the best arm movement, helps when someone is learning a new skill but not once the skill has been mastered (Schmidt & Wulf, 1997). However, if the guidance is not available at all after learning, performance drops.

Ordinarily, not every performance of a task can be acknowledged by a coach or teacher. Given the need to reduce the frequency of feedback, how often should summary feedback of several trials be given? Researchers have experimented with feedback of performance over fewer trials as well as with longer sets of about fifteen. Yao, Fischman, and Wang (1994) found that summaries over mid-sized sets of trials of about five were best compared to 15 trial summaries. One advantage of not receiving feedback from an instructor on every trial is that the learner has an opportunity to mentally estimate his or her own performance and receives less interference from others during this self-evaluation.

In our final section on simple learning, we'll take a look at research on the nature of unintentional or implicit learning. As noted above, Henry Molaison showed some signs of learning after all—but only for very specific simple tasks, and he never remembered any prior experiences with those tasks (Corkin, 1968). For example, he improved his ability to follow a dot on a spinning disc with both his preferred hand and his nonpreferred hand over several days.

Molaison's learning included improved performance on simple mazes (Milner, Corkin, & Teuber, 1968). Once, given a particularly challenging task he had done many times before, Molaison commented to one of the researchers that the task was "easier than I thought it would be" (Carey, 2008). He gradually became more familiar and comfortable with the scientists who were visiting him so frequently, despite not remembering having previously met them. So, some form of unintentional, non-conscious learning was happening over time after all (see Fig. 3.11). Let's take a look now at research on unintentional, implicit learning.

Implicit Learning

Implicit learning is the act of learning a task incidentally, without intent. It is not necessarily a conscious act, although we might become aware of implicitly learning something after the fact with improved performance. An early study on amnesiacs found evidence for this kind of unintentional learning. Warrington and Weiskrantz (1968, 1974) asked volunteers and amnesiac patients to study lists of common words for several minutes. When shown a list of words that included a mix of studied and unstudied words, however, the amnesiac patients were unable to recognize words that they had seen previously. Yet when asked to complete some word fragments with several possible answers—that is, when shown a part of a word such as "TAB__" and asked to finish the

FIGURE 3.11 On a two-handed tracking task, H.M. showed improvement similar to controls, while not remembering having attempted the task before.

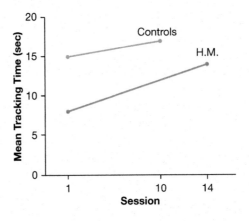

FIGURE 3.12 Amnesiacs showed the same level of recall of studied words with a cue as controls, but an inability to consciously recognize words they had studied (adapted from Warrington & Weiskrantz, 1974).

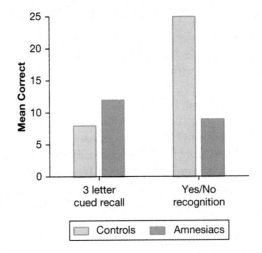

word—the amnesiac patients finished the fragments using the words they had studied earlier, at the same rate as did the volunteers. This was despite not being aware that they had seen the words previously (see Fig. 3.12).

The philosopher Bergson asserted that the past survived "in two forms," one more conscious and the other unconscious, like a habit (1911, reprinted 2004). The term "implicit learning" appears to have been first used in print by Reber in (1967). Graf and Schacter (1985) defined implicit learning as learning that is unconscious. In an implicit memory, there is no study period to reflect back to, and usually verbally stating what was learned is not possible. Teenagers may find they can mimic and master how other young adults are dancing more quickly than they can explain the moves to a younger sibling, for example. Similarly, Lewicki, Czyzewska, and Hoffman (1987) point out that few people can explain what they find attractive about the faces of other people, yet we make decisions about what we like and don't like rapidly. Some theorists see implicit learning to be largely about learned associations between concepts, ideas, and patterns, whereas explicit learning gives us the ability to state a proposition (Gawronski & Bodenhausen, 2006). So, a child might taste a new, healthy vegetable in his or her dinner meal and have a quick, automatic emotional response that gives rise to the comment of disgust, "I don't like this!"

If the process of implicit learning can't be seen or talked about, how is implicit learning to be studied? The only way to show evidence for implicit learning is to track changes in behavior, such as a participant's improving on a task over time, rather than to recall studying the skill, using reaction time and other behavioral measures. The process of implicit learning is generally seen as quick, automatic, and unconscious. The process of explicit learning is consciously controlled and is more in line with analytical thinking and complex problem-solving skills that fall under the construct of "intelligence," or abstract problem solving (Stanovich & West, 2000). As others have argued (e.g., Baddeley, 1999 p. 86), the distinction between implicit and explicit memory is not firm. The group of processes that psychologists consider to be "implicit" are defined primarily by the lack of conscious learning. They are not necessarily the opposite of "explicit" learning, as much as conscious control isn't present in those forms of learning, so the field has labeled them as "implicit."

Some characteristics of implicit learning and the resulting memories are agreed on. First, we have trouble verbalizing that which we have learned implicitly. Second, the implicit memory that results is usually not flexible, and it can't be consciously reconsidered. The process generally relies on superficial processing, such as the recognition of patterns, and generally involves simple associations. Third, the biological mechanisms underlying implicit learning play a more singular role than do those in intentional learning.

To help see the difference in research, Lewicki et al. (1987) provided a classic example of a study using an implicit learning task. In the first of two reported experiments, participants looked for a target character, a single digit, in one of the four quadrants on a screen. When they found it, they were to push a button that identified the quadrant where they had found the digit. Their performance was timed to see how quickly they could find the digit. For each trial, they did this visual search of the screen seven times: The first six were relatively easy since there were no other characters to distract the participants onscreen. In the last search, other digits were present onscreen as distractors. These trials were repeated over a twelve-hour period, which meant each participant completed 4,608 trials and pushed a button more than 30,000 times. (They did get breaks.) As is common with studies where small differences of reaction time are being examined and a lot of data are collected in a within-subjects design, this study used very few subjects—one male and two females.

Here's how implicit learning was examined in this study. Unbeknownst to the participants, there was a pattern to the placement of the digit. On the first, third, fourth, and sixth search of each trial, there was a rule to the order of where the digit would appear; and this would predict exactly where the digit would appear in the last, seventh search. During the other searches, the placement was randomly picked by the computer, as distractor trials. There were twenty-four different sequences that the computer would select from when presenting the trials to the participants. Lewicki and colleagues were essentially testing whether participants could unknowingly pick up on a complex pattern to quicken their reaction time on the final search that included distracting digits. Interviews conducted after the study found the participants to be completely unaware of the presence of any pattern. (A pilot study with the same materials had found other participants were unable to find a pattern when told about the pattern in advance, with the promise of an extra $100 if they found it.)

All three participants improved their reaction time dramatically during the twelve hours by more than a second on average. They had implicitly learned to pick up on the sequences that gave away the location of the target character in the last search of each trial. Just to make a more compelling test, in the final hours of the study, the researchers changed the rules for locating the digit, so the patterns that the participants were exposed to would no longer help. As expected, this slowed the participants' rate of response. Now, they had prior knowledge that momentarily worked against them (see Fig. 3.13). Somehow they had picked up the rules implicitly. As the researchers point out, not only did the participants learn some complex patterns without awareness, but they employed them without awareness. Both the implicit acquisition of the knowledge as well as its use appeared to be outside their control.

Implicit learning appears to be important in aspects of life outside of the laboratory. One example is the role of implicit learning in how infants learn. Unlike what adults experience, babies in the first six months of life do not have decades of knowledge or verbal skills built up during the experience of daily living. Life is mostly a matter of sensing patterns and trends in the environment and making basic connections between them; what a baby learns is likely to be heavily implicit in nature. Despite our lack of conscious awareness of this form of learning, it appears to have a fairly strong impact on what we retain, can impact how we behave later, and may be a core part of what it means to be an organism that can adapt successfully to its surroundings (Lieberman, 2000).

FIGURE 3.13   **Participants appeared to learn the sequence rules implicitly, and were disrupted when the rules suddenly changed.**

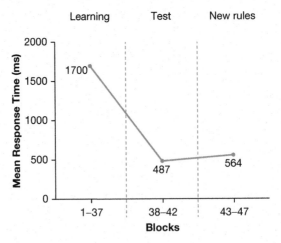

What Is Learned in Implicit Learning

Other researchers have tried to establish what is retained from implicit learning. Most see implicit learning as primarily a matter of learning simple patterns, with more conscious attention required for complex patterns. There are three theories surrounding what is learned during implicit learning. First, implicit learning may involve learning basic rules behind the structures of sentences and meaning. An early study on implicit learning found that participants could learn the artificial grammar of a fictitious language of letters (Reber, 1967). In contrast to a group of participants who had to work with randomly arranged letters, the participants who received the letters that followed a rule-based system made fewer errors, even though the rules were never explicitly taught.

Second, implicit learning may involve simply learning to pool the averages of an overall sample of items. As we engage in an activity repeatedly, we implicitly learn the general nature of the activity and its characteristics. Third, implicit learning may involve becoming familiar with the statistical patterns and regularities over time, for example, how often certain characteristics of the situation tend to appear, which cues present themselves first, or what characteristics often present themselves in combination with other characteristics. These learned patterns become units or chunks of information. At the moment, all three of these options are still considered viable theories.

Reviewing a broad amount of research, Lieberman (2000) concluded that areas of the brain inside the basal ganglia were responsible for implicit learning (see Fig. 3.14). Parkinson's and Huntington's diseases are known typically to affect the basal ganglia, and patients of either disease have an inability to learn implicitly (Lieberman, 2010; Lieberman, Chang, Chiao, Bookheimer, & Knowlton, 2004). This connection was later verified using neuroimaging studies (e.g., Lieberman et al., 2004; Poldrack et al., 2001).

FIGURE 3.14   The parts that make up the basal ganglia and related areas are nested deep inside the brain.

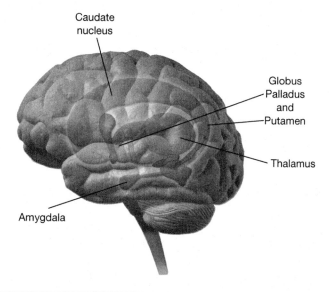

Source: Garrett (2015, Figure 11.20, p. 361).

CHAPTER SUMMARY

This chapter examined the biological basis of learning and described three research areas that involve basic forms of learning. First, the process of neurotransmission or how neurons communicate in the central nervous system was reviewed in order to provide the conceptual basis of how neurons may adapt to changes in our environment. Of most importance are the ideas that neurons communicate by releasing chemicals ("neurotransmitters") between them, and neurons have "dendrites" that accept incoming neurotransmitters. So, on a physiological level, neurons support learning in one of three ways: through changes in the amount of neurotransmitters that are released between them, by modifying existing dendrites, or by new neuron growth.

The sea slug, Aplysia, demonstrates some of the more basic aspects of nonassociative learning, or learning in which only one stimulus is involved. The sea slug can habituate to a stimulus, meaning that it will respond less after repeated exposure to the stimulus of having its gill poked. If the gill hasn't been poked in a while, it can respond at full strength again, a phenomenon known as spontaneous recovery. Additionally, if it's given a strong touch, then it becomes sensitized and will essentially overreact when given a weak touch.

Classical conditioning describes the process that results in our ability to take cues from the environment as to what is about to occur. Research on classical conditioning finds that having the novel stimulus precede the original, an unconditional stimulus and response works best for establishing that connection. Like nonassociative learning, classically conditioned associations can be habituated and spontaneously recover as well. Associations can be generalized to other similar stimuli as well.

Skill learning involves executing a series of actions on demand. Practice makes perfect, but initial progress usually is much better than later progress. Expertise in a skilled area appears to require years of practice that is aimed at eliminating mistakes. It is slower to practice an interrelated set of skills, but the learner performs better later on than when he or she has studied each skill only in isolation. Knowledge of the results of one's performance seems to matter greatly to the learning process. Guidance is helpful initially, but it needs to be tapered off; and cumulative feedback often works better than feedback on each performance.

The final form of learning discussed in this chapter was implicit learning, or learning without conscious awareness. Amnesiacs have been found to be able to make incremental performance improvements with tasks such as mazes over time, despite having no awareness of having attempted them before. What we learn implicitly seems to be relatively shallow and is hard to verbalize or reorganize. It's likely that what are learned implicitly are averages and patterns of the general nature of some stimulus.

REVIEW QUESTIONS

1. Describe the steps involved in neurotransmission. Hypothetically, what is "learning" at the neural level?

2. What is a conditional reflex you realize now that you have formed? What would be the conditional stimulus? Has the conditional reflex generalized? How would extinction work, if you wanted to weaken the reflex?

3. As a coach hired to turn around a struggling high school soccer team, what kinds of steps would you take to instill your players with the best retention of their skills? How often should the team practice? What kind of feedback should they receive?

4. Are we aware of all of the learning we acquire? How do we know that we are not learning?

KEY TERMS

FURTHER RESOURCES

- Video on sea slugs for memory research by NOVAscienceNOW: "A Memorable Snail" PBS—YouTube

- Kandel talks about his research with Aplysia: Memories Are Made of This—YouTube

- An interactive site on synapses:
  - synapses.clm.utexas.edu

- "Apollo" Robbins, stage pickpocket
  - New Yorker profile: A Pickpocket's Tale
  - also his own website: www.istealstuff.com

- A photo collection of Pavlov's dogs:
  - http://dubnaulab.cshl.edu/data/JD_dogs.html

REFERENCES

Anders, K., & Charness, N. (1994). Expert performance: Its structure and acquisition. *American Psychologist, 49*(8), 725–747. https://doi.org/10.1037/0003–066X.49.8.725

Anders, K., Krampe, R. T., & Tesch-Römer, C. (1993). The role of deliberate practice in the acquisition of expert performance. *Psychological Review, 100*(3), 363–406. https://doi.org/10.1037/0033–295X.100.3.363

Baccus, J. R., Baldwin, M. W., & Packer, D. J. (2004). Increasing implicit self-esteem through classical conditioning. *Psychological Science, 15*(7), 498–502.

Baddeley, A. D. (1999). *The Resource Library: Essentials of human memory* (1st ed.). Hove, England: Psychology Press.

Baillargeon, R. (1995). Physical reasoning in infancy. *The Cognitive Neurosciences,* 181–204.

Bassok, M. (1990). Transfer of domain-specific problem-solving procedures. *Journal of Experimental Psychology: Learning, Memory, and Cognition, 16*(3), 522.

Battig, W. F. (1979). The flexibility of human memory. In Cermak, L. S., & Craik, F. I. M. (Eds.), *Levels of processing and human memory* (23–44). Hillsdale, NJ: Erlbaum.

Bear, M. F. (2003). Bidirectional synaptic plasticity: From theory to reality. *Philosophical Transactions of the Royal Society of London. Series B: Biological Sciences, 358*(1432), 649–655.

Bergson, H. (2004). *Matter and memory.* Courier Dover Publications. Retrieved from http://books.google.com/books?hl=en&lr=&id=G9XAeb1mx6gC&oi=fnd&pg=PR7&dq=bergson+matter+and+memory&ots=4Q-T30jm8E&sig=4HuvLpVjfdQazxZP4Z60Xprs3_0

Bhatt, D. H., Zhang, S., & Gan, W.-B. (2009). Dendritic spine dynamics. *Annual Review of Physiology, 71,* 261–282.

Bouton, M. E. (1994). Conditioning, remembering, and forgetting. *Journal of Experimental Psychology: Animal Behavior Processes, 20*(3), 219.

Bransford, J., Sherwood, R., Vye, N., & Rieser, J. (1986). Teaching thinking and problem solving: Research foundations. *American Psychologist, 41*(10), 1078.

Carey, B. (2008, December 5). H. M., an unforgettable amnesiac, dies at 82. *The New York Times.* Retrieved from http://www.nytimes.com/2008/12/05/us/05hm.html

Charness, A. N., Krampe, R., & Mayr, U. (1996). The role of practice and coaching in entrepreneurial skill domains: An international comparison of LifeSpanChess Skill. In K. A. Ericsson (Ed.), *The road to excellence: The acquisition of expert performance in the arts and sciences, sports, and games* (pp. 51–80). Mahwah, NJ: Erlbaum.

Chase, W. G., & Simon, H. A. (1973). The mind's eye in chess. In *Visual information processing* (pp. 394–403). Oxford, England: Academic.

Corkin, S. (1968). Acquisition of motor skill after bilateral medial temporal-lobe excision. *Neuropsychologia, 6*(3), 255–265.

Das, E., Bushman, B. J., Bezemer, M. D., Kerkhof, P., & Vermeulen, I. E. (2009). How terrorism news reports increase prejudice against outgroups: A terror management account. *Journal of Experimental Social Psychology, 45*(3), 453–459. https://doi.org/10.1016/j.jesp.2008.12.001

Davies, S. N., Lester, R. A. J., Reymann, K. G., & Collingridge, G. L. (1989). Temporally distinct pre- and post-synaptic mechanisms maintain long-term potentiation. *Nature, 338*(6215), 500–503. https://doi.org/10.1038/338500a0

Dittrich, L. (n.d.). Henry's story. Retrieved from http://thebrainobservatory.ucsd.edu/hm_web/images/HMs_Story.pdf

Draganski, B., Gaser, C., Busch, V., Schuierer, G., Bogdahn, U., & May, A. (2004). Neuroplasticity: Changes in grey matter induced by training. *Nature, 427*(6972), 311–312. https://doi.org/10.1038/427311a

Ericsson, K. A. (Ed.) (1996). *The road to excellence: The acquisition of expert performance in the arts and sciences, sports, and games.* Mahwah, NJ: Erlbaum.

Ericsson, K. A., Krampe, R. T., & Tesch-Römer, C. (1993). The role of deliberate practice in the acquisition of expert performance. *Psychological Review, 100*(3), 363–406.

Fitts, P. M. (1964). Perceptual-motor skill learning. *Categories of Human Learning,* 243–285.

Forsyth, J. P., & Eifert, G. H. (1998). Response intensity in content-specific fear conditioning comparing 20% versus 13% CO_2-enriched air as unconditioned stimuli. *Journal of Abnormal Psychology, 107*(2), 291–304. https://doi.org/10.1037/0021–843X.107.2.291

Galdi, S., Arcuri, L., & Gawronski, B. (2008). Automatic mental associations predict future choices of undecided decision-makers. *Science, 321*(5892), 1100–1102.

Gawronski, B., & Bodenhausen, G. V. (2006). Associative and propositional processes in evaluation: An integrative review of implicit and explicit attitude change. *Psychological Bulletin, 132*(5), 692.

Gelfo, F., De Bartolo, P., Giovine, A., Petrosini, L., & Leggio, M. G. (2009). Layer and regional effects of environmental enrichment on the pyramidal neuron morphology of the rat. *Neurobiology of Learning and Memory, 91*(4), 353–365. https://doi.org/10.1016/j.nlm.2009.01.010

Glaser, R. (1996). Changing the agency for learning: Acquiring expert performance. In K. A. Ericsson (Ed.), *The road to excellence: The acquisition of expert performance in the arts and sciences, sports, and games* (pp. 347–354). Mahwah, NJ: Erlbaum.

Gould, E. (2007). How widespread is adult neurogenesis in mammals? *Nature Reviews Neuroscience, 8*(6), 481–488. https://doi.org/10.1038/nrn2147

Graf, P., & Schacter, D. L. (1985). Implicit and explicit memory for new associations in normal and amnesic subjects. *Journal of Experimental Psychology: Learning, Memory, and Cognition, 11*(3), 501.

Hayashi, Y., & Majewska, A. K. (2005). Dendritic spine geometry: Functional implication and regulation. *Neuron, 46*(4), 529–532. https://doi.org/10.1016/j.neuron.2005.05.006

Hebb, D. O. (1949). *The organization of behavior: A neuropsychological theory* (1st ed.). Wiley.

Hollis, K. L. (1997). Contemporary research on Pavlovian conditioning: A "new" functional analysis. *American Psychologist, 52*(9), 956–965. https://doi.org/10.1037/0003-066X.52.9.956

Jara, E., Vila, J., & Maldonado, A. (2006). Second-order conditioning of human causal learning. *Learning and Motivation, 37*(3), 230–246. https://doi.org/10.1016/j.lmot.2005.12.001

Kandel, E. R. (1976). *Cellular basis of behavior: An introduction to behavioral neurobiology/Eric R. Kandel.* San Francisco, CA: W. H. Freeman.

Kandel, E. R. (2001). The molecular biology of memory storage: A dialogue between genes and synapses. *Science, 294*(5544), 1030–1038.

Keetch, K. M., & Lee, T. D. (2007). The effect of self-regulated and experimenter-imposed practice schedules on motor learning for tasks of varying difficulty. *Research Quarterly for Exercise and Sport, 78*(5), 476–486. https://doi.org/10.1080/02701367.2007.10599447

Kibbe, M. M., & Leslie, A. M. (2011). What do infants remember when they forget? Location and identity in 6-month-olds' memory for objects. *Psychological Science, 22*(12), 1500–1505.

Lacks, P., & Morin, C. M. (1992). Recent advances in the assessment and treatment of insomnia. *Journal of Consulting and Clinical Psychology, 60*(4), 586–594. https://doi.org/10.1037/0022-006X.60.4.586

Lee, T. D., & Magill, R. A. (1983). The locus of contextual interference in motor-skill acquisition. *Journal of Experimental Psychology: Learning, Memory, and Cognition, 9*(4), 730–746. https://doi.org/10.1037/0278-7393.9.4.730

Lee, T. D., & Schmidt, R. A. (2008). Motor learning and memory. *Cognitive Psychology of Memory, 2,* 645–662.

Leuner, B., & Gould, E. (2010). Structural plasticity and hippocampal function. *Annual Review of Psychology, 61,* 111–140. https://doi.org/10.1146/annurev.psych.093008.100359

Leuner, B., Gould, E., & Shors, T. J. (2006). Is there a link between adult neurogenesis and learning? *Hippocampus, 16*(3), 216–224. https://doi.org/10.1002/hipo.20153

Lewicki, P., Czyzewska, M., & Hoffman, H. (1987). Unconscious acquisition of complex procedural knowledge. *Journal of Experimental Psychology: Learning, Memory, and Cognition, 13*(4), 523–530. https://doi.org/10.1037/0278-7393.13.4.523

Lieberman, M. D. (2000). Intuition: A social cognitive neuroscience approach. *Psychological Bulletin, 126*(1), 109–137. https://doi.org/10.1037/0033-2909.126.1.109

Lieberman, M. D. (2010). Social cognitive neuroscience. In *Handbook of social psychology.* John Wiley & Sons, Inc. Retrieved from http://onlinelibrary.wiley.com/doi/10.1002/9780470561119.socpsy001005/abstract

Lieberman, M. D., Chang, G. Y., Chiao, J., Bookheimer, S. Y., & Knowlton, B. J. (2004). An event-related fMRI study of artificial grammar learning in a balanced chunk strength design. *Journal of Cognitive Neuroscience, 16*(3), 427–438. https://doi.org/10.1162/089892904322926764

Maltzman, I., & Boyd, G. (1984). Stimulus significance and bilateral SCRs to potentially phobic pictures. *Journal of Abnormal Psychology, 93*(1), 41–46. https://doi.org/10.1037/0021-843X.93.1.41

Mayer, R. E., & Wittrock, M. C. (1996). Problem-solving transfer. *Handbook of Educational Psychology,* 47–62.

Miller, R. R., & Barnet, R. C. (1993). The role of time in elementary associations. *Current Directions in Psychological Science, 2*(4), 106–111. https://doi.org/10.1111/1467-8721.ep10772577

Milner, B., Corkin, S., & Teuber, H.-L. (1968). Further analysis of the hippocampal amnesic syndrome: 14-year follow-up study of H.M. *Neuropsychologia, 6*(3), 215–234. https://doi.org/10.1016/0028-3932(68)90021-3

Mineka, S., & Zinbarg, R. (2006). A contemporary learning theory perspective on the etiology of anxiety disorders: It's not what you thought it was. *American Psychologist, 61*(1), 10–26. https://doi.org/10.1037/0003–066X.61.1.10

Naveh-Benjamin, M., McKeachie, W. J., & Lin, Y. (1987). Two types of test-anxious students: Support for an information processing model. *Journal of Educational Psychology, 79*(2), 131–136. https://doi.org/10.1037/0022–0663.79.2.131

Neuman, J. (2014, July 26). Moe Norman: Golf's greatest ball striker? *Wall Street Journal.* Retrieved from http://online.wsj.com/articles/moe-norman-golfs-greatest-ball-striker-1406338027

Norman, D. A. (Ed.). (1970). *Models of human memory.* New York: Academic Press Inc.

Olson, M. A., & Fazio, R. H. (2001). Implicit attitude formation through classical conditioning. *Psychological Science, 12*(5), 413–417.

Paulman, R. G., & Kennelly, K. J. (1984). Test anxiety and ineffective test taking: Different names, same construct? *Journal of Educational Psychology, 76*(2), 279–288. https://doi.org/10.1037/0022–0663.76.2.279

Pavlov, I. P. (2015). *Conditioned reflexes: An investigation of the physiological activity of the cerebral cortex.* (G. V. Anrep, Trans.). Mansfield Centre, CT: Martino Fine Books. (Reprint of 1927 edition)

Poldrack, R. A., Clark, J., Paré-Blagoev, E. J., Shohamy, D., Creso Moyano, J., Myers, C., & Gluck, M. A. (2001). Interactive memory systems in the human brain. *Nature, 414*(6863), 546–550. https://doi.org/10.1038/35107080

Proctor, R. W., & Van Zandt, T. (1994). *Human factors in simple and complex systems.* Boston, MA: Allyn and Bacon.

Reber, A. S. (1967). Implicit learning of artificial grammars. *Journal of Verbal Learning and Verbal Behavior, 6*(6), 855–863. https://doi.org/10.1016/S0022–5371(67)80149-X

Rescorla, R. A. (1988). Pavlovian conditioning: It's not what you think it is. *American Psychologist, 43*(3), 151–160. https://doi.org/10.1037/0003–066X.43.3.151

Roediger, H. L., & Craik, F. (2014). *Varieties of memory and consciousness: Essays in honour of Endel Tulving.* New York, NY: Psychology Press.

Rosenzweig, M. R. (1984). Experience, memory, and the brain. *American Psychologist, 39*(4), 365–376. https://doi.org/10.1037/0003–066X.39.4.365

Rudman, L. A., Phelan, J. E., & Heppen, J. B. (2007). Developmental sources of implicit attitudes. *Personality and Social Psychology Bulletin, 33*(12), 1700–1713. https://doi.org/10.1177/0146167207307487

Rudy, J. W. (2013). *The neurobiology of learning and memory* (2nd ed.). Sunderland, MA: Sinauer Associates, Inc.

Salmoni, A. W., Schmidt, R. A., & Walter, C. B. (1984). Knowledge of results and motor learning: A review and critical reappraisal. *Psychological Bulletin, 95*(3), 355–386. https://doi.org/10.1037/0033–2909.95.3.355

Sarason, I. G. (1961). The effects of anxiety and threat on the solution of a difficult task. *The Journal of Abnormal and Social Psychology, 62*(1), 165–168. https://doi.org/10.1037/h0043924

Sarason, I. G. (1984). Stress, anxiety, and cognitive interference: Reactions to tests. *Journal of Personality and Social Psychology, 46*(4), 929–938. https://doi.org/10.1037/0022–3514.46.4.929

Schmidt, R. A., & Wulf, G. (1997). Continuous concurrent feedback degrades skill learning: Implications for training and simulation. *Human Factors: The Journal of the Human Factors and Ergonomics Society, 39*(4), 509–525.

Sechenov, I. (1965). *Reflexes of the brain.* Cambridge, MA: MIT Press.

Shea, J. B., & Morgan, R. L. (1979). Contextual interference effects on the acquisition, retention, and transfer of a motor skill. *Journal of Experimental Psychology: Human Learning and Memory, 5*(2), 179–187. https://doi.org/10.1037/0278–7393.5.2.179

Siegel, S. (1984). Pavlovian conditioning and heroin overdose: Reports by overdose victims. *Bulletin of the Psychonomic Society, 22*(5), 428–430. https://doi.org/10.3758/BF03333867

Siegel, S., Hinson, R. E., Krank, M. D., & McCully, J. (1982). Heroin "overdose" death: Contribution of drug-associated environmental cues. *Science, 216*(4544), 436–437. https://doi.org/10.1126/science.7200260

Siegel, S., & MacRae, J. (1984). Environmental specificity of tolerance. *Trends in Neurosciences, 7*(5), 140–143. https://doi.org/10.1016/S0166–2236(84)80124–1

Siegel, S., Baptista, M. A. S., Kim, J. A., McDonald, R. V., & Weise-Kelly, L. (2000). Pavlovian psychopharmacology: The associative basis of tolerance. *Experimental and Clinical Psychopharmacology, 8*(3), 276–293. https://doi.org/10.1037/1064–1297.8.3.276

Siegman, A. W. (1956). The effect of manifest anxiety on a concept formation task, a nondirected learning task, and on timed and untimed intelligence tests. *Journal of Consulting Psychology, 20*(3), 176–178. https://doi.org/10.1037/h0041481

Skinner, B. F. (1938). *The behavior of organisms: An experimental analysis.* Retrieved from http://psycnet.apa.org/psycinfo/1939–00056–000

Smith, M. T., & Haythornthwaite, J. A. (2004). How do sleep disturbance and chronic pain inter-relate? Insights from the longitudinal and cognitive-behavioral clinical trials literature. *Sleep Medicine Reviews, 8*(2), 119–132. https://doi.org/10.1016/S1087-0792(03)00044-3

Snoddy, G. S. (1926). Learning and stability: A psychophysiological analysis of a case of motor learning with clinical applications. *Journal of Applied Psychology, 10*(1), 1–36. https://doi.org/10.1037/h0075814

Stanovich, K. E., & West, R. F. (2000). Advancing the rationality debate. *Behavioral and Brain Sciences, 23*(05), 701–717. https://doi.org/null

Starkes, J. L., Deakin, J. M., Allard, F., Hodges, N. J., & Hayes, A. (1996). Deliberate practice in sports: What is it anyway? In K. A. Ericsson (Ed.), *The road to excellence: The acquisition of expert performance in the arts and sciences, sports, and games* (pp. 81–106). Mahwah, NJ: Erlbaum.

Stepanski, E. J., & Wyatt, J. K. (2003). Use of sleep hygiene in the treatment of insomnia. *Sleep Medicine Reviews, 7*(3), 215–225. https://doi.org/10.1053/smrv.2001.0246

Sternberg, R. J. (1996). Costs of expertise. In K. A. Ericsson (Ed.), *The road to excellence: The acquisition of expert performance in the arts and sciences, sports, and games* (pp. 347–354). Mahwah, NJ: Erlbaum.

Swinnen, S. P., Schmidt, R. A., Nicholson, D. E., & Shapiro, D. C. (1990). Information feedback for skill acquisition: Instantaneous knowledge of results degrades learning. *Journal of Experimental Psychology: Learning, Memory, and Cognition, 16*(4), 706–716. https://doi.org/10.1037/0278-7393.16.4.706

Thompson, R. F., & Spencer, W. A. (1966). Habituation: A model phenomenon for the study of neuronal substrates of behavior. *Psychological Review, 73*(1), 16.

Veteran asks for courtesy with holiday fireworks. (July 2, 2014). *USAtoday.* Retrieved November 17, 2014, from http://www.usatoday.com/story/nation/2014/07/02/ptsd-fireworks-4th-july-veterans/12024123/

Warrington, E. K., & Weiskrantz, L. (1968). A study of learning and retention in amnesic patients. *Neuropsychologia, 6*(3), 283–291. https://doi.org/10.1016/0028-3932(68)90026-2

Warrington, E. K., & Weiskrantz, L. (1974). The effect of prior learning on subsequent retention in amnesic patients. *Neuropsychologia, 12*(4), 419–428. https://doi.org/10.1016/0028-3932(74)90072-4

Winstein, C. J., & Schmidt, R. A. (1990). Reduced frequency of knowledge of results enhances motor skill learning. *Journal of Experimental Psychology: Learning, Memory, and Cognition, 16*(4), 677–691. https://doi.org/10.1037/0278-7393.16.4.677

Wright, D. L., & Shea, C. H. (1991). Contextual dependencies in motor skills. *Memory & Cognition, 19*(4), 361–370. https://doi.org/10.3758/BF03197140

Wulf, G., & Schmidt, R. A. (1989). The learning of generalized motor programs: Reducing the relative frequency of knowledge of results enhances memory. *Journal of Experimental Psychology: Learning, Memory, and Cognition, 15*(4), 748–757. https://doi.org/10.1037/0278-7393.15.4.748

Yao, W.-X., Fischman, M. G., & Wang, Y. T. (1994). Motor skill acquisition and retention as a function of average feedback, summary feedback, and performance variability. *Journal of Motor Behavior, 26*(3), 273–282.

Learning

PART

I

©iStock.com/Wavetop

Behavioral Learning

Chapter Outline

Learning Objectives

1. Explain the basic assumptions of operant conditioning theory.
2. Describe the role of reinforcement for changing the rate of behavior.
3. Identify the impact on behavior change that different schedules of reinforcement have.
4. Classify different forms of reinforcement as demonstrations of shaping, chaining, and stimulus control.
5. Explain the principle of biological constraints on reinforcement.
6. Describe avoidance conditioning as an alternate form of reinforcement.
7. Explain how operant conditioning theory explains punishment and why the theory sees limited value in punishment.

Overview

Jane Goodall observed what was a then-surprising behavior of the chimpanzees she was studying in Tanzania's Gombe Stream National Park in the 1960s. She saw a male chimpanzee trying to dig termites out of a termite mound (to eat) with blades of grass, rather unsuccessfully, and then grab a twig to dig into the mound, a more useful approach. It was commonly assumed at the time that only humans used tools. Since then, researchers like Dr. Elizabeth Lonsdorf at the Lincoln Park Zoo have been studying how chimpanzees teach their young how to use tools ("Elizabeth Lonsdorf," n.d.). Remarkably, not all groups of chimpanzees learn and pass on the same set of behaviors for getting food. They develop cultural behaviors for what they eat and how they use tools for food.

All animals can learn to associate behaviors with some goal, whether it is raising a hand to ask a question, using a pen as a tool to dig out a bank card from the side of a car seat, or avoiding traffic by taking an alternate route. In the previous chapter, we read about research on several kinds of associationistic learning and their biological basis. Simple associations, such learning to make a connection between a cue that signals an event or how to make the movements needed to execute a skill, do not necessarily require total awareness and sometimes, none at all. The study of behavioral learning attempts to explain the process of learning from a strictly observational perspective of the actions an organism takes, using behaviors as data (Skinner, 1938). This process is strictly defined as movements that the organism or "learner" is making and that can be observed by others (Skinner, 1938, p. 6).

Our focus in this chapter is behavioral aspects of learning exclusively (see Fig. 4.1). The major theory presented here, operant conditioning, combined with Pavlov's classical conditioning theory comprised behaviorism, the most popular school of thought in American psychology for most of the twentieth century.

FIGURE 4.1   **Behavioral approach to learning**

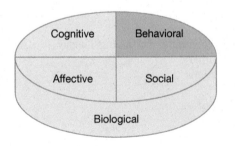

Operant Conditioning Theory

Exclusively behavioral explanations for how people and animals learn can seem very constrictive today. In modern psychology, the idea of an internal, mental world is often assumed and is the focus of much study in both humans and animals. This was not always the case. Behavioral explanations for learning are intentionally limited to what can be objectively observed in the performance of subjects. No claims can be made about motivation, goals, expectations, consciousness, personality, or knowledge. Historically, this limitation was embraced by many in the field as a way to encourage psychological research to be as scientific and rigorous as possible. Behaviorism was the catalyst that forced psychological research to get its act together and clearly define how the field would approach its topic scientifically. One of the contributions that this strict approach made was the focus on research methods that allowed for reproducibility. This meant well-thought-out experiments and clearly defined operational definitions for variables.

This approach, while narrower than the approach most psychological researchers take today, is still useful and occasionally quite relevant. Often it is worthwhile to avoid making generalizations about the conscious experience of a subject, such as animals or infants. As such, the power of the behavioral approach to describing the process of learning lies not just with reproducible research but is applicable equally to all learning organisms, human or nonhuman, and for any particular domain or activity. The broad scope of behavioral learning theories is remarkable and, as a result, remains an effective way to talk about how people and animals change their behavior based on the outcomes of their actions. The behavioral approach to learning has not become outdated so much as it is now one approach within a set of approaches. The one steadfast rule when limiting ourselves to examining learning from a behavioral perspective, is that there can be no conceptualization of the "mind" as an explanation for how an organism learns.

Operant conditioning theory, a learning theory that relies solely on observable behaviors to explain learning, describes how we learn from the consequences of behaviors. The outcome of the behaviors someone makes can alter the likelihood that the person will behave in that way again. Like the theory that was the inspiration for it (classical conditioning), operant conditioning is a content-neutral theory of learning that applies to any organism that can make an action on the environment. In operant conditioning, the behavior is usually optional or voluntary, whereas in classical conditioning the learned association can be involuntary, or reflexive. It is one of the most heavily researched psychological theories of the twentieth century. The theory has been broadly applied to situations as diverse as classroom management, drug addiction and rehabilitation, animal conservation, treatment of phobias and other anxiety disorders, and management techniques in business. The basic paradigm of the theory is that the organism can operate on the environment (whether an object, animal, or another person); and assuming there is a resulting consequence from the environment, that consequence will alter the chance that the organism will make that same behavior again.

In the late nineteenth century, Edward Thorndike carried out the first studies in "comparative animal psychology." Comparative psychology is the study of animals to gain insights into human psychology; as the name describes, the purpose is for comparison between humans and nonhumans. To find out if animals showed signs of intelligence, he built cages that included trapdoors that would open if the animal performed some basic action, like pulling a string or stepping on a lever.

First using chickens and, later, cats, he would place a hungry animal in one of his "puzzle boxes" and see how long it took the animal to get out for food (see Fig. 4.2). After the animals figured it out, he would return them to the cage. Using this method, Thorndike found that animals usually spent a lot of time trying various behaviors before accidentally finding how a specific behavior would make the door pop open. This kind of learning is known as trial-and-error learning. Once an animal had learned how to

FIGURE 4.2   Diagram of a sample puzzle box

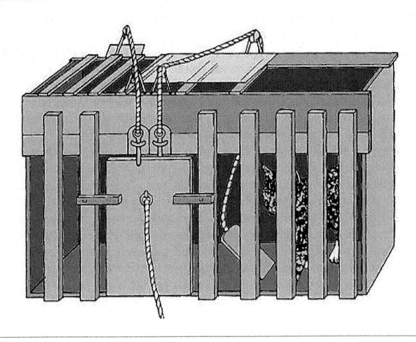

Source: By Jacob Sussman [Public domain], via Wikimedia Commons.

FIGURE 4.3   Typical "learning curve" of amount of time for a cat to escape one of Thorndike's puzzle boxes over many trials (Thorndike, 1898). In this graph, learning is indicated by a lower value over time.

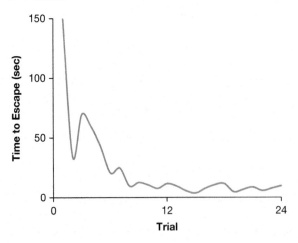

Note: Hypothetical values; are approximates.

escape, it escaped much more quickly on later trials. In other words, the time it took the animal to escape or escape latency dropped rapidly with repeated trials (see Fig. 4.3).

From this, Thorndike proposed his law of effect, stating that behaviors that lead to a "preferred" or satisfying situation are likely to be repeated. In contrast, behaviors that lead to an "annoying" or aversive situation were less likely to be repeated (Thorndike, 1911).

For Thorndike, this comparison was fairly straightforward: Animals would work to attain and preserve some situations and would try to avoid or get away from others. Situations that were satisfying tended to encourage the behavior that preceded it. By this, he did not mean satisfaction in terms of what is good for one's life or for society in general. People could engage in actions that seemed pleasing but were essentially bad habits. Nor could what any one individual finds satisfying be determined in advance; what some would find satisfying, others would find annoying.

By today's standards, such a claim may seem intuitively correct and simple. At the time however, another prevailing view was that solving a problem or puzzle required "insight," a moment of sudden realization of the solution, an idea popular with Gestalt psychologists. Thorndike had produced a principle of learning that did not appear to be due to insight but rather to acquired behaviors, and he provided a method for documenting the learning process too. An animal who developed an insight solution to escaping the cage would show a very different frequency of responding than trial-and-error learning.

Thorndike's approach required discrete, separate trials, which meant that the animal was put into the cage and the researcher had to be present to watch and wait for the animal to discover the solution. It was fairly time-intensive. This changed with B. F. Skinner's approach to behavioral learning.

B. F. Skinner, the person most identified with operant conditioning theory, took Thorndike's approach and made several improvements. The cage would house the animal more continuously instead of on a trial-to-trial basis. The cages provided a lever or switch for pressing to receive a small amount of food. The number of times the lever was pressed was recorded as the dependent variable. Skinner's adapted cage from Thorndike's "puzzle box" became known informally as a "Skinner box." (See Fig. 4.4.)

As a result, the actions of the animal could be recorded cumulatively, like an odometer, allowing for a much more nuanced look at the pattern of behavior. This technique provided some benefits. First, the continuous data recording meant the animal didn't have to be monitored continuously. Second, the data pattern could be analyzed from a more systematized perspective—that is, showing closer evidence of the relationship between the behavior and its consequence (see Fig. 4.5). Usually this consequence is the delivery of food.

FIGURE 4.4   Diagram of a Skinner box

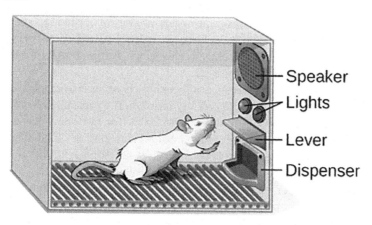

FIGURE 4.5   Example of a cumulative response graph. In this graph, more responses mean more learning is occurring.

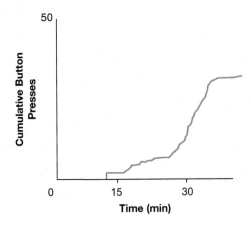

Note: Hypothetical values; are approximates.

Finally, as we will see later, it was possible to rig the cage so that the lever would not always present food, but do so only on some particular timing or schedule. This flexibility led to many conceptual developments for operant conditioning theory as well as popularizing the approach.

Skinner also encouraged psychologists to get beyond viewing all behaviors as stimulus-response driven, as Pavlov and Thorndike had done. In his view, too many actions did not seem reflexive but involved an organism taking actions to earn or avoid some consequence. His primary focus was the study of how existing behaviors could become more likely to occur or "strengthened" after the presentation of a reward, a process he named positive reinforcement. He studied the training process involved to encourage animals to make sophisticated behaviors, such as pigeons playing ping pong. He studied what happened when rewards were provided randomly to see if animals developed superstitious behavior, and examined what happened when the rewards stopped.

From the perspective of Skinner and most behaviorists, all actions by people or other animals are done because they have been rewarded or positively reinforced in the past, whether the behavior is socially desirable or not. A screaming child in a quiet store has learned that tantrums work to get what he or she wants. Students have been encouraged to take notes from better focus and exam performance. Someone who robs a bank teller successfully will tend to want to do it again.

According to Skinner, all of society is affected by these basic principles of behavioral learning. Skinner described a utopian society based on the principles of rewards rather than punishments in *Walden Two* (Skinner, 1948/2005). The focus on behavior and conditioning for learning, in this approach, is total. Knowledge itself is a kind of behavior, and the language we produce and share is behavior as well (Skinner, 1957/2015). From this perspective, language itself is knowledge, which is behavior.

Behavioral accounts of learning have relied on a popular set of techniques and tools, including pecking cages with continuous data recorders. Sometimes mazes are used with pathways to force the organism (which could be a large variety of species, not limited to a mouse, rat, cat, bird, or cockroach) to make a choice between two options that present rewards at different rates. These are called "T mazes" because they are usually in the shape of the letter T. Behavioral learning studies have included infants as well as adults, but with adults these are usually presented with more sophisticated, such as computerized financial games in which players have to make some choices between different incentives to earn small amounts of money.

Let's take a closer look at the major tenets of the theory next.

Basic Components

In operant conditioning, the individual organism reacts to cues in the environment, makes a behavior in response, and that behavior may become more or less likely to be repeated depending on how the environment responds. The individual "operates" on the environment, hence the name. When I see a vending machine, if I decide to drop some coins into it, I can be conditioned by the result to repeat this behavior at a later time if the machine provides me with what I requested. Three components must be present for operant conditioning to occur: a cue that makes clear what behaviors are accepted (e.g., a vending machine), a behavior in response (e.g., paying), and a consequence from that behavior (e.g., a bag of chips).

A behavioral response. Before any conditioning takes place, the organism has to execute a behavior. This action is in response to the antecedent cues in the environment that signal what behaviors may be acceptable. The behavior is called a response (sometimes "respondent behavior"), even though it precedes any consequence, since it is presumed that the behavior follows cues that trigger the action in the environment, such as the presence of the vending machine.

The specific action is not actually of interest, from a theoretical perspective. The likelihood of making that behavior is of interest, however: that is, the probability of making that same action when presented with the same antecedent cue later on (the rate of response or "response tendency"). Will I use the vending machine the next time I walk by it and I'm hungry? The chance of performing the action is what operant conditioning theory is attempting to explain. Additionally, the behavior itself can be helpful to others and oneself, or it may not be. Successfully robbing a bank does produce a reward, despite the negative consequences for society and personal risk to one's safety (as well as freedom). Eating salty potato chips may not be in the best interest of my health. In other words, the desirability of the behavior is irrelevant to the theory. Many "bad" or socially deviant behaviors can have a short-term reward, such as getting high.

A consequence. For operant conditioning to occur, a consequence must arrive as a result of the behavior. Several options are possible: there may be no consequence to the behavior at all, something may be presented to the organism, or something may be removed. If there is no consequence for the behavior, then the behavior and the likelihood for it occurring again is said to have become extinct. No reward or punishment occurs. The individual is now less likely to do that behavior again, since it doesn't produce any results. As we saw with classical conditioning theory, the process of extinction from a lack of a consequence applies to operant conditioning as well. This might happen when a timid student raises his hand in class and the teacher doesn't notice the hand. The student may decide it's not worth trying later on. Or, the vending machine might lock up and not deliver the chips.

Besides no consequence, two options remain. Something may be presented, or something may be removed. In operant conditioning theory, when the environment provides something as a result of an action, it is termed positive, indicating that something was added. (The vending machine provides the chips.) When the environment removes something as a result of an action, it is termed negative, indicating that something was removed. The terms positive and negative are purely mathematical, and do not indicate an emotion or the desirability of what is added or removed. That is a separate issue.

If the machine doesn't provide my snack, then isn't my losing the coins into the vending machine the something that I lost, a subtraction? While this seems sensible, this is not how operant conditioning theory views it. The payment was the necessary action in order to receive a consequence, since the vending machine is not likely to spit out a snack as I pass by. Something must be removed, such as dropping all my papers as I stretch to reach the buttons, and watching students' work fall and slip under the machine where I can't reach it.

A response tendency. Finally, the consequence has to have an impact on the likelihood of the behavior, or response tendency, for operant conditioning to be complete. Learning occurs when the response rate for that behavior has been affected. Assuming a behavior was made and a consequence occurred as a result of that behavior, one of two options is possible. The response tendency can be increased or "strengthened," meaning the behavior is more likely to occur in the future to the same cue, or it can be decreased or "weakened," meaning that the behavior is less likely to occur in the future to the same cue.

There are specific terms and research findings that are involved when the response tendency of a behavior is strengthened or weakened, and the next sections delve more deeply into these issues.

Strengthening Behavior

If a behavior produces a consequence, and the consequence increases the chance of the behavior happening again (what's called "strengthening the behavior"), the learning is called reinforcing, and the consequence itself is called a reinforcer. Keep in mind that while in casual conversation people may use the word "reinforcing" to mean something that is pleasing, from the perspective of operant conditioning theory, whether a consequence is pleasing or not is irrelevant. How desirable a consequence is does not matter; what matters is whether the probability of the behavior rises or not. Does the door open when pushed? If so, then the act of pushing the door may be reinforced. If complaining to mom and dad helps us to get what we want as children, then complaining may become reinforced, a learned strategy we can take with us into adulthood. Sometimes what is reinforcing is a behavior that gets us away from a consequence, such as lying to get out of trouble.

Reinforcement shares many of the same features as Pavlov's classical conditioning. Acquisition usually starts slowly and grows. If a previously reinforced behavior is no longer reinforced (the vending machine stops working, or the door now appears to be locked), then the behavior can follow the process of extinction and relearned more quickly if reinforcement starts again (spontaneous recovery). Likewise, the learner can generalize from one antecedent cue to another (other vending machines and doors) as well as discriminate between some cues and others.

So far, Thorndike's Law and our definition of reinforcement have only described the scenario under which operant conditioning tends to occur. What is a reinforcer, besides the consequence that makes the operant behavior more likely? Several theories have been proposed to define what is learned in reinforcement beyond Thorndike's Law of Effect. Initially, Hull (1943) and Miller (1948) proposed that the reinforcer reduced a biological need or drive. This certainly seems true for primary reinforcers that help an organism to survive. Making behaviors to provide water, food, and avoidance of pain appeases the need an organism has. But, what about other reinforcers that aren't primary needs?

The most popular theory today to explain what is meant by "reinforcement" is called Premack's principle, the idea that the relative probability of some behavior to another is what makes it reinforcing. Premack suggested that "any response A will reinforce any other response B, if and only if the independent rate of A is greater than that of B" (1959, p. 220). That is, all behaviors are on a continuum of frequency rates, and any behavior that is likely to be performed is reinforcing for a behavior that is less likely to be performed. A less probable behavior is reinforced by a more probable behavior. As such, the nature of the behaviors are not as important as their relative likelihood. For example, it is not that pressing a lever has a particularly high likelihood of being performed by a mouse so much as the likelihood of eating, which the action of working the lever affords. Whenever parents tell a child, "you can play after you have finished your homework," they are implicitly using Premack's principle. All other things being equal, doing homework has a relatively low likelihood for being chosen by a child with free time. But, if it is buttressed with a more preferable activity, then doing homework seems more worthwhile. The less preferred activity opens the door to doing the more preferred activity. This is a common way to encourage or reward a great many activities we otherwise might not do, including household chores, paying bills, or studying.

An extension of Premack's principle is the response deprivation hypothesis, which claims that the reinforcement is not strictly based on the relative rates as much as whether the rate of one behavior would restrict or hold back the rate of the other below what is normally done. That is, when a behavior is restricted past normal (for example, a child is not allowed to play any video games for a weekend), it usually becomes more reinforcing when we have the opportunity to do it (Timberlake & Allison, 1974).

Kinds of Reinforcers

Reinforcers are classified by how they are presented to the learner: by whether they are added to the situation or presented, or by whether they are removed from the situation. A reinforcer that is presented following a behavior is called a positive reinforcer to denote its additive nature, whereas a reinforcer that is removed following a behavior is called negative reinforcer, to denote how reinforcement was caused by its removal from the situation. In either case, the learner is pleased or satisfied with the result (hence, "reinforcement").

Positive reinforcers are fairly intuitive and easy to understand, since we all have experience with receiving something we want or like. They function as rewards. Positive reinforcers can be ones that support basic primary life functions, like food and water; or they can be more secondary, such as material goods, attention from someone important to us, or the opportunity to do an activity we have been wanting to do. Simple praise from another person is a positive reinforcer.

Negative reinforcers are less intuitive, but they are omnipresent nonetheless. By definition, something had to have been removed as a result of a behavior, and that removal was pleasing. This might be the removal of pain after taking medication, or this could be making a payment on a credit card to avoid the phone calls. Typically, negative reinforcers operate on escape from something unwanted or aversive, and this could include the removal of guilt or anxiety. This kind of learning is called escape conditioning, and we use these to get out of and avoid situations that are threatening or difficult. Lying, in essence, is negatively reinforced, assuming it is successful, and demonstrates that a behavior can be reinforced, but that doesn't make the behavior socially desirable or acceptable.

In the long run, behaviors can be made to preemptively try to avoid an aversive stimulus, such as taking an antihistamine before mowing the lawn. People tend to drive in their lane to avoid accidents. Escape conditioning is usually applied to situations of learning in the moment; in a longer time frame, the term avoidance conditioning is used to describe when an organism works to avoid an aversive stimulus. If successful, the behavior has become negatively reinforced. We'll take a closer look at avoidance conditioning later in this chapter.

Reinforcement is classified as conditioned reinforcement (or secondary reinforcement) when the consequence can be replaced by some other stimulus that also becomes reinforcing. For example, after a few grades have been given out in a class, an instructor can find that just praise for good work is enough on some activities. Likewise, a puppy being potty trained can be weaned off treats and be reinforced with pats and praise later on, and "good dog!" becomes reinforcing on its own. The reinforcing consequence becomes linked to other consequences in what most theorists believe is an example of classical conditioning within the operant conditioning framework. Simple examples of conditioned reinforcers are family photos and trophies we keep around our homes and places of work.

Brain Basis for Reinforcement

The basal ganglia, located deep inside the brain, is a major structure responsible for supporting learning by reinforcement (see Fig. 4.6). It is a collection of components that collects information from other areas of the cortex, the outer shell of the brain, and connects to the thalamus, which will then route information back to the cortex, including the motor cortex that is responsible for voluntary behaviors. The putamen and caudate nucleus make up the striatum, which is the channel for input into the basal ganglia.

This routing system, overall, is called the cortico-striatal system. It works as a feedback loop within the brain. This system, particularly the striatum, underlies reinforcement for actions (Shiflett & Balleine, 2011; e.g., Yin, Ostlund, Knowlton, & Balleine, 2005). Additionally, there is evidence that damage to the striatum makes one unable to learn from positive reinforcement. Cook and Kesner (1988) taught a group of rats to make a left–right direction judgment inside of a maze. Another set of rats learned a spatial judgment decision that was based on the place in the maze, but not their own left–right perspective. Lesions were made to the caudate nucleus of all of the rats. The ability to make left–right judgments was impaired in the first set of rats, but no performance problems were found with the second. They hypothesize that the caudate nucleus is needed for an organism to process spatial cues that reference the external environment relative to itself.

Neuroscientists have noted that many of the molecules involved in this learning process have ties to the process of drug addiction, implying that drug addiction is possibly a kind of accelerated learning with chemical assistance (Shiflett & Balleine, 2011). But, it's too soon to draw firm conclusions, since the exact molecular process in learning is not yet well established.

FIGURE 4.6   Diagram of the basal ganglia and related areas (from Chapter 3).

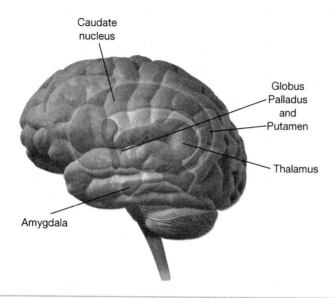

Source: Garrett (2015, Figure 11.20, p. 361).

At a neural level, the effectiveness of positive reinforcement appears to be related to the neurotransmitter dopamine (Berridge & Robinson, 1998). Neurons in the ventral tegmental area (VTA), a small region in the midbrain of mammals at the top of the stem of the brain, create the dopamine that will enter the striatum. When activated, the VTA provides a rush of arousal and excitement (e.g., Bandler, Chi, & Flynn, 1972). When a behavior results in a successful outcome, these neurons may release dopamine into the striatum. It could be that this dopamine release strengthens the association between the neurons that make the behavior and the neurons that acknowledged the result, making the behavior more likely to occur in the future, the dopamine reinforcement hypothesis. Or, it could be that the release strengthens the association between the cue and the rewarding outcome if acted on, the incentive salience hypothesis (e.g., Berridge, 2006; Robinson & Berridge, 1993). The cue itself becomes connected to the reward through the same dopamine system, and this is what provides the motivation or urge to take action.

Factors That Impact Reinforcement

A variety of factors impact the effectiveness of the reinforcer for its ability to reinforce a behavior. The timing and frequency of the reinforcer matters. Shorter delays are better. Typically, the reinforcement must be fast, for several observed reasons. First, a delay can cause the learner to fail to connect the reinforcing consequence to a behavior. Also, the consequence could be reinforced to the wrong behavior. Or, the perceived value of the reinforcer simply drops, the further out in time it might be obtained.

The timeliness of the reinforcer is particularly important with special populations, such as drug users (Critchfield & Kollins, 2001) and young children in comparison to older adults (Green, Fry, & Myerson, 1994). The need to delay reinforcement over a long period of time is sometimes necessary, but tolerating the delay can be difficult. Cocaine addicts, for example, have been found to be strongly affected by delays in reinforcement compared to controls, which seems related to their being more impulsive overall (Coffey, Gudleski, Saladin, & Brady, 2003). The delay in the reward causes a discounting of the quality or value of the reward, an effect called delay-discounting. Another study found heroin addicts discount monetary rewards at a rate twice as high as controls (Kirby, Petry, & Bickel, 1999). This effect has also been found in current smokers, who discount the value of delayed payment more than people who never smoked and ex-smokers (Bickel, Odum, & Madden, 1999).

The frequency, or how often, the learner is reinforced plays a role over the long term. Some behaviors can be continuously reinforced, so the individual earns the reinforcement with each act. Most of the time, outside of laboratory conditions, this isn't possible; parents can't reinforce their children for every appropriate behavior. Often behaviors are on a reinforcement schedule of some kind, a topic within operant conditioning theory that has been heavily researched. We will examine example schedules of reinforcement more closely in a later section of this chapter.

Other known factors that affect reinforcement include the history a learner has with a reinforcer and the schedule when it has usually been provided. Any change to an existing schedule is similar to changing the rules on the learner, and that can be met with problems. Second, learners can show resistance to being disrupted when the rate of behavior required is fairly high, a phenomenon known as behavioral momentum. Like the concept of velocity of a moving body in physics, the individual keeps up a behavior and resists change. This often occurs when we start out with easy tasks that are quick to master and begin moving on to more challenging ones. The focused effort and resistance to distraction is desirable for successfully obtaining personal goals, such as quitting smoking, for example. This means that typically it is best for learning to engage heavily in a particular activity in a particular setting (such as an office or the soccer field), so that disruptions will be less effective (Nevin & Grace, 2000). Individual motivation for the behavior matters as well and is a topic we will encounter in the next chapter.

Schedules of Reinforcement

Reinforcement works fastest when the reinforcing consequence is provided with each and every appropriate behavior, a continuous reinforcement schedule. Of course, this isn't always feasible; it's too demanding on the trainer. (Perhaps the only situation when continuous reinforcement can be provided in most real-world situations is by computer, such as video games.) Reinforcing a behavior on an intermittent or noncontinuous schedule can provide some benefits. Researchers have found this kind of partial reinforcement is not only effective but can make what is learned last for a longer period of time. They have devised schedules of reinforcement where the reinforcement is contingent on how many times a behavior has been performed or on a time interval. The performances of people or animals on these schedules are then plotted on cumulative recordings for comparison.

Putting a behavior on a noncontinuous schedule has a benefit for learning besides less work for the teacher. Perhaps counterintuitively, the frequency of the conditioned behavior will continue to stay high even if not being reinforced each time. When the behavior will not trigger reinforcement every time, the behavior becomes harder to extinguish and, instead, lasts longer. When a behavior isn't reinforced, the learner will continue trying. Intermittent reinforcement schedules make the behavior resistant to extinction, an effect known as the partial reinforcement effect. So not only does partial reinforcement allow for looser monitoring by the teacher, but also what is reinforced tends to continue.

Why this is good for the process of learning is not hard to see. It helps athletes if they continue playing the sport even after a loss. The gambling industry would have a problem if slot machines paid out with every bet. Students study a lot of information that may not make an appearance on an exam or even come up for discussion in class.

One possible reason for the partial reinforcement effect is that that learner may have trouble figuring out when the reinforcement is no longer happening. If the reinforcement doesn't happen with every relevant action, then the learner has to decide when to give up. According to the generalization decrement hypothesis (Capaldi, 1966), when nonreinforced trials (extinction) have been part of the conditioning, the learners will be kept from identifying when their behavior is being extinct from when they are going to be reinforced eventually. Some days I give my dogs a rawhide chew before leaving for work in the morning. I usually mean to, but sometimes I forget or I am running late. But, sometimes I have simply run out of chews, and I have none to give them. The dogs will continue to whine and look expectantly when I leave, because for them, the days when they will get a treat and the days when they do not, appear to be identical. Another example is playing the slots at a casino. Long periods without a payout are expected as part of the normal interaction with the machine, and those instances when a payout may occur "look" identical to those when one will not.

The four basic, most commonly studied kinds of schedules vary on two dimensions: whether reinforcement is provided at a fixed or a variable number of correct behaviors (ratio schedules) and whether the reinforcement is provided over a fixed or variable period of time (interval schedules). Initially, these were studied individually for their effects on the rates of subject response. Generally, now these may be presented concurrently, with one schedule operating through one lever in a cage while another operates on a second. This way, researchers can compare the two and see which one the subject prefers.

Ratio Schedules

One of the four basic schedules is the fixed ratio (FR) schedule. With this schedule, the learner receives reinforcement after performing the desired action a specific or fixed number of times. This schedule is not uncommon in sales promotions: the online store Amazon.com currently offers free shipping if the customer racks up $35 in purchases of stock from their warehouses. Papa John's offers customers a free large pizza for every $25 spent with their "rewards" program. Kroger, a Midwest grocery chain, offers a $0.10 discount on fuel at their attached gas stations for each $100 of groceries purchased in their store. School children might be offered a ticket for a prize after reading a certain number of pages or books. A very common reinforcement in "platformer" video games such as the Super Mario Bros. is to give the player a bonus life after the collection of 100 coins. Freelance work is often like this: Payment is made whenever the work is completed, such as writing reviews of household items for a consumer reviews website. Google's advertising payment system for YouTube can make payments based on the number of people who look at a view and do not skip through an ad.

In any case, this schedule is defined by the delivery of the reinforcement being tied to the correct number of behaviors being performed. Once completed, individuals can continue for more as they wish (see Fig. 4.7).

Researchers denote these fixed interval schedules with the number of required behaviors by using "FR" followed by the number. So, an "FR20" schedule means the animal needs to make the action twenty times before the reinforcement will be given.

FIGURE 4.7   Sample schedules of reinforcement. The tick marks indicate moments of reinforcement. As with other cumulative response graphs, an increase indicates more of a behavior, and a flat line indicates a pause.

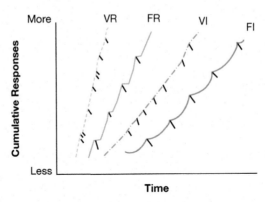

Source: Adapted from Gazzaniga, M., Heatherton, T., & Halpern, D. (2012).

Likewise, variable ratio schedules are denoted with a "VR," and fixed interval and variable interval are denoted with "FI" and "VI" in kind.

One of the notable aspects of this kind of schedule is that it tends to produce "pauses" in performing. Immediately after the reinforcing consequence, the individual tends to take a break, called a postreinforcement pause. Once I have earned a free pizza and fulfilled it, I am less likely to order more pizza the following night. A video game player might be fairly happy to receive the bonus life, but earning another will not be a top priority immediately afterward, and the pursuit of coins may slough off. Once a child receives the prize for reading, he or she is not likely to sit down and continue. Most often, the individual takes a break.

These pauses might be due to fatigue on the part of the individual, or perhaps satiation. Once I've ordered the pizza, I don't immediately need another. A comparison of schedules of reinforcement with rats indicated that the pauses are most likely due to the more pressing nature of short-term consequences over long-term consequences (Tanno & Sakagami, 2008).

With the variable ratio (VR) schedule, the learner is reinforced on some average number of performances. For example, slot machines provide a payout on some average number of pulls. Despite some advertising, the actual rate of payouts on slot machines is generally kept an industry secret. A top jackpot for a machine may run from 1 in 50,000 to 1 in 2.5 million, depending on the payout and casino ("House Edge (Gambling Lessons)," n.d.). As a result, there is some average amount of betting behavior that will cause a payout, but the player does not know how much it will be. Since the process is random as well, there is really no telling which pull will be the lucky one.

Purely commission-based sales are like this—it's not clear how many leads the salesperson must approach before gaining a sale. Several could come in a row, or there can be a dry spell.

This schedule tends to produce the highest rates of performance of all of the simplest four schedules, but it can result in burnout. Most animals and people simply cannot keep up this pattern of responding forever.

Interval Schedules

Interval schedules are reinforcement schedules that are keyed on a time period, rather than the number of behavioral responses. Fixed interval (FI) schedules of reinforcement mean reinforcement will arrive after a specific amount of time has elapsed, as long as the desired behavior has been done by then. It's a fairly common method of being paid for work: usually there is a payday, and the employee is paid for the hours worked on that day. Similarly, the knowledge a student gains is reinforced (if you will) by having the opportunity to use the knowledge on a scheduled exam.

It's a simple, common schedule to keep, but it does not necessarily encourage the best performance. As shown in Figure 4.7, the performance tends to show a scalloping function. Whatever behaviors are necessary tend to happen just prior to the scheduled reinforcement. So, for a weekly Friday quiz, this pattern would expect that students would study heavily Thursday and early Friday, but would not study after the quiz at all. This isn't a terrible concern if the quizzes are weekly, but if the course uses a traditional midterm and final exam format that are scheduled two months apart, students will often wait until about a week prior to each to really engage with the material.

This "scalloping" pattern of inactivity followed by incrementally more focus and work occurs in a number of settings. We become more alert to the boarding process as the time for boarding comes nearer. If we are waiting for a friend to pick us up, we won't bother to look until it gets close to time. As the time approaches, we will check almost continuously. This can happen waiting for a store to open, waiting for the doctor to call us at the appointed time from the waiting room, or when waiting for a bus. Waiting for a deposited check to clear the bank on a given day encourages this. With the advent of online banking, it's become easier to check and re-check whether it has been deposited—in a pattern that seems so similar to animals in a Skinner box excitedly making the behaviors necessary for the timed release of food.

In a variable interval (VI) schedule, reinforcement comes at an average time interval, but it is not scheduled as rigidly as with fixed interval. So, instead of Friday quizzes, there may be a pop quiz once a week, on any day. My dogs know that dinner for them will be in the evening but exactly when is not clear, so their attentiveness (and probably hunger) is on alert anytime in the evening that I am in the kitchen before they have been fed. Likewise, the mail is delivered once a day at a general but not specific time, so we generally check after we are sure the mail has probably been delivered. This is a very different behavior than with the FI schedules, when we might check increasingly if the delivery time were fixed.

Variable interval schedules produce a more uniform performance, but they also don't produce levels of performance like VR schedules. In fact, often the behavior rate matches the reinforcement schedule itself, a pattern called the matching law. Once people learn when they will generally be reinforced, they create a behavior pattern that keeps themselves from working unnecessarily. If mail delivery is nearly always before 1:00 p.m., then it's best to wait until after then to keep from having to check more than once in the same day. One behavioral response for one reinforcement.

Other Schedules

Researchers have experimented with a variety of schedules and combinations of schedules beyond the basic four. Reinforcing a response only after a certain amount of time has passed is known as a differential reinforcement of low rates (DRL) schedule. This schedule promotes a lower rate of responding, but with a lot of wasted efforts (Richards, Sabol, & Seiden, 1993). If DRL reinforcement is set at every 15 seconds, then a response at 14 seconds will be ignored and it will take another 15 seconds before a response is reinforced. This means the learner has to pause for a period of time that he or she must estimate. While it might make sense to try always to wait too long, such as 30 seconds, it's common to find study participants try right around the threshold, so more than half of their responses go unreinforced. As a result, the organism has to create other behaviors that take up time in between the intervals.

Alternatively, researchers can encourage bursts of high responding using a differential reinforcement of high rates (DRH) schedule, in which a fixed number of responses have to occur within a certain time frame. Because this schedule reinforces high rates of responding, this schedule typically produces higher bursts of responses than any other schedule.

Shaping

Having said all that, the concept of reinforcement depends on the behavior being present to be reinforced. It doesn't make assumptions about the learner's ability to make attempts at the desired behavior or to model the behavior of others. Thus, it's theoretically necessary for the theory to explain how reinforcement works when the learner has not yet made the behavior that would earn reinforcement. The basic idea is that a new behavior can be produced if a series of approximate behaviors can be reinforced. This is called shaping. Initially, any simple behavior that acts as a first step or attempt at the behavior is reinforced. Then, gradually, the behavior that will be reinforced has to come closer and closer to the ideal behavior. It's similar to lowering the bar for what is acceptable, and then carefully changing the rules to accept only a higher and higher standard of what will qualify for the reinforcer.

For example, no one expects a child entering kindergarten to be able to write numbers or letters perfectly on the first day. So, parents and teachers will encourage the attempt and continuous improvement by reinforcing basic actions initially. Several months in, the child will be expected to have made several months' worth of progress, and an identical behavior then will not be acceptable. Similarly, a soccer coach will encourage basic accomplishments on a "set play," such as a corner kick, but will expect more later on in the season. When training a dog to use a doggie door to eliminate outside, simply going outside might be reinforced at first. Then, investigating the door and, later, using the door as well as going outside would be reinforced.

In most formal education settings, students are not expected to have the material and skills mastered on first day of the term. Hence, obtaining the fundamental skills early on is reinforced by grades or praise; but, by the end of the term, those fundamental skills will simply be assumed. Typically, shaping involves using incremental steps for improvement that are small enough that the learner has a reasonable chance of success (and thus, reinforcement). This means not setting intermediate goals that are unrealistic. So, expecting all As the semester after a rough term of Fs and Ds might not be wise; focusing on Cs would be a smarter move for the next term.

Response Chains

Several behaviors can be taught in a sequence as well, which are called response chains or, more simply, chaining. As the term sounds, the learner is reinforced for producing not just one behavior but several in a row. These can be the same action repeatedly, but often they are several different behaviors that must be performed in a row before reinforcement. Animal shows at zoos and dog obedience competitions provide many examples of trained chains of behavior. Each trained behavior has a history of being reinforced, and each behavior is on a cue. Sometimes the cues are presented by the trainer, other times the environment naturally provides them, such as the presentation of a hoop to jump through. A prior behavior can be the cue for the next as well; often our morning routines for getting ready for the day are chained behaviors.

The three most commonly researched kinds of response chains are forward chains, backward chains, and total task chains. A total task chain is another term for calling individual behaviors at random, or a "random block" of movements as discussed in the skill-learning section of Chapter 2.

In a forward chain, the learner is taught the behaviors in the order they will later be retrieved. The chain of behaviors is broken down into steps, and each step is worked on one at a time separately and then recombined with the other steps learned so far. For example, this would mean working on the walk up to the lane to bowl a ball first, before focusing on the arm movement. Or, a child who has to memorize the preamble to the Declaration of Independence would start at the beginning ("When in the course of human events, . . .") and memorize the first section before moving on. In a forward chain, the learner gets very good at the beginning of the chain and usually ends up lost or tired, or both. This is probably by far the most common approach people make when trying to learn a response chain: start at the beginning, but it may not be the best.

In a backward chain, the learner starts with the last, final behavior and works backward from that. This approach has several advantages over the forward chain, even though it seems odd at the time. So, the child memorizing the preamble would start at the end first. Why might this be beneficial? Unlike the forward chain, when the learner studies each step, the remaining steps are familiar and easy. Simultaneously, the easier steps are at the end, when the learner is more likely to be fatigued by the performance. Finally, during learning, each attempt is more likely to end on a positive note—familiar, comfortable territory—than in forward chaining, where each new step ends someplace awkward and unfamiliar. In forward chaining, the learner faces what he or she has not learned yet with each practice. In backward chaining, each attempt should end on a success. This is why animal trainers may prefer this approach—having teaching sessions end on a high note, as the learner tires, is a big advantage.

Which of the three is best may depend on the needs of the situation. A child working on a series of multiplication problems that she will have to solve in class under a time limit might find that the total task chain (or random block) is best, assuming the in-class test presents the math problems completely randomized. If the in-class timed test looks exactly like the practice homework, then the forward or backward chains would be more appropriate. Similarly, we usually don't expect people to recall the preamble to the Declaration of Independence in a randomized fashion, hence the forward or backward chains are more appropriate.

Stimulus Control

Both of the topics of shaping and response chains involve how to encourage the learner to create the optimal behavior(s) in a given situation. But underlying these is a need for the environment (for example, a coach) to cue what behavior is wanted for the learner to accurately perceive. This relates to the issues of how the learner generalizes that cue and discriminates it from others. Altogether this involves the extent to which the cue is under stimulus control: how the behavior is influenced by different stimuli. In some situations, such as a construction worker operating heavy machinery or an orchestra following a conductor, a very precise level of stimulus control is desired, because inaccurate communication about what behaviors are necessary can be disastrous. In a classroom environment, educators talk about "prompting": setting the stage for the proper set of responses. This might involve nonverbal cues to have the class settle down (e.g., flicking the light switch), or verbal cues that acknowledge the reinforcement for doing as asked: "If we clean up quickly, we may be able to have an extra few minutes of recess."

As it was with classical conditioning (Chapter 2), the roles of generalization and discrimination apply to the antecedent cues that the learner may respond to. In operant conditioning, generalization defines the act of responding similarly to stimuli that are similar in some way. Generally, this is desirable. We want young children to learn to heed the command to "stop!" despite the exact pitch or tenor of the voice saying it. Imagine professional soccer players being unsure how to behave during a game because the soccer ball was a color they hadn't seen before. At the same time, there have to be some limits. A soccer player should be able to identify a youth ball from a professional one. In operant conditioning, discrimination defines the act of responding differently to different stimuli.

The ability to generalize and discriminate contexts appears to involve the hippocampus (Maren, 2001). Experiments using rats attempt to isolate the relevant parts of the brain by providing two similar but not identical cages (of different shapes or sizes). The different cages act as different contexts. By exposing the rats to an aversive stimulus in one cage and not the other, researchers gain some idea of whether the rats can tell the difference between the cages by how they show fear. Damage to the dorsal or upper back of the hippocampus have been found to make the rats more likely to become fearful in both contexts, rather than just one (Antoniadis & McDonald, 2000; Frankland, Cestari, Filipkowski, McDonald, & Silva, 1998; Gilbert, Kesner, & Lee, 2001). The hippocampus appears to be necessary for being able to tell different locations apart. Neuroscientists believe the hippocampus plays a role in indexing our experiences into separate memories, so our experiences don't simply run together.

Biological Constraints

From earlier examples, it might begin to sound like reinforcement, particularly positive reinforcement, can be used to train animals, children, coworkers, or spouses to do almost anything. Despite a lot of enthusiasm from psychologists of that era, it became clear after a while that the trainable behaviors had to be within the species' biological options. Whatever abilities or endowments evolution had given the animal, those are the only capabilities or talents that are available to train. In fact, those behaviors that are normal actions (behaviors such as chewing, rooting, pecking) tend to be the most easily trained.

In some cases, these "default" behaviors can overcome reinforced training over time, despite the reinforcement. The return of instinctive behaviors for reinforcement notwithstanding training is called instinctive drift. This is a situation where innately-based behaviors beat out conditioned behaviors.

In this way, a framework for operant conditioning is one of communication. Instead of replacing behavior or subverting it, the kind of learning operant conditioning is most useful for is channeling existing behavior so that it occurs when it is most appropriate and effective. In this sense, reinforcement is not a kind of manipulation as much as it is instruction.

Summary

In sum, reinforcement is one of two theoretical outcomes when the environment provides a consequence for a behavior, and it can be made on a continuous or intermittent schedule. If the behavior is not being made, shaping can be used by reinforcing approximate actions in order to arrive at the goal behavior. One behavior can be linked to another into a chain of behaviors. The training of such response chains can be done chronologically, in reverse, or in a random block. When a behavior is properly conditioned to a cue, it is said to be under stimulus control, generalizable to appropriate other similar cues and yet discriminative of inappropriate ones.

Avoidance Conditioning

Avoidance conditioning is defined as learning to make behavior to prevent or delay an aversive stimulus, and is conceptually similar to negative reinforcement, or escape conditioning. In either case, the learner has learned to make a behavior so as to avoid or get away from some consequence. This could be paying bills early to avoid a late fee, or putting on a sweater when cold. Escape conditioning refers to the act of making a behavior to remove the aversive stimulus, like twisting to get out of a tangle of bedsheets in the middle of the night. Avoidance conditioning is a broader concept that includes behaviors to prevent the aversive from presenting itself, such as going to the gym earlier in the day to avoid a crowd.

For avoidance conditioning to happen, the learner must be able to detect a cue that signals the approaching aversive stimulus. This preaversive stimulus alerts the individual to the possibility of danger or pain and may have been classically conditioned in the past. A car that is weaving while being driven is a clue to others that the driver may not be fully alert. When I notice my teenage son's bleary eyes on the way to dropping him off at school in the morning, I suspect he stayed up too late and will be a real grouch today.

Since the behavior becomes more likely as the result of avoiding something annoying, such as a crowded gym, the process is classified as reinforcement, even though an aversive is involved. An aversive stimulus is typically involved in punishment as well; but, as we will see in the next section, the aversive stimulus arrives as a result of the behavior and is usually inescapable. If I'm not paying attention and I slam my hand in the car door as I close it, there isn't a point during the consequence that I can "undo" the aversive to escape it, making the pain a punisher. However, I can be more careful next time, which is avoidance conditioning.

In some situations, the aversive stimulus has to be actively avoided, such as making sure I move my hand before closing the door. In other situations, what has been learned is passive avoidance. For example, I might not make eye contact with my boss and might remain silent when she asks for volunteers to serve on a lengthy committee.

Avoidance learning of either kind (active or passive) tends to be difficult to unlearn. A successful strategy for learning to avoid something unpleasant provides a sense of control and comfort. Having to unlearn to avoid something (e.g., confrontation, getting blood work done, paying bills on time) is often better for us in the long run. In some cases, successfully avoiding something unpleasant means not getting to develop the skills and experience we need to handle similar situations in the future (such as turning down a request from a friend or coworker).

Learned Helplessness

We make behaviors to avoid situations we dislike fairly routinely, whether trying not to stand too close to others in elevators, or choosing to sit in a quiet area of the library to study. These avoidant behaviors are an attempt by the organism to exert control over his or her environment. Positive reinforcement is similar in this sense; both involve attempting to improve a situation by gaining something pleasing or avoiding a problem.

In some cases, an organism can exert control over a situation but has learned not to try. Seligman and colleagues demonstrated that it is possible to be conditioned into being helpless (Overmier & Seligman, 1967; Seligman & Maier, 1967), a phenomenon called *learned helplessness*. As a result, someone will not try to exert control even when it's possible, due to an experience of the same situation. In this study (as well as others in this line of research), two groups of eight dogs were restrained in a manner similar to how Pavlov had done in his studies. These dogs received electrical shocks that were not physically harmful but were painful. The independent variable was whether a dog could end the shocks by pressing a panel with its head (the "escape group"), or not (the "no-escape group"), or a third control group of eight that didn't participate at this point (the "no-harness group"). In the learning phase, the dogs in the escape and no-escape conditions received sixty-four shocks at ninety-second intervals. Normally, dogs are very quick to learn that they can escape a punishing situation through some action. They are conditioned to recognize any signals that predict the shock, such as a flashing light or a buzzer. But in this study, one group was not allowed to try. The dogs in the escape condition learned that pressing the panel ended the shocks quickly; the dogs in the no-escape condition stopped trying by the thirtieth shock.

The following day, dogs from all three conditions were placed into a cage that had a partition separating one side from the other. An electrical current could be presented on either side of the box in the floor. The box was designed to be easy to escape the shock by jumping over the partition. A light would signal the side of the box where a shock was about to be delivered ten seconds later. A dog that jumped the barrier would escape the shock completely. The dependent variables were the percent of each group that failed to escape the shocks and the mean time in seconds it took them to escape in ten trials.

As shown in Figure 4.8, the dogs in the escape and no-harness condition avoided the punishment quickly; the no-harness group took longer on average, most likely because they were learning about the relationship between the light and the shock during testing. Six of the dogs in the no-escape group didn't try to escape the shock at all, or did so only once. These six were retested a week later, and five of the six failed to escape on every trial, indicating that they had learned not to try. Even when one of the no-escape dogs escaped the shock on one trial, it would revert back to no avoidance on the next (see Fig. 4.8).

Our history with a situation informs us about the likelihood of any operant behavior's being successful; behaviors that seem to have little to do with the environment are extinct (Maier & Seligman, 1976). Since actions and outcomes are completely independent, the organism is conditioned not to attempt any avoidance behaviors due to its history in this situation.

Studies like this are unpleasant due to the use of punishment with animals, but they provide a striking explanation of how people learn to exert less control over their environments in a variety of situations. Learned helplessness has also been found in humans using unavoidable loud noises. (See Abramson, Seligman, & Teasdale, 1978, for a discussion about how learned helplessness is different in humans and animals.) Seligman and colleagues' work on learned helplessness ties to a wide range of real-life experiences. People often find they have no control over some events in some part of their life, such as the death

FIGURE 4.8   When given the opportunity to escape, dogs that could not previously avoid the shock would often not try to do so.

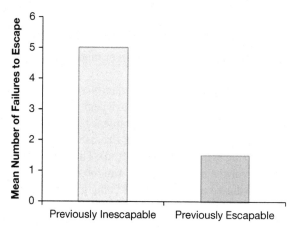

Source: Adapted from Fancher, R. E., & Rutherford, A. (2011).

of a loved one, or a chronic, serious illness. Despite what control we can exert over our lives, experiences of a loss of control can explain the helplessness that people show later. This hopelessness may manifest itself as depression, or simply "giving in" to the situation.

Learned helplessness can be unlearned, and possibly prevented. Simply by walking the dogs in a no-escape condition over the barrier, they start walking over the boundary on their own. Even better, animals can be inoculated better from learned helplessness. If animals are first exposed to shock in a situation where they can escape, then exposure to a situation they cannot escape does not seem to teach learned helplessness later (Williams & Lierle, 1986). Early experiences matter for learning that control of the situation is possible. Initial experiences in the classroom, for example, should probably provide children with success (Seligman, 1975).

Skinner and Thorndike were themselves more impressed with what reinforcement could do to shape learning than could punishment; but punishment can be instructive. Unfortunately, a reliance on aversives in learning can also lead to serious secondary problems besides learned helplessness, as we will see in the next section.

Weakening Behavior

As opposed to increasing the likelihood of a behavior, a behavior can also produce a consequence that lowers the likelihood of that behavior's happening again, or weakening it. This is the formal definition of punishment. Like reinforcement, punishment may be experienced when some aversive stimulus or activity is added after the behavior (positive punishment) or some valued object or activity is removed (negative punishment). Recall that the use of term "positive" and "negative" is not about the emotional result of punishment, but the addition or subtraction of a stimulus. Punishment, by definition, decreases the behavior, so it is always experienced as something emotionally negative.

Premack's principle can be extended to punishment. When a probable behavior is followed by a less probable behavior, the less probable behavior is punishing. A child may want to talk out of turn and disrupt class normally; but if it results in consequences he or she doesn't usually engage in, those behaviors are punishing (e.g., loss of a "good behavior" ticket, writing his or her name on the board, or a visit to the principal's office).

Positive punishment means the punishment comes in the form of the consequence presenting a situation or required activity that is irritating, harmful, or even painful. Examples of positive punishment are relatively easy to come by, simply because it is so frequently experienced. A speeding driver may be pulled over and given a ticket. Talking out of turn in class may provoke a verbal reprimand from the teacher. Using a hot oven without care may result in getting burned. A parent might give a child extra chores due to back talk.

To feel punished from the removal or omission of something valued or desired as with negative punishment is akin to a loss of privileges (Lerman & Vorndran, 2002). An aversive is not provided as part of the consequence, so much as the consequence is that an activity that is valued is removed (using Premack's principle, a behavior with a higher likelihood of occurring is no longer permitted). This can come in a range of forms, but common examples involve a cut in hours on the job or a demotion, a loss of driving privileges, losing a phone due to carelessness, or being grounded. Arguably running out of gas embodies both forms of punishment: dealing with the difficulty of being stranded, having to call for help and rearrange plans, as well as the loss of the freedom that comes with driving. We will see more on the topic of punishment after reviewing the extensive research on positive reinforcement.

As we saw in the prior section on learned helplessness, a learner can learn from punishment. For a variety of reasons that we will encounter below, B. F. Skinner saw society as overrelying on punishment as a tool for teaching, seeing reinforcement as a more optimal method for encouraging behavior. Note that punishment, by itself, does not indicate a more correct or optimal action. This is part of the problem Skinner and others have cited. The sole use of punishment to change and correct behavior doesn't communicate what should occur, just what should not. Admonishing a child to stop being so messy, for example, doesn't focus on how or why he should keep his room clean. Scolding doesn't encourage cleaning so much as punish being messy. It can be subtle, but the direct message of the punishment is aimed at ending a behavior, even if the punisher's goal is to encourage some other behavior.

In contrast to reinforcement, there has been a long history of debate about both the effectiveness as well as the disadvantages of the use of punishment, as we will see next. The use of punishment among people is so common that it's possible to intuit a number of the disadvantages. One disadvantage, discussed above, is that punishment tends to stop a specific behavior rather than to discourage a range of related behaviors; and it may be contextually specific to the situation. When people learn where a police officer is likely to be parked along a stretch of road looking for speeders, people will slow down—but often only in that area or only when they have spotted the police officer.

Effective Punishment

A recent literature review of research on punishment and its effectiveness has found several problems (Lerman & Vorndran, 2002). For instance, the use of punishment in real-world situations, such as classrooms, the workplace, clinics, or at home, can be complicated. Punishers vary tremendously. Also, an undesirable behavior that needs to be suppressed might be reinforced on one schedule while punishment is being administered alongside it. But most research studies on punishment rely solely on electric shock and animals to evaluate punishment, and usually not with concurrent schedules. So the reinforcement schedule is being extinct while the punishment schedule begins—a kind of research confound. There has not been extensive, high-quality research on the use of punishment in applied settings, despite the clear need. Also, it's not certain how many studies have found punishment to be ineffective, because they are not submitted for publication or are not accepted due to the lack of results. This is a problem in terms of gauging the overall effectiveness of the use of punishment.

Advocating the use of punishment is a problem, as Vollmer (2002) notes. While trained behaviorists and clinicians are aware of the nuances and issues surrounding the use of punishment, many of the people who might decide to carry it out will not be highly trained. Without clear guidelines that would stem from having extensive, applied research findings available, it is difficult to offer solid advice to those people (foster parents, teachers, nurses) who would administer the punishment.

But, it's clear humans and animals can learn from punishment, even when a behavior is also being reinforced. In some cases, a behavior must be stopped (self-injury, for example), and some form of punishment may have to be used. Under what arrangements has punishment been found to be effective?

First, research has repeatedly found that the punishment has to be introduced at full strength to encourage a response to be suppressed (Lerman & Vorndran, 2002). It cannot be slowly increased, step-by-step, or else the learner can habituate to the punishment. This is a mistake many parents make by first cajoling, then scolding, and then yelling at a misbehaving child. By then, the child has begun ignoring the verbal reprimands. The escalation of punishment is a problem, since the punisher doesn't get what is desired at a lower level, becomes angry, and escalates it until it's gone overboard.

The habituation to a punisher tends to hold true only for mild punishers; stronger punishers do not usually have this problem. This presents an ethical quandary in real-world situations. Generally, caregivers, parents, and teachers will want to use the least amount of punishment necessary to suppress the behavior; yet research finds escalation to be a problem, so it's unclear where the optimal amount lies. Often, practitioners have to rely on common practices or guidelines from others, instead of from research findings, to determine what is appropriate and safe at this time.

Since nearly all research on punishment has relied on a single form of punisher (electric shock), it's not clear that other kinds of punishments may or may not hold to this same pattern. There is some evidence that smaller amounts of punishment may be effective after larger punishments have been used, or if there is another alternative behavior that is being reinforced at the same time.

Second, the punishment has to be delivered with each misbehavior, every time, in what's called a "continuous schedule," as we will see in the next section. The learner has to find that the behavior will, without a doubt, produce the punishing consequence. This is, of course, an issue in real-world settings. Most punishments are on an intermittent, occasional schedule. Often, when a behavior that is punished sometimes continues to occur, the caregiver may move to a continuous schedule of punishment. Unfortunately, research has found that a behavior that has been punished intermittently will tend to resist a continuous schedule (Lerman & Vorndran, 2002). As a result, the intensity of punishment may have to be increased, which can run into an escalation problem described earlier.

Third, the punishment has to be delivered immediately after the undesired behavior, without delay. This makes clear which behavior specifically produced the punishing consequence. Of course, the person being punished may avoid the punishment, sometimes by simply running away. Even delays of 30 seconds have been found to reduce the effectiveness of punishment when used with adults (Banks & Vogel-Sprott, 1965). Young children may forget the behavior even took place a few minutes ago, and it's not entirely clear that animals can recall the past at all (Roberts, 2002). This presents a problem, since often the individual responsible for punishment may not be around when the behavior occurs, or a complete lack of delay may not be possible. What may be needed is a process to "bridge" when a behavior occurred with the use of punishment; but here, again, applied research on these techniques is sparse (Lerman & Vorndran, 2002). Activities such as recording the behavior for discussion later might be useful in some situations.

The immediate timing of a punisher may not always be appropriate. Most behaviors are already being reinforced, and if the punishment arrives *before* the reinforcement, then the effectiveness of the punishment is reduced (or even ignored). Consider a teacher who, knowing Timothy is about to talk out of turn and say something inappropriate because he usually does, frowns at him and uses his name firmly just as Timothy blurts out some foul language in front of the class. The class reacts in shock and laughter a second later, which Timothy enjoys. The reinforcing attention may completely negate the on-time-delivery of the punishment from the teacher. For effectiveness, the punishment has to follow the reinforcement for the behavior.

It can be helpful to create a conditioned punisher, a cue that signals that a punishment is eminent if the behavior continues. This includes something as simple as using the word "no." When a conditioned punisher has been established, then the cue can be used in other environments as well, generalizing the punishment. However, research on conditioned punishers is still considered fairly preliminary (Lerman & Vorndran, 2002)

Finally, some other alternative behavior must be reinforced. Ideally it should be some behavior that is logically or physically incompatible with the punished behavior. For example, if a child is being punished for wandering around the classroom, then the child should also be reinforced for sitting properly. Performing the reinforced behavior makes the punished behavior impossible, and the combination of the two consequences clearly conditions the child toward the wanted behavior.

Indirect Issues With Punishment

Some of the concerns regarding the use of punishment are not necessarily about the effectiveness of punishment itself, but the by-products or secondary effects that stem from it. Generally, these have to do with the negative emotions associated with it, and actions the punished individual may take in response to being punished.

Unlike reinforcement, the emotional nature of being punished can become a major issue for this approach to learning, particularly positive punishment. Whether something we like is removed or something aversive is added, people and animals can become upset. This may seem obvious, but this effect of punishment isn't present in reinforcement and is noticeable. When told to write their name on the board, students may emotionally react with fear, shame, or anger. Few people enjoy being pulled over by the police and waiting as other people drive by, watching. Regardless of the manner or form, punishment involves creating a situation that is unwanted or disliked, and a negative emotional reaction is not surprising.

In what may stem from the emotional reaction, retaliation against the punisher or anyone else nearby is possible with punishment and virtually never exists with reinforcement; we are rarely angry when our actions produce an outcome that is satisfying. The punished individual can seek to get back at the situation or person that delivered the punishment. This can be trivial, such as punching a countertop after standing up and feeling the sharp, unexpected pain from ramming the top of your head into an open cabinet door in your kitchen. Or it can be much more severe, such as carrying out acts of violence against people in some authoritative position (parents, teachers, work supervisors, politicians, police officers).

Similarly, punished individuals may seek to simply continue the behavior, but in other contexts—a kind of escape. Instead of learning not to do the behavior at all, the punished animal or person will just do it somewhere else where the punisher is not around. This could include learning not to cuss around parents, for example, instead of not cussing at all. Essentially, punishment can become a situation that encourages avoidance learning of the punisher, rather than suppressing the action entirely. Ironically, avoidance conditioning from escaping punishment is quick and easy to learn, and it can be more effective than the punishment itself.

Often, the issue at hand with retaliation and avoidance is that the punished individual does not necessarily learn that the behavior provoked the punishment. More often, the punished individual learns that the behavior plus the presence of the punisher provoked the punisher. What the learner may have learned is the nature of the punisher. For a parent or a teacher, for instance, this is not an ideal framework for communication. It removes the onus of the behavior from the individual and places it on the situation, and what is learned is essentially misdirected.

Another potential downside to punishment is total withdrawal of the individual from the situation. As we saw with learned helplessness, a punished individual may essentially give up regarding the situation and completely stop interacting with the environment. Repeated, poor scores in one class could trigger a student to decide to simply give up across all classes, like a generalized form of learned helplessness. While this does not always occur with the use of punishment, the risk of total withdrawal increases with the frequency of its use.

Punishment can present problems for the person administering the punishment as well. Since punishment works best when the punishment is delivered with every single instance of the behavior, the person relying on punishment to teach proper behavior constantly has to monitor the situation, which can be fatiguing or simply not possible. Additionally, compliance on the part of the punisher can be an issue. The individual in the punishing role is often aware of at least some of the problems with punishment. As a result, often the individuals who are supposed to mete out punishment according to school policy (or police department policy, or what-have-you) will not apply the consequences evenly. Since not everyone is equally engaged or committed to seeing this approach through, the end result is not uniform. For example, a school district may rely on a student color-coding system that indicates how well each child is performing. Each child starts the school day on "green" and then moves to different colors as they misbehave, down to "black." Enough of the "black" marks may mean a loss of privileges, parent conferences, or suspension. There is no formal way to recover or move back up the color chain, so it's purely a system of punishment. As a result, different teachers are likely to carry this system out unevenly. Some are sure to use it constantly, but others will apply it only in truly bad, egregious situations; or allow kids to move back up; or use the system only during formal instruction time. (People can be pretty creative or intentionally lazy with implementing systems in which they do not see the merit.)

Decelerators

What can be missed in debates about whether punishment is appropriate or effective, either in child rearing, in education, or in public policy on criminal behavior, is that punishment can take a lot of forms. Some of those forms may be more suitable or necessary depending on the situation. Below are kinds of decelerators, forms of behavior control for the purpose of slowing down or stopping some behavior. Some, but not all of them, involve punishment.

One way to end a behavior is not to allow it to be reinforced any longer (extinction). Technically, this approach is not punishment, since a stimulus is not being added or removed as a result of the behavior. An assumption of operational conditioning theory is that all behaviors are done for the purpose of earning or avoiding a consequence. If a child has discovered that she likes the attention from the teacher that comes from disrupting the class, then she will do it when she wants that attention. Her teacher could start by withholding the attention—ignoring it.

This approach may or may not be possible. First, if the actions are dangerous (e.g., standing on a desk), highly disruptive (e.g., screaming), or considered immoral (e.g., yelling inflammatory curse words at others), then immediate action has to be taken. Second, the strength of one reinforcer tends to be greater than the strength of one extinction, especially if the reinforcement was not continuous in the past. So, extincting a behavior can take a while. Finally, because the reinforcement is no longer being provided, emotional outbursts called extinction bursts can occur. Behavior can regress, as well, to earlier actions that seem immature. Essentially, when extinction is occurring, the rules of reinforcement are being changed, and the individual is likely to get upset for a period of time. When someone tries the extinction approach, he or she has to be willing to stick with it for a while, because to give in at some point means to reinforce on a new schedule, making the behavior even more resistant to extinction.

Another decelerator is overcorrection, which means to have the individual make restitution by fixing the problem and making it better, or by having the individual demonstrate the correct steps (this is known as "positive-practice overcorrection"). Someone who is arrested for painting on the school walls, for example, could be brought in on a Saturday to repaint.

A decelerator that similarly involves promoting the proper behavior is escape extinction. The individual cannot dodge the work or activity, but must do it—no escape is allowed. A child who refuses to eat a healthy dinner, but likes to skip the meal, and then snack late into the night might be told he or she must eat dinner before leaving the table from now on. No exceptions until enough dinner has been eaten. While not enjoyable to administer, it makes a point and forces the individual to give up learned avoidance responses.

Response blocking is the term for not allowing a behavior to occur by restraining the individual. When is this necessary? When the individual is about to do something that will injure himself or others. Like escape extinction, the goal is not to allow the undesired action to occur.

One unusual but potentially effective method of curtailing interest in a reinforcer is stimulus saturation. (Sometimes this technique is referred to informally as a kind of "reverse psychology.") If an individual is overly focused on a reinforcer, and it's disrupting other activities, the stimulus saturation approach calls for providing as much of the reinforcer as possible—overloading the individual with it—until he or she has had enough and interest in it wanes. A kid who has a strong need for attention from peers and spends class time using jokes for the attention could be asked to bring a joke to class each day to write on the board. (There are a lot of days in the school year.)

Some decelerators are forms of negative punishment. A response cost is a behavior that produces a cost each and every time it is done, such as a late fee for not paying a bill on time. Some classroom teachers use tokens such as tickets as rewards for good behavior, and they can take them away as part of a planned response cost for undesirable behavior. Time-outs are a form of negative punishment, in that the child is removed from participation with the group for a short period of time. Of course, this approach assumes that the child doesn't like the isolation; however, some children find the isolation reinforcing.

Decelerators that involve positive punishment include verbal reprimands (scolding) and spanking and other forms of corporal punishment. The use of rare, sharp verbal reprimands is known to help focus mild misbehavior in a classroom environment, such as calling someone's name sharply and telling them to focus. Corporal or physical punishment in school settings is against the law in most U.S. states, but it is legal for parents to use in all fifty states. There is controversy surrounding it within the media. However, the majority of psychological research is against the practice, certainly as a primary parenting tool for a number of reasons. First, there is a high risk of all of the disadvantages of punishment occurring with the presentation of a physical aversive from a parent. Second, physical punishment is readily mimicked by the child with his or her peers and siblings, which means the use of physical force becomes taught as a method for handling relationship problems with others. It's not uncommon that the use of physical punishment is used during a period of high emotional strain from the parent as well, when smarter, saner thinking does not prevail. Avoiding its use entirely helps to make sure any application of it is not done during duress. Simply put, there are many other disciplinary options than hitting a child, and usually other options provide similar results without resorting to the use of violence.

With any decelerator that relies on punishment, it's important that a more appropriate behavior be reinforced. Ideally, the reinforced behavior should make the punished behavior impossible to do. With the reinforcement of incompatible behavior, the desired action is encouraged while the undesired action is discouraged. So, if a child is being punished for getting up out of her seat and wandering around the room, then she should also be reinforced for sitting properly. If a child is forgetting to put his name on his homework, then in addition to the point deduction (punishment), he should also be reinforced when he gets it correct. Without this reinforcement, the punisher is relying on avoidance learning to encourage the child to sit properly or to remember to put down his name. It's more direct to simply reinforce the desired behavior.

Overview of Operant Conditioning Theory

The basic components of operant conditioning theory are straightforward, but grasping them presents us with problems since they are sometimes misused in the media and casual conversation. In response to some cue in the environment, an organism (the learner) makes a behavior that may or may not invite a response from the environment. This operant behavior has a particular baseline rate of strength that could be high, low, or in-between. The behavior might receive a consequence from the environment, which will then strengthen the likelihood of the behavior's happening again (reinforcement) or weaken it (punishment). If there is no noticeable consequence to the behavior, then the behavior is being extinct, from the perspective of operant conditioning theory. Figure 4.9 shows the four possibilities when a consequence results from a behavior.

FIGURE 4.9   A table of operant conditioning situations, by whether a stimulus is presented or removed and whether the behavior is strengthened or weakened

	Behavior	
Stimulus	**Strengthened**	**Weakened**
Presented	*Positive Reinforcement*	*Positive Punishment*
Removed	*Negative Reinforcement*	*Negative Punishment*

Source: Adapted from Seligman, M. E., & Maier, S. F. (1967).

Notice that operant conditioning does not claim that learning might occur. The consequence of a behavior will exert an influence on the base rate of the behavior, although this may not always be true, as we will see in the next chapter. Additionally, every behavior we make is done because of prior experience from the consequences of that behavior: behavior is never done purposelessly. The learner is working toward an improved state of affairs or is trying to avoid a worse one. Finally, since what is being taught and learned is the relative frequency of behaviors, the overall desirability or societal value placed on a behavior does not matter. Even behavior that might provoke a punishment may be reinforced in other ways. As a result, a child may find the attention he or she gets from acting out in class reinforcing, despite the negative consequences that follow. Getting a tattoo is painful, but the reinforcement for it outweighs the short-term punishment.

CHAPTER SUMMARY

Operant conditioning theory attempts to explain human and animal learning using strictly behavioral observations. Reinforcement is when an individual gives a behavioral response to a cue in the environment that results in a consequence that makes that response *more* likely to happen again. Punishment is when an individual gives a behavioral response that makes that response *less* likely to happen again. In either case, a stimulus can be presented as part of the consequence (positive reinforcement or positive punishment), or a stimulus can be removed (negative reinforcement or negative punishment). If a desired behavior is not being made yet, the trainer can shape the behavior by reinforcing smaller behaviors that gradually approximate the desired behavior. Ultimately, all reinforcement is restricted to those behaviors that the animal or human is normally capable of biologically.

Reinforcement is typically not continuous, and behaviors on a noncontinuous reinforcement schedule show a benefit of being more resistant to extinction. Commonly studied schedules include ratio schedules that involve reinforcement for a fixed or average number of behaviors and interval schedules that involve reinforcement for a fixed or average length of time.

In addition to positive reinforcement, operant conditioning theory also attempts to explain avoidance conditioning and punishment. Avoidance conditioning involves making a behavior to escape from an unwanted consequence, and success here means being reinforced for avoiding something. Of course, sometimes we avoid situations that it would be better for us to confront.

Punishment can be effective, but it has a number of drawbacks. Among other problems, punishment can become habituated, can produce anger and other negative emotional responses, can provoke a dislike of the punisher, and can result in avoidance conditioning rather than ending the behavior. These are typically most true for positive punishment. To be effective, punishment has to be strong, delivered without delay after the undesired behavior, each time it occurs. It is best if the learner has no interest in

improving on his or her own, and an optimal behavior should be reinforced simultaneously.

Operant conditioning restricts itself to the observerable and has become a strong theory in its own right. It is now one of the older learning theories within the field of psychology. It isn't that operant conditioning has been debunked or discarded, but rather that theory and research have moved beyond it. New theory includes the social context, such as learning from watching others; motivations and goals; as well as mental representations of knowledge—as we will find in the next chapters.

REVIEW QUESTIONS

1. What is the primary driver of all learned behavior, according to operant conditioning theory?

2. Can punishment be used to increase the frequency of a behavior? Why not?

3. How can shaping, response chains, and stimulus control be used to communicate to a learner that which needs to be performed?

4. Can any behavior be taught with any animal using reinforcement techniques? Why not?

5. What are the four primary kinds of schedules, and how do they impact the frequency of behaviors?

6. Both avoidance conditioning and punishment involve an aversive stimulus or situation, but in different ways and to different effects. Explain the difference.

KEY TERMS

Antecedent cues   81

Avoidance conditioning   84

Backward chain   91

Basal ganglia   84

Behavioral momentum   86

Behavioral response   81

Caudate nucleus   84

Comparative psychology   77

Conditioned reinforcement   84

Consequence   81

Continuous reinforcement
   schedule   86

Corporal punishment   101

Cortico-striatal
   system   84

Decelerators   100

Delay-discounting   86

Delays   85

Differential reinforcement of
   high rates   90

Differential reinforcement of
   low rates   89

Discriminate   82

Discrimination   92

Dopamine   85

Dopamine reinforcement
   hypothesis   85

Escape conditioning   84

Escape extinction   100

Escape latency   78

Extinction   81

Extinction bursts   100

Fixed interval   89

Fixed ratio   87

Forward chain   91

Generalization   92

FURTHER RESOURCES

- A dog that dances to the Grease soundtrack with her trainer:
  - https://www.youtube.com/watch?v=n936e073z58 andfeature=youtu.be

- "What Shamu Taught Me About a Happy Marriage": A *New York Times* article on dolphin training techniques and marriage:
  - http://www.nytimes.com/2006/06/25/fashion/ 2510ve.html?pagewanted=alland_r=0

- "It's a bird! It's a plane!" An article by B.F. Skinner describing his research on training pigeons to guide missiles:
  - http://www.army.mil/article/111511/It_s_a_bird_ It_s_a_plane_/

- An NPR story on approaching drug addiction as a matter of changing habits:
  - http://www.npr.org/blogs/health/2015/01/05/ 371894919/what-heroin-addiction-tells-us-about- changing-bad-habits

- A parent asks the police to supervise his spanking of his daughter. Would an operant conditioning theorist be supportive of this technique for improving behavior?
  - http://www.today.com/health/florida-father-asks- police-supervise-daughters-spanking–1D80400270

REFERENCES

Abramson, L. Y., Seligman, M. E., & Teasdale, J. D. (1978). Learned helplessness in humans: Critique and reformulation. *Journal of Abnormal Psychology, 87*(1), 49.

Antoniadis, E. A., & McDonald, R. J. (2000). Amygdala, hippocampus and discriminative fear conditioning to context. *Behavioural Brain Research, 108*(1), 1–19. https://doi.org/10.1016/S0166–4328(99)00121–7

Bandler, R. J., Chi, C. C., & Flynn, J. P. (1972). Biting attack elicited by stimulation of the ventral midbrain tegmentum of cats. *Science, 177*(4046), 364–366. https://doi.org/10.1126/science.177.4046.364

Banks, R. K., & Vogel-Sprott, M. (1965). Effect of delayed punishment on an immediately rewarded response in humans. *Journal of Experimental Psychology, 70*(4), 357–359. https://doi.org/10.1037/h0022233

Berridge, K. C. (2006). The debate over dopamine's role in reward: The case for incentive salience. *Psychopharmacology, 191*(3), 391–431. https://doi.org/10.1007/s00213–006–0578–x

Berridge, K. C., & Robinson, T. E. (1998). What is the role of dopamine in reward: Hedonic impact, reward learning, or incentive salience? *Brain Research Reviews, 28*(3), 309–369. https://doi.org/10.1016/S0165–0173(98)00019–8

Bickel, W. K., Odum, A. L., & Madden, G. J. (1999). Impulsivity and cigarette smoking: Delay discounting in current, never, and ex-smokers. *Psychopharmacology, 146*(4), 447.

Capaldi, E. J. (1966). Partial reinforcement: A hypothesis of sequential effects. *Psychological Review, 73*(5), 459–477. https://doi.org/10.1037/h0023684

Coffey, S. F., Gudleski, G. D., Saladin, M. E., & Brady, K. T. (2003). Impulsivity and rapid discounting of delayed hypothetical rewards in cocaine-dependent individuals. *Experimental and Clinical Psychopharmacology, 11*(1), 18–25. https://doi.org/10.1037/1064–1297.11.1.18

Cook, D., & Kesner, R. P. (1988). Caudate nucleus and memory for egocentric localization. *Behavioral and Neural Biology, 49*(3), 332–343. https://doi.org/10.1016/S0163–1047(88)90338-X

Critchfield, T. S., & Kollins, S. H. (2001). Temporal discounting: Basic research and the analysis of socially important behavior. *Journal of Applied Behavior Analysis, 34*(1), 101–122.

Elizabeth Lonsdorf, primatologist, emerging explorer. (n.d.). *National Geographic.* Retrieved from http://www.nationalgeographic.com/explorers/bios/elizabeth-lonsdorf/

Frankland, P. W., Cestari, V., Filipkowski, R. K., McDonald, R. J., & Silva, A. J. (1998). The dorsal hippocampus is essential for context discrimination but not for contextual conditioning. *Behavioral Neuroscience, 112*(4), 863–874. https://doi.org/10.1037/0735–7044.112.4.863

Gilbert, P. E., Kesner, R. P., & Lee, I. (2001). Dissociating hippocampal subregions: A double dissociation between dentate gyrus and CA1. *Hippocampus, 11*(6), 626–636. https://doi.org/10.1002/hip0.1077

Green, L., Fry, A. F., & Myerson, J. (1994). Discounting of delayed rewards: A life-span comparison. *Psychological Science, 5*(1), 33–36.

House Edge (Gambling Lessons). (n.d.). Retrieved April 6, 2017, from http://vegasclick.com/gambling/houseedge

Hull, C. L. (1943). *Principles of behavior: An introduction to behavior theory.* Retrieved from http://doi.apa.org/psycinfo/1944-00022-000

Kirby, K. N., Petry, N. M., & Bickel, W. K. (1999). Heroin addicts have higher discount rates for delayed rewards than non-drug-using controls. *Journal of Experimental Psychology: General, 128*(1), 78–87. https://doi.org/10.1037/0096–3445.128.1.78

Lerman, D. C., & Vorndran, C. M. (2002). On the status of knowledge for using punishment implications for treating behavior disorders. *Journal of Applied Behavior Analysis, 35*(4), 431–464. https://doi.org/10.1901/jaba.2002.35–431

Maier, S. F., & Seligman, M. E. (1976). Learned helplessness: Theory and evidence. *Journal of Experimental Psychology: General, 105*(1), 3–46. https://doi.org/10.1037/0096–3445.105.1.3

Maren, S. (2001). Neurobiology of Pavlovian fear conditioning. *Annual Review of Neuroscience, 24*(1), 897–931.

Miller, N. E. (1948). Studies of fear as an acquirable drive: I. Fear as motivation and fear-reduction as reinforcement in the learning of new responses. *Journal of Experimental Psychology, 38*(1), 89.

Nevin, J. A., & Grace, R. C. (2000). Behavioral momentum: Empirical, theoretical, and metaphorical issues. *Behavioral and Brain Sciences, 23*(1), 117–125.

Overmier, J. B., & Seligman, M. E. (1967). Effects of inescapable shock upon subsequent escape and avoidance responding. *Journal of Comparative and Physiological Psychology, 63*(1), 28.

Premack, D. (1959). Toward empirical behavior laws: I. Positive reinforcement. *Psychological Review, 66*(4), 219–233. https://doi.org/10.1037/h0040891

Richards, J. B., Sabol, K. E., & Seiden, L. S. (1993). DRL interresponse-time distributions: Quantification by peak deviation analysis. *Journal of the Experimental Analysis of Behavior, 60*(2), 361–385. https://doi.org/10.1901/jeab .1993.60–361

Roberts, W. A. (2002). Are animals stuck in time? *Psychological Bulletin, 128*(3), 473–489. https://doi.org/10.1037/0033–2909 .128.3.473

Robinson, T. E., & Berridge, K. C. (1993). The neural basis of drug craving: An incentive-sensitization theory of addiction. *Brain Research Reviews, 18*(3), 247–291. https://doi .org/10.1016/0165–0173(93)90013-P

Seligman, M. E., & Maier, S. F. (1967). Failure to escape traumatic shock. *Journal of Experimental Psychology, 74*(1), 1.

Seligman, M. E. P. (1975). *Helplessness: On depression, development, and death* (Vol. xv). New York, NY: W H Freeman/Times Books/ Henry Holt and Co.

Shiflett, M. W., & Balleine, B. W. (2011). Molecular substrates of action control in cortico-striatal circuits. *Progress in Neurobiology, 95*(1), 1–13. https://doi.org/10.1016/ j.pneurobi0.2011.05.007

Skinner, B. F. (1938). *The behavior of organisms: An experimental analysis*. Retrieved from http://psycnet.apa.org/ psycinfo/1939–00056–000

Skinner, B. F. (1948). Superstition in the pigeon. *Journal of Experimental Psychology, 38,* 168–172.

Skinner, B. F. (2005). *Walden Two.* Indianapolis, IN.: Hackett Publishing Company, Inc. (Original work published 1948)

Skinner, B. F. (2015). *Verbal behavior.* Mansfield Centre, CT: Martino Fine Books. (Original work published 1957)

Tanno, T., & Sakagami, T. (2008). On the primacy of molecular processes in determining response rates under variable-ratio and variable-interval schedules. *Journal of the Experimental Analysis of Behavior, 89*(1), 5–14. https://doi .org/10.1901/jeab.2008.89–5

Thorndike, E. L. (1898). Animal intelligence. *Nature, 58,* 390.

Thorndike, E. L. (1911). *Animal intelligence: Experimental studies.* New York, NY: Macmillan.

Timberlake, W., & Allison, J. (1974). Response deprivation: An empirical approach to instrumental performance. *Psychological Review, 81*(2), 146–164. https://doi .org/10.1037/h0036101

Vollmer, T. R. (2002). Punishment happens: Some comments on Lerman and Vorndran's review. *Journal of Applied Behavior Analysis, 35*(4), 469–473. https://doi.org/10.1901/ jaba.2002.35–469

Williams, J. L., & Lierle, D. M. (1986). Effects of stress controllability, immunization, and therapy on the subsequent defeat of colony intruders. *Animal Learning and Behavior, 14*(3), 305–314.

Yin, H. H., Ostlund, S. B., Knowlton, B. J., & Balleine, B. W. (2005). The role of the dorsomedial striatum in instrumental conditioning: Striatum and instrumental conditioning. *European Journal of Neuroscience, 22*(2), 513–523. https:// doi.org/10.1111/j.1460–9568.2005.04218.x

Social Learning

Chapter Outline

Learning Objectives

1. Explain how observational learning is defined and expands operant conditioning theory.

2. Identify how modeling, attributions, self-efficacy, and self-regulation play roles in the effectiveness of observational learning.

3. Explain Piaget's theory of cognitive development.

4. Describe Vygotsky's theory of the role of social context supporting learning development.

Overview

A rash of bank robberies took place in the Midwestern rural town where I was living while I was attending graduate school. The crime wave began with one person who robbed a bank by riding up to the drive-thru on a bicycle, proffering a note, and then riding off with the teller's cash. Once the news of this robbery was broadcast on the local news, a rash of other people did the same thing ("copycat crimes"). The area still has a reputation for their "bicycling bank robbers."

On a more individual level, becoming a parent can lead to many examples of the power of learning by imitation. Most parents have had the unfortunate experience of hearing one of their children spontaneously produce foul language that he or she overheard a parent use, without knowing what the words specifically meant (other than perhaps, "anger"). Likewise, we monitor what children are exposed to on television and online with the expectation that they will learn from what they see. The use of celebrities in advertisements is expressly to encourage us to imitate people held in high regard in society for the purpose of sales.

In this chapter, we'll look at theories about how we learn from watching others and how to model effectively when we want to teach others (see Fig. 5.1). Then we'll look at the two major theories of cognitive development, the changes in our ability to think and reason that come with age.

Learning by Watching Others

FIGURE 5.1   Quadrant of four perspectives on learning

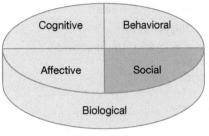

After the peak years of research on classical and operant conditioning, popular areas of research on learning extended in several directions, and the terminology used in one branch of study sometimes mirrored the terms in another. The emphasis in this chapter is on the social and motivational components of learning, including affect, but these approaches have been named differently in the past. Social learning theory (Miller & Dollard, 1941; sometimes known as the "social cognitive theory" of learning (see Aronson, Wilson, & Akert, 2012; Bandura, 1986). Social learning theory focuses on the individual's specific behaviors and the environment as does operant conditioning; but it includes cognitive and personal factors that interact as well (Schunk, 1991), including how people learn from watching others, what motivates people, and their beliefs about their own abilities. The tenets of social learning theory provided principles that bridged older behaviorist learning theories with the more contemporary theories researchers investigate today (Bandura, 1986; Rosenthal & Bandura, 1978).

The basic tenets of social learning theory expressed a view beyond the pure stimulus-response-consequence learning of the past. As you might guess, social learning theory asserts that someone can learn by observing others and watching the outcome that they receive. This doesn't fit neatly into the trial-error learning that Thorndike employed, or operant conditioning, which posits that all learning is due to directly experienced consequences. Perhaps surprisingly, Thorndike himself did not see the learning of associations' stimuli and responses to be a complete accounting of learning. In his writings on education, he emphasized issues of fatigue, personality, attitudes, interests, and even culture as influencing the learning process (Joncich, 1968). He saw his experimental work as a scientific attempt to turn the application of psychology to learning.

Early social learning theorists had noted that some learning occurred without any behavioral change at all. Learners can collect observations that are put to use at a later time, a phenomenon called latent learning. Tolman and Honzik (1930) let two groups of rats explore a maze; one group was fed within the maze, but the other group was not. As you would expect, the rats who were fed learned the maze quickly and made few directional errors. After ten free-explore trials, some in the other set of rats were given food in the maze. Suddenly they were able to navigate the maze as quickly as the rats who had been fed in the maze during the earlier trials. Learning can happen without reinforcement, and this result contradicted the basic process of operant conditioning as well.

Hence, social learning theorists concluded that performing an act that shows learning is not the same as the act of learning. We observe someone else, and learn from what that individual does and the outcomes of his or her actions. Of course, the information learned by observation has to be stored somewhere, if it's not used immediately. In some cases, people may form expectations about what to expect that are entirely based on rumor. You may have had the experience of being told an instructor was "easy," or "hard," or "fair," just to find out something entirely different after taking the class.

Social learning theory accepts the presence of mental acts such as attention, perception, and memory in the process of storing observed information, apart from just the motor actions taken in performing an action. In order for a consequence to have any effect at all on learning, the learner has to be explicitly aware of it. Essentially, that cognition has a role in learning, which we will focus on exclusively in the next chapter.

Social learning theorists see the consequence stemming from a behavior as only one part of the learning process. The learner can influence the environment in a number of ways. In fact, not only do we continually adapt to our environment, but also we make major changes to what is going on around us. While all of the smaller actions may be described using principles of reinforcement and punishment, an individual can exert change on his or her environment as well. Learning is not unidirectional. The learner can exert reinforcements and punishments on the coach or teacher, or can avoid the activity completely by choice. We tailor our environments as best as we can while choosing those activities that fit us best in the long run. Along with this level of interactivity between an individual and his or her environment, an individual also brings purpose and goals into the situation, often having expectations and desires for what he or she wants out of a situation.

In fact, someone may be waiting for punishment and, if it is not delivered, the behavior becomes reinforced *in the absence of punishment.* One study randomly assigned six-year-old boys to watch a film of a boy and his mother. The independent variable was whether the boy was either rewarded or punished by his mother for playing with some toys, or whether no consequence was shown in the film, or whether there was no film. Then, all of the boys were left alone with the same toys after being warned not to play with them. Whether the boys deviated from the warning was observed through a one-way mirror. The two sets of boys most likely to ignore the warning were the ones who had watched the boy in the film being rewarded and the ones who had seen no consequence for playing with the toys (Walters & Parke, 1964). Being told to not play with something and then removing the likelihood of being caught seemed to encourage the behavior as much as reinforcing it did.

Observational Learning

The idea that learning could happen by observation, called observational learning or vicarious learning, was originally an extension of operant and classical conditioning (e.g., Bandura & Walters, 1963). A specific action was not always required, and in some cases the observer learned without either any direct reinforcement for themselves or even the presence of a model.

From the perspective of social cognitive theorists, operant and classical conditioning didn't explain observational learning for several reasons (Rosenthal & Zimmerman, 1978). Conditioning by making simple associations wasn't able to explain how the knowledge was transferred from the person demonstrating an action to an observer. Second, it was hard to see how generalization of the stimulus could explain the process, since what the observer was examining was not simply the stimulus itself and the traits of the stimulus were not shared. Some behaviorists have focused on generalization to explain observational learning, and this requires having to stretch generalization as a concept very broadly. For example, a behaviorist could see a child imitating his or her parents because, in general, the child is reinforced for doing what they say (Mazur, 2012). The problem with this approach is that there is no concrete, specific stimulus for "obedience" that the child would be looking for as a cue. Third, the social situation affects the content of what is learned, perhaps by focusing attention. For example, someone could be modeling the same action, making a golf swing, but focusing the attention of the observer on the movements of the swing or details of his or her clothing for performance. In other words, the social context affects what is focused on and thus learned. Finally, combined with the concept of latent learning, it seemed clear to the social cognitive theorists that reinforcement can be fairly indirect, and learning could be a covert (nonbehavioral) mental activity.

Learning seemed to take on two new forms: (1) learning both reinforcements and punishments vicariously by watching others and (2) imitation (Rosenthal & Zimmerman, 1978). In order to explain imitation, it becomes necessary to describe psychological constructs that had not been part of operant condition theory, such as "attention," "retention," and "motivation."

Imitation

The act of imitating the gestures of others arrives very early on. Infants can repeat basic gestures that mirror the reflexes they are born with a day or two after birth (Meltzoff & Moore, 1997). Researchers studying infant imitation have used head movements, the act of sticking out the tongue, and facial expressions. In the case of facial features, infants are imitating expressions that they cannot see themselves perform! Meltzoff and Moore (1977) have suggested that infants must have to connect the pattern of muscle movements in facial expressions they see to those they feel they are making. Imitation during infancy increases toward age two, even after a delay of one day (Barr, Dowden, & Hayne, 1996). Animals show an ability to imitate early on, as well (Hayes & Hayes, 1952; Heyes, 2001, 2012).

One proposed biological mechanism for the act of imitation comes in the form of mirror neurons. Neurons in a particular area of the motor cortex have been found to activate not only when a macaque monkey holds an object and plays with it, but also when simply watching another monkey play with the object. In essence, the motor cortex appears to be simulating or "mirroring" the observed action. Imitation at a neural level can be automatic, causing the observer to incorporate what is seen to some extent without intent (Heyes, 2011). How many and what kind actions mirror neurons respond to and whether there are differences across species are not firmly established at this time.

It is believed that mirror neurons do not react simply to imitate what is seen, but they also act as a bridge between the sensory and motor systems. Information about what is observed is being, at least in part, translated into motor functions (Iacoboni, 2009). But the exact role mirror neurons play in imitation is less clear. Possibly mirror neurons help the perceiver to understand the goal of the actions of the individual he or she is watching, but this hypothesis is not considered to be well supported (Heyes, 2010). Possibly the associative learning, such as what classical conditioning describes, produces neurons that respond to interactions with others. Essentially, mirror neurons are the result and become part of how we interact socially.

Modeling

Learning from a model can affect behaviors in a lot of ways. We can learn a new behavior from a model. Teaching a child how to throw a Frisbee involves a lot of modeling. A child's initial attempts to throw a Frisbee usually involve tossing it overhanded or trying to bowl it into the air. Modeling can influence those behaviors we already do, by increasing how often we do them, or increasing a similar set of behaviors. Once a child has figured out how to toss the Frisbee with enough spin to make it float a distance, someone can model how to throw it at an angle so the disc "banks" in flight; or how to throw it at the right angle into the wind so that it returns to the thrower; or how to catch the disc in unusual ways (over the shoulder, between the legs). Of course, not everything we learn from a model will be positive—a model can teach and encourage activities that are not desirable, such as smoking.

Social cognitive theorists do not assume that people automatically learn from something that is modeled for them. According to Bandura (1986), modeling reinforces behavior in four ways: attention, retention, production, and motivation. Each element matters. First, for modeling to be effective, the observer has to be paying explicit attention. Imagine a kindergarten teacher demonstrating how to write the letters of the alphabet to his students. If the observer's attention is elsewhere, then what the model does is unimportant. Modeling does not appear to be a largely implicit learning process. Instead, it helps if the modeler is particularly vivid, at least for an infant observer. Waxler and Yarrow (1975) found infants were more likely to imitate their mothers if the mothers were more enthusiastic and varied their style often. It appears that infants are using the act of watching others to make the basic associations from what they see to the movements necessary to mimic them (Ray & Heyes, 2011). Not everything that can be imitated happens at the same rate, either. Rodgon and Kurdek (1977) found infants and toddlers did not imitate gestures and vocalizations equally, although gestured imitation was much more common overall. For infants, at least, learning by imitation is stronger when the model is live, rather than on television (Barr & Hayne, 1999).

Of course, the learners not only have to observe and to mimic; but for true learning, they must then store the movements for later use (retention). The acts of observing and mimicking have to be powerful enough that the learner creates a memory of the event.

The observer has to have time to practice the modeled behavior as well, so the kindergarteners will need to practice the motions necessary to produce the letters. Without an opportunity to practice, there is no possibility for feedback, which tends to help learning at all skill levels (Shute, 2008).

Production involves reproducing the steps necessary to optimally learn the behavior. Essentially, the observer enacts the motions necessary to make the behaviors, internalizing the actions. By teaching a set of motor skills to 128 children through several instructional conditions, Weiss and Klint (1987) found that children watching a model who talked through the demonstrations and encouraged practice of the skills or practice of the verbal instructions did much better than those watching the model alone. Having ten-month olds practice using a tool (a cane to reach a toy) rather than just watching it, meant they understood more quickly the purpose of another person using the tool (Sommerville, Hildebrand, & Crane, 2008). The researchers concluded that using the tool personally means constructing an understanding of the motor skills necessary to reach a goal.

One advantage of production is that the practice of retrieval appears to extend retention of the memory. Infants who choose to imitate (practice) are more likely to remember the behavior when given a cue later (Hayne, Barr, & Herbert, 2003). In the same study, the practice also allowed the behavior to generalize to new cues a day later as well. Switching from the original cue, an animal puppet, to a new animal puppet was an acceptable cue for infants who had practiced the behavior. Practice appears to encourage generalization in infants. Barr, Rovee-Collier, and Campanella (2005) found six-month-old infants could remember something they had imitated more than two months earlier, if they had practiced it repeatedly.

Finally, the observer has to be motivated to find that what the model is demonstrating is worth paying attention to. The model often has to convince the observers that the actions are worth following. If motivated to find the information useful or interesting or fun, then the learners are more willing to pay attention and give a better effort.

What makes a model effective? Similarity and relevance appear to play major roles in dictating what observers find most compelling. We are most persuaded by models who are similar to ourselves, present information relevant to our needs, and appear to be competent. Some amount of prestige helps too. Research has found it is important that the observing learners see the demonstrator as similar to themselves, in terms of age, gender, or their perceived needs (Rosenthal & Bandura, 1978). Personality has not been found to matter as much.

Learners also identify most strongly with models who seem similar to themselves, such as the same gender (Perry & Bussey, 1979). This "same-sex imitation effect" appears to be a particularly strong trait of children, who are forming their gender identities at the same time (Martin & Ruble, 2004). Hence, gender cues tend to be picked up by the observers as part of learning how to behave. They are motivated to be like others who are like themselves (Leaper & Friedman, 2007). This can be problematic because it means children will most readily focus on the gender-stereotypical behaviors presented by a model, as they will be more likely to make an effort to emulate those models who are similar to their own gender. Bussey and Perry (1982) found rejection of opposite-sex behavior to happen with boys more often than girls, but both sexes accept modeled same-sex behavior equally. Hence, the boys may listen more closely to the male astronomer's discussion about how to think about science, which reinforces the long gender imbalance in the sciences. Most likely, the best approach to countering this tendency is occasionally to use models who break gender stereotypes, to bring attention to the irrelevance of gender for most activities, and to use multiple models.

Some characteristics of the performance itself matters. Learners are more impressed by a model who appears to be competent and has prestige. A model who is uncertain, makes mistakes, and has trouble executing the necessary steps does not inspire as much confidence or attention as opposed to someone who has confidence and exudes experience. Schulz, Hooppell, and Jenkins (2008) found models who produced direct effects from their actions were more effective as modelers among preschoolers and toddlers than models who produced "probabilistic" results (i.e., it usually worked, but not always). By age three, children will choose to mimic actions that produce better results (Want & Harris, 2001).

Similarly, prestige helps convince learners that the person they are watching has information that is likely to matter. One study found high-status peers had more of an impact on learning from a demonstration than low-status peers among handicapped students (Sasso & Rude, 1987). Observers have been found to imitate high-prestige models and the models' response style more than low-prestige models, such as those who appear professional and have a doctorate rather than individuals who seem messy and inexperienced (Bauer, Schlottmann, Bates, & Masters, 1983).

Seemingly counterintuitively, highly competent performances may not always be the best call. Braaksma, Rijlaarsdam, and van den Bergh (2002) found observers tend to learn best from the models who present themselves at their observers' skill level, even if that means being less competent. As such, children who were weak writers found themselves learning more from models who presented themselves as having had only a modest amount of competency. In contrast, children who had good writing skills learned more from the more competent models. How does this study mesh with the general adage, "models should be competent"? Perhaps competency matters, but similarity matters more. An instructor has to tailor his or her demonstrations to the audience and their existing capabilities, first and foremost. If faced with learners who are already fairly skilled, the model has to take that proficiency into account and present a demonstration at their level.

The best model of this complex level of interactivity is represented by Bandura's model of reciprocal causation (or "reciprocal determinism," Bandura, 1986; see Fig. 5.2). Rather than being a simple passive observer of the environment, a learner "perceives" the environment and chooses how to interact with it. The successes and failures that the individual experiences then change the perception of the person and his or her own abilities over time. The beliefs that we have about our abilities will influence how much we pay attention to and struggle with the strategies we will use to learn something. For example, someone can adopt a sense of confidence about some activities (e.g., programming a computer), while learning to be bothered by others (e.g., public speaking), so choosing to work from home to write computer programs may maximize strengths while limiting perceived weaknesses. Even the weaknesses themselves are perceived, since individuals can only really judge themselves based on past performance and current expectations rather than in any true absolute sense.

FIGURE 5.2   Reciprocal causation (Bandura, 1986)

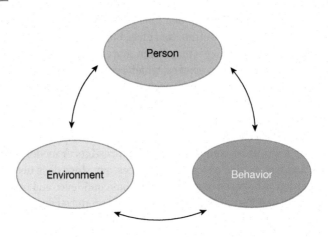

To summarize, social cognitive theory incorporates social elements with learning, such as the assumption that we can learn by watching others. What is learned may be completely internal and can be stored for later use. While the environment influences us, we can also influence the environment. How we attempt to exercise that control may be heavily governed by how we perceive the situation as a whole and our own abilities.

Social cognitive theorists assume that our behavior is directed toward a goal of some kind and that we will work toward it. We manage our time and efforts to try to make that goal a reality. The perception of ourselves as achieving that goal becomes very important, because if we believe we have that ability, we will take steps to reach the goal. If we do not believe we are capable, then we do not. The level of engagement with the learning process will be affected by the strength of this perception as well.

Attribution Theory

Motivation is also affected by the perception of the results or outcome of the effort. According to attribution theory (Weiner, 1985), people attribute the results of their actions to be due either to their own efforts or to factors outside their control. We make attributions about where the source or *locus* of the effort resides.

In making a judgment about whether he or she expects to be able to do the work necessary for the outcome, a learner will consider where he or she believes the control of the work will be. Can the performance be ascribed solely to him- or herself? Is that control something that can be maintained over time? Are there aspects of the work that cannot be directly controlled?

A belief that the work can be primarily attributed to one's own personal ability is called an internal attribution. A belief that the work will be due to luck, fate, random chance, or other situational factors is called an external attribution. As you might guess, someone is more likely to engage in the work necessary to learn if they make an internal attribution about it. Internal attributions also encourage people to make more of an effort and to try to overcome obstacles. In contrast, if the effort is seen as being a matter of happenstance, then the individual has little reason to make a strong commitment to the task. The effect of the attribution will continue after the work is done as well. An individual who successfully completes a task and makes an internal attribution about the effort will have a sense of pride about the work, but someone who sees it as luck will not. It helps if the internal attribution is viewed as long-lasting and controllable. This means the individual sees one's own ability as the primary cause for doing the work that can promote learning.

One example of the decision process in making an attribution about the source of the effort needed is small-group work. Group work is popular in education for a number of reasons. Many contemporary work environments employ teams, so group work allows time to practice those skills. Also, it gives the instructor an opportunity to allow students to make more of the decisions about their own learning. Group work is known to encourage social bonding and peer support as well (Blaney, Stephan, Rosenfield, Aronson, & Sikes, 1977). Of course, the attributions made about the assigned work become cloudy in comparison to individual work. In a solo situation, the student knows he or she is completely responsible for the effort. In a group environment, it is less clear how much control any one person will be able to employ, and for how long. As a result, students often have mixed feelings about group work assignments. Prior negative experiences with group work are not likely to help, either, since that history informs the attribution-making process.

One prediction from attribution theory makes learning from mistakes more challenging. Heider (1944) and other attribution theorists found that people tend to use a self-serving bias when making attributions about their own work. People would readily make an internal attribution about efforts that resulted in success (such as getting a high score on a test) but would make an external attribution about unsuccessful efforts (getting a low score on a test). In one case, the individual takes credit; but in the other, where mistakes may have been made, the person will gravitate toward blaming situational issues (bad lighting, extraneous noise, a test that was too difficult). Note that either or even both attributions may, in fact, be true; but the perception will drive the next steps in dealing with the result. Someone who becomes frustrated from a disappointing experience may want to blame the situation, but it does mean lifting any sort of responsibility off oneself. External attributions can serve as excuses that allow people not to learn from mistakes, not to persist, and not to change strategies.

For this reason, teachers and coaches are often advised to give feedback that is focused on improvement and on those factors that are controllable, regardless of how successful the outcome is. Focusing the learning on what can be improved in his or her own performance encourages what has been called a growth mindset (Dweck, 2007), a frame of mind that is aimed at improvement through hard work and dedication.

Self-Efficacy Theory

If someone sees the work as controllable by themselves, what goes into the decision that he or she can do the work? Self-efficacy theory (e.g., Bandura, 1997) is defined as the confidence a person has in his or her ability to perform some task under some set of conditions. It is not considered to be the same as self-esteem or self-worth, which are usually thought of as the value we place on ourselves. Similarly, it is not one's self-concept, which is the information and knowledge we have about ourselves. Self-efficacy is that sense of certainty, high or low, for being able to accomplish a specific activity, such as completing a college-level course in calculus with a passing grade, or driving home safely in bad weather, or juggling part-time work and school and family.

A high self-efficacy and a high expectancy judgment affects whether one will engage in a task, regardless whether it can be done. Realistically, it's a perception, and not necessarily reality. A low self-efficacy influences a decision not to engage. Conversely, a high self-efficacy for a task induces a willingness to take on challenging goals, to make more of an effort, and to focus more accurately on the learning process.

This means that a teacher providing a challenging learning activity may have to counter a low self-efficacy and enhance self-confidence in order to increase the likelihood that the task can be accomplished. There are several known factors that feed into the confidence judgment of self-efficacy. First, prior successes and failures play a role in one's estimation of confidence, and often only those successes and failures that were relatively recent (Bandura, 1986, 1997). Second, the successes and failures of others, the group as a whole, also matters since we can learn vicariously. It's hard to feel self-confident about a task when we can witness others struggling and failing. Third, one's current emotional state also matters; a negative affective state can drag down the sense of confidence.

While neuroscientists do not necessarily study self-efficacy directly, they do study the act of the individual's engaging in a behavior versus experiencing someone else as engaging in a behavior. They do observe brain functioning as someone makes a simple motion to manipulate an object and contrast that motion to when someone else does it for them. The supplemental and presupplemental motor-related areas of the brain are activated by voluntary movement, which appear to be used for planning and then executing an action. When an individual makes the decision to make a movement, activation occurs in the insula (Farrer & Frith, 2002).

Self-Regulation Theory

Conscious attempts at learning imply that we can exert some control over the learning process. What is the nature of self-control? Several researchers have studied the act of self-regulation to find out more about how people approach a task, such as learning, and maintain their effort over time until the project is completed. While we will look at self-regulation concepts and theories as they apply to learning, self-regulation as a topic also overlaps with other topics in psychology, including productivity in the workplace, and problems with what is often called executive functioning in neurophysiology.

Self-regulation is thought to involve several steps, beginning with defining the task (Mischel, Cantor, & Feldman, 1996). For learning, this may involve comprehending directions for an assignment, evaluating what to study, and making judgments about what areas will require the most effort and time. Next, the student will then set goals and make plans for how to reach those goals, whether short-term (e.g., "I need to skim the chapter for the quiz tomorrow") or long-term (e.g., "I need to improve my writing skills"). The plans we make will involve selecting strategies we think will help us reach our goals and can include the different learning strategies we have encountered so far. Then we enact the strategies and put them to use. Not everything will go as planned, so we then must adapt to our experiences as we see how our strategies pan out.

The COPES model is a fuller model of self-regulation (Greene & Azevedo, 2007). In this model, we start with a set of conditions that make up the situation we find ourselves in. The strategies we use are the operations we make on our situation to try to reach our goals. This will produce results, or products, that are then subject to our own evaluations as well as evaluations of others, like an instructor. All of this is subject to a number of expectations or standards that can affect the process as a whole, such as how much time we think we have, what the nature of a class or assignment is like, and our beliefs about our own self-efficacy.

During this process, we engage in self-monitoring and self-control. Self-monitoring is the continual sense of how the process is going relative to our standards and pondering if something needs to change. It's considered to be a continuous process, and it repeats itself. As we go, we use our self-control to execute various actions and adapt as needed.

Development of Learning

Two theorists proposed explanations for how children develop their capability to learn by interacting with their environment, including others around them. Swiss biologist and developmentalist Jean Piaget believed that children build their understanding of their world through reflection and interaction. Their understanding of the world increases and becomes more complex with age, a tenet of constructivism. Their age-based advances in understanding, he proposed, were not merely a matter of improvements in quantity, but in quality as well. Russian psychologist Lev Vygotsky proposed a corollary theory to Piaget's, establishing a framework for understanding the role of society, culture, and family in how a child learns.

For the remainder of this chapter, let's look at these two theories of learning development.

Piaget's Theory of Cognitive Development

Jean Piaget used an unusual (for the early twentieth century) methodology for developing his understanding of how children learn and reason. At the time that he began his research, the primary approach to the study of children and how they think would have been early research on intelligence and intelligence testing. At that time, the foundational work on intelligence testing was in understanding at what ages children typically gave the correct answer to practical questions. Piaget, in contrast, was interested in the wrong answers that children produced, particularly since some children would consistently give the wrong answer to some questions. Instead of simply dismissing them as wrong, he wondered why children were producing the answers they gave.

To do this, he used an unorthodox method of research for the time, when behaviorism and rigid animal research were popular in American psychology. He devised puzzles and problems for children to work on and watched how they formed their answers. He would ask them questions about their thinking (e.g., Piaget, 1954, 2013a, 2013b; Piaget & Inhelder, 1958/2013, 1969). Nowadays, we might see his approach as an interview style or a kind of ethnography that is focused on learning about children's problem-solving abilities. For example, if a child claimed that spreading out a set of pennies meant there were now magically more pennies, he and his research assistances would ask why. While Piaget's work is now highly regarded and popular, his own children were less taken with it, since they were frequently subjects in his studies. None of his children chose to go to college.

Of course, exploring how children thought about their world meant accepting that their mental behavior could be studied, a concept which was not accepted within the behaviorist community either. It was some time before Piaget's work was "discovered" and popularized in North America, starting with Flavell's 1963 English translation of his French writings.

Primary Assumptions

Piaget's approaches to understanding how children learn are basic tenets of constructivism. As presented in Chapter 1, constructivism sees the knowledge we accumulate about the world as constructed by ourselves. This semantic information becomes prior knowledge that we use to understand our world moving forward. Piaget saw children as actively engaged in their learning (Piaget, 2013a). Instead of simply responding to stimuli around them, they were, like beginning scientists, testing out the world around them. Any parent who has experienced his or her baby dropping a spoon from the baby's high chair repeatedly just to hear the sound and watch the parent fetch it will have a sense of how this might work.

Children's knowledge of the world is created. Combined with dropping the spoon and other events, such as tripping and falling, and observing how most things tend to fall down, children begin to construct an understanding of gravity. Likewise, they will learn about people from those they interact with, read about, and observe on television. They start to form a base of knowledge about animals stemming from their experiences as well.

If children develop knowledge and ability to learn by interacting with the environment, then interaction with the physical environment around them is essential. For Piaget, playtime is a child's work. They must explore what is around them to learn how to manipulate their world. Banging, throwing, shrieking, rolling, stacking, knocking things over—these activities are part of the learning experience in the early years of life. While they lack the rigor of modern scientific techniques, children are naive scientists, exploring for themselves how things work, forming basic understandings of the world as they experience life each day.

Of course, this interaction with the world is not going to be completely isolated. While children may form their "naive theories" about the world, if you will, they learn much through their interactions with others. By socializing with peers as well as adults, they learn about differences people have in understanding the world. They develop an understanding that others may have a different perspective of an event witnessed by all. They will find that not everyone has a completely accurate idea of what may have gone on. They will learn to spot logical inconsistencies in their own and others knowledge.

So, how do children learn from interacting with the environment? Piaget claimed there are two primary processes: assimilation and accommodation. Assimilation describes any situation in which a child uses preexisting knowledge to respond successfully to the situation. For example, an infant sees a ball, and uses her reflexive ability to grab the ball successfully. The knowledge the child possesses has successfully been molded to the environment to achieve a goal. Assimilation doesn't end with infancy. We constantly assimilate what we know about the world to solve math problems, navigate city roads, merge into freeway traffic, and resolve disagreements. Being able to adequately handle situations using what we already know means we are in a state of equilibrium, according to Piaget.

Of course, what we currently know isn't always enough. Accommodation describes situations in which we have to adapt our existing knowledge to fit a situation in which something unexpected happened. Perhaps the ball is wet, and as the infant grasps it, it slips out of her fingers, surprising her. A math problem stumps us. Due to lane closures from construction work, we find getting to our destination taxing and difficult. Accommodation means the child either must modify existing knowledge or form new knowledge for the situation. Perhaps the infant decides this slippery ball will take two hands, a new strategy for situations like this. Tomorrow, we'll take a different route entirely. Being puzzled or surprised by a result is the basis of becoming aware of a need to alter what we know—our existing skills are not enough. Piaget called these situations a state of *disequilibrium*, a state of confusion that produces the motivation to better understand what is going on. Today, it's clear to researchers that Piaget's emphasis on interaction with the physical environment is certainly important. However, it is important to keep in mind that children learn much by observing, and those with severe physical disabilities still develop cognitively without the same level of interaction other children have (Bebko, Burke, Craven, & Sarlo, 1992; Brainerd, 2003).

Accommodation is the act of learning, while assimilation is the use of that learning. (A mnemonic to help remember how the two terms operate is to remember that with aSSimilation, existing knowledge *Stays the Same*, whereas with acCommodation, *knowledge must Change*.) Assimilation and accommodation work simultaneously with each other, rather than being opposites. As children engage in activities, they both use and modify their existing knowledge. Being in a state of equilibrium, a surprising event forces us into disequilibrium, until we can resolve the issue successfully and return to equilibrium. These terms are not precisely defined, and might be thought of best as a framework for discussion (Chapman, 1988; diSessa, 2006).

Piaget's Stages of Cognitive Development

The idea that children can mentally process more information as they grow up, primarily due to changes in brain development, is not particularly controversial. What Piaget proposed went beyond this idea: he proposed that children at specific ages think differently from other ages, mostly likely due to the maturation of the brain. The qualitative differences in thinking ability occurred in four fixed stages, and each child moves through them sequentially. So, it is not just that the computational power of the brain is being increased over time, but the brain is gaining new computational abilities as well, like additional hardware, if you will.

His theory is a classic stage theory. At each stage, there is a qualitative change (a difference in kind, not just amount) in thinking. At each stage, there are structural features that limit a child's ability to learn and think. Each stage builds on the prior one in a fixed order, universally. According to Piaget, any one stage completely influences all thinking and learning in the child's life, regardless of content area or domain. A rigid, dogmatic interpretation of Piaget's stage theory hasn't held up well over time. Recent research has found that all the tenets of his theory are not always completely true, although the basic thesis of a sequence of phases remains (Chapman, 1988; Ginsburg, Cannon, Eisenband, & Pappas, 2006). It may be better to think of the stages as general trends, since specific ages can vary (Kuhn & Franklin, 2006). It's not clear that each stage is as universal to all children or as rigid over time and domain as he believed (Arnett, 2014; Klaczynski, 2001).

Let's take a closer look at the kinds of thinking Piaget proposed children are capable of at different ages, keeping the focus primarily on those developments that affect a child's ability to learn.

Sensorimotor Stage (birth until eighteen–twenty-four months). Piaget believed that infants lacked the ability to mentally represent the external world. So, without mental representation, the behaviors of infants are primarily reflexive, innate behaviors (e.g., sucking, grasping) that are useful for survival. Reflexes are automatic muscular responses to environmental stimuli. This means that the infant does not have a capacity for thought, planning strategies, a memory for past events, or language. The baby has reflexive behaviors that are triggered in response to environmental cues. Everything is in the present.

Another consequence of a lack of mental representation is that the infant will not have object permanence. If an infant loses sight of an object, Piaget believes the infant no longer knows it exists. If all infant behaviors are responses to environmental cues and nothing more, then anything that does not provide any cues (a hidden object) is simply gone.

This focus on the present continues for most of the first year of life. In the early months, voluntary movements are focused on the infants' own bodies, such as sucking on fingers; but in time, objects around them will become included without forethought or any particular goals. Piaget named this period the sensorimotor stage. Around the end of the first year, the infants start to understand cause-and-effect relationships in what they do. An infant in a high chair will learn that smacking a spoon on the tabletop makes a noise and will test this repeatedly. (It also causes parents to make a fuss.)

Piaget mapped out advances in infant movements as they age. After one month of age, infants engage in primary circular reactions: an action produces an interesting result, so it's repeated. Grasping a finger or sucking a thumb is an example of this. Between 4–8 months, infants engage in secondary circular reactions by using other objects to try to create an effect, such as putting other objects in their mouths. While Piaget believed they did not have a specific goal in mind, the behavior seemed a little more intentional. After 8 months to 1 year, infants can coordinate several behaviors to make something happen, such as pushing a bowl out of the way of some toy car keys. This stage marks the beginning of behavior that is more goal-like. At this point, infants have started to learn object permanence—just because something is hidden doesn't mean it no longer exists—and they may pursue something that fell under a blanket or rolled under a chair. By year one, an infant can engage in tertiary circular reactions, which involve testing reactions while including some novelty. The child begins to actively experiment with the environment: testing sounds of different objects when hit against the floor, watching what happens when different objects are dropped off the table.

Infant development is not necessarily quite as restricted as Piaget believed; recent research indicates that object permanence may develop by two to three months (Baillargeon, 2004; Cohen & Cashon, 2006). Also, while language will not develop until two years or later, nonverbal communication does start by twelve months of age (Mandler, 2007).

Preoperational Stage (eighteen–twenty-four months to seven years). As children develop the ability to mentally represent the world around them, gaining object permanence for instance, they develop language and learn symbolism. Pretend play becomes all encompassing. I remember having to keep toy cars from my youngest son during meals, because he would play with them and never eat. At that age, he realized he could turn his spoon into a car, and so much for the toy car prohibition. A child who has entered that stage can form basic plans, chain behaviors together to accomplish a goal, and can start to put together the words to explain the goal. The ability to form mental representations is behind these developments. They can now represent one thing (an event or object) with a symbol (a word or a gesture). However, Piaget noted that the thinking ability in this age-set is not always logical, so he named it the preoperational stage.

Children in this cognitive stage show several unique thinking traits. Perhaps most fundamentally, they tend to show a rigid thinking style, often bounded by the sensory experience of a situation. First, they show centration, focusing on a single aspect of a problem, rather than grasping several interacting factors. So, a child might understand that he lives in his hometown, but not the state or country where his hometown exists. This appears both in their estimations of quantity and their ability to understand the perspectives of others. Piaget demonstrated that children in the younger group of preoperational stage will reason about the quantity of the number of pennies, amount of clay, or liquid by the visual appearance of the objects. So, if a row of pennies is spread out, there is a greater visual appearance of them, so there must be more. The number of pennies doesn't matter to them. Piaget called this a lack of conservation, meaning that the properties of an object were not conserved or held constant as the perceptual nature of the object underwent a change. If liquid is poured into a tighter, taller glass, they focus on the height of the liquid (the new watermark) and will believe there is now more liquid, magically. They are not able to consider the change in volume of the glass at the same time. Similarly, children in this age set can have trouble sorting a mixed set of objects by any one category.

Second, early preoperational children have trouble seeing the world from perspectives that they do not have, a trait called egocentrism. So, they are likely to answer grandmother's question over the phone by nodding their heads. It's not impossible for them to understand another's perspective, but it seems to take some effort. If they witness some event, like a fight in the playground, they will assume that everyone else has witnessed it too (and had similar emotional reactions to it).

Modern research has not completely supported the idea that preschoolers are completely egocentric. Preschoolers can hold pictures in a manner that others can see them and can answer spatial questions (Newcombe & Huttenlocher, 1992), but it may not be until age 5 that they can answer questions about whether an object is to someone else's "left" or "right" accurately.

Concrete Operations Stage (ages six–seven until eleven–twelve). Major advances in thinking ability happen during the concrete operations stage, so named because the thinking takes on a more logical nature. Concrete operational thinkers show several improvements from their preoperational days. They can focus on multiple elements of a problem, ending centration, so they show conservation of an object's traits despite minor changes to its appearance. They can classify objects by two or even three dimensions. They handle multiple perspectives better, and will realize they may have to validate their understanding of a situation with others by asking them about what they experienced. It's interesting to note that the early teen years, right after this age period, have a very high emphasis on social interaction and influence from peers. An engaged social teen wouldn't be possible if he or she believed that his or her perspective were the only one to be had.

Piaget believed the advances were mostly restricted to concrete events and objects rather than abstractions, an assertion that has mixed support today. So, while their ability to handle objects logically improves, understanding algebraic variables and hypothetical, impossible situations will not have improved. Counterfactual thinking (e.g., "What if 9/11 had not occurred? What might be different now?") is not likely to produce well-reasoned answers. They will have trouble accepting logic problems that are purely hypothetical, such as, "If all pencils are umbrellas, and all umbrellas are beans, then are all pencils beans?"

When children move into the concrete operations stage, their thinking processes begin to take the form of logical operations that enable them to integrate various qualities and perspectives of an object or event. Such operational thought enables several more advanced abilities. For example, children now realize that their own viewpoints and feelings aren't necessarily shared by others and may reflect personal opinions rather than reality. Accordingly, they know they can sometimes be wrong and thus begin to seek out external validation for their ideas, asking such questions as, "What do you think?" and "Did I get that problem right?"

Formal Operations Stage (ages eleven or twelve through adulthood). In Piaget's final suggested stage, formal operations, children become able to reason logically about abstract concepts and can reason hypothetically. This stage develops as a matter of maturation according to Piaget, but modern research has found that this stage is heavily dependent on formal education and cannot be assumed. Thinking at this stage means they can embrace counterfactual ideas, reason about abstract ideas (e.g., "Are our existing copyright laws fair or not?") and understand the meanings behind parables. Abstract mathematical concepts like infinity and negative numbers become understandable. For the first time, these children can approach a hypothesis systematically, analyzing a problem by tackling each variable in turn, and making predictions. There is a reason most experimental science is taught in high school. Conscious awareness of own thinking—metacognition—also appears during this stage. A teenager can question whether he or she has contradicted him- or herself. With this ability to reason hypothetically, teens may propose idealistic solutions to real-world problems that may not be practical or possible.

While Piaget left this stage as his final transition into adult-like thinking, research indicates that much of what he described in the formal operational stage may not be the norm for daily reasoning of adults. Most adults do not use formal rules of logic but rely heavily on experience when dealing with the world (Birney, Halford, & Andrews, 2006; Kuhn & Franklin, 2006). Taking classes in a particular area has been shown to increase logical thinking in that area (Lehman & Nisbett, 1990). Taking social science classes improves reasoning about statistics, whereas natural science and humanities classes increase reasoning about conditional logic instead.

To conclude our review of Piaget's theory of cognitive development, it's important to note that his primary contribution was the idea of constructivism. Beginning as children, we actively seek to learn about the world, constructing our own understanding of what is happening around us by using what we already know or by forming new knowledge.

Educational Implications

What does Piaget's theory of cognitive development mean for education? First, Piaget's belief that play is "children's work"—that learning is the result of active exploration of the environment—has meant the creation of instructional methods that allow children to find knowledge for themselves. Discovery learning is the approach of providing a situation that is "sandboxed," meaning that children are provided the necessary tools to re-create some algorithm or result and are encouraged to figure out a principle. The activity is led by the students. Open-ended learning in this manner might either use physical objects, such as balls to simulate the movements of the solar system, or be computer-based and virtual (Moreno, 2006; Moreno & Mayer, 2007; Pease & Kuhn, 2011; Wirkala & Kuhn, 2011).

Despite the well-meaning intention, this approach has its critics (e.g., Kirschner, Sweller, & Clark, 2006). The amount of structure children need will depend on their age, as well as experience in the subject matter. As you might guess, children below the formal operations stage could be at a disadvantage with so little structure, since they lack the systematic approach it takes to evaluate variables individually. It is also necessary that children have mastered the basic concepts before being able to make useful predictions and design experiments. Philosophically, it might not be necessary for children to learn about science by recreating the situations in which scientific principles were learned. While not a problem in itself, it may be unnecessary. I can operate a car well without knowing how internal combustion engines were invented. Students seem to benefit from more structure that guides the activities as well as helps with developing the explanations for why certain results have been achieved. A meta-analysis of fifty-five studies of the use of "manipulatives," such as blocks, to learn math principles seems to confirm that manipulatives help in learning abstract math principles (Carbonneau, Marley, & Selig, 2013).

However, it's also possible for students to develop a completely incorrect understanding for why something occurs the way it does, even when using props. Some knowledge is simply complicated and counterintuitive on its face. Consider that the earth is closer to the sun in winter in the northern hemisphere rather than in the summer. The correct explanation for the seasons is not necessarily what a student would initially propose, since the idea of moving closer to a heat source for warmth is so intuitive.

Inquiry learning, instead, is a variation on discovery learning that shows more promise (Minner, Levy, & Century, 2010). The teacher guides activities by asking students to consider what they know about a topic, asking them to make some predictions, and then gathering information to draw some conclusions (Mantzicopoulos, Samarapungavan, & Patrick, 2009; Patrick, Mantzicopoulos, & Samarapungavan, 2009). So, a fourth-grade science teacher might ask students to think about what they know about plant growth; to make some predictions about sunlight, water, or the dirt matter supporting growth; and then to engage in research or a study to test some hypotheses. After collecting evidence, they can then discuss what their findings mean. KWL charts are a form of inquiry learning. Students are asked to make a table of what they "Know" about a subject; "What" they would like to learn about it; and. after an activity, to describe what they have "Learned." It's a structured journaling method to track learning. Notice that this kind of activity embeds feedback about student progress into it, which can help the educator tremendously. Even with more structured activities, students can still form misconceptions; tracking learning through KWL charts and by other means helps the teacher to monitor the process.

A second major implication of Piaget's theory has been to encourage the use of disequilibrium to spark the conflict that will provoke children to have to accommodate a new understanding. The idea is to present puzzling or surprising results with the hope that this will naturally inspire them to rethink what they know (e.g., Frazier, Gelman, & Wellman, 2009; Gelman, 2009). For example, fifth-graders might be asked to draw a basic solar system including the sun, moon, and earth and their orbits. Most children will know the moon orbits the earth, and most of them will know it orbits earth monthly. From this, a teacher can ask, "So how often do we have a solar eclipse?" which most students know is fairly rare. The teacher might follow up with, "So why don't we have a solar eclipse every month?" This question could spark some discussion over what might be occurring, since a simple model of the solar system would expect a monthly solar eclipse.

Discussing results with peers can also trigger disequilibrium (Palincsar, 1998). Once students find out that several people (some of them friends!) have radically different ideas about the basic movements of the solar system, it begins to call into question whether they themselves truly have the correct answer or not. Additionally, children are more willing to ask questions of and challenge the beliefs of their peers. So, discussing an issue in small groups is another instructional method that can spur disequilibrium (Mercer, 1996; Slavin, 2011). Here too, notice that an educator will still have to watch for misconceptions. Not every group of children will land on the known, correct answer for some phenomenon.

Finally, Piaget's stages have encouraged teachers to adopt different teaching strategies for children of different ages. It's clear that what works for one age-set is not necessarily going to work for another. Abstract ideas are usually very challenging for younger children, for instance, and complicated interacting systems will probably need to be reduced to basic components before teaching a whole system. For example, focusing on the basic movement of the sun, earth, and moon prior to introducing the phases of the moon is critical.

Piaget focused almost exclusively on the development of cognitive abilities as the individual experiences them, chronicling the universal nature of cognitive change over time (Chapman, 1988). As we have seen with formal operational thinking, however, thinking abilities can vary by experience through gained knowledge in a subject. Also, a primary filter for constructing our understanding of the world stems from interactions—not with objects but with other people such as our parents. Lev Vygotsky attempted to describe the role that people play in helping children interpret their environment, as we will see in the next section.

Social Context of Cognitive Development

Lev Vygotsky (1896–1934), a Russian psychologist, held a view of cognitive development that explicitly included the social aspects of learning. The adults in a child's life are involved and generally viewed as responsible for helping that child understand the world around him or her. Teachers, parents, guardians, siblings, and others take on the role of providing explanations and insights into how to think about the world and strategies for navigating it. Vygotsky saw individual people as part of a matrix or interconnected web of other people (R. Miller, 2011), and a child in that web will rely on others to construct his or her reality. Philosophically, Vygotsky proposed something very different from Piaget. Vygotsky believed that children did not possess mental representations of the world, so much as that a child "co-constructs" mental structures of the world with others (Galotti, 2016). This is a fairly controversial view today, and can be seen as harkening back to behaviorism. It is possible, however, to see contributions from Vygotsky's perspective to our understanding of the nature of cognitive development without accepting or rejecting the issue of where mental representations reside.

Vygotsky drew attention to the highly social nature of a child's learning to handle a troublesome problem. Imagine tutoring a child in understanding how to calculate the area of a square and a triangle. It's not something most children will teach themselves. An adult might ask probing questions, trying to see what is confusing the child, and ask for some simpler tasks, such as "Can you find the length of side x? How about y?" before performing the calculation. The adult will pause and wait for the child to perform these tasks before trying to integrate those results into the formula for computing area. There might be discussions or interruptions along the way, but ultimately the adult provides a strategy to achieve something the child would not have likely resolved on his or her own. For an older child who has encountered this material before, the adult might take a different approach: "Let's review what you did last week. Can you transfer what you learned then to this?," which is more of a metacognitive strategy for remembering.

Vygotsky proposes that the adult is providing cognitive tools to understand and resolve the problem. Like using a hammer and nails for building, cognitive tools are mental concepts and strategies that we impart to others to help them solve a problem (Vygotsky, 1980). These tools are passed along in formal education or through information conversations with family and friends.

For Vygotsky, language was very important as a cultural tool. Besides communication with others, language is used internally to talk us through a difficult task. Whereas young children might use language for communication initially, children use their language to

FIGURE 5.3   A diagram of the "zone of proximal development"

ZPD

Easy but
Unchallenging

Too Difficult;
Frustration

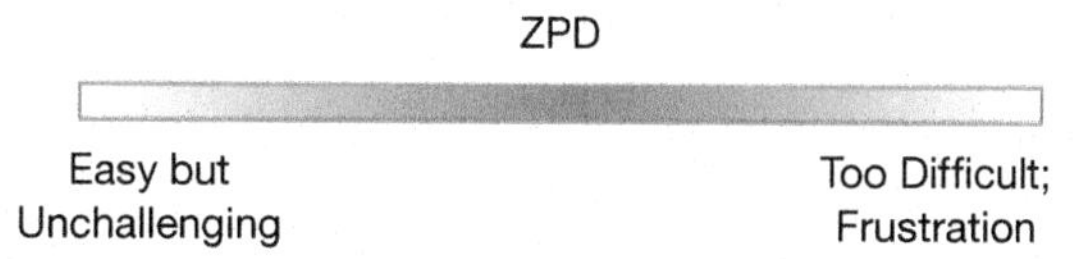

express their own thoughts after age two. They begin to use self-talk as they work through a task. As we get older, the self-talk becomes private, inner speech that we engage in as our own cognitive guide.

A child, Vygotsky believed, has a range of cognitive functioning for some task or domain—a zone of proximal development (see Fig. 5.3). This zone can range from a low, comfortable level of tasks that a child finds easy to complete independently (perhaps single-digit addition) up to those tasks that a child possibly can do, but only with help from someone else (perhaps double-digit multiplication). The child doesn't have an existing average ability so much as a range that he or she is capable of. Easy tasks, those at the lower end of the zone, do not promote much growth at all. Those at the higher end that require assistance provide the challenge that encourages growth. This zone will change over time as the child matures.

What a teacher (or any adult providing assistance) is engaging in when teaching a child is finding and working on increasing that child's zone of proximal development. If children spend too long at the lower end, they will become bored and disinterested; yet at the upper limits, they can become highly anxious and threatened. Starting with easy tasks and migrating as far as possible before easing off is a common teaching strategy, particularly in tutoring. You might be able to see the similarity between this approach and learning how to swim or play a sport. There's a maximal level of performance that we might want to push ourselves to, but typically it's not wise or safe to engage in the activity only at that level. It's frustrating and demoralizing. Tasks that are so hard that they are impossible are virtually useless (Vygotsky, 1980).

So, the adult provides guidance through a process known now as scaffolding, meaning that the adult provides the extra support to help accomplish a task. This could be physical—helping to hold the paintbrush and brush a line at the right pace—or mental, providing the mental steps needed to solve the problem. While the examples I have used so far are all academic, the same principles could easily be adapted to social problems, such as negotiating an argument between friends. Teachers spend hours learning and creating physical and mental ways to try to communicate strategies to students for how to tackle a problem. A first-grade teacher might use scissors or string; a college professor might use a syllabus. Both act to try to frame the situation with support to succeed.

If learning depends on the social context, then this does mean that different cultures will have different values to impart, and the tasks and cognitive tools that are shared will be different. For example, it was not uncommon when I was a young child to spend several grades learning how to write in cursive (you may have seen this on papers handed back to you by the adults around you). As a teenager, high schools usually offered a typing (now called keyboarding) class. These skills seem to have become less mandatory, as keyboarding skills have moved to online programs, and handwriting is usually left for learning letters only.

CHAPTER SUMMARY

In this chapter, we looked at the phenomenon of social learning, or learning by watching others. Originally an extension of operant conditioning, social learning theory was an attempt to explain learning that occurred without a direct consequence to the individual. The act of imitation can be observed both in early childhood and with other primates, so it appears to be a very basic form of learning. One proposal is that a set of neurons, or "mirror neurons," may play out what we experience others doing, enabling us to mentally simulate the actions of others. The person we are observing, or the "model," must take on several steps, for learning from him or her to be successful. The observers must pay attention, store the model's movements, repeat them later, and see the whole enterprise as worth doing.

A social learning theorist sees the learning situation as complex, compared to how a strict behaviorist sees it, because the learner will have goals in mind, can enact certain behaviors, and can modify the environment ("reciprocal causation"). The learners may ascribe beliefs about the cause of some result to the situation or to themselves ("attributional theory"), which may or may not be accurate. Learners enter a situation with beliefs about their own abilities to perform related tasks ("self-efficacy"), which can lead to their choosing not even to try. And finally, learners can learn to "self-regulate," a metacognitive skill that lets them control what strategies they employ to see a task through.

In the second half of the chapter, we looked at two major theories that describe how children develop their abilities to learn. Piaget believed children constructed their own learning about the world much as amateur scientists would, and that they would experiment with applying knowledge they already have ("assimilation") by adjusting their knowledge when it appeared to be insufficient ("accommodation"). He believed that there were qualitative differences in how children could conceptualize the world, and he grouped those differences into four broad stages.

While Piaget's perspective emphasized biological changes as the driver for cognitive development, Vygotsky's perspective emphasized the social aspects of childhood learning. Others support our understanding of the world at a young age, and provide "cognitive tools" or strategies to interpret, understand, and construct understanding. Vygotsky believed children have an optimal range of learning, where the task is not too simple to be boring, but not so difficult that they give up easily (a "zone of proximal development").

In the next chapter, we'll examine the emotional and motivational aspects of learning.

REVIEW QUESTIONS

1. In your own words, how does the idea of "observational learning" through imitation violate a strict behaviorist paradigm of stimulus-response conditioning?

2. A teacher is going to introduce his kindergarteners to oil paints and brushes for the first time. He wants to model how to use the materials without making a big mess. What advice on effective modeling would you give him?

3. Some people believe violence in the media (e.g., movies, shows, video games) can cause people to become more violent. Some believe that entertainment simply reflects our violent tendencies or fantasies. What does "reciprocal determinism" suggest about this situation?

4. What might be some ways that a teacher can counter some low self-efficacy beliefs about the content of the class, for example, in a statistics course?

5. Do you see Piaget's or Vygotsky's theories having the greater impact on explaining how a parent or a teacher should educate a child? Why?

KEY TERMS

FURTHER RESOURCES

- Weblink: The first of a series of videos including interviews with Piaget and children completing Piagetian tasks:
  - https://www.youtube.com/watch?v=I1JWr4G8YLM

- Weblink: Discussion and illustration of mirror neurons (NOVA):
  - https://www.youtube.com/watch?v=Xmx1qPy08Ks

- Weblink: Several neuroscientists are interviewed discussing mirror neurons (audio, NPR):
  - http://www.npr.org/templates/story/story.php?storyId=4729505

- Weblink: Albert Bandura is interviewed and discusses a number of his theories, including self-efficacy:
  - https://www.youtube.com/watch?v=S4N5J9jFW5U

REFERENCES

Arnett, J. J. (2014). *Adolescence and emerging adulthood.* New York, NY: Pearson. Retrieved from http://www.jeffreyarnett.com/aea4efmfinalpages.pdf

Aronson, E., Wilson, T. D., & Akert, R. M. (2012). *Social psychology* (8th ed.). Boston, MA: Pearson.

Baillargeon, R. (2004). Infants' physical world. *Current Directions in Psychological Science, 13*(3), 89–94.

Bandura, A. (1986). *Social foundations of thought and action: A social cognitive theory.* Englewood Cliffs, NJ: Prentice Hall.

Bandura, A. (1997). *Self-efficacy: The exercise of control.* New York, NY: Macmillan. Retrieved from https://books .google.com/books?hl=enandlr=andid=eJ-PN9g_o-ECan doi=fndandpg=PR7anddq=bandura+1997+self-efficacy +theoryandots=zxPJKVic3handsig=T9KWZ4U6_oaCC 4ID1QwwodJrnIE

Bandura, A., & Walters, R. H. (1963). *Social learning and personality development.* New York, NY: Holt, Rinehart & Winston.

Barr, R., Dowden, A., & Hayne, H. (1996). Developmental changes in deferred imitation by 6- to 24-month-old infants. *Infant Behavior and Development, 19*(2), 159–170. https://www.dropbox.com/s/b05y5j73zxz2mgm/Barr%20 et%20al_2005_Retrieval%20Protracts%20Deferred%20 Imitation%20by%206-Month-Olds.pdf?dl=0

Barr, R., & Hayne, H. (1999). Developmental changes in imitation from television during infancy. *Child Development, 70*(5), 1067–1081. https://doi.org/10.1111/1467-8624.00079

Barr, R., Rovee-Collier, C., & Campanella, J. (2005). Retrieval protracts deferred imitation by 6-month-olds. *Infancy, 7*(3), 263–283. https://doi.org/10.1207/s15327078in0703_3

Bauer, G. P., Schlottmann, R. S., Bates, J. V., & Masters, M. A. (1983). Effect of state and trait anxiety and prestige of model on imitation. *Psychological Reports, 52*(2), 375–382. https://doi.org/10.2466/pr0.1983.52.2.375

Bebko, J. M., Burke, L., Craven, J., & Sarlo, N. (1992). The importance of motor activity in sensorimotor development: A perspective from children with physical handicaps. *Human Development, 35*(4), 226–240.

Birney, D. P., Halford, G. S., & Andrews, G. (2006). Measuring the influence of complexity on relational reasoning: The development of the Latin Square Task. *Educational and Psychological Measurement, 66*(1), 146–171.

Blaney, N. T., Stephan, C., Rosenfield, D., Aronson, E., & Sikes, J. (1977). Interdependence in the classroom: A field study. *Journal of Educational Psychology, 69*(2), 121–128. https://doi.org/10.1037/0022-0663.69.2.121

Braaksma, A., Rijlaarsdam, G., & van den Bergh, H. (2002). Observational learning and the effects of model-observer similarity. *Journal of Educational Psychology, 94*(2), 405–415. https://doi.org/10.1037/0022-0663.94.2.405

Brainerd, C. J. (2003). Jean Piaget, learning research, and American education. Retrieved from http://psycnet.apa.org/ psycinfo/2003-02627-011

Bussey, K., & Perry, D. G. (1982). Same-sex imitation: The avoidance of cross-sex models or the acceptance of same-sex models? *Sex Roles, 8*(7), 773–784. https://doi.org/10.1007/ BF00287572

Carbonneau, K. J., Marley, S. C., & Selig, J. P. (2013). A meta-analysis of the efficacy of teaching mathematics with concrete manipulatives. *Journal of Educational Psychology, 105*(2), 380.

Chapman, M. (1988). *Constructive evolution: Origins and development of Piaget's thought.* Cambridge, England: Cambridge University Press. Retrieved from https://books .google.com/books?hl=enandlr=andid=7WgCnXmdX1MC andoi=fndandpg=PR7anddq=Chapman+1988+piagetand ots=jJwsPNvJ8randsig=x11K56JT58Cjsqoh3BjjboTLjbM

Cohen, L. B., & Cashon, C. H. (2006). Infant cognition. *Handbook of Child Psychology.* Retrieved from http:// onlinelibrary.wiley.com/doi/10.1002/9780470147658.chpsy 0205/full

diSessa, A. A. (2006). A history of conceptual change research: Threads and fault lines. In R. K. Sawyer (Ed.), *The Cambridge handbook of the learning sciences* (pp. 265–281). Cambridge, England: Cambridge University Press.

Dweck, C. S. (2007). *Mindset: The new psychology of success* (Rep Upd ed.). New York, NY: Ballantine Books.

Farrer, C., & Frith, C. D. (2002). Experiencing oneself vs. another person as being the cause of an action: The neural correlates of the experience of agency. *Neuroimage, 15*(3), 596–603.

Flavell, J. H. (1963). *The developmental psychology of Jean Piaget.* Ardent Media. Retrieved from https://books.google. com/books?hl=enandlr=andid=Zj-jrNHbbSUCandoi=fnd andpg=PR7anddq=flavell+1963+piagetandots=XtyaZvp QrKandsig=VM6Klavt2hx53uMoGmn-FsRxKQw

Frazier, B. N., Gelman, S. A., & Wellman, H. M. (2009). Preschoolers' search for explanatory information within adult–child conversation. *Child Development, 80*(6), 1592–1611.

Galotti, K. M. (2016). *Cognitive development: Infancy through adolescence* (2nd ed.). Thousand Oaks, CA: SAGE.

Gelman, S. A. (2009). Learning from others: Children's construction of concepts. *Annual Review of Psychology, 60,* 115–140.

Ginsburg, H. P., Cannon, J., Eisenband, J., & Pappas, S. (2006). Mathematical thinking and learning. *Blackwell Handbook of Early Childhood Development,* 208–229.

Greene, J. A., & Azevedo, R. (2007). A theoretical review of Winne and Hadwin's Model of Self-Regulated Learning: New perspectives and directions. *Review of Educational Research, 77*(3), 334–372. https://doi.org/ 10.3102/003465430303953

Hayes, K. J., & Hayes, C. (1952). Imitation in a home-raised chimpanzee. *Journal of Comparative and Physiological Psychology, 45*(5), 450–459. https://doi.org/10.1037/h0053609

Hayne, H., Barr, R., & Herbert, J. (2003). The effect of prior practice on memory reactivation and generalization. *Child Development, 74*(6), 1615–1627. https://doi.org/10.1046/j.1467-8624.2003.00627.x

Heider, F. (1944). Social perception and phenomenal causality. *Psychological Review, 51*(6), 358–374. https://doi.org/10.1037/h0055425

Heyes, C. (2001). Causes and consequences of imitation. *Trends in Cognitive Sciences, 5*(6), 253–261. https://doi.org/10.1016/S1364-6613(00)01661-2

Heyes, C. (2010). Where do mirror neurons come from? *Neuroscience and Biobehavioral Reviews, 34*(4), 575–583. https://doi.org/10.1016/j.neubiorev.2009.11.007

Heyes, C. (2011). Automatic imitation. *Psychological Bulletin, 137*(3), 463–483. https://doi.org/10.1037/a0022288

Heyes, C. (2012). What's social about social learning? *Journal of Comparative Psychology, 126*(2), 193–202. https://doi.org/10.1037/a0025180

Iacoboni, M. (2009). Imitation, empathy, and mirror neurons. *Annual Review of Psychology, 60*(1), 653–670. https://doi.org/10.1146/annurev.psych.60.110707.163604

Joncich, G. M. (1968). *The sane positivist: A biography of Edward L. Thorndike* (1st ed.). Middletown, CT: Wesleyan University Press.

Kirschner, P. A., Sweller, J., & Clark, R. E. (2006). Why minimal guidance during instruction does not work: An analysis of the failure of constructivist, discovery, problem-based, experiential, and inquiry-based teaching. *Educational Psychologist, 41*(2), 75–86.

Klaczynski, P. A. (2001). Analytic and heuristic processing influences on adolescent reasoning and decision-making. *Child Development, 72*(3), 844–861.

Kuhn, D., & Franklin, S. (2006). *The second decade: What develops (and how).* Wiley Online Library. Retrieved from http://onlinelibrary.wiley.com/doi/10.1002/9780470147658.chpsy0222/full

Leaper, C., & Friedman, C. K. (2007). The socialization of gender. In J. E. Grusec & P. D. Hastings (Eds.), *Handbook of Socialization: Theory and Research* (pp. 561–587). New York, NY: Guilford Press.

Lehman, D. R., & Nisbett, R. E. (1990). A longitudinal study of the effects of undergraduate training on reasoning. *Developmental Psychology, 26*(6), 952.

Mandler, J. M. (2007). On the origins of the conceptual system. *American Psychologist, 62*(8), 741–751. https://doi.org/10.1037/0003-066X.62.8.741

Mantzicopoulos, P., Samarapungavan, A., & Patrick, H. (2009). "We learn how to predict and be a scientist": Early science experiences and kindergarten children's social meanings about science. *Cognition and Instruction, 27*(4), 312–369.

Martin, C. L., & Ruble, D. (2004). Children's search for gender cues cognitive perspectives on gender development. *Current Directions in Psychological Science, 13*(2), 67–70.

Mazur, J. E. (2012). *Learning and Behavior* (7th ed.). Boston, MA: Pearson.

Meltzoff, A. N., & Moore, M. K. (1977). Imitation of facial and manual gestures by human neonates. *Science, 198*(4312), 75–78.

Meltzoff, A. N., & Moore, M. K. (1997). Explaining facial imitation: A theoretical model. *Early Development and Parenting, 6*(3–4), 179–192. https://doi.org/10.1002/(SICI)1099-0917(199709/12)6:3/4<179::AID-EDP157>3.0.CO;2-R

Mercer, N. (1996). The quality of talk in children's collaborative activity in the classroom. *Learning and Instruction, 6*(4), 359–377.

Miller, N. E., & Dollard, J. (1941). *Social learning and imitation* (Vol. xiv). New Haven, CT: Yale University Press.

Miller, R. (2011). *Vygotsky in perspective.* Cambridge University Press. Retrieved from https://books.google.com/books?hl=enandlr=andid=uCFEW1T_k3cCandoi=fndandpg=PR7anddq=miller+vygotskyandots=Rb9x10YAQYandsig=zFUEQ-dwUVT9eQFN0AyLdoH3uzY

Minner, D. D., Levy, A. J., & Century, J. (2010). Inquiry-based science instruction—what is it and does it matter? Results from a research synthesis years 1984 to 2002. *Journal of Research in Science Teaching, 47*(4), 474–496.

Mischel, W., Cantor, N., & Feldman, S. (1996). Principles of self-regulation: The nature of willpower and self-control. In E. T. Higgins & A. W. Kruglanski (Eds.), *Social psychology: Handbook of basic principles* (pp. 329–360). New York, NY: Guilford Press.

Moreno, R. (2006). Learning in high-tech and multimedia environments. *Current Directions in Psychological Science, 15*(2), 63–67.

Moreno, R., & Mayer, R. (2007). Interactive multimodal learning environments. *Educational Psychology Review, 19*(3), 309–326.

Newcombe, N., & Huttenlocher, J. (1992). Children's early ability to solve perspective-taking problems. *Developmental Psychology, 28*(4), 635.

Palincsar, A. S. (1998). Social constructivist perspectives on teaching and learning. *Annual Review of Psychology, 49*(1), 345–375.

Patrick, H., Mantzicopoulos, P., & Samarapungavan, A. (2009). Motivation for learning science in kindergarten: Is there a gender gap and does integrated inquiry and literacy instruction make a difference. *Journal of Research in Science Teaching, 46*(2), 166–191.

Pease, M. A., & Kuhn, D. (2011). Experimental analysis of the effective components of problem-based learning. *Science Education, 95*(1), 57–86.

Perry, D. G., & Bussey, K. (1979). The social learning theory of sex differences: Imitation is alive and well. *Journal of Personality and Social Psychology, 37*(10), 1699–1712. https://doi.org/10.1037/0022–3514.37.10.1699

Piaget, J. (1954). *The construction of reality in the child.* New York, NY: Basic Books.

Piaget, J. (2013a). *Play, dreams and imitation in childhood* (Vol. 25). New York, NY: Routledge. Retrieved from https://books.google.com/books?hl=enandlr=andid=jk49prxDZ6gCandoi=fndandpg=PP2anddq=piaget+andots=Ynnva33Bgpandsig=tlPERBb3pFoA7yFU06r-dPAWGNA

Piaget, J. (2013b). *The construction of reality in the child* (Vol. 82). Routledge. Retrieved from https://books.google.com/books?hl=enandlr=andid=PpfGxMDZP-4Candoi=fndandpg=PP2anddq=piaget+andots=LLuGNodNrdandsig=ZuY6ciake9NzttJU9aKicRBtUA8

Piaget, J., & Inhelder, B. (2013). *The growth of logical thinking from childhood to adolescence: An essay on the construction of formal operational structures.* New York, NY: Routledge. (Original work published 1958)

Piaget, J., & Inhelder, B. (1969). *The psychology of the child.* New York, NY: Basic Books. Retrieved from https://books.google.com/books?hl=enandlr=andid=GSXRDQAAQBAJandoi=fndandpg=PR1anddq=inhelder+piaget+andots=Kt9GohdLQrandsig=1qp-cP_Ej043Jtl_ueYB4TOqbfU

Ray, E., & Heyes, C. (2011). Imitation in infancy: The wealth of the stimulus. *Developmental Science, 14*(1), 92–105. https://doi.org/10.1111/j.1467-7687.2010.00961.x

Rodgon, M. M., and Kurdek, L. A. (1977). Vocal and gestural imitation in 8-, 14-, and 20-month-old children. *The Journal of Genetic Psychology, 131*(1), 115–123. https://doi.org/10.1080/00221325.1977.10533280

Rosenthal, T. L., & Bandura, A. (1978). Psychological modeling: Theory and practice. *Handbook of Psychotherapy and Behavior Change: An Empirical Analysis, 2,* 621–658.

Rosenthal, T. L., & Zimmerman, B. J. (1978). *Social learning and cognition.* New York, NY: Academic Press. Retrieved from http://www.getcited.org/pub/101859873

Sasso, G. M., & Rude, H. A. (1987). Unprogrammed effects of training high-status peers to interact with severely handicapped children. *Journal of Applied Behavior Analysis, 20*(1), 35–44. https://doi.org/10.1901/jaba.1987.20–35

Schulz, L. E., Hooppell, C., & Jenkins, A. C. (2008). Judicious imitation: Children differentially imitate deterministically and probabilistically effective actions. *Child Development, 79*(2), 395–410. https://doi.org/10.1111/j.1467-8624.2007.01132.x

Schunk, D. H. (1991). *Learning theories: An educational perspective* (Vol. xi). New York, NY: Macmillan.

Shute, V. J. (2008). Focus on formative feedback. *Review of Educational Research, 78*(1), 153–189. https://doi.org/10.3102/0034654307313795

Slavin, R. E. (2011). Cooperative learning. *Learning and cognition in education.* (pp. 160–166), Boston, MA: Elsevier.

Sommerville, J. A., Hildebrand, E. A., & Crane, C. C. (2008). Experience matters. *Developmental Psychology, 44*(5), 1249–1256. https://doi.org/10.1037/a0012296

Tolman, E. C., & Honzik, C. H. (1930). Introduction and removal of reward, and maze performance in rats. *University of California Publications in Psychology, 4,* 257–275.

Vygotsky, L. S. (1980). *Mind in society: The development of higher psychological processes.* M. Cole, V. John-Steiner, S. Scribner, & E. Souberman (Eds.) (Rev. ed.). Cambridge, MA: Harvard University Press.

Walters, R. H., & Parke, R. D. (1964). Influence of response consequences to a social model on resistance to deviation. *Journal of Experimental Child Psychology, 1*(3), 269–280. https://doi.org/10.1016/0022–0965(64)90042–6

Want, S. C., & Harris, P. L. (2001). Learning from other people's mistakes: Causal understanding in learning to use a tool. *Child Development, 72*(2), 431–443. https://doi.org/10.1111/1467-8624.00288

Waxler, C. Z., & Yarrow, M. R. (1975). An observational study of maternal models. *Developmental Psychology, 11*(4), 485–494. https://doi.org/10.1037/h0076683

Weiner, B. (1985). An attributional theory of achievement motivation and emotion. *Psychological Review, 92*(4), 548–573. https://doi.org/10.1037/0033–295X.92.4.548

Weiss, M. R., & Klint, K. A. (1987). "Show and tell" in the gymnasium: An investigation of developmental differences in modeling and verbal rehearsal of motor skills. *Research Quarterly for Exercise and Sport, 58*(3), 234–241. https://doi.org/10.1080/02701367.1987.10605455

Wirkala, C., & Kuhn, D. (2011). Problem-based learning in K–12 education: Is it effective and how does it achieve its effects? *American Educational Research Journal, 48*(5), 1157–1186.

©iStock.com/Prochkailo

Affect and Motivation in Learning

Chapter Outline

Learning Objectives

1. Define emotions and distinguish between emotions for their encouraging or discouraging roles for learning.

2. Describe motivation and summarize the classic ("drive") theories of motivation.

3. Distinguish between modern motivational theories.

4. Summarize how motivational theories can explain how learning can be impacted by educational policy.

Overview

Without motivation to achieve, it's hard to make much of an effort to learn, and our emotions can work for or against us when we are trying to accomplish our goals. I can remember struggling as an undergraduate when I transferred from a small community college into a large state university; my immature view of some of my classes was that the professor was there to trick us up and hold us back. For those classes, setting aside my negative emotions was a barrier to applying myself successfully to the class work. The resulting grades were more of a reflection of my emotions about the classes than my abilities. Of course, such an attitude doesn't help the student much, since the grades travel with the student, not the professor. And looking back now, a lot of my feelings about the classes had to do with the anonymity that comes from taking very large lecture classes and not having a sense of "place" in the new environment. In this chapter, we consider the role that affective states have on learning (see Fig. 6.1).

Attempting to provide a structure to emotions and affect has been a theoretical challenge within the field for as long as the discipline has been studied; William James asked in 1884, "What is an emotion?" The study of affective phenomena (affect, emotions, moods) can be challenging because the terms "affect," "emotion," and "mood" are not considered synonymous, yet there is overlap between them, and the terms can be used inconsistently. Generally speaking, an emotion is a specific state of feeling that is temporary and occurs as part of an event (Russell & Barrett, 1999). For example, I feel rage after I bump my head against a cabinet door edge, for the second time. Common emotions are anger, fear, jealousy, pride, and love (Ekkekakis & Dafermos, 2012). An emotion usually involves an event or is tied to a specific object or person. In other words, emotions are episodic. They are thought to be brought on by some event and are about that event.

A key part of the brain that is responsible for producing emotions appears to be the amygdala (LaBar & Cabeza, 2006; LeDoux, 2000; see Fig. 6.2), possibly through the regulation of the neurotransmitter norepinephrine (Tully & Bolshakov, 2010). The amygdala takes information from two other places in the brain: directly from the sensory system via the thalamus, and from the cerebral cortex. Information from the thalamus reaches the amygdala quickly and acts as a rapid way to spark arousal in a fearful situation. Information will also leave the thalamus to go to the visual and auditory cortices for processing and can also trigger an emotion as a result of that processing. This

FIGURE 6.1 Quadrants of learning

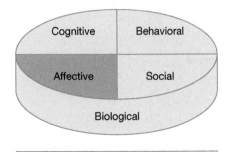

FIGURE 6.2   Diagram of the brain including prefrontal cortex, amygdala, thalamus

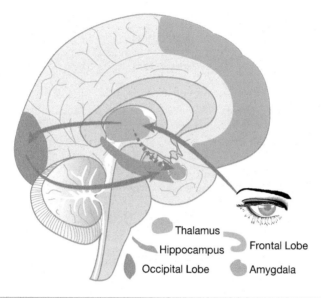

Thalamus

Hippocampus   Frontal Lobe

Occipital Lobe   Amygdala

Source: Human brain parts during a fear amygdala hijack from optical stimulus, https://commons.wikimedia.org/wiki/File:EQbrain_optical_stim_en.jpg, licensed under CC BY-SA 3.0.

second pathway is slower than the first. fMRI research has found the amygdala to be responsive to facial expressions of happiness, anger, and fear; but it is the most sensitive to fear. The amygdala seems to play a large role in becoming classically conditioned by fear of some situation or object (Büchel & Dolan, 2000). This fear conditioning can be conscious or implicitly learned (e.g., Critchley, Mathias, & Dolan, 2002). Other emotions are known to involve other areas of the brain, and many emotions may not have one brain pattern at all (for a discussion of these issues, see Barrett, 2006).

There is a physiological component to emotions, as the autonomic part of the peripheral nervous system either may produce an accelerated heart rate, pupil dilation, and sweating when we are frightened or may calm those same actions when we are relaxed. However, there is a cognitive component to the experience, too, which will involve the frontal cortex. According to the Schachter-Singer two-factor theory of emotions, we cognitively name the physiological response with an emotional label as we experience it (Schachter & Singer, 1962). We are quick to the interpretation our arousal based on what is happening in that moment of that event (e.g., receiving a pink slip at work), so the cognitive part of the experience is the defining component of what emotions are. Since there is a cognitive element to emotions, this does open up the possibility of misattributing the arousal to the wrong source, a situation called misattribution of arousal.

In contrast to an emotion, a mood is a long-term emotional state. It may not have a specific event that triggered it or a target for it, such as feeling content or angry for a period of hours or days (Russell, 2003). Affect or ("core affect") is the most general term, and it implies a core dimension of emotions and mood, such as pleasure, tension, and energy (or arousal).

Many attempts have been made to map emotions onto some affective dimensions (see, e.g., Lang, Greenwald, Bradley, & Hamm, 1993). One of the more popular approaches is

FIGURE 6.3 Diagram of circumplex map of emotion (adapted from Russell & Barrett, 1999)

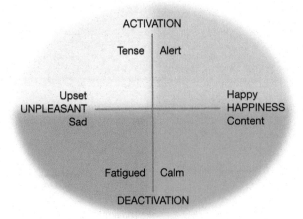

Source: Adapted from Russell, J. A., & Barrett, L. F. (1999).

to use two continuums: a pleasure-displeasure dimension of valence, which is viewed as running from negative emotions such as sad and upset to positive emotions such as happy and content. The other is a sleepy-activated dimension of arousal, running from unaroused emotions such as fatigue and calm to aroused emotions such as tense and alert (Russell & Barrett, 1999; see Fig. 6.3). There is fMRI and behavioral evidence that each dimension happens along different pathways in the brain. Events that triggered an aroused state tend to activate the amygdala and the hippocampus, whereas events that triggered differences in valence were processed in the prefrontal cortex (Kensinger & Corkin, 2004).

Emotions During Learning

In general, emotions such as fear, including apprehension and anxiety, are common negative emotions that inhibit learning. To the extent that stress from a difficult task is involved in the learning process, dejection, sadness, and grief may result from frustration as well. Frustration is a specific feeling that results from being thwarted from a goal by an obstacle (Dollard, Miller, Doob, Mowrer, & Sears, 1939). It can be temporary, and it usually increases in intensity the closer the learner is to the goal. Experiencing computer problems might not cause me too much worry early in the morning of a day that I have a presentation to make, but having computer problems in the minutes prior to the presentation can be extremely frustrating. In some cases, the frustration can spill over into aggressive acts, but this will not always be the case (Berkowitz, 1989; Miller, 1941).

We can express frustration at an early age. By monitoring the actions and autonomic nervous systems of fifty-six four-month-olds, Lewis, Hitchcock, and Sullivan (2004) were able to assess how infants react to situations that cause frustration. After establishing a baseline of arm movements, the infants find that moving an arm triggers the playback of a video clip that they enjoy. After enough time to have learned about the connection, the video playback stops responding to arm movements. Researchers then analyze the arm movements, facial expressions, and physiological changes that result. Lewis and colleagues (2004) believe that by four months of age, infants can coordinate behavior and facial movements to express frustration.

Frustration isn't necessarily all bad. In a later study, Lewis, Sullivan, & Kim, (2015) wanted to see whether emotional expressions of frustration and anger at a very young age could indicate persistence at a task at a later age. They observed infants playing with their mothers at two months of age. Then at five months, the researchers introduced a frustrating event as in Lewis et al. (2004), described above. They then measured the infants' displays of anger and sadness. When the children turned two, the now-toddlers were observed at play again, and the researchers disrupted play time by asking each mother to call her child to her and, if ignored, to pick the child up from play. The pause was temporary and repeated once. The researchers found that the displays of anger from frustration at the age of two months was associated with how hard the then-toddlers persisted in returning to play when the mothers interfered. Displays of emotion can signal progress toward a goal, and may be part of a developmental process.

If a learning activity is not challenging enough or if it seems irrelevant, boredom can result. Typically activities need to be within the realm of "proximal development" (Vygotsky, 1978) for successful engagement, meaning that the activity is not too easy or too difficult without support. Or, the task may not appear to the learner to be worth performing—it doesn't appear to provide future benefits or seems pointless. Ironically, the learner is by definition the least qualified to make the evaluation whether the task is beneficial, yet motivation plays a role in the emotion that is produced by the assigned activity.

Anxiety, a persistent, stressful worry about performance during the learning process, is usually due to a pressing secondary goal of evaluation. Evaluation might be simultaneous with the learning, or the anxiety can stem from the evaluation that will occur after learning. According to the Yerkes-Dodson law (Yerkes & Dodson, 1908; see Fig. 6.4), a mild amount of anxiety, such as having to execute a task in front of another person, is relatively normal and helps to energize the learner. This low level of

FIGURE 6.4   The Yerkes-Dodson law describes the level of expected performance based on task difficulty and arousal level (Diamond et al., 2007). Performance on simple tasks improves with arousal, but performance on difficult tasks improves only with a moderate amount of arousal.

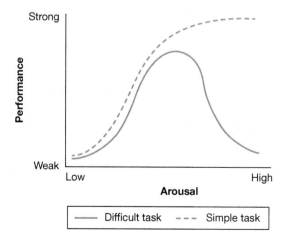

anxiety is known as facilitating anxiety and is generally seen as helpful when the task is well earned. Having the attention of others or being evaluated will tend to improve performance for activities that are routine enough that we need the extra incentive to do well. However, when a task is difficult, the extra emotion is debilitating anxiety and performance drops.

The problem of anxiety during learning is when anxiety increases from a mild amount that can be energizing to a level that interferes with the individual's ability to concentrate and work on developing the necessary skills. Persistent worry detracts from the ability to process information and to focus on the task at hand and can possibly be accompanied by physiological reactions such as increased heart rate, sweating, dizziness, and inability to sleep (Cassady, 2010). On the other hand, being extremely relaxed doesn't help learning and focus either. Being a little nervous may provide the elevated arousal that stimulates attention. Mild amounts of anxiety appear to be facilitating, but high amounts are debilitating. The critical threshold between normal, mild anxiety from having to execute some action versus more debilitating anxiety seems to be when the learning activity has become a psychological threat to one's well-being. The material may be available but anxiety blocks the individual's retrieving it. This may be a completely psychological threshold—that is, in the eye of the beholder—but once the concern becomes about the self-worth of the individual, attention will no longer be on the task alone but also on managing the rise of anxiety.

Negative emotions do not always hamper learning, however; in some cases, what might be considered "negative emotions" can be used to spur engagement with the material. Becoming concerned about the plight of a group of people under persecution, for example, can make the material more readily learned and memorable. Such motivated reasoning, sometimes called "hot cognition" (Ayduk, Mischel, & Downey, 2002; Metcalfe & Mischel, 1999), describes someone whose interest in the material makes him or her highly involved and more focused on the strengths of the issues (Kunda, 1990). Worry for others, concern from empathy, or anger over a social injustice can prompt close attention and study. This assumes that the motivated reasoning stems from a goal of accuracy rather than confirming a biased view from the material.

But then, emotions can play a helpful role in learning. Learning new concepts, discovering new insights, and mastering tasks can produce emotions like a feeling of satisfaction, pride, or a development of resilience–a sense of self-confidence from solving problems.

One positive affective state during learning is flow, a pleasurable state of being completely absorbed and involved in some activity (Csikszentmihalyi, 1990; Csikszentmihalyi, Abuhamdeh, & Nakamura, 2014). A person experiencing flow is completely engaged in the task at hand, and comes with an awareness of the current activity and the joy at engaging in it, like an "optimal experience." Self-consciousness is lost. In what is known as "time expansion," time seems to stop, and a longer time is spent on the activity than is realized. To experience flow, the individual has a clear sense of what the task involves, with a feeling of being in control, and feedback is clear so the person has a straightforward sense of the next steps. It is thought that the confluence of emotion and the perception of the expansion of time is occurring in the anterior insular cortex, a part of the cerebral cortex that connects the thalamus and amygdala (Tse, Intriligator, Rivest, & Cavanagh, 2004).

So, emotions can play a helpful or damaging role on the learning process, regardless of the specific pleasurable or displeasurable nature. In some cases, emotions run alongside the activity and encourage attention; in others, they interfere with learning.

Most likely, we can maximize the likelihood of positive emotions during learning if we provide opportunities to activities that the learner is interested in. While flow can be a rewarding experience during an activity, making progress toward personal future goals is also a positive experience. According to self-determination theory (SDT), the ability to act on our own and engage in a problem or task with the encouragement of others as we see fit enhances personal motivation to learn (Deci & Ryan, 2000). Competence, relatedness, and autonomy are necessary needs for human motivation. According to SDT, what holds most of us back from autonomy and developing more personally motivating goals for ourselves is the presence of external pressures from others. These pressures include deadlines and threats, monitoring or surveillance for performance, and external rewards. Parents, teachers, and coaches have to support and develop the potential for individual motivational goals, rather than purely externally provided structures meant to motivate, or "controlled motivation."

Controlled motivation produces pressure to behave in expected ways, particularly when the behavior has not been internally accepted by the learner. In contrast, motivation that is autonomous and intrinsic in nature has been shown to produce better performance on exams, for example (Wang, 2008), and, in general, show more psychological well-being (Deci & Ryan, 2008). Conditions that produce controlled motivation tend to produce lower self-esteem and higher feelings of depression and anxiety. Kasser and Ryan (1993) found career choices that are made by college students who are focused specifically on financial rewards were negatively correlated with their mental health.

In a situation in which you are teaching someone how to do something, what can you do to encourage positive emotional reactions to learning, while minimizing the negative ones?

Motivation

Motivation is more than an affective state, although emotions definitely play a role in feeling motivated. Motivation is not easy to define; there have been over one hundred definitions (Kleinginna & Kleinginna, 1981). The effects of being motivated are fairly well known: It affects how long someone will work on a task, the amount of effort applied to the task, and the strategies and direction someone will take to accomplish the task. Motivation is not viewed as just an affective state, but as a force that focuses energy and effort to achieve some result or goal. Being motivated can produce a variety of moods: elation, pride, frustration, disappointment, even boredom. It is usually seen as a force that is the combination of multiple needs, biological drives, instincts, and external factors that encourage the initiation of tasks and direction (Pinder, 2008). The difference between the effort a person usually gives versus someone's highest performance can be simply the result of how motivated they are (e.g., Klehe & Anderson, 2007). That is, motivation is what distinguishes a typical performance on a task from an optimal one (Sackett, Zedeck, & Fogli, 1988). Motivation is always present in our lives, but we are not always in a situation in which we can do what we are currently motivated do to.

Besides the struggle of defining motivation, documenting the relationship between motivation and ability is complicated (Dalal & Hulin, 2008). The actions people take to initiate or complete a task are often multidimensional and can even seem contradictory. The various smaller tasks a student may do in the course of an hour when writing on a paper make it difficult to identify exactly which behaviors lead to an accounting of motivation's role in completing the work. The most basic formula for how much effort is applied is an interaction between how valued the result is and whether the person believes the result is possible (Vroom, 1982).

Being motivated means focusing more directly on a task to be learned, applying greater attention to it, persisting in the face of challenges, and taking steps to do a better job at it. Motivation is an underlying phenomenon in all attempts to learn and master some knowledge or skill. Despite the ubiquitous importance of motivation, it is not one of the more heavily researched areas in psychology, possibly because of the challenges in defining and observing it.

Intrinsic/Extrinsic Kinds

Motivation has traditionally been divided into one of two kinds: intrinsic motivation, or being motivated by personal interests, goals, and desires ("inherent satisfaction," Deci & Ryan, 2000, p. 260), and extrinsic motivation, being motivated by external reinforcements and punishments (see Fig. 6.5). Watching someone's behavior may not always tell us which kind of motivation is behind his or her actions, but whether a person engages in an activity without a clear reinforcement or reward is a likely clue. Like the mastery goal orientation, someone relying on intrinsic motivation will generally be more interested in personal growth and improvement over social recognition. The primary driver of intrinsic motivation may be simple curiosity, since it drives what we find interesting (Silvia, 2008). Someone who follows her bowling score over time to track progress, regardless of her rank in the league, is likely to be intrinsically motivated. Someone looking to gain a trophy or monetary reward is driven by extrinsic motivation. Someone who is intrinsically motivated to write poetry may be disappointed to not get his work published, but will continue writing out of sheer enjoyment and interest in it. Intrinsic motivation is more likely to produce feelings of flow, and may indicate that the activity is in line with a person's future goals, as self-determination theory suggests.

Because extrinsic motivation is tied to external reinforcements, a clear connection to operant conditioning exists. Any system of external reinforcements, whether grades, money, or prestige, is inherent in extrinsic motivation. And this is the essential issue or problem that many find with using incentives to motivate people: They do not capitalize on the existing internal motivations people have. They are seen as coercive. It would be better to excite students about the material they are studying rather than to have to construct elaborate plans for reinforcing learning (e.g., syllabi).

In some cases, adding an external reinforcement when people engage in an activity for personal pleasure can decrease the desire to do the activity once the external reinforcement is removed, a result known as an overjustification effect. In a meta-analysis of 128 studies, external reinforcement was found to reliably undermine intrinsic motivation (Deci, Koestner, & Ryan, 1999), a problem that exists more for children than young adults. Activities become less interesting. Deci and colleagues (1999) hypothesize that external

FIGURE 6.5   Intrinsic and extrinsic motivation

rewards and their structure remove the ability for individuals to take responsibility for their own actions. Additionally, the external reward structure means more monitoring and evaluation, so there is less autonomy or freedom to work as one chooses. Evidence for a reduction in brain activity in the pleasure and engagement centers (striatum and lateral prefrontal cortex) after a reward was removed was found by Murayama, Matsumoto, Izuma, and Matsumoto (2010). This change was not seen for individuals doing a task who had not been rewarded in the first place.

However, the contrast between intrinsic and extrinsic motivation is probably not an either/or situation. Typically we do not have much time to focus on pursuits that are intrinsically motivating. It's more likely that we choose between extrinsic motivations, so intrinsic motivation shows itself in what activities we chose to adopt and adhere to (for example, whether to pursue a college degree and which major to attempt).

Classic Motivational Theories

Many older, classic theories about what motivates us are based around the concept of "needs," hypothesized motivators that humans seek out to satiate, usually for a sense of pleasure or satisfaction. A need may or may not have a fixed biological basis in the brain; they are usually thought of as abstract deficiencies or desires that people seek to address. For example, humans seem to need at least a minimal amount of arousal, or excitement, and are motivated to seek it out through many forms of entertainment (Heron, 1957). Activities that do not stimulate arousal become boring, and become another form of punishment just through the lack of interest.

For a period of time, theorists explored the possible needs that humans share. Abraham Maslow (1943) proposed that there are more than one kind of human motivational need. Some needs are deficiency needs and exist as problems that drag people down and de-motivate them until they can be resolved. For example, money can be a deficiency need. Having barely enough to live on will make acquiring the means to get by very motivating, a top priority. However, once enough money has been earned to be comfortable, additional money might be enjoyed but does not bring the same level of motivation as having an insufficient amount did. Deficiency needs are akin to psychological holes in the ground. Once filled in, there isn't as great a desire to continue seeking to resolve it. Many needs that allow us to exist comfortably and safely are deficiency needs: shelter, safety, food, and water. Usually the lack of one of these is felt as an irritant, and resolving it returns us to merely a satisfactory or adequate state, emotionally.

In contrast, growth needs are those needs that involve personal growth, such as taking on new challenges, learning something new, mastering new skills, and experiencing new pleasures. Growth needs do not have an end point like deficiency needs do, and involve more creativity and enjoyment. The interest in maintaining and pursuing them continues, such as enjoying reading a good book, playing music, talking to friends, or taking a class. Pursuing these needs produces much stronger feelings of pleasure and satisfaction than resolving deficiency needs.

Maslow also postulated that needs could exist in a kind of hierarchy. That is, resolving some lower needs was necessary before being able to focus on higher ones. Maslow proposed a sequenced set of five needs: at the lowest, most basic level, physiological needs, then safety and security needs, love and belonging, self-esteem, and then the need to self-actualize (personal growth and discovery). He claimed that people are motivated by only one of the five needs at any one time. More basic, deficiency needs had to be resolved before the individual could move on to higher growth needs. Maslow's contribution that there may

FIGURE 6.6   Alderfer's ERG theory

---

be a hierarchy of needs has withstood the test of time, but other aspects of his framework are debated. Alderfer proposed an alternative to Maslow's classic motivation theory.

Alderfer's ERG theory (1969; 1972) claims there are three basic needs instead of Maslow's five, and that all are activated simultaneously (see Fig. 6.6). The lowest basic need, existence, includes physiological needs such as food and water and material needs. At the existence level of basic needs, the goal is to simply have enough resources. Having enough does not drive any desire for more. Relatedness involves the need to relate to other people and to belong to a group that respects and values our input. Relatedness involves acceptance and understanding by others. The opposite of relatedness, according to Alderfer, is not anger but a lack of connection with others. Unlike existence needs, the more relatedness needs are satisfied, the more we desire them.

Relatedness includes the need to feel and appear competent at what we do. The hypothesized need for competency involves wanting to have a positive sense of self-worth, the value we place on ourselves and our contributions to groups we participate in (such as a class, with friends, or coworkers).

Growth includes a need for creativity and developing new capabilities. To satisfy growth needs, we need to take on problems that require us to use our existing capabilities fully and develop new capabilities. Finding those opportunities to explore what we are capable of is important. This level of needs is similar to what Maslow described as "self-actualization"—operating at the highest level of his needs hierarchy.

Each level of basic needs is more abstract as we move up the levels. Like relatedness needs, the more we satisfy our growth needs the more we desire growth. Unlike Maslow's hierarchy, Alderfer proposed that an individual can be motivated by any of the three categorical kinds of needs at any one time; so someone who is experiencing poverty or homelessness can still pursue a growth need.

If someone experiences frustration and difficulties with one of the higher needs, then the individual will refocus on satisfying a lower, more concrete need, in what is called the frustration-regression hypothesis. For example, a student surprised by a low score on an exam (with learning within a Growth level of needs) may then check with other students ("How did you do? I did not do well!") or focus on friends or family (the Relatedness level) for a time.

Modern Motivational Theories

Modern motivational theories may incorporate the idea of psychological needs, but they are more concerned with the cognitive and social aspects of what people find motivating (or demotivating). Modern motivational theories examine the role that expectations about one's personal ability play in deciding whether to attempt a task, the personal value one places on the expected reinforcement or gains from doing a task, and personal interest in an outcome. In the next sections, we will look more closely at each of these concepts in turn before ending with a contemporary theory that tries to integrate most modern motivational theory.

Control Theories

Some theorists have focused on how the perception of control in the learning situation can improve motivation, citing the need to feel competent, have some amount of freedom or autonomy, and relatedness with others in order to feel willing to ask for help (Connell & Wellborn, 1991). Missing one of those elements means lower motivation and performance (Connell, Spencer, & Aber, 1994). Ellen Skinner (1995) has proposed that school-age children have beliefs about what actions produce outcomes, whether they have access to the resources that let them make those actions, and a general sense of control that they can produce desired events. She and her colleagues have found that having some motivation can lead to more competency, since having some motivation encourages seeking out resources and asking for help (Marchand & Skinner, 2007). In contrast, students who are low in motivation tend to hide and conceal their problems, making their overall situation direr. Seeking out help and hiding problems are both viewed as coping strategies for dealing with a task. Concealment means disengaging from the activity and could be a sign of anxiety or boredom.

Some neuroscientists investigate self-control as volition, which they define as exerting voluntary control over behaviors (Haggard, 2009). When neuroscientists observe brain functioning as people think about several possible actions and when to perform them, they find activation occurs in the motor cortex, the band across the cerebral cortex in the parietal lobe. When conflicts arise, as an individual tries to decide between several actions, the dorsal anterior cingulate cortex becomes activated (Reeve & Lee, 2012).

Perceived Task Value

Of course, some people may believe themselves capable of doing the task, but they may not value the outcome. Perceived task value is the worth that someone assigns to a task ("Is it worth doing?") and is a subjective judgment. Typically, perceived task value is considered to be a matter of the type of motivation and personal interests.

Interests

There are many individual differences in the values people will assign to a particular outcome. The value someone attaches to a particular result can be difficult to predict, possibly because it will depend on many factors. Individual interests matter beyond the situation itself. We are more likely to be predisposed to value those activities that already interest us (Hidi & Baird, 1986; Renninger & Su, 2012). When the learning activity attracts us more, we focus better on understanding more thoroughly, such as recalling the main ideas and thinking more deeply about the material (Schiefele, 1999). Interests have to be maintained and developed over time. That is, once they have been sparked, it usually requires focused attention so that the interest persists and eventually becomes predisposing (Hidi & Renninger, 2006).

Goal-Setting Theory

E. C. Tolman (1949, 1957) took a decidedly unorthodox view of the behaviorists' stimulus-response conditioning theories that were popular during his day. He believed that once an individual had learned to associate a stimulus with a response, the individual could then use that association intentionally as a goal. Once I know that inserting money into the vending machine provides a carbonated drink, I may later purposively use that association to get a drink. Essentially the learning becomes goal-directed.

The setting of a goal, some objective that a person works to achieve (Murayama, Elliot, & Friedman, 2012), has a long history in the study of learning and motivation. This is in great part because having a goal seems to change the learning process greatly. Goals vary widely: They may be short-term or long-term, they may be work and career-related or more for personal growth. Generally, goals are effective only if they are truly obtainable (Bandura, 1997).

Goals benefit learning in many ways. Having a goal directs attention and effort. Of all of the optional actions someone can take at any given time, a goal provides direction for choosing what to do next so that we leave irrelevant actions aside (Locke & Latham, 2006). People achieve more with difficult goals over easy ones or goals that are vague. Difficult goals have an advantage of requiring more commitment and intensity, providing for more consistent behavior in choosing related actions over a period of time.

With more commitment comes more tenacity to stick with the goal. People with a goal will be more cognitively engaged in their chosen activities, thinking more about the strategies they plan to use. People with a goal tend to persist longer and work harder to overcome obstacles. This persistence also increases with more difficult goals. Usually, specific goals help with the development of techniques and strategies more than more general, ambiguous goals do. Setting a specific target for calories eaten or hours exercised tends to work better than simply wanting to "get healthier." The specific nature of the goal means more concentrated effort and more ease in picking the exact behaviors necessary to achieve the goal (Locke & Latham, 1990).

One reason why having a goal may work so well is that goals require some amount of self-management (Rousseau, 1997). It gives the individual an opportunity to accomplish something, provided the necessary effort is taken. Having the autonomy to make choices about the course of action is its own incentive; the ability for individuals to decide for themselves how they want to reach the goal provides its own motivation.

Of course, simply achieving a goal produces beneficial effects, including emotional satisfaction and an improved sense of accomplishment. People who achieve a goal are likely to raise their own standards the next time they set a goal, as self-efficacy increases (Bandura, 1986, 1989).

Despite this, being motivated does not mean performance is sure to follow (Pinder, 1998). A number of factors for reaching the goal can be outside of the individual's control. For example, someone who is motivated to do well in band and transfers to a new school may find more competition for the top seats in the group.

So, it's not purely a matter of designing a goal well to motivate people. The goals people choose and the reasons they have for the goals they pursue can vary along several different perspectives or orientations. When describing the goals people might try to achieve, researchers have historically divided the goal setting into two kinds: mastery goals and performance goals (Murayama et al., 2012). These different perspectives result in different outlooks on the learning process as well as different choices in strategies and persistence. Mastery goals are those that are about personal bests and trying for success; performance goals are aimed for success, but only in terms of comparison with others, some comparison group. They are more motivationally extrinsic in nature than mastery goals (Grant & Dweck, 2003).

A mastery goal describes the situation in which the individual is personally interested in the achieving the goal largely out of interest and a desire for growth. The individual with this orientation is looking to master the necessary skills; and, while acknowledgement from others may be appreciated, it isn't needed for the learning to occur. Constructive, honest feedback is appreciated, because the individual is looking to improve. If needed, the goal can be revised when the person believes he or she lacks the necessary ability (Ilies & Judge, 2005).

A performance goal describes the situation in which the individual is pursuing the goal primarily as a matter of wanting to achieve a certain status or rank. More than wanting to be a better clarinetist, the person wants to be the first clarinet player. The goal is a means to a social end, not a matter of learning itself. This individual does not truly want honest feedback about his or her performance, since what is desired is merely status. Selection of strategies will be done only in terms of what it takes to "get ahead" rather than to improve. Alternatively, the goal selected may be purely for the purpose of avoiding failure, perhaps by picking a goal that will minimally provide success but risks very little.

The difference between mastery and performance orientations is important, albeit subtle in some cases. The question becomes why the goal has been selected, which can be entirely internal and may not be a fully conscious decision. Whether we are considering a goal for ourselves or are teaching someone else, it's important to look for the signs between the two, since they signal our willingness to learn from our mistakes, listen to feedback, and persist.

Individuals who are motivated by either mastery or performance goals are all interested in pursuing the goal to a point of success, but the reference point for success varies from one orientation to the other. Some goals, though, are not aimed at success but at the avoidance of failure; these are known as work-avoidance goals. Achieving the goal is not as important as not appearing to be incompetent to others. This alternate orientation completely changes the choice of strategies to achieve this form of "success." Success becomes secondary to the true goal of attempting to manage the impression others have. Shortcuts look more enticing.

Here, the individual directs behaviors to the goal of avoiding work and chooses strategies to keep from getting deeply involved with the activity. Use of a work-avoidance goal usually means the individual has not been convinced of the value of the work, either in terms of personal interest or expected gains to be achieved (such as a high grade in the course). This kind of behavior, in a group, will result in the person's not pulling his or her weight and doing as little as possible to get by, a phenomenon known as social loafing (Karau & Williams, 1993; Latané, Williams, & Harkins, 1979). For coaches and teachers, positioning important, necessary goals so they do not encourage work avoidance is one of the biggest challenges they will face.

One extreme strategy that comes from having a work-avoidance goal is self-handicapping. This strategy involves intentionally setting up the situation so that failure is not just possible, but likely, a result of some self-made obstacle. For example, a student could accept a babysitting job the night before an exam and conveniently leave the textbook at home. When the exam doesn't go well, the student has a ready excuse—an inability to study due to the babysitting job. Of course, this is not the case when accidents and mistakes happen; but an intentional self-sabotage attempt, like a learned helplessness, provides a ready-made reason for failure. The strategy is motivated by a desire to place the blame for the consequence on an external situation, rather than on any personal inability or lack of effort.

So then, what makes for the best goals? The best goals for encouraging focused attention are challenging or difficult instead of being easy (or having no goal at all) and are specific and clear in their objectives, rather than being ambiguous. The goal must be realistically within reach. It's important that the individual is committed to the goal. There should be some form of reinforcement for reaching the goal.

Additionally, there is a need for helpful feedback as the person works toward the goal (Locke & Latham, 2006; Shute, 2008). Helpful feedback explains the difference between the current level of performance and the eventual goal. In a way, the feedback is meant to eliminate ambiguity and uncertainty, so the learner better knows what need to be done. The feedback also helps reduce the mental load on the learner, especially early on in the learning process. The guidance helps to focus the learner on what matters. Finally, the feedback is believed to help correct existing mistakes.

With all of these benefits, there are some conditions to goals. First, the person has to be aware of the goal and what needs to be done. A teacher could have many grand expectations for his students' learning, but if those expectations are not communicated, then it's unlikely the expectations will be effective as goals. Second, the goal has to be achievable, and not simply a high bar that would be convenient. Someone who struggles with low grades is not likely to benefit from deciding to get perfect exam scores from here on out. Finally, the person must accept the goal as worth working for. Simply assigning a goal to a student does not mean the student will find the goal worth achieving.

Expectancy-Value Theory

One theory attempts to integrate many of the different perspectives on motivation and is best considered to be a social-cognitive theory. Expectancy-value theory sees motivation to take on a task as the result of three decisions people make regarding the offered arrangement (e.g., the workload listed on a syllabus that will be required for a particular grade). It focuses on the social nature of obligations, contracts, and requests and what people think about them. Expectancy theory attempts to explain how an individual will evaluate the quality of a proposal to make some effort before becoming motivated to do it. While it touches on the social contract that exists between a person or organization who is making the offer and the learner or worker, oftentimes the same proposal is made to a group of people at one time, such as in a classroom, on the job, or on a sports team. The social aspect of the arrangement also affects the motivation of the people involved.

Expectancy-value theory approaches the motivation someone has to engage in a task, such as studying to earn a high grade in a class, as the result of three cognitive decisions. Hence this theory sees motivation as a primarily cognitive process, which is quite different from Maslow's and Alderfer's conceptualizations of motivation. Expectancy theory assumes that more effort will mean more performance; hence more motivated students will learn more by accepting more learning opportunities, as more motivated workers will be more productive.

With operant conditioning, the environment offers reinforcements for making certain behaviors to a cue. With expectancy theory, the entire transaction is subject to purview by the learner. As the teacher or coach, I may offer an arrangement: Complete these exams and this paper at these levels of competency, and I will award you a suitable grade (which will let you continue on your academic path). Expectancy theory claims that the motivation you experience from my offer will come from your estimation of the value of

FIGURE 6.7   Expectancy-value theory. The amount of effort put into achieving an outcome is based on three decisions: the potential to produce the required effort, the relationship between the effort and the outcome, and the value of the outcome.

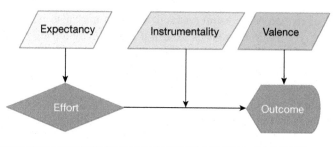

a good grade from this class, from your estimation of whether I will be fair and timely in evaluating your work, and finally, from whether you believe you could meet or exceed the requirements of those assignments themselves (see Fig. 6.7). Let's look more closely at these three decisions.

Expectancy

Expectancy is the perception of the relationship between the effort the learner is being asked to make and the resulting performance. In other words, it is the individual's evaluation as to whether he or she can produce the performance in the first place. Someone might value an outcome quite strongly (high valence) and believe the offer is real (high instrumentality), and yet not believe that he or she is capable of the necessary effort. The individual asks, "Am I capable?" and the answer to that question will determine whether the person is willing to try at all. From this perspective, an individual, at least, has to be convinced as part of the arrangement that he or she can do the required work; it is not enough simply to offer a reinforcement for some behavior. An educator or coach may have to reaffirm in the minds of the students and players that he or she will provide support along the way, for instance. In research, a judgment of expectancy is evaluated on a score of from 0 to 1.

What do we use as the basis of our judgments of expectancy? Expectancy judgment appears to be based on whether we attribute the results of our efforts to ourselves or to uncontrollable events, and to our own sense of confidence for the task (self-efficacy) and the domain in general (Eccles & Wigfield, 2002).

Instrumentality

Instrumentality is the perceived relationship between one's own performance and whether the outcome will actually be obtained. Is the outcome that has been promised really dependent on performance? It is a perception and an evaluation of the trust or faith the individual being asked to do the work has in the person or system offering the deal.

If we assume that every time a teacher makes an offer, the students are completely convinced that the teacher will follow through, then this part of expectancy theory might seem like a nuance. But, the reality is that students evaluate the "bargain" being offered to them based in part on whether they believe the teacher will, in fact, carry through.

Similarly, this could be applied to a promise from a friend—did she pay you back the last time you loaned her money? When your parents promise to send money, do they remember or do they tend to forget? Marketing involves some amount of instrumentality, too. If a commercial touts a new product from a company you have tried before and not liked, it's much harder to trust the claims about this new product.

Awareness of the expected reinforcement schedule may also play a role in deciding instrumentality. If reinforcement is expected occasionally during the task, on some schedule, we can see the schedule of reinforcement to be a factor in deciding whether the ability to perform will be likely. For example, some people are aware of themselves and what motivates them enough to know that going to college for four to six years before earning the primary reinforcer, a bachelor's degree, is not right for them. Likewise, some students may find that the traditional midterm–final exam format of many lecture courses does not provide enough incentive to study regularly. So, when they see that format on a syllabus, they know they will need to give themselves a more rigorous study schedule in order to succeed.

Researchers will attach probabilities to participants' perception of instrumentality from low to high, using 0 to 1 as 0% to 100%. Theoretically, the relationship could even be negative, if a person believed that making a performance would result in the exact opposite result!

Instrumentality can be affected by our observation of others who are in the same situation. Equity theory (Adams, 1963) explains how and when people lose motivation by what they see happening to others compared to themselves in group settings. It is based on the relative effort made and the gains earned in comparison to other people. Initially it was aimed at describing financial compensation from work (Pritchard, 1969), but has been extended to any circumstance in which rewards for accomplishments can be compared with others. The basic assumption of equity theory is that people compare the effort they are putting into an activity and what outcomes they are getting out of the situation with what other similarly situated people are doing and receiving. The basic premise is one of social comparison, the evaluation of our experiences with similar others. This social comparison can affect the perceived instrumentality of the outcomes based on the applied effort.

When making social comparisons about the work we are doing, we monitor two processes: the effort or "inputs" we provide and the results or "outcomes" that we receive from our efforts. We monitor these both for ourselves as well as for other people we can observe, such as classmates. Mentally, we create two kinds of ratios: our inputs divided by the outcomes, and the inputs over outcomes of other people. These are then compared. Hence, a student will notice if she struggles to do all of the required work on time for a course, submits it, and finds out other students either turned the work in late, did it with less care, or perhaps didn't do it at all, and the difference had no effect whatsoever on the resulting grades given in the class. In this case, the student will believe that her inputs (effort) were much higher for the same outcomes as everyone else. She then experiences an inequity.

This comparison of ratios is entirely perceptual. It could be that there are other situational factors that she is not aware of. Other students could be doing completely different kinds of work, or perhaps her understanding of the nature of the assignments was incorrect. The reality will not matter; her motivation to continue maintaining a high standard of effort will be undermined.

In a way, the observation of others and their experiences under the same bargain of inputs-outcomes could be seen as a concurrent validation of the instrumentality of the bargain. What is the relationship between the effort and the work for others? Is it the same as what I understood for myself?

Equity theory assumes that equity (meaning "fairness") is a desired state that everyone wants, and it assumes that when inequity is perceived, dissatisfaction and tension result. If one student is carrying the workload for a group of students, then that student might be unhappy when it becomes clear that one grade is assigned to the entire group, regardless of each individual group member's effort. When tension occurs, we are motivated to reduce the tension. With the increase in tension, people are even more motivated to try to reduce the inequity and the tension.

How might this be done? Usually in one of three ways. First, someone who believes he or she is working too much for the same outcomes as everyone else can decrease his or her effort, by reducing the inputs. By not working as hard, the perceived ratio will not be as imbalanced relative to others. A second option is to ask for more consideration to be made to the imbalance, for example, asking a teacher to consider the difference in workload and take that into account. This is known as changing the outcomes. Finally, it is possible to alter the perceptions of the relative ratios, and reframe them mentally. While the individual may be working more than the others, perhaps it is also of more importance to that individual than to the others. Perhaps it's something he or she enjoys excelling at. Maybe there are other components of the work that the person has not yet taken into account. This is called reconsidering the ratios. It is a purely cognitive change, in contrast to the other two that will involve some behavioral action.

However, research into equity theory has found that not everyone is equally as sensitive to inequity (Huseman, Hatfield, & Miles, 1987). The imbalance bothers some people more than others. Some people simply accept being underappreciated and do not mind; they are aware of the inequity, but it doesn't appear to cause any real tension. Other people want a better ratio regardless of the level of equity; that is, even when everything is perfectly fair, they would like to tip the scales in their direction and benefit even more.

What does this mean for learning? The person supervising the learning situation has to be sensitive to the students' perceptions of inputs and outcomes. For example, opportunities for extra credit should be made available to the entire class. If a special arrangement or accommodation is made for one person, it needs to be clear to others (if they need be aware of it at all) that there is a reason for the arrangement beyond favoritism. When someone believes incorrectly that he or she is doing more workload than others for the same results, the supervisor has to help the individual reconsider the ratios, perhaps by pointing out work that the others will be responsible for later, or work that the others are doing that was not taken into account.

In sum, instrumentality is the perception of how strong the association between the required effort and the outcome is. Equity theory claims that in group situations, people are aware of the relative ratio of work they must do for reinforcement compared to the work others must do for their reward. Where there is an imbalance, people may be motivated to work less hard or to complain.

Valences

Perceived task value or valence for the outcome is the final component of expectancy-value theory. The valence is not just the overall difficulty of the task but the features of the work itself and how they align with our interests (Feather, 1995). Eccles and Wigfield (2002) believe there are four components to the valence judgment people make to decide whether a task is motivating. First is "attainment value," or how important doing well on the task is for the individual. Second is the "intrinsic value" of the task, a judgment of how much enjoyment he or she will receive from doing it. Third, how well the task aligns with our future goals (self-determination theory) is known as "utility value." And finally, the individual takes into account the "cost" of the task. Engaging in the activity will mean effort, use of resources, time, and energy, and will mean giving up other activities. Because of the possible cost of doing the activity, the valence can be positive or negative—someone may see the outcome as simply not satisfying. Researchers often score participants' ratings of valence from low to high (0 to 1) as a way to measure their value.

Neuroscientists do not approach task value in the same manner. While Eccles and Wigfield (2002) view task valence as a combination of four different evaluations, neuroscientists approach "value" as a singular, convergent experience of reward. This reward can result from encountering an object or event, whether it is an innate biological response, such as drinking water, or a learned one, such as earning a high grade (Reeve & Lee, 2012). When people encounter experiences they have previously learned to find rewarding, the orbitofrontal cortex is activated, which probably aides them in deciding between options and which actions to pursue (Rushworth, Behrens, Rudebeck, & Walton, 2007). The orbitofrontal-striatal circuit appears to be a system for comparing values across many stimuli and in different environments (Montague & Berns, 2002). Rewards for different options can vary by type, size, salience, and immediacy (Reeve & Lee, 2012). The different options and their rewards are compared in the orbitofrontal-striatal circuit, which converts all rewards to a common scale across all options, not unlike comparing prices on items in the grocery store. This appears to be what allows people to pick and choose what actions they would like most to pursue.

Expectancy theory, then, claims that there are three perceptual evaluations that people make before choosing to find a potential task motivating. The importance or value of the outcome, the relationship between the work required and the reality of the outcome, and an estimation of one's own ability to make the effort are all considered. Researchers who use this theory will calculate the overall motivational force of a task by multiplying all participants' scores on all three factors against each other. Of course, if any one of those evaluations is zero, then the entire deal is off.

For people looking to encourage learning, expectancy theory claims that it's important that the outcomes be desirable by the people being asked to take on the activity (Pritchard, DeLeo, & Von Bergen, 1976). No busywork. The rules for the expected work should be clear, and the actions necessary to complete the work need to be seen as controllable. The amount of effort required needs to appear to be within the realm of possibility. This last factor may mean making clear that support and feedback will be provided along the way, particularly if the task is seen as a challenging one.

Work Design Theory

Given these kinds of research findings, it would be good if there was a theory for describing how work should be designed so that learners would be more likely to find it motivating. Work design theory (sometimes called task design theory or job characteristics theory) combines much of what we have discussed about motivation so far and provides a framework for designing tasks so that they are more likely to spur motivation (Hackman & Oldham, 1976; see Fig. 6.8). Work design theory assumes that the context of the work matters and that the design of a job or task can facilitate motivation. From this perspective,

FIGURE 6.8   Diagram of work design theory

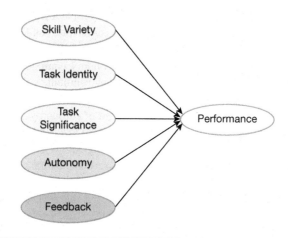

work design theory can be used by teachers, coaches, and managers to tailor the design of a task so that it is enticing to the population they would like to have embrace it. Ultimately the teacher of a class has more power over the design of an assignment than the students themselves, so this may be a natural way to combine motivational theory with a target that is controllable (the task itself).

Work design theory claims there are three general aspects of a job or task that can be prepared in a way to enhance motivation: the job characteristics, the autonomy granted to the learner or "worker," and the task feedback to the learner. Autonomy and task feedback both involve how the work should be allowed to be carried out, rather than any specific design feature of the work. It should seem familiar at this point: Some amount of self-determination and clear, constructive feedback is desired by the learner. So, work should be designed with some amount of choice involved, as well as periods of guidance from an instructor or mentor as to the quality of the work.

Of the job characteristics, there are three traits that a task should employ in order to encourage motivation, according to work design theory: skill variety, task identity, and task significance. We have seen some form of these in earlier presentations of motivational theory. Skill variety is the extent to which an assortment of skills, activities, and talents is required in the task. More variety is encouraged, and use of a single skill repeatedly is to be avoided. Task identity is the degree to which the learner can identify the required work, similar to idea of clearly stated objectives from goal theory. Are the expectations of the work identifiable to the learner? This trait also mirrors the "expectancy" decision from expectancy theory. Finally, task significance is whether the task seems to involve something of importance to the learner, similar to the notion of "valence" from expectancy theory.

An assumption of the model is that not every individual looking at the same task will view all five traits equally; any one person will value or desire more of some than others because of individual differences. But, if a task is designed with all five in mind, it should be more likely to encourage people to take it on. One study, using activities designed to mirror a work environment, found the model to explain 25% of the variance in performance, 34% of the satisfaction people had in the task, and 24% of the commitment people had to the company (Humphrey, Nahrgang, & Morgeson, 2007).

Motivation in Education

What does the plethora of motivational theories mean for education? Whether we take the perspective of self-efficacy theory, or perceived control, or self-determination theory, learners who believe they have control over the results they are striving for feel more competent (Wigfield, Cambria, & Eccles, 2014). Autonomy, competency, and relatedness are all necessary for support in the school and home environments so children become fully engaged in learning activities. Whenever possible, intrinsic motivation should be facilitated so personal interest can coincide with the development of autonomy and competency.

Children tend to enter elementary school feeling high levels of self-confidence in their abilities, a feeling that declines through secondary school (Wigfield, Eccles, Mac Iver, Reuman, & Midgley, 1991). In some ways, the weaker optimism is simply more realistic, but the self-efficacy beliefs can become fairly negative. Likewise, children in elementary school will typically display mastery goal orientations, but this reverts to performance goal orientations by middle school. In some part, this is due to the developing social awareness that occurs in the years after age eight and in the teen years, which permits more social comparison with peers. Additionally, participation in group activities such as sports, band, and academic competitions invite social comparisons. As a result of the adoption of performance goal orientations and weaker self-efficacy for schoolwork, motivation for academic goals tends to decline during those years. While these are overall trends, not every child fits this pattern; and it's not necessarily a requirement of the childhood experience.

Many of the recommendations for creating a classroom environment that encourages motivation for academic achievement will seem sensible given theories such as goal-setting theory and work-design theory. In a comprehensive literature review, Stipek (1996) found the studies of student engagement support providing activities to students who are at the appropriately challenging level and varying them from time to time to keep up interest and allow for the development of different skills. The criteria for success must be clear and achievable, and the teacher must believe that all of the students can achieve success with effort, since the students will use their interactions with the teacher as a form of feedback. Feedback on how to improve must be provided, with rewards for success that are based on task completion, improvement, and effort. The rewards are primarily used for information about progress and mastery, not control, to encourage whatever intrinsic motivation is present.

The use of rewards to force specific types of learning and rigid expectations of mastery in the form of high-stakes, standardized testing that began with the No Child Left Behind law and continued with Race to the Top has been decried by the theorists who developed self-determination theory. Those theorists say that such external forces intended to produce compliant behavior are counter to a basic understanding of motivational theory (Deci & Ryan, 2008). External programs with rewards of bonuses and punishments of firings and school closures are likely to have many negative effects on student motivation and learning. In fact, certain negative effects appear to have occurred. During the high-stakes testing regime, more students have dropped out of school. Some school districts either have stopped recording students as dropouts in order give the appearance of higher attendance, or have discouraged some students from taking the tests at all. At the level of the teaching, teachers are having to focus only on material that will appear on the tests, and they are teaching skills on how to take tests, which is not a terribly pertinent task in most career paths. As can happen in business environments, high levels of control though punishments and incentives ignore intrinsic motivation and autonomy needs—and can backfire.

CHAPTER SUMMARY

In this chapter, we have looked at the act of imitation as a form of learning; affective states and learning; and classic as well as modern motivational theories. The basic act of imitation can be viewed as a kind of learning from one who models how to complete some task. Positive emotional states like flow can help learning, while negative emotions such as anxiety and frustration are signs of difficulty and can impede progress.

To feel as if the results of the task are part of one's own increasing competency, it's important that the individual believe the results of the effort can be attributed to him- or herself. What motivates someone to accomplish a task has been viewed as a matter of meeting a hierarchical set of psychological needs (Maslow, Alderfer), or as cognitive and social evaluations about the nature of the work and outcome. For example, what are the individual's expectations about the nature of the work, the value of the results of the task, or the likely relationship between the performing the work and the outcome? Much of the process of motivation stems from the action of setting a goal initially, ideally one that is challenging and accepted by the individual.

REVIEW QUESTIONS

1. What is the difference between an affective state, an emotion, and a mood?

2. Have you experienced *flow* when working on an activity? What activity was it? Do you think there is a relationship between doing an activity that lines up with your future goals well, as self-determination theory suggests, and experiencing flow? Or, are they produced by separate sources?

3. What is the difference between feeling intrinsically motivated when doing a task versus feeling extrinsically motivated?

4. Consider an opportunity you turned down. It could be a job, an extra credit assignment, or an offer for a date. Apply expectancy-value theory to your decision to find out what nixed the deal. What was your achievement expectation for the offer? The perceived task value or valence? Or instrumentality?

KEY TERMS

FURTHER RESOURCES

1. Weblink: Abraham Maslow talks about self-actualization:
   - https://www.youtube.com/watch?v=7DOKZzbuJQA

2. Weblink: A discussion of video games on Maslow's hierarchy of needs:
   - https://www.acxiom.com/game-video-games-maslows-hierarchy-needs-big-data/

3. Weblink: A quiz on Maslow's hierarchy:
   - https://www.purposegames.com/game/maslows-hierarchy-of-needs-quiz

4. Weblink: Animated explanation of expectancy theory:
   - https://www.youtube.com/watch?v=dPr8F6rbfdw

REFERENCES

Adams, J. S. (1963). Towards an understanding of inequity. *The Journal of Abnormal and Social Psychology, 67*(5), 422.

Alderfer, C. P. (1969). An empirical test of a new theory of human needs. *Organizational Behavior and Human Performance, 4*(2), 142–175.

Alderfer, C. P. (1972). *Existence, relatedness, and growth; Human needs in organizational settings* (1st ed.). New York, NY: Free Press.

Ayduk, O., Mischel, W., & Downey, G. (2002). Attentional mechanisms linking rejection to hostile reactivity: The role of "hot" versus "cool" focus. *Psychological Science, 13*(5), 443–448. https://doi.org/10.1111/1467-9280.00478

Bandura, A. (1986). *Social foundations of thought and action: A social cognitive theory.* Englewood Cliffs, NJ: Prentice Hall.

Bandura, A. (1989). Human agency in social cognitive theory. *American Psychologist, 44*(9), 1175.

Bandura, A. (1997). *Self-efficacy: The exercise of control.* New York, NY: Macmillan. Retrieved from https://books.google.com/books?hl=en&lr=&id=eJ-PN9g_o-EC&oi=fnd&pg=PR7&dq=bandura+1997+self-efficacy+theory&ots=zxPJKVic3h&sig=T9KWZ4U6_oaCC4ID1Qwwod JrnIE

Barrett, L. F. (2006). Are emotions natural kinds? *Perspectives on Psychological Science, 1*(1), 28–58. https://doi.org/10.1111/j.1745-6916.2006.00003.x

Berkowitz, L. (1989). Frustration–aggression hypothesis. *Psychological Bulletin, 106*(1), 59–73. https://doi.org/10.1037//0033-2909.106.1.59

Büchel, C., & Dolan, R. J. (2000). Classical fear conditioning in functional neuroimaging. *Current Opinion in Neurobiology, 10*(2), 219–223. https://doi.org/10.1016/S0959-4388(00)00078-7

Cassady, J. C. (2010). *Anxiety in schools: The causes, consequences, and solutions for academic anxieties* (Vol. 2). New York, NY: Peter Lang.

Connell, J. P., Spencer, M. B., & Aber, J. L. (1994). Educational risk and resilience in African-American youth: Context, self, action, and outcomes in school. *Child Development, 65*(2), 493–506. https://doi.org/10.1111/j.1467-8624.1994.tb00765.x

Connell, J. P., & Wellborn, J. G. (1991). Competence, autonomy, and relatedness: A motivational analysis of self-system processes. In M. R. Gunnar & L. A. Sroufe (Eds.), *Self processes and development* (pp. 43–77). Hillsdale, NJ: Erlbaum.

Critchley, H. D., Mathias, C. J., & Dolan, R. J. (2002). Fear conditioning in humans: The influence of awareness and autonomic arousal on functional neuroanatomy. *Neuron, 33*(4), 653–663. https://doi.org/10.1016/S0896-6273(02)00588-3

Csikszentmihalyi, M. (1990). *Flow: The psychology of optimal experience*. New York, NY: HarperPerennial.

Csikszentmihalyi, M., Abuhamdeh, S., & Nakamura, J. (2014). Flow. In *Flow and the foundations of positive psychology* (pp. 227–238). Springer Netherlands. Retrieved from http://link.springer.com/chapter/10.1007/978-94-017-9088-8_15

Dalal, R. S., & Hulin, C. L. (2008). Motivation for what? A multivariate dynamic perspective of the criterion. *Work Motivation: Past, Present, and Future, 27*, 63–100.

Deci, E. L., Koestner, R., & Ryan, R. M. (1999). A meta-analytic review of experiments examining the effects of extrinsic rewards on intrinsic motivation. *Psychological Bulletin, 125*(6), 627–668. https://doi.org/10.1037/0033-2909.125.6.627

Deci, E. L., & Ryan, R. M. (2000). The "what" and "why" of goal pursuits: Human needs and the self-determination of behavior. *Psychological Inquiry, 11*(4), 227–268. https://doi.org/10.1207/S15327965PLI1104_01

Deci, E. L., & Ryan, R. M. (2008). Self-determination theory: A macrotheory of human motivation, development, and health. *Canadian Psychology/Psychologie Canadienne, 49*(3), 182.

Diamond, D. M., Campbell, A. M., Park, C. R., Halonen, J., & Zoladz, P. R. (2007). The temporal dynamics model of emotional memory processing: A synthesis on the neurobiological basis of stress-induced amnesia, flashbulb and traumatic memories, and the Yerkes-Dodson law. *Neural Plasticity, 2007*. Retrieved from https://www.hindawi.com/journals/np/2007/060803/abs/

Dollard, J., Miller, N. E., Doob, L. W., Mowrer, O. H., & Sears, R. R. (1939). *Frustration and aggression* (Vol. viii). New Haven, CT: Yale University Press.

Eccles, J. S., & Wigfield, A. (2002). Motivational beliefs, values, and goals. *Annual Review of Psychology, 53*(1), 109–132. https://doi.org/10.1146/annurev.psych.53.100901.135153

Ekkekakis, P., & Dafermos, M. (2012). Exercise is a many-splendored thing but for some it does not feel so splendid: Staging a resurgence of hedonistic ideas in the quest to understand exercise behavior. In E. O. Acevedo (Ed.), *The Oxford handbook of exercise psychology* (pp. 295–333). New York, NY: Oxford University Press.

Feather, N. T. (1995). Values, valences, and choice: The influences of values on the perceived attractiveness and choice of alternatives. *Journal of Personality and Social Psychology, 68*(6), 1135.

Grant, H., & Dweck, C. S. (2003). Clarifying achievement goals and their impact. *Journal of Personality and Social Psychology, 85*(3), 541.

Hackman, J. R., & Oldham, G. R. (1976). Motivation through the design of work: Test of a theory. *Organizational Behavior and Human Performance, 16*(2), 250–279. https://doi.org/10.1016/0030-5073(76)90016-7

Haggard, P. (2009). The sources of human volition. *Science, 324*(5928), 731.

Heron, W. (1957). The pathology of boredom. *Scientific American*. Retrieved from http://psycnet.apa.org/psycinfo/1958-00206-001

Hidi, S., & Baird, W. (1986). Interestingness—A neglected variable in discourse processing. *Cognitive Science, 10*(2), 179–194. https://doi.org/10.1207/s15516709cog1002_3

Hidi, S., & Renninger, K. A. (2006). The four-phase model of interest development. *Educational Psychologist, 41*(2), 111–127. https://doi.org/10.1207/s15326985ep4102_4

Humphrey, S. E., Nahrgang, J. D., & Morgeson, F. P. (2007). Integrating motivational, social, and contextual work design features: A meta-analytic summary and theoretical extension of the work design literature. *Journal of Applied Psychology, 92*(5), 1332–1356. https://doi.org/10.1037/0021-9010.92.5.1332

Huseman, R. C., Hatfield, J. D., & Miles, E. W. (1987). A new perspective on equity theory: The equity sensitivity construct. *Academy of Management Review, 12*(2), 222–234. https://doi.org/10.5465/AMR.1987.4307799

Ilies, R., & Judge, T. A. (2005). Goal regulation across time: The effects of feedback and affect. *Journal of Applied

Psychology, 90(3), 453–467. https://doi.org/10.1037/0021-9010.90.3.453

Karau, S. J., & Williams, K. D. (1993). Social loafing: A meta-analytic review and theoretical integration. *Journal of Personality and Social Psychology, 65*(4), 681–706. https://doi.org/10.1037/0022-3514.65.4.681

Kasser, T., & Ryan, R. M. (1993). A dark side of the American dream. *Journal of Personality and Social Psychology, 65*(2), 410–422. https://doi.org/10.1037//0022-3514.65.2.410

Kensinger, E. A., & Corkin, S. (2004). Two routes to emotional memory: Distinct neural processes for valence and arousal. *Proceedings of the National Academy of Sciences, 101*(9), 3310–3315. https://doi.org/10.1073/pnas.0306408101

Klehe, U.-C., & Anderson, N. (2007). Working hard and working smart: Motivation and ability during typical and maximum performance. *Journal of Applied Psychology, 92*(4), 978–992. https://doi.org/10.1037/0021-9010.92.4.978

Kleinginna, P. R., Jr., & Kleinginna, A. M. (1981). A categorized list of motivation definitions, with a suggestion for a consensual definition. *Motivation and Emotion, 5*(3), 263–291. https://doi.org/10.1007/BF00993889

Kunda, Z. (1990). The case for motivated reasoning. *Psychological Bulletin, 108*(3), 480–498. https://doi.org/10.1037/0033-2909.108.3.480

LaBar, K. S., & Cabeza, R. (2006). Cognitive neuroscience of emotional memory. *Nature Reviews. Neuroscience, 7*(1), 54–64.

Lang, P. J., Greenwald, M. K., Bradley, M. M., & Hamm, A. O. (1993). Looking at pictures: Affective, facial, visceral, and behavioral reactions. *Psychophysiology, 30*(3), 261–273.

Latané, B., Williams, K., & Harkins, S. (1979). Many hands make light the work: The causes and consequences of social loafing. *Journal of Personality and Social Psychology, 37*(6), 822.

LeDoux, J. E. (2000). Emotion circuits in the brain. *Annual Review of Neuroscience, 23*, 155–184.

Lewis, M., Hitchcock, D. F. A., & Sullivan, M. W. (2004). Physiological and emotional reactivity to learning and frustration. *Infancy : The Official Journal of the International Society on Infant Studies, 6*(1), 121–143.

Lewis, M., Sullivan, M. W., & Kim, H. M.-S. (2015). Infant approach and withdrawal in response to a goal blockage: Its antecedent causes and its effect on toddler persistence. *Developmental Psychology, 51*(11), 1553–1563. https://doi.org/10.1037/dev0000043

Locke, E. A., & Latham, G. P. (1990). *A theory of goal setting & task performance.* Englewood Cliffs, NJ: Prentice Hall.

Locke, E. A., & Latham, G. P. (2006). New directions in goal-setting theory. *Current Directions in Psychological Science, 15*(5), 265–268. https://doi.org/10.1111/j.1467-8721.2006.00449.x

Marchand, G., & Skinner, E. A. (2007). Motivational dynamics of children's academic help-seeking and concealment. *Journal of Educational Psychology, 99*(1), 65–82. https://doi.org/10.1037/0022-0663.99.1.65

Maslow, A. H. (1943). A theory of human motivation. *Psychological Review, 50*(4), 370.

Metcalfe, J., & Mischel, W. (1999). A hot/cool-system analysis of delay of gratification: Dynamics of willpower. *Psychological Review, 106*(1), 3–19. https://doi.org/10.1037/0033-295X.106.1.3

Miller, N. E. (1941). I. The frustration-aggression hypothesis. *Psychological Review, 48*(4), 337–342. https://doi.org/10.1037/h0055861

Montague, P. R., & Berns, G. S. (2002). Neural economics and the biological substrates of valuation. *Neuron, 36*(2), 265–284. https://doi.org/10.1016/S0896-6273(02)00974-1

Murayama, K., Elliot, A. J., & Friedman, R. (2012). Achievement goals. In R. M. Ryan (Ed.), *The Oxford handbook of human motivation* (pp. 191–207). New York, NY: Oxford University Press.

Murayama, K., Matsumoto, M., Izuma, K., & Matsumoto, K. (2010). Neural basis of the undermining effect of monetary reward on intrinsic motivation. *Proceedings of the National Academy of Sciences, 107*(49), 20911–20916. https://doi.org/10.1073/pnas.1013305107

Pinder, C. C. (1998). *Work motivation in organizational behavior.* Upper Saddle River, NJ: Prentice Hall.

Pinder, C. C. (2008). *Work motivation in organizational behavior* (2nd ed.). New York, NY: Psychology Press.

Pritchard, R. D. (1969). Equity theory: A review and critique. *Organizational Behavior and Human Performance, 4*(2), 176–211. https://doi.org/10.1016/0030-5073(69)90005-1

Pritchard, R. D., DeLeo, P. J., & Von Bergen Jr., C. W. (1976). A field experimental test of expectancy-valence incentive motivation techniques. *Organizational Behavior and Human Performance, 15*(2), 355–406. https://doi.org/10.1016/0030-5073(76)90046-5

Reeve, J., & Lee, W. (2012). Neuroscience and human motivation. In R. M. Ryan (Ed.), *The Oxford handbook of human motivation* (pp. 365–380). New York, NY: Oxford University Press.

Renninger, K. A., & Su, S. (2012). Interest and its development. In R. M. Ryan (Ed.), *The Oxford handbook of human motivation* (pp. 167–187). New York, NY: Oxford University Press.

Rousseau, D. M. (1997). Organizational behavior in the new organizational era. *Annual Review of Psychology, 48*(1), 515–546.

Rushworth, M. F. S., Behrens, T. E. J., Rudebeck, P. H., & Walton, M. E. (2007). Contrasting roles for cingulate and orbitofrontal cortex in decisions and social behaviour. *Trends in Cognitive Sciences, 11*(4), 168–176. https://doi .org/10.1016/j.tics.2007.01.004

Russell, J. A., & Barrett, L. F. (1999). Core affect, prototypical emotional episodes, and other things called emotion: Dissecting the elephant. *Journal of Personality and Social Psychology, 76*(5), 805–819. https://doi.org/10.1037//0022-3514.76.5.805

Russell, J. A. (2003). Core affect and the psychological construction of emotion. *Psychological Review, 110*(1), 145–172. https://doi.org/10.1037/0033-295X.110.1.145

Sackett, P. R., Zedeck, S., & Fogli, L. (1988). Relations between measures of typical and maximum job performance. *Journal of Applied Psychology, 73*(3), 482–486. https://doi.org/10.1037/0021-9010.73.3.482

Schachter, S., & Singer, J. (1962). Cognitive, social, and physiological determinants of emotional state. *Psychological Review, 69*(5), 379–399. https://doi.org/10.1037/h0046234

Schiefele, U. (1999). Interest and learning from text. *Scientific Studies of Reading, 3*(3), 257–279. https://doi.org/10.1207/s1532799xssr0303_4

Shute, V. J. (2008). Focus on formative feedback. *Review of Educational Research, 78*(1), 153–189. https://doi.org/10.3102/0034654307313795

Silvia, P. J. (2008). Interest—The curious emotion. *Current Directions in Psychological Science, 17*(1), 57–60.

Skinner, E. A. (1995). *Perceived control, motivation, & coping.* Thousand Oaks, CA: SAGE.

Stipek, D. J. (1996). Motivation and instruction. *Handbook of Educational Psychology,* 85–113.

Tolman, E. C. (1949). *Purposive Behaviour in Animals and Men.* Berkeley: University of California Press.

Tolman, E. C. (1959). *Principles of purposive behavior.* In S. Koch (Ed.)., *Psychology: A study of a science* (Vol. 2, pp. 92–157). New York: McGraw-Hill.

Tse, P. U., Intriligator, J., Rivest, J., & Cavanagh, P. (2004). Attention and the subjective expansion of time. *Perception & Psychophysics, 66*(7), 1171–1189. https://doi.org/10.3758/BF03196844

Tully, K., & Bolshakov, V. (2010). Emotional enhancement of memory: How norepinephrine enables synaptic plasticity. *Molecular Brain, 3*(1), 15. https://doi.org/10.1186/1756-6606-3-15

Vroom, V. H. (1982). *Work and motivation.* Malabar, FL: Krieger.

Vygotsky, L. S. (1978). *Mind in society: The development of higher psychological processes* (14th ed.). Cambridge, MA: Harvard University Press.

Wang, F. (2008). Motivation and English achievement: An exploratory and confirmatory factor analysis of a new measurement for Chinese students of English learning. *North American Journal of Psychology, 10*(3), 633–646.

Wigfield, A., Cambria, J., & Eccles, J. S. (2014). Motivation in education. *The Oxford handbook of human motivation,* 463–478.

Wigfield, A., Eccles, J. S., Mac Iver, D., Reuman, D. A., & Midgley, C. (1991). Transitions during early adolescence: Changes in children's domain-specific self-perceptions and general self-esteem across the transition to junior high school. *Developmental Psychology, 27*(4), 552–565. https://doi.org/10.1037/0012-1649.27.4.552

Yerkes, R. M., & Dodson, J. D. (1908). The relation of strength of stimulus to rapidity of habit-formation.

©iStock.com/gradyreese

Cognitive Learning

Chapter Outline

Learning Objectives

1. Describe the basic characteristics of short-term memory.

2. Explain the assumptions of Baddeley's working memory model and how the components of the model function together.

3. Summarize the consciously active strategies that people can use to optimize their learning.

4. Explain the neurobiological basis of the formation of memories.

Overview

In this chapter, we begin the bridge between "learning" and "memory." As you may remember from Chapter 1, three key cognitive processes are commonly acknowledged in learning and memory: encoding, storage, and retrieval. We encode information from our environments, store some of that information, and attempt to retrieve it later. Learning seems to include encoding and a temporary storage, while memory includes both storage and retrieval (see Fig. 7.1).

One famous Russian man was able to memorize complex mathematical formulas after only seven minutes of study (Luria, 1968; Wilding & Valentine, 1997). His technique was to turn the formula into meaningful people and objects, turning the formula into a story. For example, his story for this formula, which he was able to recall fifteen years later at a surprise test, included "Neiman (N) came out and jabbed the ground with his cane (.)" (Luria, 1968, p. 43; see Fig. 7.2). As you can see, part of his strategy to retain the information was how he studied it. This chapter explores the different ways we actively study information in the hopes of improved retention of the information for later retrieval.

The focus of the research and theories presented in this chapter is primarily cognitive in nature. This approach highlights the mind and brain as a powerful computational machine (see Fig. 7.3).

Recall the Atkinson-Shiffrin model of memory (Chapter 1). We are now clearly in their second stage of the model. We are moving into the middle stage, "short-term memory store," a temporary holding place for information that we need for only a short period while we process it. While I will use the stage name of "short-term memory" (STM) frequently, this chapter is focused primarily on the active, conscious process of study that we can engage in inside of this mental space. Once information is lost from the short-term memory store, it can't be readily recovered.

Research on short-term memory has typically focused on one of two kinds of questions, generally speaking. The first is what are the naturally occurring capacities of short-term memory? How much can the short-term

FIGURE 7.1   Learning is assumed to include the processes of encoding and storing, while memory includes storing and retrieval.

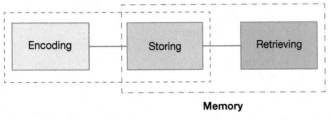

Learning

Encoding — Storing — Retrieving

Memory

FIGURE 7.2   Example of a complex formula that Shereshevskii could recall. Could you recall this after only seven minutes of study, and again fifteen years later?

$$N \cdot \sqrt{d^2 \times \frac{85}{vx}} \cdot 3 \sqrt{\frac{276^2 \cdot 86x}{n^2 v \cdot \pi 264}} \; n^2 b = sv \frac{1624}{32^2} \cdot r^2 s$$

Source: Adapted from Wilding, J. M., & Valentine, E. R. (1997).

FIGURE 7.3   Quadrant of four perspectives of learning

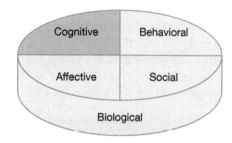

memory store hold? How long does information last in short-term memory? This approach primarily documents the technical aspects of what short-term memory is capable of and the underlying biological system.

The second question is how we self-regulate our conscious efforts at learning. When we choose what to learn, how do we decide when we have learned enough? Are we accurate when we decide we have studied enough? Can we improve learning? One theorist has called this a matter of "willful encoding," that is, a combination of applying attention, organizing information in a meaningful way, and rehearsing or practicing the material to be learned (Watkins, 1989).

The stored information or memories that result from cognitive learning will be the focus of the next set of chapters, when we examine retrieval and long-term memories. But first, to understand how we consciously control what is in our short-term memory store, we need to know a little about the nature of the short-term store itself.

Short-Term Memory Store

Before looking at how we process information in the short-term memory store, we should consider the evidence that short-term memory exists.

Logically, we know there is a need for coordinating activities, such as paying attention to information in our surroundings, as well as recalling prior knowledge in real time or on the fly. Consider the professional basketball player who must quickly and accurately coordinate sensory information about the other players around and the location of the ball, while forming strategies for the next play, keeping in mind the rules of the game. The player has to willfully choose to focus on the game and ignore distractions, and will most likely also have thoughts about how well or poorly the game is going. But once the game is over, it's not necessary to retain the specific information needed for every moment of the game, and much of it is lost.

For some time, many psychologists assumed that memory essentially acted as a single depository, that is, a place where all learned content was stored, like a memory bank. While it was clear that this was not what the underlying biological structure was like (one brain area that held all of one's memories), on a strictly cognitive or mental level, it was commonly believed that memory was simply a single storage area for learned associations.

The idea that there is an area of memory that has some limited abilities and is used only temporarily is supported by two lines of evidence: trends in recall performance for lists of words, and memory deficits from patients who have experienced some brain damage. First, when given a longer list of twenty words or more, and given time to recall them in a free recall task, the likelihood of a particular word's being recalled depends somewhat on where it was in the list (see Fig. 7.4).

As you can see in Figure 7.5, words that are at the beginning or ending of a list have an advantage when being recalled. This is known as the serial position curve, since it documents the average recall for words based on their sequential position in the original list (Rundus, 1971). Those words that "bookend" the list are remembered better (see Fig. 7.5). The primacy effect is the name for the improved performance for words at the beginning of a list. The recency effect is the name for the improved performance for words at the ending of a list, since those words were presented last. Usually only the last few words seem to benefit from the recency effect. Items in the middle have neither benefit and seem to interfere with each other.

The serial position curve has some implications for daily life. When someone gives you a long list of instructions to follow, such as a recipe or road directions, the first steps and the last may be easier to recall; but the ones in the middle can become jumbled and lost. The curve may mean that there is a benefit for job applicants who are interviewed early on or later in a series of interviews, since they may be fresher in the minds of the interviewers. It is possible that our system for conducting jury trials is also structured to take advantage of these memory effects, even though jury trials have been around longer than when these effects were documented. Since the burden of proof is on the prosecutor to demonstrate that the defendant is guilty of the accusations (as the defendant is presumed innocent), the prosecutor presents his or her arguments from the onset of a trial, and will usually rebut the defense's claims just before jury deliberations begin.

FIGURE 7.4   Give yourself two minutes to memorize this word list. Hide the list, and recall the words in any order. Were you more likely to recall words at the beginning and ending of the list than the middle?

COLD	SHORT	NEED	ROUND	LARGE
HAND	WIND	DIRTY	SMOOTH	CAKE
SLEEP	TREE	QUEEN	BUG	STUPID
SHEEP	PAIN	BLACK	DAY	WASH

FIGURE 7.5   The serial position curve. Words at the beginning and ending of a list show a preference in recall.

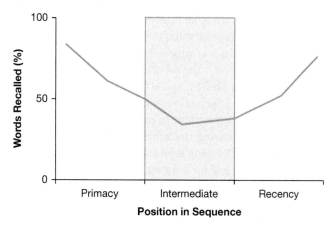

The most common explanation for these results is that those items at the beginning of the list experience less interference with other items, since they do not have as many other words to compete with in our minds, and there is a longer opportunity for the person to mentally think about them. Many memory researchers view this effect to indicate the beginning of a long-term memory store.

The words at the end of the list are also favored, possibly because they are residing in the short-term memory store. Additionally, this short-term memory store can be disrupted. The recency effect can be interfered with by having participants complete a new task, such as counting backward from ninety-nine by threes, or solving a division problem. Many researchers view this recency effect and how it is susceptible to interference by a dual task as evidence of a temporary, limited memory store that holds only a few items (Davelaar, Goshen-Gottstein, Ashkenazi, Haarmann, & Usher, 2005).

In addition to the serial position curve, the other line of evidence for a short-term memory store comes from patients who have experienced brain damage. Patients with brain damage that affects the portions of the brain that involve memory can show deficits in short-term memory or in forming long-term memories. Mr. Moliason, or "H.M.," as described in Chapter 3, is an example of someone who retained his existing long-term memories and short-term memory processing; but he lost the ability to turn short-term memories into new long-term memories. Other patients, such as "K.F.," had difficulties with short-term memory alone (Shallice & Warrington, 1970). Taken together, most researchers today believe there is some sort of temporary holding spot for information before it will be stored as a long-term memory.

Processing Information in the Short-Term Memory Store

The topic and nature of the processing we can conduct in short-term memory has received much attention from researchers over the past fifty years. This temporary holding place permits us to remember a password long enough to enter it into a website, or translate someone's oral directions into where to turn next. Calculating the tip to leave at a restaurant requires short-term processing; most "mental math" does, particularly if there are several steps. This temporary holding spot allows us to formulate our thoughts before we speak our minds, to remember at the end of a sentence what it was we were reading about, and to reconstruct a past event and ask questions of ourselves about it ("Was that what really happened? Or am I just imagining it that way?"). It is a phase in learning that we are more consciously aware of and can control. We can regulate what happens to information that reaches this temporary stage.

We are capable of several kinds of processing of the information in the short-term memory store. Selective attention is the act of directing attention to important sensory information (what Atkinson and Shiffrin called the "sensory buffer") for more processing. We organize or rearrange information in the short-term memory store to solve a problem, consider possible alternatives, or to make a prediction of what might happen next. Rehearsal is the act of repeating the information in the short-term memory store. Rehearsal aids learning both by keeping information in the temporary short-term memory store for longer, and by building up a strong memory to help with retrieval later on.

Features of the Short-Term Memory Store

The short-term memory store has a limited capacity. When people are asked to try to remember too much information, some information is lost by displacement, the loss of older information as newer information is added. The short-term memory store is like a small bookshelf with the space to hold maybe a dozen books. As too many books are added, some will start to fall off.

An early test of short-term memory was devised by a schoolteacher named John Jacobs with the intent of measuring intelligence (1887). This "digit span test" requires the participant to follow a string of digits and recall them, and as the name implies, the number of digits increases in time. You can test yourself using the table in Figure 7.6. The task is to read the digits in a row, hide them, and then write them down in the same order as you read them. How far can you go before you start experiencing difficulties? What does it feel like to experience an overload of information and try to recall it? Odds are you have experienced this kind of information overload before. While information in short-term memory can fade, information can also be bumped or overridden by other information.

FIGURE 7.6   Digit span self-test

• 312	Read a number, then recall it on a scratch sheet of paper. At what point does the length get too difficult to overcome?
• 8409	
• 71661	
• 671396	
• 2718459	
• 92373729	
• 541710378	
• 1353964620	
• 33680765785	
• 868794129665	

Source: Adapted from Peterson, L., & Peterson, M. J. (1959, p. 193).

A measure of short-term memory is usually included on professional tests of intelligence today. The Wechsler Scales of Intelligence include a basic digit span test as well as a "reversed" digit span test, where the test taker has to recall the digits in reverse order. A particularly difficult version of the digit span test is to hear a string of mixed letters and numbers and to have to recall the numbers and letters separately and in order. However, "intelligence" as a construct is viewed today as a much broader range of abilities and skills than just how many items one can retain over a short time.

Exactly how large short-term memory is for similar kinds of items like numbers was described by George Miller (1956) in a review of the relevant literature. It appears to be seven, plus or minus two items—or five to nine—for a normally healthy adult. While this seems fairly limiting, we can often go farther by finding ways to "group" information based on a visual pattern, rhyme, or by meaning. For example, if one of the rows in the table in Figure 7.6 included your personal phone number, then your ability to remember that row might be quite high, despite its length; or, if the numbers were simply sequential (1 2 3 4 5), a pattern you are very familiar with. Grouping information by pattern or meaning is called chunking, and is a technique we use to work around the short-term memory limit. Memory experts often use a chunking technique to remember unusually long sequences of numbers or other information. Incidentally, without any patterns at all, the true capacity of the short-term memory store might be closer to four (Cowan, 2005).

While a visual pattern can help us to retain a sequence of similar items more readily (e.g., 100100100100), often people use what they already know about a situation or domain to work around the short-term memory limit. The amount of knowledge someone acquires over the course of their lifetime is hard to estimate, and might always be more than we think. This is particularly true for domains in which we have reached some level of mastery. Someone who has closely followed a sports team for years will have an uncanny ability broadly to consider and think about different issues affecting the team's play, in no small part because of the deep reservoir of knowledge the person can draw from. To be clear, it is not generally expected that an expert in an area has a larger-than-normal short-term memory capacity, but that he or she has the prerequisite body of knowledge that allows for grouping of larger batches of knowledge.

The information in short-term memory also has a limited duration. Without continually revisiting the information, the longest the material will be available in short-term memory is about thirty seconds (Atkinson & Shiffrin, 1971). Under optimal laboratory conditions with absolutely no outside visual or auditory distractions whatsoever, forty-five seconds is possible. This is why researchers who want to examine long-term memory but not short-term memory will, after a study session, have participants complete a secondary diversion task that takes about half a minute to complete. This secondary task wipes out recency effect for the studied material.

The exception to this limited duration stems from the potential for conscious control. This stage of the memory system is unique in that we can choose to think continuously about and practice information in short-term memory. This ability to replay or rehearse information for as long as desired is unique to short-term memory.

Causes of Information Loss in Short-Term Memory

In sensory memory, information that isn't accessed is seen as lost or decayed. For information in short-term memory, however, there are more options, hypothetically. First, decay can still occur. Having conjured up an image of where I remember leaving my car keys, if I stop thinking about it, the image should fade automatically over time.

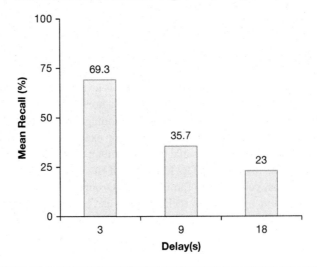

FIGURE 7.7   Averaged results for Experiment 2 from Peterson and Peterson (1959). Recall rate drops with more time spent counting backward between learning and testing.

Source: Adapted from Wickens, D. D. (1970).

Second, information in working memory can be interfered with by other information, particularly if within the same sensory modality. When different, related information share a sensory modality, they can conflict with each other. The classic demonstration of this is from a set of researchers (Brown, 1958; Peterson and Peterson, 1959) who devised this technique for showing interference at about the same time. Peterson and Peterson (1959) asked participants to memorize units of three random letters of the alphabet. Before the testing, they had to count backward from a three-digit number by threes aloud. The longer participants spent counting backward, the fewer random letter units they could recall (see Fig. 7.7). Essentially, information that has been held in short-term memory only a little while is forgotten in less than a minute.

This finding will seem unsurprising to just about anyone who has thought about something briefly and then, after being interrupted, tries to recall what it was. Additionally, that information from a sensory modality can conflict with information from the same sensory modality seems intuitive, particularly considering the problems we have with multitasking when using overlapping sensory activities, such as texting and driving.

What was less expected is the ability for the meaning of information to provoke interference as well. Wickens (1970) found evidence that the interference in short-term memory could be based on the meaning of the information being retained. Using an adapted version of the Peterson and Peterson (1959) technique, he asked participants to memorize a list of words with a similar theme or semantic category (e.g., all words about vegetables, say, or vehicles). After a distraction activity, they were asked to write down as many words as they could recall from that list in a free recall task. Wickens then repeated this procedure two more times for new words, but from the same theme as the first list. Recall dropped significantly across the three lists. He termed this effect proactive inhibition.

Studying information from the same general topic—not an identical list—produced interference. Considering only the word lists themselves, each list of words to memorize represented a new and separate trial, so no interference across lists should occur. From

FIGURE 7.8   Repeatedly studying words from the same category produced lower recall over trials, but recall rates recovered somewhat when the category changed (Wickens, 1970).

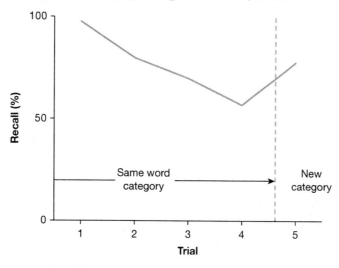

Source: Adapted from Salamé, P., & Baddeley, A. (1982).

Note: Hypothetical values; are approximates.

the perspective of the participant, each list of words is still partially activated in the mind when the next list is presented. The brain doesn't necessarily stop processing information simply because we have shifted our awareness away from it. So, the preceding information from the first and second lists begins to drag on the person's ability to distinguish and remember new words from older words within the same semantic category.

On the fifth trial, Wickens presented another list of words, but those words were from a new category. That is, the topic of the word list for Trial 5 would be different from that in the prior four trials. As shown in the graph, suddenly recall performance rebounded to levels similar to the first list (see Fig. 7.8). He termed this effect a release from proactive inhibition.

One way to explain this result is that material that is similar in nature will likely share similar cues for accessing that information, so remembering "all the words were vegetables" isn't specific enough and will include words that weren't on the list. When we switch to a new topic, the mental hints and connections we make to that topic will be less likely to overlap with what we just studied.

What are the implications of this for study? Most likely, this implies that taking breaks from studying one kind of material is necessary now and then. The brain needs time to process and mentally distinguish between lots of new information on a topic. The break can involve switching to another, unrelated area, so moving from one class to another after a while helps the memory system to organize a lot of similar information.

Baddeley's "Working Memory" Model

To review, the information in our short-term memory store seems to have a fixed amount of material that it can hold. We can consciously select the information from our sensory buffer to transfer into short-term memory, where we can organize and rehearse it. The information won't stay for very long unless we continue to rehearse the material.

Information in STM can decay from a lack of awareness, or be interfered with by other related information.

Looking over the discoveries about the nature of short-term memory, Baddeley and Hitch (1974) proposed a multicomponent theory to bring them together. Their theory of working memory describes the structure of the short-term memory store and explains the processes that interact with it. Baddeley proposed that what had been investigated as short-term memory was, in fact, several smaller systems that hold information and interact in order to allow us to manipulate information as part of our conscious thinking efforts. He used dual tasks to discover what combinations of activities caused selective interference between them. In this way, he was able to learn more specifically what each kind of process he was studying was doing.

According to working memory theory, short-term memory store is not a passive storage area, but an active area for conscious thought, like the desktop or workbench. Information from both sensory memory and long-term memory is brought together for combination and transformation to solve problems, simulate situations, and make predictions. What was novel about Baddeley's suggestion was that short-term memory was not just a single storage space, but an area for work produced by several interacting systems.

Verbal Information

Baddeley proposed that one of the client systems in working memory was the phonological loop, his term for the part of the memory system that was dedicated to storing and replaying language information, primarily phonemes. Phonemes are the specific sounds we make for the words we use, such as *ah*, *oh*, and *eh*, ("bat," "boat," and "get"). The phonological loop can hold the sounds of speech for a little while, helping us to process what we read and the language we hear as well as the speech we make. It can be used to actively rehearse or practice information. As long as rehearsal continues, then the material can stay in the phonological loop indefinitely. You might have experienced hearing your voice internally as you read, or as you think about things you need to accomplish on a given day. This nearly automatic embrace of language codes in short-term memory has been studied extensively, as we will see below.

The existence of the phonological loop was based on a variety of findings about short-term memory and how it handles language. One way to study the nature of a memory store is to try to selectively interfere with how it normally functions. This is done by asking participants to complete a normal memory task, such as studying a list of words to recall, while exposing them to some other set of stimuli that they are asked to ignore (a dual-task study). This might be music, or an overheard conversation, or perhaps words in a foreign language. The goal of this approach is to find out what kinds of stimuli interfere with the learning task. The nature of the material that causes performance to suffer says something about the nature of short-term memory itself.

Early on, researchers found that short-term memory was extremely accommodating to verbal information. Whether read or heard, the short-term memory stage seemed to automatically register speech sounds. It doesn't matter whether the information was heard, spoken, read silently, or observed by reading someone's lips (Shulman, 1971). Researchers have found that instrumental music was somewhat disruptive, but noise is not (Salamé & Baddeley, 1982). The material that interferes most with short-term memory tasks is speech, even if that speech is not pertinent to the task at hand. This effect is known as the irrelevant speech effect. In fact, the speech can be in a language that the person does not know (see Fig. 7.9).

FIGURE 7.9   Averaged results of Experiment 2 from Salamé and Baddeley (1982). The presence of words that are irrelevant to the task increases errors in recall.

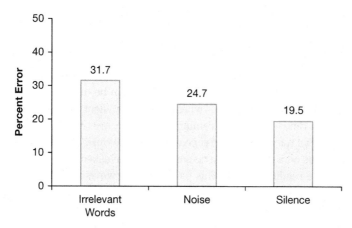

This is why people lose focus so easily when working on a thoughtful task and others are speaking nearby or a television is blaring the news. Short-term memory appears to be primed for encoding language sounds and is easily disrupted by speech that we might just as soon ignore. Combined with the limited capacity of short-term memory, you can see why people often prefer to study and work in relatively quiet spaces, or at least ones where they can control the level of disruption themselves.

Naturally, researchers have found they have to be very careful about the kind of instructions they give to participants when they need to cue the end of study time and the beginning of the recall period. If someone wanted to study short-term memory, giving verbal instructions such as "Please write down what you remember now" not only enters short-term memory, but it can also displace other information that is there.

Conrad (1964) found when asking people to recall strings of letters that the mistakes they made were usually based on the sound of the letter—so T instead of D—but they were never based on the look of the letter, like Q for O. Rehearsing strings of items that are phonetically similar (e.g., P, E, G) also decreases recall performance relative to other items, but it doesn't seem to occur for items that are visually similar (e.g., O, Q, D). The effect of phonetically similar items causing trouble with recall is referred to as phonological-similarity effect. Baddeley found that long sequences that sounded entirely alike (e.g., CGBVT instead of KHXWQ) produced great difficulty. This difficulty extended to words that sounded alike as well, and likewise did not relate to the similarity of the meaning of the words on the list. Here are some examples to read and repeat back, without looking (Kintsch & Buschke, 1969):

- pen day few cow pit bar hot sup (control)

- high great big long tall broad large wide (semantic-similarity)

- man mad mat map can cat cap cad (rhyming-pattern test)

Often the rhyming set of words is not only more difficult but also produces more errors.

Another limitation is that a list of longer words is more difficult to remember than the same size group of shorter words—the word length effect (Baddeley, 1992). The relationship is linear. As the lengths of words get longer, the likelihood of those words being recalled drops. Words that can be spoken more rapidly are more likely to be recalled. Chunking can't explain this difference, since the number of units should be the same. Remembering longer words means more syllables have to be rehearsed. It's possible that the longer length of some words means that there is more time-based decay when recalling them (Cowan et al., 1992); but not everyone agrees (Nairne, 2002).

Researchers have found that short-term memory can be disrupted internally, as well. Simply by repeating a word or phrase—whether aloud or silently—people find they have a much more difficult time focusing and retaining what they are trying to concentrate on. For example, a participant may be asked to repeatedly say the word "the" out loud while memorizing a list of words on a page. Or participants might be asked to count "one, two, three" to themselves while reading essays. This technique, known as articulatory suppression, effectively reduces people's ability to process what they are focusing on (Jurgens, 2002; Page & Norris, 1998). I encourage you to try it now on what you are reading in this book! Odds are, it will force you to have to reread the material because of a lack of comprehension.

Taken together, the discovery of the irrelevant speech effect, articulatory suppression, and similarity-based interference led researchers to hypothesize that short-term memory relied heavily on phonetic speech codes. Additionally, researchers began to suspect that short-term memory for verbal information is rehearsed in a physical manner, subvocally, silently. As we try to remember material, we exercise subvocal muscles to inwardly rehearse, an act called subvocal rehearsal. This would explain why phonetically similar items would become harder to retain. The muscle movements were too similar for them to stand out, and mistakes would be made or information lost. This would also explain why forcing someone to say pointless words would interfere with subvocalization (Baddeley, Thomson, & Buchanan, 1975).

Baddeley proposed that the phonological loop has several uses. We need it to keep our place when reading something difficult or solving math problems. It acts as a consciously controlled gateway to long-term memory. We use it for learning new words. For developing readers, Service (1992) found the best predictor for English language skills for children over two years of age was a test that required hearing fake non-words and repeating them back. The storage part of the phonological loop appears to be ready by about four years of age (Hitch et al., 1983; Hulme & Tordoff, 1989). PET scan evidence indicates that subvocal rehearsal involves the front and temporal lobes of the left hemisphere, including Broca's area (Paulesu, Frith, & Frackowiak, 1993; Salmon et al., 1996).

Spatial Memory

Baddeley proposed a second client process he called the visuospatial sketchpad. This subsystem involves processing and manipulating visual information, including imagery as well as spatial coordinates. It is used during navigation tasks, such as gathering information about landmarks and distances from a map. This includes generating a view of a scene and some objects in various positions within it as one might do while listening to someone describe an event or while reading a story. Imagining a scene with your eyes closed is a matter of using the visuospatial sketchpad. For example, trying to decide if a particular piece of furniture will fit through the front door and how it might have to be held to make it pass will require the visuospatial sketchpad. Playing video games will also make use of spatial memory and thinking.

FIGURE 7.10 Sample stimuli from Shepard and Metzler (1971)

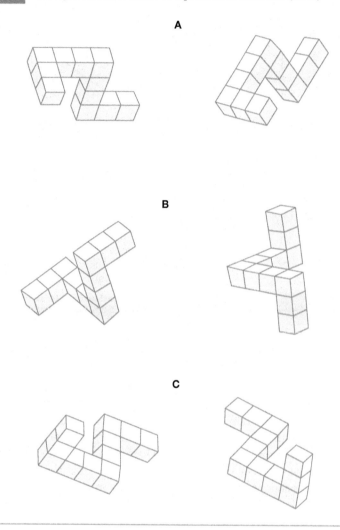

A

B

C

Shepard and Metzler (1971), in a classic study, examined our ability to mentally simulate objects and manipulate them by rotating them. They presented participants with drawings of formations of blocks and asked participants to evaluate whether each drawn block formation was the same as a paired block formation shown on the page, except that it was rotated (see Fig. 7.10).

They found the length of time needed to evaluate the pairs of items that were indeed rotations of the same formation increased as the calculated amount of rotation in degrees between the formations increased (see Fig. 7.11). That is, people took longer to evaluate the objects that were drawn at a 180-degree rotation from themselves in comparison to, say, objects that were drawn at 50-degree rotations from themselves. It appears that much of mental imagery simulates the workings of actual, real objects, even though the objects being rotated are only imagined. The visuospatial sketchpad appears to be used to simulate spatial environments.

FIGURE 7.11   As the implied angle of rotation between block patterns of the same shape increased, so did the time to mentally calculate a correct answer (Shepard & Metzler, 1971).

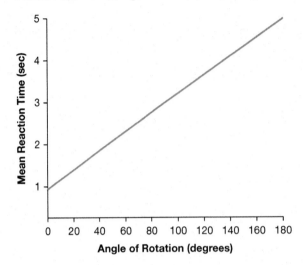

Essentially, processing of imagery appears to be analog in nature, or similar to what we experience in daily life.

Like the phonological loop, the visualspatial sketchpad has a limited capacity (Luck & Vogel, 1997). As a result, people find that diagramming and making doodles often help to relieve the burden on visualspatial thinking. Also like the phonological loop, some of the evidence for it comes from tasks that evaluate for interference (Logie, Zucco, & Baddeley, 1990). In another classic study of mental imagery, Brooks (1968) asked participants to imagine the shapes of capital letters. Then, they were asked to imagine themselves situated at one corner-edge of the letter and move in a particular direction. As they reached any corners of this imagined letter, they were to indicate the turn they would need to make in order to continue. For example, someone imagining themselves walking along the top of the edge of a capital letter F from left to right would need to make a right turn at the first edge, and then a right turn again before making a left turn (see Fig. 7.12).

Brooks evaluated interference by allowing participants to respond to the direction of the turn they made by either pointing to a card ("Yes" or "No," a spatial task) or orally providing their answer. Brooks found that requiring participants to point to their answers slowed their performance and produced more errors. Essentially, asking participants to complete two visual tasks at the same time impacts performance.

This is the basis of much of the warnings from cognitive psychologists that people should not text and drive. As Brooks (1968) demonstrated, texting and driving are both spatial tasks, and they rely on the same client process, the visuospatial sketch in working memory, which causes problems such as momentary inattentive blindness that can be deadly while driving.

While visual memory is an important part of the working memory system, there is not as much research as there is with verbal memory, for a few reasons. There isn't a set of standardized stimuli like letters and words for researchers to use as visual stimuli. Plus, naming an object puts information into the phonological loop, and Western

FIGURE 7.12   Sample diagram of Brooks's (1968) imagined stimuli

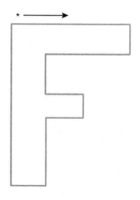

Source: Adapted from Baddeley, A. D., & Longman, D. J. A. (1978).

subjects are known for labeling all kinds of objects including ambiguous ones relatively quickly. At that point, articulatory suppression has to be used to stop the phonological loop (Lupyan, 2008).

Researchers have found that visual and spatial tasks tend to produce neural activity in the occipital lobe and are lateralized differently in the hemispheres (Farah, 1989). Generating mental imagery can rely on the posterior of the left hemisphere, while rotation of mental images depends on the posterior of the right hemisphere.

Episodic Buffer

The third client component to Baddeley's working memory model is the most recently proposed and the least researched. The **episodic buffer** bridges working memory with long-term memory and acts as a temporary storage for holding information from long-term memory for playback, such as personal events from the past. It can connect to and include information from the phonological loop and visuospatial sketchpad as well, so information can be mixed and combined here. Information that we have already learned and are merely recalling is not as likely to experience interference. Like the other client processes, the episodic buffer is expected to be of limited capacity.

Central Executive

The server system, the **central executive**, does not store information but acts as the mediator between the client subsystems. It applies attention where it is needed, and is necessary for reasoning, developing solutions to a problem, comprehending, making corrections, suppressing information that is irrelevant, and coordinating information across the three client subsystems. Like a business CEO, it decides what information can be ignored and what information needs to be pursued. It is the part of thinking that is involved in evaluating whether a strategy isn't working and needs to be replaced by another.

Evidence for the central executive has been developed through studies of interference. Since the central executive is involved in planning and reasoning, the success of a secondary, unrelated activity that keeps someone from being able to plan ahead would show evidence for a central executive unit in working memory. In one study, chess experts were asked to engage in a number of interference tasks such as articulatory suppression and having to generate random numbers (Robbins et al., 1996). Chess is typically seen as an activity that requires a fair amount of strategizing and planning. The ability of the experts to play chess was hampered, not by interference with the phonological loop, but by the random number generation.

It is believed that central executive functioning relies most on the frontal lobes of the brain, since they are what are most activated, in both hemispheres during central executive tasks (D'Esposito et al., 1995).

Conscious Learning

Baddeley's working memory model proposes that the short-term memory store includes a range of interacting systems and processes. The central executive is at least somewhat under our conscious control. What do we know about the conscious act of rehearsal? Are there successful strategies that we can adopt when we want to learn something deeply?

One way to see the importance of the issue of self-control over learning is that students with a history of strong academic performance tend to engage in learning behaviors that are different from students who have performed weakly academically. People who don't seem to have a lot of tools at their disposal for studying get stuck fairly quickly. Perhaps you can remember a former version of yourself that had difficulties studying before you were able to reach the level where you are today.

Weaker learners may have no varying strategies at all in how they approach material (Zimmerman, 1990; Zimmerman & Martinez-Pons, 1988). That is, their basic approach will not change from one course to the next or from one kind of activity to another. The approach they typically use is solely one of repetition (Karpicke, Butler, & Roediger, 2009), which is considered to be a very shallow method of learning something, prone to easy forgetfulness and interference. If there are multiple strategies, they are viewed as being of equal quality. All are equally appropriate, which means that weak learners may not distinguish between when each strategy is more appropriate than others. Finally, it's normal to be overconfident in what we think we have learned (as we will see later in this chapter). However, weak learners don't check to see if they are overconfident, and they lack the strategies to adapt if they find out they are.

In the remainder of this section of the chapter, we will look at research on five topics that relate to actively controlling our learning. For each, you will find strategies you can use to enhance your study. First, we will look at the issue of amount of time studied, or "rehearsal time," for improving how much we learn. Then we will consider what research says about how often we should try to study, the frequency of rehearsal. We then will explore how self-testing has been shown to help with learning, as a way of practicing remembering, essentially. Our fourth focus area is on the strategies we can choose to mentally rehearse material. Finally, we will finish by examining a theory of self-regulation in learning as a way to review and interrelate the separate areas of research on active study.

Rehearsal Time

When studying, I have to consider how much time will I need to expend on this, and do I know whether or not I am done yet? The amount of time we should spend studying is often a flash point for conflict between teachers (of any kind) and their students. One assumption is the more study time we put into actively learning, the more we will learn—Ebbinghaus's total time hypothesis.

While the amount of time invested in studying is likely to be related to the amount retained, it's not clear that this is the only factor or constraint. Some people find they can remember material from some domains better than others, and the total time hypothesis side-steps any issues of how we should study as well, including deciding when we have studied enough.

Metacognitive researchers have found one of the first judgments people make when deciding to focus their attention on something to be learned is an estimate of how easy or difficult the material will be to learn, an ease-of-learning or EOL judgment (Jacob & Nelson, 1990; Nelson & Jacob, 1988). This is usually a momentary reflection prior to starting to study, as the student looks over the material and tries to "size up" the difficulty of the material. This EOL judgment does affect how a person studies that material. Participants who have rated material as more challenging by making a judgment of difficulty before studying will spend more time on the material they see as more troublesome.

So, we appear to quickly evaluate the difficulty of the material prior to deciding how much time and energy to put into the task. The next question will come during study: Have I studied enough? (Jacob & Nelson, 1990; Nelson & Dunlosky, 1991). The estimation of whether we have learned the material well enough, a judgment-of-learning or JOL, needs to be accurate in order for people to stop when it's appropriate. Presumably, people use their JOLs to control their learning and to monitor their progress. Having an inaccurate JOL that leads us to being overconfident could be disastrous at exam time. Having overestimated the amount learned can lead to an *illusion of knowing*, a term meaning that the learner feels that he or she has mastered the material but, in reality, has not.

So, what is known about how people use their JOLs when studying, and are they accurate? Can the accuracy of JOLs be improved?

Leonesio and Nelson (1990) found a 0.3 correlation between JOLs and recall performance—a positive correlation, but a fairly modest one. Lichtenstein, Fischhoff, and Philips (1982) found people to be overconfident in their JOLs, overall. The best learners have the most accurate JOLs (Thiede, 1999). Given an entire test of items, people have a tendency to be overconfident (that is, to have higher JOLs than later performance would expect) by about 30 percent. Typically, JOL accuracy for any one item is better than the overall trend.

One factor that has been found to affect the accuracy of JOLs is the timing of a JOL: whether it is made immediately after study, or after a short delay (Nelson & Dunlosky, 1991). Research has found the delayed-JOL technique to reduce overconfidence. Essentially, the student studies, and before deciding whether to quit, waits for a short period of time, hides the information, and then makes a JOL. The belief is that delayed JOLs are more effective because the JOL is tapping into the material from long-term memory after a short delay, instead of from short-term memory for an immediate JOL. Usually if it's worth studying, the student wants the information to be held in long-term memory, so assessing its presence in short-term memory is not an effective indicator of whether that has occurred. A short delay or break helps make sure the JOL is accessing the material in long-term memory instead.

Repetition of Rehearsal

While it's helpful to know that we can improve our estimates of our learning, it's worth considering how often we should sit down to study in the first place. Does the frequency of practice and study help? Generally, learning is strengthened by the amount of time material is repeatedly studied (Bjork, 1970). Although, repetition doesn't always improve learning. For example, if someone doesn't pay attention to the material during numerous exposures, then details are frequently lost (Nickerson & Adams, 1979). It doesn't help if rote or maintenance rehearsal is used for learning. Participants who have been asked to repeat a word numerous times find they retain less, start to find the repeated word nonsensical, and are slower to make decisions about the word than if they were asked to repeat it only a few times (for a review, see Greene, 1987).

If repetition generally helps learning, how should the frequency of repetition be scheduled? Are fewer, longer sessions better or worse than shorter, more frequent sessions? This question is often framed as a matter of massed practice, or studying a lot in one session, versus spaced practice, or studying in shorter sessions that are spread out over time. The extreme form of massed practice is known informally as "cramming."

Research has explored both of the approaches. When doing this kind of work, researchers compare not just the performance rates of different study patterns but the amount of time the different approaches require as well: the ratio of performance to time spent helps to determine the best approach on balance. Called the distributed practice effect (or spaced effect), people learn most optimally—with the most improvement in the least amount of time—when they have frequent, short, study sessions.

Baddeley (the same person who developed the working memory model) and his colleges helped the British Post Office create a program of study schedules to teach postal workers a new set of postal codes that had to be typed using a physical keyboard. Four schedules were created and were the primary independent variable: two 2-hour sessions each day (the most intensive schedule), one 2-hour session each day or two 1-hour sessions each day, and one 1-hour session a day (the least intensive). Postal workers were assigned at random to each of these conditions. Baddeley and his colleagues monitored their correct keystrokes per minute as well as how many hours the postal workers put into the class. What they found was that those who had been engaged in the least intensive schedule learned as much as those who had been enrolled in the most intensive schedule. However, they did so in about 30 percent less time (see Fig. 7.13)! Additionally, they retained the skills better than did the more intensively scheduled workers when retested several months later (Baddeley & Longman, 1978).

FIGURE 7.13   Shorter practice times increased the speed of learning (Baddeley & Longman, 1978).

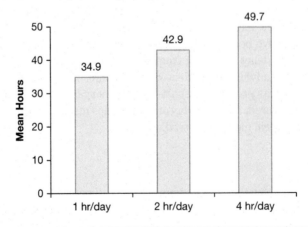

Source: Adapted from Craik, F. I., & Tulving, E. (1975, p. 268).

Why is distributing the practice sessions better? There are a number of possible explanations. First, having repeated practice sessions means that at the beginning of each practice, the learner has to remember where he or she left off last. In a way, repeated sessions require the learner to review. The shorter sessions might also lead to less proactive interference, since the material is absorbed in smaller chunks. An operant conditioning explanation would note the more frequent practice sessions as countering the postreinforcement pauses that come with a fixed interval schedule. Instead of studying for a particular class once a week, studying for a little bit each day means a steadier rate of behavior.

There is a downside to distributed practice. While each session can be shorter, the practices are spread over a greater amount of time. Sometimes, such as the week prior to final exams, we don't have the luxury of spreading out our study time. In Baddeley's postal worker experiment described above, the postal workers in the least intensive schedule were the least happy with the schedule to which they had been assigned. While it took them only fifty-five hours on average to complete the course, and the most intensive took an average of eighty hours, the fifty-five hours meant fifty-five sessions over eleven weeks of training. In contrast, most intensive group was done much earlier: at eighty hours, they finished in about four weeks.

Why does distributed practice work better than massed? It might be due to habituation. With repeated exposure to the same stimulus, we start to pay less attention to it, something Hintzman and Block (1973) found. So, repetitions aren't processed as strongly as the first (Zechmeister & Shaughnessy, 1980). It could be a conscious process. If someone believes that he or she has mastered the material, then they may consciously give it less effort. When participants are asked to rehearse words aloud, they are less likely to repeat a word aloud the second time they encounter it (Rundus, 1971). Even how dilated someone's pupils are is related to whether visual stimuli are massed or spaced (Magliero, 1983). If visual information on a slide is shown repeatedly without any delay, eye dilation shrinks, indicating less attention. If visual information is shown after a delay, eye dilation grows.

Another possibility is that distributed practice allows people to encode the information differently each time, an encoding-variability explanation (Estes, 1955). The idea here is that each time the information is encountered, the person generates a different memory from encountering it, so, essentially, there are multiple versions or copies of that information present in memory to refer to. Having multiple copies of the information then makes finding any one copy of it easier, once retrieval is necessary (Hintzman, 1988; Landauer, 1975).

Probably spacing out practice has several benefits, rather than just one or two, since most accounts haven't successfully explained all of the related research (Benjamin & Tullis, 2010).

Strategies During Rehearsal

So far, findings indicate that more study time is usually better, and we use metacognitive judgments to decide how difficult the material will be and whether we feel we have studied enough. Accuracy is an important factor in these judgments. Practicing retrieval, whether by summarizing the material or testing oneself, is known to enhance learning. But what about the act of study itself? What is the best way to rehearse the material?

A number of successful strategies are reliant on using a semantic or meaning-based approach to the material to be learned, and we will explore these strategies first.

Afterward we'll consider some additional strategies that are not based on semantic processing but use other tricks to help make the material more meaningful.

The power of semantic-based processing, that is, studying material for its meaning, was proposed originally by Craik and Lockhart (1972). The authors suggested that there was more than one form of rehearsal and that they were not all created equal. To test this, Craik and Tulving (1975) asked participants to make some judgments about the words in a list. The independent variable in this study was the judgments the participants had to make. It involved three prompts: evaluating a word for whether it was capitalized (a visual judgment), evaluating a word for whether it rhymed with another word (a phonetic judgment), and evaluating a word for whether it successfully completed a sentence with a missing word (a semantic judgment). In each case, they gave a Yes or No answer to the prompt. Then, the participants were given a surprise recall test. As shown in Figure 7.14, phonetic processing an item outperformed visually processing it; but semantic processing a word made it much more likely to be recalled. Note that this affect worked whether the word was an acceptable fit for the sentence or not. Processing the material for meaning provided a benefit even if the word did not correctly fit the sentence. Semantic-based processing provided an overall benefit even when an item did not make semantic sense.

Craik and Tulving (1975) referred to the benefit from semantic processing as deep processing, implying that the act of rehearsing a word by its meaning enhanced the learning process. Visually processing a word was a form of shallow processing. As we will discuss further later in this text, much of the information in our long-term memory is semantic in nature, so processing material deeply means thinking about it with more elaborate consideration and engaging more prior knowledge. These terms are general concepts that infer this approach to learning and do not themselves represent exact forms of thinking, per se. We don't have quantitative ways for distinguishing the two forms of processing.

According to their levels of processing theory, Craik and Lockhart (1972) suggested that deep processing was the result of elaborative rehearsal, a form of rehearsal that involved adding or using existing knowledge to enhance what was being maintained in short-term memory. This from of rehearsal was in direct contrast to maintenance rehearsal, or rehearsal that simply involves repeating the material.

FIGURE 7.14   Processing for the meaning of a word improved recognition for the word over rhyming or upper/lowercase tasks (Craik & Tulving, 1975).

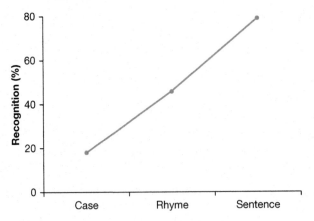

Note: Hypothetical values; are approximates.

Researchers began to pursue the idea that rehearsal could be improved by how we thought about the material to be learned. This is usually done by presenting participants with material to remember, often lists of words, and asking some of them to study the list in a particular way (e.g., "Imagine how useful each item would be if you were stranded on an island") while the others study them as they normally would or in a shallow manner (e.g., "Count the number of vowels in each item"). After completing a task meant to cause displacement of material from short-term memory, the participants would be asked to recall as many words as possible; and the results between the groups would be compared.

One strategy that provides a learning boost is considering how each word applies to oneself, the self-reference effect, over simply repeating them (Rogers, Kuiper, & Kirker, 1977). This works even for the words that do not seem directly relevant to us. Why does this strategy enhance learning through the act of connecting each word to the one topic in the world that you know the most about: yourself? This is more likely to embed the information more deeply into your existing base of knowledge, providing more connections for ways to try to remember the words later. One advice from this finding is that asking questions like "What do I think of this?" "How does this relate to me?" and "Didn't something like this happen to Aunt Martha?" seems to enhance learning.

A related strategy involves thinking of how a particular object would help with survival on an island or when lost in the desert. Even if there are no immediate applications to surviving in the wild, survival processing appears to encourage us to think of the functions of what we are thinking about, and that boosts learning as well (Nairne & Pandeirada, 2010; Nairne, Thompson, & Pandeirada, 2007).

Like the self-reference effect, the generation effect seems to rely on prior knowledge, too. The generation effect is the learning benefit that comes from making up our own cue words for each item, rather than using someone else's cue words (MacLeod, Pottruff, Forrin, & Masson, 2012; McCabe, 2015). In a cue-target word association task, people have a higher recall if they get to pick the cue words they use themselves. You may have experienced this if you have ever tried to study from someone else's notes rather than your own. It's not terrible, but it's not like using your own.

Some techniques involve adding a structure to the material, essentially arranging it. Giving material some sort of organization involves assigning an overarching meaning to the information, whether by a visual pattern, rhyming, or the semantic information. The benefits for learning may stem from the act of generating an organization for some material, a kind of elaborative rehearsal. It can also stem from the cues that will be present among the learned items. Groups of words will provide hints to each other since they have been organized by some similar feature, and there will be hints across the groupings based on some presumed contrast. For example, given a set of words to study, partitioning them into words that seem related (nouns and verbs, or foods and cars and toys) will create both reminders within each group for retrieval later and contrasts that can help.

What specific kinds of organizing are there? Chunking, as a method for overcoming the basic capacity problem of short-term memory, applies here to describe grouping based on some similarity, whether semantic or sensory patterns, such as rhyming or visual patterns (Chase & Ericsson, 1982). A related strategy, the hierarchy technique, involves arranging objects into series of classes. While this may sound like chunking, this kind of organization involves explicitly separating items by some feature, whether creating a table, listing concepts, or making outlines such as concept maps.

Another way of remembering specific items is to focus on how each item is different from the others, a technique known as distinctiveness, also known as the

von Restorff effect (Restorff, 1933; Wallace, 1965). This strategy is based on the finding that when given a list of words, people show a higher recall for words that are different from the rest of the words in some way.

All of the organizing strategies so far are generally most useful when there is some pattern of similarity that can be used to group or cluster related information. Sometimes a pattern of similarity is simply not apparent, though. Randomly generated passwords, phone numbers, postal codes, and names of parts of human anatomy may all lack a kind of coherent structure to rely on. In these cases, other techniques rely on "artificial" forms of organization, or imposed structure that isn't really present in the original information but can act as a reminder for recall later. These nonsemantic strategies are generally referred to as **mnemonics** (pronounced *ni-mon-icks*).

One famous method for remembering objects is to imagine a familiar space, like a room, or a house, or a town, and imagine placing items in different locations (McCabe, 2015). This approach, called the **method of loci** (or location), adds spatial information that is not necessarily a part of the objects themselves but is added in order to create a series of hints and cues for recall.

Another approach, the **first-letter technique**, involves spelling a word with the first letter of each object that needs to be remembered, like an acronym, such as HOMES (for the names of the Great Lakes, or OCEAN for the Big Five personality factors). The first letters might be used to create a full sentence. Instead of a word or sentence, the items can be linked together in a story, the **narrative technique**.

The **keyword method** involves connecting the list of objects to an already learned series or sequence (Bellezza, 1996). For example, the sequence of one-two-three-four and so on can have the set of objects tied to each. Each number in the sequence is the cue for the object. An example of this would be one-SHOE, two-FLOUR, three-CEREAL, and so on.

Forming Memories

Over the preceding chapters, we have looked at four approaches to learning: behavioral change, social context, motivation and affect, and cognitive awareness. Underneath all of these theories are the neurological structures that support learning. At some point, what we learn is stored and can become available for retrieval. What we have learned becomes "memories," which are typically thought of as information that we have learned that is momentarily outside of conscious awareness.

It may be surprising to learn that we do not know where memories that are not simple reflexes, like concepts and knowledge, are stored in the brain. We have not been able to observe the cells that are involved when a child learns the difference between kinds of volcanoes, or a college student grasps differentials in calculus class. We may never be able to. Possibly, the information is distributed throughout the brain. The concept for "photogenesis," for example, might be a network of neurons throughout the brain that coordinate in order to store the concept (Lashley, 1950). This is why someone can experience damage to a specific part of the cerebral cortex and still function well overall. Usually, people do not sustain a contusion to the brain and suddenly lose everything they know about chemistry, for example.

Having said that, there is some evidence that parts of the brain are key for some kinds of knowledge, if not for specific concepts themselves. There is an individual who struggled to name fruits and vegetables after a brain injury, but nothing else (Hart,

Berndt, & Caramazza, 1985). Others have lost the ability to name furniture, or current celebrities, or familiar people (Lucchelli, Mugga, & Spinnier, 1997; Miceli et al., 2000; Yamadori & Albert, 1973) while retaining all other knowledge.

The problem of observing a memory is harder than it initially appears. A "memory" involves a lot of bits of information, including sensations, motivations and emotions, associated behaviors, and other knowledge that makes sense of the information or past event. Neuroscientists try to examine the process of learning by studying how a group of neurons are changed after an experience. They try to do this by trying to alter the learning process without affecting how the memory might be used, since the goal is to study learning and avoid altering performance.

Consolidation

Most memory researchers believe that engaging in a learning experience produces "memory traces" within the brain. These memory traces are pathways in the brain that involve parts of the experience that will be, as a whole, what we would refer to as the "memory." A learning experience is believed to produce both memory traces that are short-term and traces that are long-term. The short-term memory traces decay very quickly and tend to be easy to disrupt, most likely due to the active nature of the learning process. Baddeley's model of working memory and other models can be seen as a way to try to conceptually capture this process. If a short-term memory trace is disrupted, perhaps by a blow to the head or distraction by another activity, the information is not stored. Long-term memory traces on the other hand, which tend to decay much more slowly, are not as vulnerable to disruption. A problem with retrieving the information is more likely to be a temporary inability to access the information.

The difference between the two kinds of traces is viewed as a matter of memory consolidation (Müller & Pilzecker, 1900). Over time, a memory trace becomes more "consolidated" and more resistant to disruption as a result. This phenomenon is known as consolidation theory, and is largely the norm. Of what we experience, some amount of the information is stored for the long term, and that long-term information becomes more stable over time. (One exception is the act of retrieval, which can alter the long-term memory, as we will explore below.)

To study how we form memories biologically, neuroscientists can employ behavioral tests to encourage learning and then attempt to manipulate brain functioning (Rudy, 2013). Behavioral tests can involve inhibitory avoidance conditioning, by giving a rat a shock when it moves to one side of a cage. It is then removed from the cage. When it is returned to the cage, if it avoids the side it was shocked on, then learning is believed to have occurred. Another approach is Pavlovian fear conditioning. A sound is played while the rat is in the cage, and a shock is delivered. The rat will usually freeze. If the rat freezes the next time a sound is played, then the rat is said to have learned. Another approach that doesn't involve shock is the water-escape task (Morris, 1984). A rat is allowed to swim in a pool of water. Eventually it will find a hidden platform that it can walk on underneath the surface. Typically, each time the rat is put back into the pool, it will find the platform more quickly, showing learning.

Neurological Research

Given these methods for encouraging learning, how are specific chemical processes or brain regions explored for their role in forming the memory?

One option is to damage a portion of the brain with the intent to see whether the rodent can still show a memory of the learning event when returned to the cage or pool. Stereotaxic surgery involves inserting an electrode or needle into a small area of the rodent's brain. An electric current or a chemical can be delivered so that the neurons of that part of the brain are damaged.

As a technique, stereotaxic surgery has a known problem that chemical solutions tend not to be precise enough. An entire area can be damaged, including nearby ones. Genetic engineering involves much more precise changes by altering the DNA of a fertilized egg (which is then transferred into an animal for birth) so that particular genes are altered. Those particular genes will be ones known to be responsible for how much of a particular chemical process involved in forming memories are produced. The offspring will now have a mutation that will mean a difference in how some chemical is genetically expressed. This approach has become more sophisticated over time, such that a researcher can suppress the activity of a particular gene for just one area of the brain for a particular period of development.

CHAPTER SUMMARY

The cognitive approach to learning focuses on how we can consciously learn through focused attention and thoughts. Short-term memory (STM) is the name for the temporary memory store that is consciously available to us but limited in how much it can hold. We can rehearse (mentally repeat) information in STM as long as we want, but ordinarily information can exit STM rather quickly. Information in STM can fade through decay or interference with other material.

The most popular model for the conscious control we have over the STM store is Baddeley's working memory model. He proposed that several systems act as clients to a server system, which allows for some multitasking with cognitive problems. These client systems are the phonological loop, which primarily processes phonemic information; the visual-spatial sketchpad, which primarily processes spatial and visual information; and the episodic buffer, which allows for rehearsal of past events from long-term memory. The central executive acts as the server to these client systems and coordinates the information across them.

Since we have conscious control over what goes on in STM, we can study those techniques that are known to help learning. We looked at three general strategies: rehearsal time, repetition, and rehearsal strategies. More rehearsal time is generally better, the total time hypothesis. However, people alter their study time based on metacognitive judgments about how easy they perceive the material will be to learn (ease-of-learning) and, afterward, whether or not the material has been successfully learned (judgment-of-learning). Judgments of learning are more accurate when they are made after a short delay. Repetition, or repeated practice, appears to be most effective when spaced out over time. And finally, rehearsal strategies tend to be more effective when they involve elaborative rehearsal, or focus on the meaning of the material, rather than rote repetition (maintenance rehearsal), according to levels-of-processing theory.

The neurobiological aspect of encoding for storage is called consolidation, the term for a memory trace becoming more stable and longer lasting. Neuroscientists study learning by attempting to disrupt the consolidation process using stereotaxic surgery and genetic engineering.

In the next section, Part II, we will begin looking at different forms of memory, focusing more on the "storage" and "retrieval" aspects of learning and memory.

REVIEW QUESTIONS

1. Let's say you have a fairly technical presentation to make at your job to a lot of people who need to know more about what you'll be talking about, and yet they are fairly unfamiliar with the basics. How should you go about preparing the presentation knowing about the limits of short-term memory?

2. Baddeley's model of working memory has four key components to it. Pretend each component was a person. How would you describe each working memory "personality"?

3. Have you ever experienced proactive interference while studying? How can you combat it?

4. A friend of yours is finding college to be much more difficult than he expected. He knows you are in a class on "learning and memory" and wants to know what you have learned that might help him. What do you suggest?

5. What is meant by "consolidation"? How do neuroscientists research how memories are formed?

KEY TERMS

FURTHER RESOURCES

1. Weblink: World Memory Championships:
   - http://www.worldmemorychampionships.com

2. Weblink: World memory champion describes what it takes to be a memory expert:
   - https://www.yahoo.com/news/blogs/sideshow/u-s—memory-champion-nelson-dellis-shares-his-secrets-for-strengthening-your-mind-194920556.html

3. Weblink: The first American world memory champion explains how to memorize anything using his "major system" technique:
   - https://www.youtube.com/watch?v=mI96Ph-yHcA

4. Weblink: The connection between memory and sleep (National Science Foundation, video):
   - https://www.youtube.com/watch?v=ObuaXhtKbVY

REFERENCES

Atkinson, R. C., & Shiffrin, R. M. (1971). *The control processes of short-term memory.* Citeseer. Retrieved from http://citeseerx.ist.psu.edu/viewdoc/download?doi=10.1.1.398.2237&rep=rep1&type=pdf

Baddeley, A. (1992). Working memory. *Science, 255*(5044), 556–559. https://doi.org/10.1126/science.1736359

Baddeley, A. D., & Hitch, G. (1974). Working memory. *Psychology of Learning and Motivation, 8,* 47–89.

Baddeley, A. D., & Longman, D. J. A. (1978). The influence of length and frequency of training session on the rate of learning to type. *Ergonomics, 21*(8), 627–635.

Baddeley, A. D., Thomson, N., & Buchanan, M. (1975). Word length and the structure of short-term memory. *Journal of Verbal Learning and Verbal Behavior, 14*(6), 575–589.

Bellezza, F. (1996). Mnemonic methods to enhance storage and retrieval. *Memory,* 345–380.

Benjamin, A. S., & Tullis, J. (2010). What makes distributed practice effective? *Cognitive Psychology, 61*(3), 228–247. https://doi.org/10.1016/j.cogpsych.2010.05.004

Bjork, R. A. (1970). Repetition and rehearsal mechanisms in models for short-term memory. *Models of Human Memory,* 307–330.

Brooks, L. R. (1968). Spatial and verbal components of the act of recall. *Canadian Journal of Psychology/Revue Canadienne de Psychologie, 22*(5), 349–368. https://doi.org/10.1037/h0082775

Brown, J. (1958). Some tests of the decay theory of immediate memory. *Quarterly Journal of Experimental Psychology, 10*(1), 12–21.

Chase, W. G., & Ericsson, K. A. (1982). Skill and working memory. *Psychology of Learning and Motivation, 16,* 1–58.

Conrad, R. (1964). Acoustic confusions in immediate memory. *British Journal of Psychology, 55*(1), 75–84.

Cowan, N. (2005). Working memory capacity limits in a theoretical context. In *Human learning and memory: Advances in theory and application. The 4th Tsukuba international conference on memory* (pp. 155–175). Retrieved from https://books.google.com/books?hl=en&lr=&id=GMB5AgAAQBAJ&oi=fnd&pg=PA155&dq=cowan+2005+working+memory+capacity&ots=qsUetm__eF&sig=QHxN1_c7t_OwbF6RnHv9cay6XLM

Cowan, N., Day, L., Saults, J. S., Keller, T. A., Johnson, T., & Flores, L. (1992). The role of verbal output time in the effects of word length on immediate memory. *Journal of Memory and Language, 31*(1), 1–17.

Craik, F. I. M., & Lockhart, R. S. (1972). Levels of processing: A framework for memory research. *Journal of Verbal Learning and Verbal Behavior, 11*(6), 671–684.

Craik, F. I. M., & Tulving, E. (1975). Depth of processing and the retention of words in episodic memory. *Journal of Experimental Psychology: General, 104*(3), 268–294. https://doi.org/10.1037/0096-3445.104.3.268

Davelaar, E. J., Goshen-Gottstein, Y., Ashkenazi, A., Haarmann, H. J., & Usher, M. (2005). The demise of short-term memory revisited: Empirical and computational investigations of recency effects. *Psychological Review, 112*(1), 3–42. https://doi.org/10.1037/0033-295X.112.1.3

D'Esposito, M., Detre, J. A., Alsop, D. C., Shin, R. K., Atlas, S., & Grossman, M. (1995). The neural basis of the central executive system of working memory. *Nature* (London), *378*(6554), 279–281.

Estes, W. K. (1955). Statistical theory of distributional phenomena in learning. *Psychological Review, 62*(5), 369.

Farah, M. J. (1989). The neural basis of mental imagery. *Trends in Neurosciences, 12*(10), 395–399. https://doi.org/10.1016/0166-2236(89)90079-9

Greene, R. L. (1987). Effects of maintenance rehearsal on human memory. *Psychological Bulletin, 102*(3), 403–413. https://doi.org/10.1037/0033-2909.102.3.403

Hart, J., Berndt, R. S., & Caramazza, A. (1985). Category-specific naming deficit following cerebral infarction. *Nature, 316*(6027), 439–440.

Hintzman, D. L. (1988). Judgments of frequency and recognition memory in a multiple-trace memory model. *Psychological Review, 95*(4), 528–551. https://doi.org/10.1037/0033-295X.95.4.528

Hintzman, D. L., & Block, R. A. (1973). Memory for the spacing of repetitions. *Journal of Experimental Psychology, 99*(1), 70–74. https://doi.org/10.1037/h0034761

Hitch, G. J., Halliday, M. S., Hulme, C., Voi, M. E. L., Routh, D. A., & Conway, A. (1983). Working memory in children [and Discussion]. *Philosophical Transactions of the Royal Society of London B: Biological Sciences, 302*(1110), 325–340. https://doi.org/10.1098/rstb.1983.0058

Hulme, C., & Tordoff, V. (1989). Working memory development: The effects of speech rate, word length, and acoustic similarity on serial recall. *Journal of Experimental Child Psychology, 47*(1), 72–87. https://doi.org/10.1016/0022-0965(89)90063-5

Jacob, R., & Nelson, T. O. (1990). Do different metamemory judgments tap the same underlying aspects of memory? *Journal of Experimental Psychology: Learning, Memory, and Cognition, 16*(3), 464–470. https://doi.org/10.1037/0278-7393.16.3.464

Jacobs, J. (1887). Experiments on "prehension." *Mind*, (45), 75–79.

Jurgens, U. (2002). Neural pathways underlying vocal control. *Neuroscience and Biobehavioral Reviews, 26*(2), 235–258. https://doi.org/10.1016/S0149-7634(01)00068-9

Karpicke, J. D., Butler, A. C., & Roediger, H. L., III. (2009). Metacognitive strategies in student learning: Do students practise retrieval when they study on their own? *Memory, 17*(4), 471–479. https://doi.org/10.1080/09658210802647009

Kintsch, W., & Buschke, H. (1969). Homophones and synonyms in short-term memory. *Journal of Experimental Psychology, 80*(3, Pt. 1), 403.

Landauer, T. K. (1975). Memory without organization: Properties of a model with random storage and undirected retrieval. *Cognitive Psychology, 7*(4), 495–531. https://doi.org/10.1016/0010-0285(75)90020-1

Lashley, K. S. (1950). *In search of the engram*. Retrieved from http://smash.psych.nyu.edu/courses/spring16/learnmem/papers/Lashley1950.pdf

Leonesio, R. J., & Nelson, T. O. (1990). Do different metamemory judgments tap the same underlying aspects of memory? *Journal of Experimental Psychology: Learning, Memory, and Cognition, 16*(3), 464.

Lichtenstein, S., Fischhoff, B., & Phillips, L. (1982). Calibration of probabilities: The state of the art to 1980. In D. Kahneman, P. Slovic, & A. Tverski (Eds.) *Judgement under uncertainty: Heuristics and biases*. New York, NY: Cambridge University Press.

Logie, R. H., Zucco, G. M., & Baddeley, A. D. (1990). Interference with visual short-term memory. *Acta Psychologica, 75*(1), 55–74. https://doi.org/10.1016/0001-0918(90)90066-O

Lucchelli, F., Mugga, S., & Spinnier, H. (1997). Selective proper name anomia: A case involving only contemporary celebrities. *Cognitive Neuropsychology, 14*(6), 881–900.

Luck, S. J., & Vogel, E. K. (1997). The capacity of visual working memory for features and conjunctions. *Nature, 390*(6657), 279–281. https://doi.org/10.1038/36846

Lupyan, G. (2008). From chair to "chair": A representational shift account of object labeling effects on memory. *Journal of Experimental Psychology: General, 137*(2), 348–369. https://doi.org/10.1037/0096-3445.137.2.348

Luria, A. R. (1968). *The mind of a mnemonist: A little book about a vast memory*. Cambridge, MA: Harvard University Press.

MacLeod, C. M., Pottruff, M. M., Forrin, N. D., & Masson, M. E. (2012). The next generation: The value of reminding. *Memory & Cognition, 40*(5), 693–702.

Magliero, A. (1983). Pupil dilations following pairs of identical and related to-be-remembered words. *Memory & Cognition, 11*(6), 609–615. https://doi.org/10.3758/BF03198285

McCabe, J. A. (2015). Learning the brain in Introductory Psychology: Examining the generation effect for mnemonics and examples. *Teaching of Psychology, 42*(3), 203–210.

Miceli, G., Capasso, R., Daniele, A., Esposito, T., Magarelli, M., & Tomaiuolo, F. (2000). Selective deficit for people's names following left temporal damage: An impairment of domain-specific conceptual knowledge. *Cognitive Neuropsychology, 17*(6), 489–516.

Miller, G. A. (1956). The magical number seven, plus or minus two: Some limits on our capacity for processing information. *Psychological Review, 63*(2), 81–97. https://doi.org/10.1037/h0043158

Morris, R. (1984). Developments of a water-maze procedure for studying spatial learning in the rat. *Journal of Neuroscience Methods, 11*(1), 47–60. https://doi.org/10.1016/0165-0270(84)90007-4

Müller, G. E., & Pilzecker, A. (1900). *Experimentelle beiträge zur lehre vom gedächtniss* (Vol. 1). JA Barth. Retrieved from https://books.google.com/books?hl=en&lr=&id=5Rd CAQAAMAAJ&oi=fnd&pg=PA15&dq=(Mueller+%26+P ilzecker,+1900)&ots=09PL1jheUM&sig=LsMw8g9NQFE QkQyOYbU9qwxARG4

Nairne, J. S. (2002). Remembering over the short-term: The case against the standard model. *Annual Review of Psychology, 53*(1), 53–81.

Nairne, J. S., & Pandeirada, J. N. (2010). Adaptive memory: Ancestral priorities and the mnemonic value of survival processing. *Cognitive Psychology, 61*(1), 1–22.

Nairne, J. S., Thompson, S. R., & Pandeirada, J. N. S. (2007). Adaptive memory: Survival processing enhances retention. *Journal of Experimental Psychology: Learning, Memory, and Cognition, 33*(2), 263–273. https://doi.org/10.1037/0278-7393.33.2.263

Nelson, T. O., & Dunlosky, J. (1991). When people's judgments of learning (JOLs) are extremely accurate at predicting subsequent recall: The "delayed-JOL effect." *Psychological Science, 2*(4), 267–270. https://doi.org/10.1111/j.1467-9280.1991.tb00147.x

Nelson, T. O., & Jacob, R. (1988). Allocation of self-paced study time and the "labor-in-vain effect." *Journal of Experimental Psychology: Learning, Memory, and Cognition, 14*(4), 676–686. https://doi.org/10.1037/0278-7393.14.4.676

Nickerson, R. S., & Adams, M. J. (1979). Long-term memory for a common object. *Cognitive Psychology, 11*(3), 287–307. https://doi.org/10.1016/0010-0285(79)90013-6

Page, M. P. A., & Norris, D. (1998). The primacy model: A new model of immediate serial recall. *Psychological Review, 105*(4), 761–781. https://doi.org/10.1037/0033-295X.105.4.761-781

Paulesu, E., Frith, C. D., & Frackowiak, R. S. (1993). The neural correlates of the verbal component of working memory. *Nature; London, 362*(6418), 342–345.

Peterson, L., & Peterson, M. J. (1959). Short-term retention of individual verbal items. *Journal of Experimental Psychology, 58*(3), 193.

Restorff, H. von. (1933). Ueber die Wirkung von Bereichsbildungen im Spurenfeld. Analyse von Vorgängen im Spurenfeld. I. Von W. Köhler und H. v. Restorff. *Psychologische Forschung.* Retrieved from http://psycnet.apa.org/psycinfo/1934-01527-001

Robbins, T. W., Anderson, E. J., Barker, D. R., Bradley, A. C., Fearnyhough, C., Henson, R., . . . Baddeley, A. D. (1996). Working memory in chess. *Memory & Cognition, 24*(1), 83–93. https://doi.org/10.3758/BF03197274

Rogers, T. B., Kuiper, N. A., & Kirker, W. S. (1977). Self-reference and the encoding of personal information. *Journal of Personality and Social Psychology, 35*(9), 677.

Rudy, J. W. (2013). *The neurobiology of learning and memory* (2nd ed.). Sunderland, MA: Sinauer Associates, Inc.

Rundus, D. (1971). Analysis of rehearsal processes in free recall. *Journal of Experimental Psychology, 89*(1), 63–77. https://doi.org/10.1037/h0031185

Salamé, P., & Baddeley, A. (1982). Disruption of short-term memory by unattended speech: Implications for the structure of working memory. *Journal of Verbal Learning and Verbal Behavior, 21*(2), 150–164. https://doi.org/10.1016/S0022-5371(82)90521-7

Salmon, E., Van der Linden, M., Collette, F., Delfiore, G., Maquet, P., Degueldre, C., . . . Franck, G. (1996). Regional brain activity during working memory tasks. *Brain, 119*(5), 1617–1625. https://doi.org/10.1093/brain/119.5.1617

Service, E. (1992). Phonology, working memory, and foreign-language learning. *The Quarterly Journal of Experimental Psychology Section A, 45*(1), 21–50. https://doi.org/10.1080/14640749208401314

Shallice, T., & Warrington, E. K. (1970). Independent functioning of verbal memory stores: A neuropsychological study. *Quarterly Journal of Experimental Psychology, 22*(2), 261–273. https://doi.org/10.1080/00335557043000203

Shepard, R. N., & Metzler, J. (1971). Mental rotation of three-dimensional objects. *Science, 171*, 701–703.

Shulman, H. G. (1971). Similarity effects in short-term memory. *Psychological Bulletin, 75*(6), 399–415. https://doi.org/10.1037/h0031257

Thiede, K. W. (1999). The importance of monitoring and self-regulation during multitrial learning. *Psychonomic Bulletin & Review, 6*(4), 662–667.

Wallace, W. P. (1965). Review of the historical, empirical, and theoretical status of the von Restorff phenomenon. *Psychological Bulletin, 63*(6), 410–424. https://doi.org/10.1037/h0022001

Watkins, M. J. (1989). Willful and nonwillful determinants of memory. In H. L. Roediger, III, & F. I. M. Craik (Eds.), *Varieties of memory and consciousness: Essays in honour of Endel Tulving* (pp. 59–71). Hillsdale, NJ: Erlbaum.

Wickens, D. D. (1970). Encoding categories of words: An empirical approach to meaning. *Psychological Review, 77*(1), 1–15. https://doi.org/10.1037/h0028569

Wilding, J. M., & Valentine, E. R. (1997). *Superior memory.* Hove, East Sussex, UK: Psychology Press. Retrieved from http://www.netlibrary.com/urlapi.asp?action=summary&v=1&bookid=10206

Yamadori, A., & Albert, M. L. (1973). Word category aphasia. *Cortex, 9*(1), 112–125. https://doi.org/10.1016/S0010-9452(73)80020-6

Zechmeister, E. B., & Shaughnessy, J. J. (1980). When you know that you know and when you think that you know but you don't. *Bulletin of the Psychonomic Society, 15*(1), 41–44. https://doi.org/10.3758/BF03329756

Zimmerman, B. J. (1990). Self-regulated learning and academic achievement: An overview. *Educational Psychologist, 25*(1), 3–17. https://doi.org/10.1207/s15326985ep2501_2

Zimmerman, B. J., & Martinez-Pons, M. (1988). Construct validation of a strategy model of student self-regulated learning. *Journal of Educational Psychology, 80*(3), 284–290. https://doi.org/10.1037/0022-0663.80.3.284

Memory

©iStock.com/LUHUANFENG

Retrieval

Chapter Outline

Learning Objectives

1. Compare "retrieval" with "remembering" and "knowing."

2. Explain the phenomenon called "feeling-of-knowing" or FOK.

3. Describe the role of cues in retrieval.

4. Compare prospective memory to retrospective memory, and explain how prospective memory relies on retrieval cues.

5. Explain the biological mechanisms behind retrieval.

6. Explain how retrieving a memory can enhance the retention of that memory.

7. Summarize how situational cues can encourage retrieval of associated memories.

Overview

We don't just use memories as a guide to the past; we also use them to remember what to do in the future. Errors in retrieval can be relatively minor or merely embarrassing; consider the former Governor of Texas, Rick Perry, who announced during a live debate that as president, he wanted to eliminate three federal government agencies and forgot one of them when he went to list them off (CNBC, and The Associated Press, 2016). In other cases, errors in retrieval can be fatal. About 37 infants die in cars each year because of extreme heat temperatures ("Heat Stroke | KidsandCars.org," n.d.), and often those are due to inattention. Infant car seats face the rear of the car to avoid airbag deployment in the front of vehicles, so they are not visible to the driver. Parents driving to work, distracted by other obligations and their own thoughts, can completely unintentionally forget to drop the child off at day care while the infant sleeps, then park at work, and head in for the day ("Fatal Distraction," 2009). The emotional devastation for the parent is terrible. Recently, safety experts have begun recommending the use of reminders to help parents remember that a child is in the back, and companies have started selling alert systems, too ("Walmart Selling Car Seat That Alerts Parents When a Child Is Left Behind," 2015). In this chapter, we look at how retrieval works and begin the process of looking at when it doesn't, a topic we conclude in Chapter 11 on Forgetting.

To briefly review where we have been so far, we have seen that learning can be approached and explained from a purely behavioral perspective, a social perspective, an affective and motivational perspective, and a cognitive perspective. When it comes to retrieval, these different perspectives still apply and, in some cases, interact with each other to affect our ability to retrieve memories. The serial position curve (from Chapter 7) and the experiences of some people with brain injuries have convinced most memory researchers that there tends to be a short-term memory store and a long-term memory store. The memories that are stored for the long-term tend to be distributed somewhat throughout the brain, often connecting different areas. Any one memory may be spread throughout different areas of the brain, and these fragments of the whole are often referred to as traces. When we attempt to retrieve a memory, we are relying on our ability to find these memory traces and create a whole memory that we can use in short-term memory to solve a problem or complete a task.

Some basic distinctions are needed as we begin. In memory research, the words "retrieval," "remembering," and "knowing," do not mean the same thing. Retrieval means the general act of recalling or recognizing something from memory. Remembering, however, specifically applies to situations when we retrieve personal memories of events. Knowing refers to retrieval of information that we have learned and may or may not be retrieved with memories of events. This chapter solely focuses on general issues of memory retrieval. We will delve into remembering and knowing in the next two chapters.

Retrieving Memories

When it is a conscious effort, retrieval is an experience that does not use our senses as a primary source. Retrieval is clearly an important part of learning and memory; encoding and storing information without being able to retrieve it is pointless (Roediger, 2000; Roediger & Guynn, 1996). In some cases, retrieval can occur without encoding: People can remember an event that didn't happen to them, or perhaps they merge one or more events into a new memory that isn't all that accurate.

Retrieval is the standard we use to judge learning (Rajaram & Barber, 2008), and it tends to occur as a background activity as we retrieve information over the course of a day. In many learning and memory studies, retrieval is studied separately from encoding and storing, but generally all three work together in a more or less fluid process.

The Experience of Retrieval

Let's consider the process of retrieval from the perspective of conscious awareness, the time it takes, and how we don't always retrieve what we have stored.

Retrieval is thought to occur in both explicit (conscious and controllable) and implicit (automatic, subliminal) modes. While a clearly controlled effort can be used to retrieve information, much information (e.g., how to walk, drive, form words and sentences) is retrieved relatively effortlessly. The classic levels of processing effect, discussed in Chapter 7, don't appear when implicit retrieval is tested instead of explicit retrieval (e.g., Graf & Mandler, 1984; Jacoby & Dallas, 1981). Implicit retrieval may operate under a different set of rules or conditions than explicit retrieval.

Retrieval takes time. It is not instantaneous, and this can be a problem in a variety of situations. For example, lecturers are infamous for not waiting long enough for a group of students to respond to a question. Some studies have found teachers wait barely one second before rephrasing or repeating a question (Rowe, 1987). As you may guess, one second is typically not enough time to form a response to a spontaneous question, especially if having to respond in front of peers. If retrieval (of, say, a motor skill) needs to be rapid, then more automatic retrieval has to be trained for.

Does retrieval precisely tell us how much one has stored? That is, is there a perfect one-to-one relationship between what someone can retrieve and what he or she has, such that we can tell exactly from what can be retrieved how much was stored? Unfortunately, no. How much information is accessible to us, that which we can retrieve, is not the same as how much we have available for us to retrieve. As anyone who has recently studied for a test knows, some well-learned material will not be retrievable at the moment of a test, but it often is immediately afterward, as we saw with Rick Perry's well-publicized gaffe. What is available for us to retrieve is much larger than what we can access at any one time. Tulving and Pearlstone (1966) found that people could remember more words from a list when a category for the word list was provided, rather than not. The information was stored, but not necessarily accessible.

Given that retrieval takes time, it makes sense that we have mental shortcuts that help us quickly determine if deciding whether some bit of information is available for retrieval.

Feeling of Knowing

Since controlled retrieval is not immediate but takes time, and there is too much information in the world to simply know everything, it makes sense that people would develop the ability to make a quick assessment of what they might know before making the effort to retrieve some information. Attempting to make a quick estimate of whether we would be able to recognize something without conducting retrieval is called a feeling of knowing judgment, abbreviated to FOK (Dunlosky & Metcalfe, 2009). It is metacognitive in nature, since the individual is asking him- or herself about the state of his or her knowledge.

Hart (1965) pioneered this idea and the research technique behind it. He would ask people to answer a general-knowledge question, such as "Who was the fifth U.S. President?" If a person could answer correctly, then that was the end of the trial. If the person answered the question incorrectly, then he would ask the person if they thought they could pick out or recognize the right answer on a multiple-choice question. The answer to this second question is the "feeling of knowing" measurement. After this FOK judgment was given, usually a percent of certainty from 0 percent up to 100 percent, Hart would provide the individual with an actual multiple-choice question to test how accurate their feeling of knowing judgment was. Hart found that people were generally accurate in what they could recognize, even though they couldn't retrieve the information originally. Essentially, the feeling of knowing paradigm is to ask someone to recall information, then judge whether they could recognize it, and then attempt the recognition. Hence, this research technique is called the RJR method.

Reder (1987) found evidence that FOK judgments are automatic. When subjects were explicitly asked to make FOK judgments while playing a trivia game, the game wasn't any slower than a control group that was not explicitly asked to make FOK judgments. Given that we have the metacognitive ability to rapidly assess what we might recognize, what do we use FOK judgments for? Reder (1988) sees feeling of knowing judgments as a strategy search: the result of the judgment helps us decide whether to look up the information or to continue thinking about the answer. Another view of FOK judgments is that we use them to decide whether continuing to think about the answer is worth the effort at all (Kolers & Palef, 1976). This approach sees FOK judgments as more about retrieval termination. If there is no chance we would know the answer, then why bother searching at all? Nelson, Gerler, and Narens (1984) provide some evidence that FOKs are used to end searching by correlating the strength of the FOKs with the amount of time people spent thinking of an answer to a question. The time taken was positively correlated with FOK scores, meaning that people tend to invest time in the questions to which they think they may know the answer.

The ability to make accurate FOK judgments appears to reside in the frontal lobes of the brain. Janowsky, Shimamura, and Squire (1989) found FOK judgments were not as accurate from patients with Korsakoff syndrome (brain damage because of excessive alcohol consumption) when the damage had included the frontal lobes. Patients with frontal lobe lesions that were in the right medial prefrontal cortex have been found to have less accurate FOK judgments (Schnyer et al., 2004).

Theories of Feeling of Knowing

What are the psychological processes believed to underlie making a FOK judgment? One early theory was that when we make a FOK judgment, we attempt to retrieve the memory directly and assess the "strength" of the memory (Hart, 1967). This direct-access explanation has not withstood the test of time, in part because FOK judgments are made more quickly than attempting to retrieve the original memory (Reder, 1987, 1988), an odd finding if FOK judgments were based on the same process as directly accessing a memory. General familiarity with a topic seems to be a better explanation for FOK, so researchers have moved to looking at FOK as a more indirect way of accessing the presence or strength a memory.

Two other hypotheses have been proposed to explain how FOK judgments indirectly access information accurately while being faster than accessing the memory directly. According to the cue familiarity hypothesis, people use a shortcut or heuristic to get a quick sense of whether the memory might be available. Say I am asked, "What was the name of the lead actress in *Forrest Gump?*" and I can't immediately recall it. I should first consider whether I am familiar with the domain of the question in general. Have I seen this film? Do I remember much about the film? Have I seen it recently enough to maybe be able to recall it? The answers to these questions would be the basis of the FOK judgment. I know I have seen the film a few times, once a month or so ago, so my FOK judgment might be fairly high. In other words, the cue familiarity hypothesis suggests that we consider whether we would be likely to have the answer given what we generally know.

This hypothesis has some evidence behind it. When people have a high FOK judgment (so they believe they can retrieve the answer), and they turn out to be wrong, the wrong answer tends to come from the correct domain (Krinsky & Nelson, 1985). So, answering the question with a similar but incorrect actress despite my high FOK judgment would indicate that I was using familiarity with the domain as my indicator for whether I might have the memory. This explanation has been further supported by Reder (1987, 1988), who has found that being primed for a particular domain by being exposed to the material from that domain tends to increase FOK judgments. Researchers have manipulated how familiar a cue is to participants using repeated exposures, and find the FOK judgments tend to correlate with how familiar the participants are with the cues (Metcalfe, Schwartz, & Joaquim, 1993).

Another intriguing possibility is the target accessibility hypothesis, which claims that instead of directly accessing the memory, we attempt to retrieve a few details about the memory and then take into account how easy it was to recall them. This hypothesis suggests that instead of domain familiarity, I might consider whether I can remember anything about the lead actress in *Forrest Gump*, such as other movies or shows she may have appeared in, things her character said or did, her appearance, or comments I've heard others say about her. Do I feel like I know a lot about her life or career? If so, then I would be more likely to make a high FOK judgment since I can retrieve a lot of pertinent details quickly. The extra information we retrieve tells us something about how accessible the information is (Koriat, 1993, 1995). The more relevant details we can recall, the higher the FOK judgment.

So which is correct? It's not clear at this time. It could be both. One study found people seemed to start with cue familiarity and, given a positive feeling of familiarity, will move to target accessibility as a follow-up strategy (Koriat & Levy-Sadot, 2001). Basically, using accessibility happens only with a strong sense of familiarity. FOK judgments may involve a sequence of strategies that we invoke before deciding to make a full attempt at retrieval.

While FOK judgments may help us decide whether to start or continue a retrieval search (for an answer we could recognize), we haven't examined the core process of attempting to retrieve the information itself using prompts or "cues," which we turn to now.

Retrieval Cues

While FOK judgments refer to the process of deciding whether we might recognize an answer, the process of attempting to retrieve a memory is generally viewed as a matter of using retrieval cues, prompts or stimuli, to help recall a memory. Retrieval cues are any kind of information we use to activate a memory trace to see if we can access a memory. Usually, retrieving memories does not retrieve the memory alone. A lot of other information will be recovered with it, including emotions, general stereotypes, beliefs, and expectations (Lindsay, 2008).

Trying to retrieve a memory can create new memories as well. For example, trying to remember someone's name for an embarrassingly long time during an unexpected conversation in a restaurant might become its own memory. Recalling an event for a friend can create a memory of "telling the story" that might be more memorable than the event itself (E. J. Marsh & Tversky, 2004). (There is a biological explanation for this phenomenon later in this chapter.)

Retrieval cues can be external to us or internal in nature; we often rely on external cues for recall and recognition tasks in educational environments on tests and other assessments. Internal cues can be those produced by our own mental strategies, as we saw in the prior chapter, using organizational techniques and mnemonics, for example. Recall performance is improved when the recall is prompted with some retrieval cues (Tulving & Pearlstone, 1966). Your own notes from class act as a kind of retrieval cue for what went on in class.

Having more cues rather than fewer also helps recall. Hamilton and Rajaram (2003) asked participants to memorize lists of words and measured their recall as the dependent variable. For the independent variable, they manipulated the presence and number of retrieval cues. As shown in Figure 8.1, performance was highest for the recognition task, which means the answer was explicitly cued by being present in the prompt. Performance was worst for free recall (no cues whatsoever). But providing the category plus an initial letter (two cues) increased recall over providing the category only. As with playing a trivia game, more hints about the answer tend to be better than fewer hints.

Restated in terms that memory researchers use, the presence of retrieval cues alters the accessibility of the memory. It is interesting to consider what this relationship between retrieval cues and retrieval performance means in real-world situations, such as coaching or teaching. Of course, when someone is being introduced to new material and is just beginning to practice it, many cues are probably helpful. But later, the instructor must consider the amount and quality of the hints in the retrieval cues to gauge whether a satisfactory level of learning has been reached. Multiple-choice exams provide more external retrieval cues, and

FIGURE 8.1   Retrieval is higher with more cues (Hamilton & Rajaram, 2003).

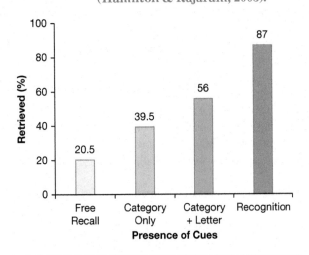

Source: Adapted from Hamilton, M., & Rajaram, S. (2003).

hence are easier for memory retrieval than essay exams. Are there ever too many retrieval cues, or can there be too few? Using essay exams in some situations, such as when there is a lot of "breadth" to the material and hence a lot of detail, may be too difficult. Perhaps the highest level of external retrieval cues is an open-book test. Ironically, open-book tests can produce poor performances. Students take a long time sifting through all the material and get easily distracted by the irrelevant information. This could be the result of both too many retrieval cues as well as a low incentive to memorize the basics in advance. Too many retrieval cues can make the memory task too easy to demonstrate learning, and they may defeat the motivation to learn. Interestingly, while trying to avoid presenting too many external retrieval cues is a teaching issue for educators and coaches, the presence of too many internal retrieval cues (from knowing a subject well) is never viewed as a problem.

Prospective Memory

The importance of retrieval cues is usually discussed in terms of retrieving events and memories from the past, or retrospective memory. But, retrieval cues and the difference between internal and external cues can be readily seen in prospective memory, the need to remember actions that we intend to take in the future, something that we do almost continuously in daily life. Often, we have to remember actions and plans that we can't execute immediately, and instead have to put off, for one reason or another, until a better time. (I tend to think of things I need to get done at home when I'm not at home.) Remembering a future action means having to store both the action as well as the time and place that the action needs to occur. An error in retrieval for prospective memory means forgetting to do the action when we were supposed to.

Prospective memory involves both the action or task itself as well as the processes that are needed to make the action. This includes the objective of the task (cleaning clothes), the behavior (unloading the washing machine and loading the dryer), and place and time (at home, this evening). Often the information in a prospective memory is small, but that doesn't make the task simple. In one study, people reported an average of 15.5 plans per week and, at the end of the week, about 25 percent of them were not completed for a variety of reasons (R. L. Marsh, Hicks, & Landau, 1998).

While nothing terrible is likely to happen from my forgetting to change over the laundry, forgetting to do some actions can be fatal (Einstein et al., 2005). This can include forgetting to drop off a sleeping infant at child care before heading to work and leaving the child in the car during the workday; forgetting to turn off the stove and starting a fire; forgetting to put down the landing gear on an airplane when descending; or forgetting to take medication (e.g., Woods et al., 2009).

Prospective memories may be self-generated and a matter of self-regulation and self-control; but some are assigned to us by others. The priority for prospective memories can vary a lot, from critical to a much lower, "someday," status. Sometimes prospective tasks can compete with each other. Some tasks are single, isolated actions like mailing a bill payment or taking out the garbage, whereas others have a host of interrelated actions that are necessary, such as preparing a presentation. Some have fixed, rigid deadlines, whereas others can be postponed or ignored. Some tasks are fairly vague (e.g., "lose weight").

Models of Prospective Memory

One model of prospective memory proposes that there are five basic stages involved in trying to remember future events (Zogg, Woods, Sauceda, Wiebe, & Simoni, 2012).

The first is forming the intent to make some action. This is deciding what task needs to be done, such as picking up prescription refills. The second stage is the retention interval, or the delay before the task can be executed (Hicks, Marsh, & Russell, 2000). During this delay, we monitor for the right opportunity to implement the task, so we look for cues (time, place, other people).

The third stage is detecting the right cues that tell us it's time to enact something we had meant to do. The available retrieval cues help to trigger the awareness that the task needs to be completed. So, we can set up cues that will help us to remember, such as alarms and to-do lists. Future tasks come in two varieties, which affect the usefulness of retrieval cues: those that are time-based, and those that are event-based (Hicks, Marsh, & Cook, 2005). Time-based prospective memories might have to be done either at a particular time, a pulse, such as "show up for class at 2:00;" or within a certain window of opportunity, a step, such as "before the store closes." Between pulses and steps, pulses are easier to remember, since they are cued by a specific time; and people can set up external retrieval cues to help them, such as phone alarms or a daily planner.

Event-based prospective memories are cued by an object, person, or event, such as "I need to ask her about the class I missed when I see her." Event-based prospective memories are usually easier to remember than time-based ones (Hicks et al., 2005), because there is an event or cue that is presented to us, and we do not have to monitor the passage of time. This is why time management experts recommend turning time-based prospective memories into event-based ones whenever possible. For example, to help remember to mail a box tomorrow, put the box by the front door and place your car keys on it. Another example would be making sure to remember to drop off an infant at child care by putting one shoe next to the child in the back seat before driving. The task of needing to drop off the child becomes an event if we step out of the car at work and realize we only have one shoe on.

In many ways, what seems to help prospective memory is more of a reliance on external rather than internal retrieval cues, particularly if the cue is time-based, since those require monitoring. People will make time-based prospective memories easier by migrating them to memory aids, like alarm clocks, other people, and other external reminders (Kim & Mayhorn, 2008).

The fourth stage Zogg and colleagues (2012) proposed was to remember what the task was once the retrieval cue had been noticed. It's one thing to remember that something needed to happen at two o'clock, and another to remember what it was. Perhaps the benefit of event-based prospective memories as external retrieval cues spans the second through the fourth stages. They require less monitoring of the passage of time; they present themselves externally to us; and they may integrate what needed to happen as part of the presented event. In the fifth and final stage, the behavior is executed.

To review the chapter so far, retrieving a memory can be performed automatically or explicitly, and the cues we use to trigger the retrieval may be internal to us or in the external environment. Because retrieving a memory takes time, we can make a quick FOK judgment to decide whether some information is accessible to us and worth mentally searching for. FOK judgments may be based on our general knowledge of the domain in question or how readily details come to mind. Some memories we need to retrieve are not past memories but future actions that we need to perform. Often the biggest challenge can be forgetting a prospective memory during the delay between forming the intent and realizing when the opportunity to perform the action has arrived.

Now let's take a look at the biological basis of retrieving memories.

The Biological Basis of Retrieving Memories

As we found at the end of our last chapter, memory traces "consolidate" over time. Essentially, they become less vulnerable to disruption as they age. This consolidation appears to be the biological mechanism behind what we refer to as a long-term memory: a memory trace that is relatively inert and inactive, until we choose to retrieve it.

This conception of storing memories for the long-term and later retrieving them is what most people think of as the complete process of learning and memory. But, things are not always as simple as they first appear. Neurobiologists have found that while time helps to consolidate a memory, the simple act of retrieving the memory can make the memory vulnerable to change. The act of retrieving a memory can make it unstable and malleable again. After retrieval, the memory appears to be consolidated again, stored for a later time. Instead of thinking of memories as something printed on a page for us to refer to later, like a recipe in a cookbook, we probably should think of memories as notes stored on a computer. The memories or notes are relatively static but, once reopened, can be edited. Let's examine the critical research that revealed this possibility.

Disrupting Long-Term Traces

It appears to be possible to disrupt the process of consolidation. Misanin, Miller, and Lewis (1968) found that delivering a shock while a rat retrieves a memory could disrupt the memory itself, causing it to be forgotten. Rats were taught to fear a shock using a standard fear-conditioning technique based on classical conditioning: the rats learned that a sound would precede the shock. The following day, the rats were tested to see if they remembered the sound, which they did. At the time of the retrieval, however, some of the rats were, without warning, given a new shock. When brought back for a second round of testing later, the rats who had experienced the shock during retrieval displayed no memory of the original fear conditioning by not responding to the sound that they had originally learned to associate with shock. The researchers saw this as evidence that it is possible to disrupt a memory during retrieval, altering it or possibly erasing it. This result seemed to conflict with the basic assumption of consolidation theory.

Lewis (1979) interpreted those findings by claiming that essentially time or consolidation don't matter, but the state of activity for a memory does (Nadel, Hupbach, Gomez, & Newman-Smith, 2012). According to his active trace theory, whether a memory is being formed (learned) or is being retrieved, it is active; and once active, it is malleable and can be altered. This view states that new information and long-term information are held in an active memory state, and information in an active state can be disrupted. Once the memory becomes inactive, then it is less vulnerable to disruption.

Active trace theory is not the only known explanation for the flexibility that comes with retrieval. Like Lewis (1979), Przybyslawski and Sara (1997) found that when a rat was required to retrieve a memory and was injected with a particular chemical (an NMDA antagonist), the rat did not show the learned behavior the following day. The injection worked for up to ninety minutes after memory retrieval, but no later. After conditioning rats with a fear, Nader, Schafe, and LeDoux (2000) used a protein synthesis inhibitor (anisomycin) following the retrieval of the fear memory; and they found it had a large impact on a memory test after a day. Essentially, half of the rats who froze at the sound of an auditory cue that they had learned preceded a shock forgot about the cue because of the injection. This was not an immediate effect. The memory was still functionally retrieved, up to four hours later; but it disappeared over a twenty-four-hour delay. Nader and colleagues (2000) concluded that the protein synthesis inhibitor caused forgetting by stopping protein from being created between neurons in the memory system.

So, the forgetting that can come with retrieval was not immediate, and was due at least in part to the role of protein for neurotransmission. Nader (2003) proposed, in what is known as **reconsolidation theory**, that retrieved memories have to be "reconsolidated," or consolidated again, and that this happens at the level of the synapses between neurons. When a memory is retrieved, the synapses involved in the memory trace become weakened. It's possible for the entire memory to be lost at this point, as the "strings" of the memory together loosen. Fortunately, this does not normally happen, because the act of retrieval triggers the proteins that will synthesize the memory trace or re-form the memory trace. Nader's reconsolidation theory implies that retrieving a memory causes a kind of amnesia at the cellular level of the existence of a memory, before it is repaired. The act of retrieval both unwinds existing connections and then attempts to solidify them, according to this theory.

What possible advantages would such a system provide? Why might retrieving memories make them unstable and pliable? One interpretation of this conflict is that "learning" and "memory" are not necessarily distinctions that the brain uses (Spear, 1973). Spear suggested the two terms are an artificial distinction we use to conduct research studies and classroom experiences. But, the brain simply treats retrieval like any other experience, including new ones: Some old information brought to attention, and new information may be available to be integrated into it (Dudai & Eisenberg, 2004). The brain essentially opens the memory for updating and revision as needed, like a file stored on a computer, rather than a printed page that is unalterable. Hence, what we call reconsolidation is simply a matter of old and new information being brought together before the memory is re-stored. The present is integrated with the past. This perspective on reconsolidation theory is known as **trace updating** (McKenzie & Eichenbaum, 2011).

An implication of reconsolidation theory and trace updating is that memories can be altered and disrupted, or intentionally made to be forgotten. This is a natural result of how the brain adapts to new information. In some situations, it can even be desirable to have memories disrupted and forgotten. It would be helpful if someone who experiences cravings for a psychoactive drug that they are addicted to could unlearn the cues and triggers that spark the craving, for example. This should lower the likelihood of relapsing into a pattern of abusive use of the drug. Perhaps someone who was experiencing posttraumatic stress disorder could erase some of the memories that were the basis of the anxiety and fear.

One research team allowed rats to learn to feed themselves cocaine. By stopping the flow of protein in the amygdala during a drug memory retrieval, the team could cause the rats to forget about the cues that related to using the cocaine (Lee, 2008; Lee, Di Ciano, Thomas, & Everitt, 2005; Lee, Milton, & Everitt, 2006). While intentional "memory erasure" is theoretically possible, drug treatments have not been developed yet to the point of being effective (Besnard, Caboche, & Laroche, 2012; Bossert, Marchant, Calu, & Shaham, 2013; Sorg, 2012).

Having a better idea of the process underlying memory retrieval, let's look at research that has found consciously using retrieval can strengthen memories and situational influences on retrieval.

Retrieval to Improve Learning

Having a better understanding of the biological basis of retrieval helps to understand how retrieval appears to improve learning. Testing seems to enhance memory. As we saw in the last chapter, distributing study time helps with learning, possibly because with each practice we are forced to remember what it is we had been studying. What if we simply practiced retrieving material as part of the study process, instead of waiting for an exam? According to Roediger and Karpicke (2006b), "testing not only measures knowledge, but also changes it, often greatly improving the retention of the tested knowledge" (p. 181). Retrieving a memory changes the accessibility of that memory (R. A. Bjork, 1975).

Many researchers have found that practicing retrieval, by itself, enhances learning (for overviews, see E. L. Bjork & Bjork, 2011; deWinsanley & Bjork, 2002). The retrieval-practice effect is the benefit of retrieval because of using retrieval as a part of practice. Broadly speaking, the neural pathway we use to retrieve information will not be identical to the pathways we use to encode and store information. Since the goal of most learning is retrieval, practicing retrieval as a part of learning would involve incorporating the end-goal of the learning process. Imagine reading about how to drive a car but not practicing the act of driving until the test. While we might not imagine that as a good idea, we tend to do exactly that when it comes to learning academic subjects. Additionally, practicing retrieval, particularly after a delay, is likely to make our estimates of learning or JOLs more accurate. Bjork and Bjork (2011) refer to this as creating "desirable difficulties" when learning.

The testing effect involves a memory boost that comes from a specific form of retrieval practice. The testing effect describes better memory performance on a recall test following a recognition test. The testing effect can be more beneficial than rereading the material, in some situations (Campbell & Mayer, 2009; Vojdanoska, Cranney, & Newell, 2010; Zaromb & Roediger, 2010). The use of self-testing as a part of study has been found to reduce overconfidence (Dunlosky & Rawson, 2012), and has been shown to lead to greater mental organization of the material on a second test of free recall questions (Zaromb & Roediger, 2010). Researchers who have studied this effect recommend self-testing as a part of the study process rather than only reviewing. Those "check yourself" self-quizzes at the end of the chapters in textbooks are apparently useful after all. Now, the advice to self-test instead of rereading does not apply if the material was too difficult to comprehend in the first place or if attention had wandered. Arguably the material was not processed at a level of attention that the self-quiz would help solidify what was learned. Presumably a self-quiz would help to make an accurate JOL, however.

Repeated Retrieval

If retrieval can improve learning, then do repeated attempts at retrieval improve learning as well? Should we quiz ourselves several times when studying?

What is retrieved in free recall tasks changes over several attempts, without any renewed attempt at study. The accessibility of memories shifts rather quickly, despite the same amount of available memories. Just attempting to recall information repeatedly, the total amount remembered tends to improve; but oddly, the exact items remembered may change with each attempt as well. Ballard (1913) called this "remembering without relearning" (see Erdelyi & Becker, 1974). Sometimes researchers refer to this phenomenon as hypermnesia.

We tend to retrieve more if we try repeatedly. Brown (1923) found with repeated attempts at retrieval, there was inter-test forgetting; that is, not every item recalled on one test would be remembered on the next. Then, on a further test, some of those items would be recovered. There is an overall improvement—the recovery of items exceeds the forgetting of them, but the set of items recalled each time fluctuates. Essentially, the repeated attempts at retrieval seem to expand memory accessibility.

FIGURE 8.2   In a replication and expansion of Brown's 1923 study, Roediger and Payne (1985) found retrieval to increase over attempts, using several methods of recall.

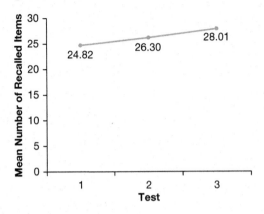

Source: Adapted from Roediger, H. L., & Payne, D. G. (1985).

In some situations, it may simply be a matter of the time permitted for retrieval (Roediger & Thorpe, 1978; see Fig. 8.2). Having one long period for recall could produce the same number of items as several shorter recall periods (Erdelyi & Becker, 1974). This may mean that it is not necessarily the multiple attempts but the overall amount of time that is given for retrieval that benefits performance. But, some have theorized that during the repeated testing, learners build more cues to the material, changing how accessible the information is, a slightly different hypothesis (Payne, 1986).

Does repeated retrieval work as a planned study technique? In fact, it may be what is behind the benefits of the distributed practice effect for study. Each study session involves retrieving information from the prior session, invoking a retrieval-practice effect through scheduling.

How does repeated retrieval fare relative to repeated study? Spitzer (1939) found two attempts at retrieval improved performance on a multiple-choice test, particularly if the first attempt came immediately after study. Possibly less forgetting could occur this way, as if what had been learned had become inoculated from forgetting. So, should we simply retest ourselves repeatedly instead of restudying? Perhaps not. Spitzer offered some fairly contemporary advice in 1939 when he suggested that while recall via tests helps with retention, students have to be provided with an opportunity to correct their ideas, and that tests should be used as tools for learning rather than simply measuring achievement.

Perhaps the most thorough attempt to clarify the use of repeated retrieval on memory performance was an experiment Roediger and Karpicke (2006a; see Fig. 8.3) performed. They provided participants with essays on science topics and asked them to recall information from them in a format that was like an essay test. The design was meant to be realistic by simulating what teachers might normally ask students to do. They assigned the participants to one of several study and test patterns: either four study sessions, or three study sessions followed by one practice test, or one study session followed by three practice tests. Each participant then took a final exam.

The best results on the final exam were when it was scheduled five minutes after studying. But, if the final was a week later, the pattern of one study session plus three practice tests beat all others by about 20 percent. Studying three times with a single

FIGURE 8.3   Incorporating at least one practice test means remembering more and forgetting less (Roediger & Karpicke, 2006a).

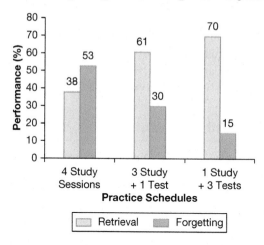

Source: Adapted from Roediger, H. L., & Karpicke, J. D. (2006).

Note: Hypothetical values; are approximates.

practice test also performed well. Essentially, incorporating at least one practice retrieval into the act of studying helps retain the material for a longer period of time, and several practice retrievals can help even more.

So, practicing retrieval helps solidify what we are learning and reduces overconfidence. Repeated retrieval helps as well. Why does practicing retrieval help memory?

Theoretical Explanations for Retrieval Benefits

Several theoretical explanations have been offered to explain why retrieval tends to improve memory for the long term. Possibly, the processes of being tested is not the same as learning, so if the goal is to pass a test, then incorporating testing as part of the learning process makes for a strong match between the activity of learning and testing (Thomas & McDaniel, 2007). This explanation is a claim that performance is enhanced when the learning situation closely resembles the situation required for performance.

Another possibility is that the initial testing creates multiple retrieval routes to access the information. McDaniel and Masson (1985) gave material to participants that had to be learned phonetically or semantically and then gave them a recall test that cued them with either phonemic information or semantic information. Half of the time, the cues matched how they had learned the information; half of the time, they did not. On a second, later test, the participants who had been tested initially using cues that didn't match how they had learned performed better, regardless of whether it was phonetically or semantically. Possibly, the act of retrieval forced by testing produces elaborations from the initial act of encoding. This principle is behind the advice educators often give to parents to encourage children to practice their math skills in a grocery store and at restaurants, for example.

A final possibility is that the effort involved in retrieval helps with learning. Recall testing is more difficult than recognition testing since it requires generation, so it should strengthen the memory better than recognition testing, which McDaniel, Roediger, and Mcdermott (2007) found. Trying to generate material after a study period by writing a summary or explaining what was learned to a roommate may be more effective for learning than a multiple-choice test.

In sum, practicing retrieval as part of learning can improve learning. This appears to occur for a variety of reasons: Retrieval during learning simulates the later retrieval during performance, makes external cues more salient, and enhances the internal organization of the information. Recalling the information is better than simply recognizing it.

This leads us to a particular issue that has been heavily researched in the retrieval literature. To what extent does the situation we are in help or hinder our ability to retrieve?

Situational Effects on Retrieval

The context itself provides cues that produce interactions between encoding and retrieval. In this section, we will examine three known contextual effects on retrieval due to the context of learning: encoding specificity theory, the match between the physical context of encoding and retrieval, transfer-appropriate processing, the match between the mental processes at encoding and at retrieval, and collaborative memory, encoding and retrieval around other people.

In most of the studies we have discussed so far, the researchers vary the encoding that takes place during the performance task, and the manner of retrieval is held constant (a standardized test, for example). Craik and Tulving's (1975) levels of processing study is a good example of this. Three types of encoding were compared to find possible differences in retrieval. This approach is beneficial for comparing different kinds of encoding, since the retrieval cues are held constant. Altering the kinds of retrieval cues, particularly to make them either congruous or incongruous with the encoding, can illuminate how accessibility to the information can be altered after information has been encoded.

Encoding Specificity Principle

The encoding specificity principle claims that retrieval is best when the context of the retrieval matches the context of encoding. This idea is contrarian to the levels-of-processing theory, which claims learning is improved simply by the way we encode information. Encoding specificity predicts an improvement when retrieving information, if the available retrieval cues match or are similar to the environment in which we learned the material. So, taking an exam in the same classroom where you have been attending class should aid your performance. Having to take it in another room might mean the loss of potential reminders that are provided by the environment in which you were exposed to the material. The match between the cues available at encoding and retrieval matters.

Thomson and Tulving (1970) demonstrated this by asking participants to study lists of words under conditions that varied for how strong a cue each target word would receive, and whether the same cue words used to study from would be present at recall. So, for one independent variable, a cue might be provided with the target word to be remembered, and the strength or quality of that word varied. The list of words might be presented without any cue words to act as a hint during recall of the target words (e.g., BLACK, by itself), or it might include cue words that were weakly associated with the target words (e.g., train-BLACK), or it might include cue words that were strongly associated with the target words (e.g., white-BLACK).

In a second independent variable, the cue words presented during encoding were not necessarily the same as the cue words presented during retrieval (a free recall test).

FIGURE 8.4 Congruency between the cue used at learning and retrieval matters more than whether the cue is a strong or weak one (Thomson & Tulving, 1970).

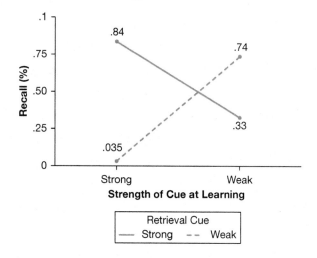

Source: Adapted from Thomson, D. M., & Tulving, E. (1970).

If a participant had learned the words with cues, there might not be any at the recall, or it could be cue words that changed in their strength. The key research question was whether the strength of the cue word mattered more than the match between the cues at encoding and retrieval.

As shown in Figure 8.4, Thomson and Tulving (1970) found that the strength of the association between the cue and target words was not as important as the match between learning and retrieval. A strong cue word wasn't as helpful if it wasn't present during encoding. Hence, the claim of the encoding specificity principle—that the match or congruence of the context of encoding and retrieval matters; and the better the match, the better the retrieval (Tulving, 1985).

But what is meant by "context"? What elements of the situation of learning act as retrieval cues later? Three aspects of the learning context are known to influence retrieval cues: the physical context, our physiological state, and mood at the time of learning.

Place-Dependent Cues

First, the physical context during encoding is itself known to provide retrieval cues, also known as **place-dependent cues**. A particularly dramatic example of this principle was conducted by Godden and Baddeley (1975; see Fig. 8.5). Participants memorized thirty-six words and were asked to free-recall them. But the contexts of the encoding and retrieval were manipulated independently of each other. One group of participants studied the list on dry land and took the test out of water, as one usually does. Another group put on scuba suits and studied the list and was tested on them completely underwater. In two other conditions, the learning and retrieval conditions didn't match. Some participants studied the list on land, but were tested underwater; and some studied the list underwater, and were tested on land. As you might guess, the participants in the matching environments recalled more information than the participants in the groups that had to alternate environments, regardless of whether it was on land or under water.

FIGURE 8.5   Retrieval was highest when the conditions of retrieval matched the conditions of learning (Godden & Baddeley, 1975).

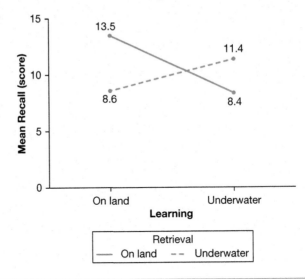

Source: Adapted from Godden, D. R., & Baddeley, A. D. (1975).

Does this principle work in classrooms as well? Smith (1979) held the room used for studying and testing constant, or changed it—and got similar results. Smith and Vela found that imagining being in the same room helped, however. If the context changes, people can rely on internal cues through imagination to help overcome some of the difference (Smith & Vela, 2001).

It should be noted that this particular effect occurs during tests of recall, but not on tests of recognition (Smith & Vela, 2001). If external cues are provided as part of the testing process, then a reliance on the environment is less necessary. So, taking a standardized test like the SAT, ACT, or GRE in a new room doesn't necessarily aid retrieval, but that should be overcome by the cues present on the test itself. When unsure, imagining the environment in which the material was initially learned might help ameliorate the lack of environmental cues.

State-Dependent Cues

Another source kind of situational retrieval cues are state-dependent cues or the physiological state of the body itself at the time of learning. This includes overall physiological arousal (feeling tired or awake) as well as the presence of drugs and alcohol in the body during learning. In several studies, participants studied lists of words 20 minutes after having smoked marijuana or tobacco that tasted like marijuana (J. E. Eich, 1980; J. E. Eich, Weingartner, Stillman, & Gillin, 1975). Retrieval was tested using both free recall tests and a recall test that presented general category names as hints. Participants were smoking either the same drug or the alternative during recall. When the physiological state was changed (tobacco-marijuana or marijuana-tobacco), performance worsened in the free recall tests. This was interpreted to mean that matching learning and retrieval conditions is important, but mostly for those situations in which there are fewer external cues, like a free recall test. Also, it's important to note that recall was best when the participants were not high from marijuana when learning or retrieving. Marijuana itself is not a memory enhancer.

Mood-Dependent Cues

Another kind of situational congruence between encoding and retrieval can be mood. People often find it easier to recall happy memories when they are feeling happy. Likewise, when feeling down, people find it easy to recall sad memories—a cyclical issue for people who are clinically depressed (Blaney, 1986). However, experimentally studying this relationship is difficult, since it involves manipulating the moods of the participants. Techniques that have been tried include hypnosis, using happy or sad music or videos, or measuring the current emotional state of participants using rating scales (not a true manipulation). Eich and Metcalfe (1989) asked participants to read target words by themselves ("cold") or generate them from cues ("hot-???") while listening to pleasant or unpleasant music. Participants recalled words in a free recall test while listening to music that matched or did not match the music during learning. Whether the moodiness of the music matched during learning and retrieval mattered only for those target words that participants had to generate during learning, not the ones that were just read. Seemingly, mood matters more if the material is self-generated than just read.

In a follow-up study, Eich, Macaulay, and Ryan (1994; see Fig. 8.6) manipulated the mood of participants while they were doing a task. The researchers then induced the same or a different mood and asked them to recall events from the task. Their findings were that people readily remembered events that matched their mood, and later on, they were better at recalling the events that matched their mood at retrieval. These results still held more for free recall tests than recognition tests.

Transfer-Appropriate Processing

So, retrieval is helped if the physical context matches the context of learning. However, transfer-appropriate processing is a view of the encoding specificity principle that reframes the issue of context as one of mental processes. Instead of seeing the match as a matter of encoding and retrieval cues, transfer-appropriate processing postulates that

FIGURE 8.6 Retrieval was highest when the emotional condition at retrieval matched the emotional condition at learning (Eich, Macaulay, & Ryan, 1994).

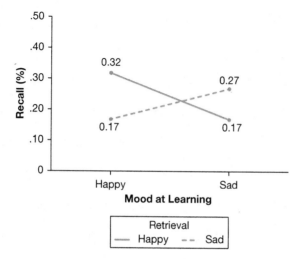

Source: Adapted from Eich, E., & Metcalfe, J. (1989).

what is important is for the cognitive processes that are engaged during testing to match those that were engaged during learning (Roediger & Blaxton, 1987; Blaxton, 1989). This explains Smith's (1979) finding that simply imagining the original context helps retrieval. It is not the congruity of the external cues per se, so much as the contiguity of the mental processes that are sparked by retrieval cues.

Whether we look at parallels in encoding and retrieval as a matter of cues or processes, this phenomenon has implications for educators and coaches. There is a responsibility for the instructor to create learning situations that evoke the kinds of thinking that will be expected in retrieval situations. This implies that an instructor should keep the context of the final performance in mind and craft learning situations that prepare the students to perform well in that context. Similarly, a student may need to take some ownership over contextual cues and physiological state in order to be optimally ready to learn and perform.

Retrieval in Groups

Until this point, all the retrieval situations we have considered focused only on the individual. Retrieval can occur in a social context and may usually do so (Weldon, 2001). In many situations, retrieval happens with others, whether other members of a study group, coworkers, or family. When it comes to retrieval, are groups better than individuals? Groups are expected to perform at higher levels than individuals alone, when making decisions, hence the saying "two heads are better than one." Is this true for memory retrieval?

Collaborative Memory

The study of groups' retrieval and how groups alter the processes of retrieval is called collaborative memory. In collaborative memory research, groups may work together by taking turns or by participating in any order they like; and the results from these collaborative groups are contrasted to nominal groups. A nominal group is not a traditional group, but rather an experimental control group. The individuals in the nominal group work alone, but their results are pooled together. The participants in a nominal group may not be aware that their results are being pooled with other participants. The use of nominal groups is to provide a control for the social interaction of the collaborative groups. Groups should recall more than individuals since two people working apart will recall more than either one alone (Vollrath, Sheppard, Hinsz, & Davis, 1989).

If collaborative groups impede performance, then the use of groups to retrieve information is viewed as a process loss, meaning that the drop in performance is due to the process of using a group (Steiner, 1972). Collaborative memory researchers have found that using groups to retrieve information can alter retrieval performance, and not always in positive ways. Overall, collaborative memory researchers have found that collaborative groups produce more answers than nominal groups, but the overall performance is not better. Collaborative groups are more overconfident and produce more wrong answers. In some cases, collaborating groups recall fewer items than the nominal groups (Basden, Basden, Thomas, & Souphasith, 1997; Weldon & Bellinger, 1997).

The disruption that comes from collaborative groups appears to be isolated to the process of retrieval. Weldon and Bellinger (1997) had participants study word lists alone and then asked them to recall the information individually or in a group. The group recall is akin to studying alone and then taking a test together. Results are scored by forming nominal groups from those who recalled alone and adding up all nonredundant right answers. Weldon and Bellinger found the average nominal group score was higher than that of any one person working alone, so any process loss wasn't due to encoding or storage processes. But, the collaborative groups performed worse than the nominal groups, by recalling fewer correct words. The drop in performance because of attempting retrieval in a collaborative group setting is referred to as collaborative inhibition.

Collaborative inhibition isn't the only kind of process loss that occurs in collaborative memory. First, a higher number of wrong answers (sometimes called "false intrusions") are introduced in collaborative memory retrieval over nominal groups as well (Basden, Reysen, & Basden, 2002). Possibly members of a collaborative group go along with errors because they don't want to state openly that someone else in the group is wrong. A desire for cohesion can dampen the group performance. Second, one study found collaborative groups were more accurate when using a simulated police interrogation than individuals acting alone, but the collaborative groups were more overconfident in their wrong answers (Stephenson, Abrams, Wagner, & Wade, 1986). Third, collaborative groups tend to be prone to the misinformation effect, spreading around incorrect information as part of conforming to the group (Schneider & Watkins, 1996). Some studies use a planted confederate in the group, who tries to spread wrong information. They find that it alters the group performance as well as recall later on—the misinformation becomes long-term (Roediger, Meade, & Bergman, 2001). Reconsolidation and trace updating theories would predict this, since the act of retrieval makes the original memories available for updating. The presence of wrong information during recall may be consolidated with the original memory.

Explanations for Collaborative Inhibition

So, what exactly causes collaborative inhibition? Explanations for collaborative inhibition come in two general forms: social explanations and cognitive explanations.

A social explanation for collaborative inhibition is that in a group retrieval setting, motivation to do well as an individual is reduced; and the group members do not coordinate well, creating a social loafing situation (Kerr & Tindale, 2004; Latané, Williams, & Harkins, 1979). Social loafing is the name for a situation in which the individual members of a group try less hard at an activity (e.g., clapping their hands or singing) than when performing alone. Evidence for this explanation includes a study by Paulus and Dzindolet (1993), who found that if the collaborative groups were informed that other groups were conducting the same task and were not doing as well as they were, then the group would relax and not work as hard.

However, the idea that reduced motivation due to the social situation doesn't explain every research finding. Weldon, Blair, and Huebsch (2000) offered rewards to improve motivation, and the collaborating groups still were not able to beat the nominal groups, although overall recall improved. Additionally, recall improves when people work alone after a group recall effort, which implies that there is a cognitive element to the disruption beyond just loafing (Finlay, Hitch, & Meudell, 2000).

Four possible cognitive explanations have been introduced. First, according to the retrieval strategy disruption hypothesis, it's possible that our own internal retrieval cues are the best for retrieval (Dahlström, Danielsson, Emilsson, & Andersson, 2011), and the retrieval cues from others are disruptive. In other words, the external retrieval cues from others may conflict with our own internal retrieval cues, as the encoding-specificity principle would suggest. One study that supports this explanation found that if participants are given lists of words that have been organized differently for each participant, collaborative inhibition rises when the participants collaborate on retrieval

(Basden et al., 1997). This primarily occurs for free recall tests, which makes sense if each person is relying on his or her own internal retrieval cues. Basden and colleagues found recall for the material increased if the participants were allowed to recall words on their own, after a group recall attempt. Words that were forgotten are suddenly remembered, indicating that the group context is the issue.

If the retrieval cues that others use are a problem, then encoding the same retrieval cues might eliminate the issue according to this hypothesis. This result has been found with paired-associate recall tasks. Collaborative inhibition doesn't occur when everyone learns the same external retrieval cues (Finlay et al., 2000).

Second, participants might choose to share less in a group by setting a very high threshold for what they will openly share, what is sometimes called "production blocking." According to the evaluation apprehension hypothesis, group members do not want to introduce mistakes, so they elect to not share as much (Diehl & Stroebe, 1991). Participants have also been found to wait to introduce ideas, so the social context is disrupting the timing of their own retrieval as each member works around the others. Ironically, while members might hold back some information to avoid making mistakes, collaborative memory groups tend to produce more errors.

Third, it could be the exposure to what other people recall strengthens the memory for the words that have been presented, while weakening the memories for the words that haven't been recalled yet. This effect, known as the part-set cueing effect, describes how people perform worse for material they haven't yet recalled when freely given some of the answers unexpectedly. Imagine being given some hints or answers on an exam. It seems like this would be helpful, but it appears to disrupt the process of retrieval by causing a strengthening of the available information at the cost of information that hasn't been retrieved yet. Reconsolidation theory would expect that the introduction of answers during retrieval would create a new learning experience and that material would become strengthened. Information that was not available for review becomes less strong in contrast.

Finally, it may be a matter of cognitive overload. Simply the act of having to coordinate retrieval with others introduces extra performance demands, so the retrieval process is more difficult. With increases to the size of the group, there is more difficulty with performing efficiently and acting cohesively as a group (Steiner, 1972). Something that most of us have experienced at one time or another is the challenge that comes from trying to contribute while in a group.

Reducing Collaborative Inhibition

Collaborative memory situations can't always be avoided; work teams are expected to make presentations together and students are sometimes asked to perform in group exams. Are there ways to reduce collaborative inhibition?

Collaborative inhibition may occur more with some tasks than others (Rajaram and Pereira-Pasarin, 2010). Recall tasks that involve recalling general knowledge tend to be more affected by collaborative inhibition than recalling events. Specific events tend to involve very specific cues, such as time and place, whereas general knowledge may involve more interconnectedness between concepts and beliefs. As a result, internal retrieval cues may be more important and more readily disrupted by collaborative inhibition with recall tests of general knowledge. But, personal memories are less affected by the group.

The number of people in the collaborative group does matter. Inhibition seems to present itself with groups of three or more; pairs, or dyads, do not show as much collaborative inhibition (Basden, Basden, & Henry, 2000; Rajaram & Pereira-Pasarin, 2010; Weldon & Bellinger, 1997).

As we saw earlier, collaborative groups perform better on cued recall tasks, such as paired-associate word lists (Weldon et al., 2000). The presence of external retrieval cues seems to help focus the group on those specific prompts. Finally, having a shared experience of encoding helps too. Collaborative groups can beat nominal groups in recall, if the collaborative members studied together initially (Andersson & Rönnberg, 1995).

Maybe a collaborative group made up of friends would show more efficiency. Friends do show less collaborative inhibition, although nominal groups still perform better (Andersson & Rönnberg, 1995). Friends benefit from having an existing communication system and may share a base of knowledge from shared past experiences. Friends may also benefit from a greater leeway to disagree with each other than strangers.

In sum, the context of retrieval and its match to the context of learning influences retrieval. Improved retrieval occurs when there is a congruity between the physical location, physiological state, and mood at encoding and retrieval. In all likelihood, it is not the specific match between encoding and retrieving cues so much as the congruity between mental processes that are engaged in encoding and retrieval. This occurs even for collaborative groups, where the presence of others only at the time of retrieval seems to produce lower recall and more incorrect answers. Collaborative inhibition seems to be worst when the recall task involves general knowledge, free recall without cues, and the group members are not friends and did not study together.

CHAPTER SUMMARY

In this chapter, retrieval was presented as a critical part of the learning and memory process, since it is the measure by which we regard all learning. Because more information is available to us than we can access at any one time, and retrieval takes time and effort, people often make a rapid FOK judgment to decide if they could recognize an answer if presented with one. These FOK judgments tend to be fairly accurate, and can be based on how familiar we are with the domain of the question in general as well as whether we can easily retrieve other pertinent details about the possible answer.

We use retrieval cues as prompts to guide the retrieval of information. Some are externally provided, and some are internally generated. Generally, more cues are better for retrieval than fewer. Remembering to perform some future action, or prospective memory, relies heavily on both kinds of cues. Researchers find external cues are better to rely on for prospective memory tasks since we do not have to internally monitor for the presence of the cue.

Biologically, the distinction between encoding and retrieval may not matter, since the neurons responsible for storing a memory will allow for updating when a memory is activated. A memory can be disrupted on a chemical level.

Retrieving information aids learning, and repeatedly retrieving information provides an additional boost. This can be because retrieval strengthens a memory through additional effort, or because retrieval simulates a performance situation, or because repeated attempts at retrieval will provide more overall time for retrieval. Repeated attempts at retrieval will also develop additional retrieval cues. In any case, researchers recommend building retrieval into practice as a way of enhancing learning.

The situation we are in during encoding influences retrieval, and this includes the cues that are present in the physical environment, our physiological state, and our mood. Matching or congruous cues at encoding and retrieval enhance performance, and this is likely because the cues at retrieval will trigger the mental processes incurred during encoding. This can present a challenge when we study alone, but are asked to recall information in a group setting. Collaborative retrieval can cause process loss, as groups of people recalling information together will provide fewer correct answers, more incorrect answers, and be more overconfident in their performance than nominal, working-independently groups. There are some strategies to limit these problems, including studying together or engaging in collaborative retrieval only during recognition tasks.

Retrieval Strategies

Another way to review the chapter is to assemble some empirically based strategies that help retrieval.

1. Retrieval takes time, and not every memory that is available can always be retrieved. More than one attempt may be necessary.

2. Part of learning should involve practicing retrieval. Recognition tasks help, but recall tasks are best, probably because they take more effort. Summarize what you have been studying to yourself or explain it to someone.

3. If information will be retrieved in a particular setting, then attempt to encode the information in that setting as well. When this isn't possible, mentally simulate where you were during learning. Try to be in the same physiological state during performance as during study. Relax, sleep well, and restrict the use of psychoactive substances during learning and performance.

4. External retrieval cues can be helpful since they don't rely on our internal monitoring. When feasible, turn internal retrieval cues into external ones (notes, alarms, other reminders) so that you are not dependent solely on your own internal cues.

5. Retrieving information around others is best if everyone works separately and then pools their answers, *unless* the group studies together as well.

REVIEW QUESTIONS

1. According to active trace theory, why does retrieving a memory make it malleable to change?

2. What is the difference between the availability of memories and the accessibility of memories?

3. What is an FOK judgment, and how do people use them when deciding whether to retrieve information?

4. What is the difference between an external and an internal retrieval cue? Which kind appears to be better for remembering to do future tasks, and why?

5. What explanations are there for the memory boost from practicing retrieval?

6. Knowing about the encoding specificity principle, how might that affect trying to learn and remember a skill that you expect to have to use in many different situations? Alternatively, how would it apply to making a speech in a class?

7. Are group tests a good idea or not?

KEY TERMS

FURTHER RESOURCES

1. Weblink: Rick Perry forgets:

   o https://www.youtube.com/watch?v=mv9LBUG4KsE

2. Weblink: "Partial recall: Can neuroscience rewrite our most traumatic memories?" (New Yorker):

   o http://www.newyorker.com/magazine/2014/05/19/partial-recall

3. Weblink: Dr. Eleanor Maguire talks about the neuroscience of memory:

   o https://www.youtube.com/watch?v=gdzmNwTLakg

4. Weblink: The five steps to "getting things done":

   o http://gettingthingsdone.com/fivesteps/

REFERENCES

Andersson, J., & Rönnberg, J. (1995). Recall suffers from collaboration: Joint recall effects of friendship and task complexity. *Applied Cognitive Psychology, 9*(3), 199–211.

Ballard, P. B. (1913). Obliviscence and reminiscence. *British Journal of Psychology.* Retrieved from http://psycnet.apa.org/psycinfo/1913-10033-001

Basden, B. H., Basden, D. R., & Henry, S. (2000). Costs and benefits of collaborative remembering. *Applied Cognitive Psychology, 14*(6), 497–507.

Basden, B. H., Basden, D. R., Thomas, R. L., & Souphasith, S. (1997). Memory distortion in group recall. *Current Psychology, 16*(3), 225–246.

Basden, B. H., Reysen, M. B., & Basden, D. R. (2002). Transmitting false memories in social groups. *The American Journal of Psychology, 115*(2), 211–231. https://doi.org/10.2307/1423436

Besnard, A., Caboche, J., & Laroche, S. (2012). Reconsolidation of memory: A decade of debate. *Progress in Neurobiology, 99*(1), 61–80.

Bjork, E. L., & Bjork, R. A. (2011). Making things hard on yourself, but in a good way: Creating desirable difficulties to enhance learning. *Psychology and the real world: Essays illustrating fundamental contributions to society.* In M. A. Gernsbacher, R. W. Pew, L. M. Hough, & J. R. Pomerantz (Eds.), (pp. 56–64). New York, NY: Worth.

Bjork, R. A. (1975). Retrieval as a memory modifier: An interpretation of negative recency and related phenomena. In R. L. Solso (Ed.), *Information processing and cognition: The Loyola Symposium* (pp. 123–144). Hillsdale, NJ: Erlbaum. https://www.amazon.com/Information-Processing-Cognition-Loyola-Symposium/dp/0470812303/ref=sr_1_1?ie=UTF8&qid=1499481558&sr=8-1&keywords=Information+processing+and+cognition%3A+The+Loyola+Symposium

Blaney, P. H. (1986). Affect and memory: A review. *Psychological Bulletin, 99*(2), 229–246. https://doi.org/10.1037/0033-2909.99.2.229

Blaxton, T. A. (1989). Investigating dissociations among memory measures: Support for a transfer-appropriate processing framework. *Journal of Experimental Psychology: Learning, Memory, and Cognition, 15*(4), 657.

Bossert, J. M., Marchant, N. J., Calu, D. J., & Shaham, Y. (2013). The reinstatement model of drug relapse: Recent neurobiological findings, emerging research topics, and translational research. *Psychopharmacology, 229*(3), 453–476.

Brown, W. (1923). To what extent is memory measured by a single recall? *Journal of Experimental Psychology, 6*(5), 377.

Campbell, J., & Mayer, R. E. (2009). Questioning as an instructional method: Does it affect learning from lectures? *Applied Cognitive Psychology, 23*(6), 747–759.

CNBC, and The Associated Press. (2016, December 13). Rick Perry's Energy Department "Oops" Moment. *The New York Times.* Retrieved from https://www.nytimes.com/video/us/politics/100000004820721/rick-perrys-energy-department-oops-moment.html

Craik, F. I. M., & Tulving, E. (1975). Depth of processing and the retention of words in episodic memory. *Journal of Experimental Psychology: General, 104*(3), 268–294. https://doi.org/10.1037/0096-3445.104.3.268

Dahlström, Ö., Danielsson, H., Emilsson, M., & Andersson, J. (2011). Does retrieval strategy disruption cause general and specific collaborative inhibition? *Memory, 19*(2), 140–154.

deWinsanley, P. A., & Bjork, R. A. (2002). Successful lecturing: Presenting information in ways that engage effective processing. *New Directions for Teaching and Learning, 89,* 19–31.

Diehl, M., & Stroebe, W. (1991). Productivity loss in idea-generating groups: Tracking down the blocking effect. *Journal of Personality and Social Psychology, 61*(3), 392.

Dudai, Y., & Eisenberg, M. (2004). Rites of passage of the engram: Reconsolidation and the lingering consolidation hypothesis. *Neuron, 44*(1), 93–100.

Dunlosky, J., & Metcalfe, J. (2009). *Metacognition.* Thousand Oaks, CA: Sage. Retrieved from http://psycnet.apa.org/psycinfo/2009-16200-000

Dunlosky, J., & Rawson, K. A. (2012). Overconfidence produces underachievement: Inaccurate self evaluations undermine students' learning and retention. *Learning and Instruction, 22*(4), 271–280.

Eich, E., Macaulay, D., & Ryan, L. (1994). Mood dependent memory for events of the personal past. *Journal of Experimental Psychology: General, 123*(2), 201.

Eich, E., & Metcalfe, J. (1989). Mood dependent memory for internal versus external events. *Journal of Experimental Psychology: Learning, Memory, and Cognition, 15*(3), 443–455. https://doi.org/10.1037/0278-7393.15.3.443

Eich, J. E. (1980). The cue-dependent nature of state-dependent retrieval. *Memory and Cognition, 8*(2), 157–173.

Eich, J. E., Weingartner, H., Stillman, R. C., & Gillin, J. C. (1975). State-dependent accessibility of retrieval cues in the retention of a categorized list. *Journal of Verbal Learning and Verbal Behavior, 14*(4), 408–417.

Einstein, G. O., McDaniel, M. A., Thomas, R., Mayfield, S., Shank, H., Morrisette, N., & Breneiser, J. (2005). Multiple processes in prospective memory retrieval: Factors determining monitoring versus spontaneous retrieval. *Journal of Experimental Psychology: General, 134*(3), 327.

Erdelyi, M. H., & Becker, J. (1974). Hypermnesia for pictures: Incremental memory for pictures but not words in multiple recall trials. *Cognitive Psychology, 6*(1), 159–171.

Fatal Distraction: Forgetting a Child in the Backseat of a Car Is a Horrifying Mistake. Is It a Crime? | KidsandCars.org. (2009, March 8). Retrieved from http://www.kidsandcars.org/2016/07/08/fatal-distraction-forgetting-a-child-in-the-backseat-of-a-car-is-a-horrifying-mistake-is-it-a-crime/

Finlay, F., Hitch, G. J., & Meudell, P. R. (2000). Mutual inhibition in collaborative recall: Evidence for a retrieval-based account. *Journal of Experimental Psychology: Learning, Memory, and Cognition, 26*(6), 1556.

Godden, D. R., & Baddeley, A. D. (1975). Context-dependent memory in two natural environments: On land and underwater. *British Journal of Psychology, 66*(3), 325–331.

Graf, P., & Mandler, G. (1984). Activation makes words more accessible, but not necessarily more retrievable. *Journal of Verbal Learning and Verbal Behavior, 23*(5), 553–568.

Hamilton, M., & Rajaram, S. (2003). States of awareness across multiple memory tasks: Obtaining a "pure" measure of conscious recollection. *Acta Psychologica, 112*(1), 43–69.

Hart, J. T. (1965). Memory and the feeling-of-knowing experience. *Journal of Educational Psychology, 56*(4), 208.

Hart, J. T. (1967). Second-try recall, recognition, and the memory-monitoring process. *Journal of Educational Psychology, 58*(4), 193–197. https://doi.org/10.1037/h0024908

Heat Stroke | KidsandCars.org. (n.d.). Retrieved from http://www.kidsandcars.org/how-kids-get-hurt/heat-stroke/

Hicks, J. L., Marsh, R. L., & Cook, G. I. (2005). Task interference in time-based, event-based, and dual intention prospective memory conditions. *Journal of Memory and Language, 53*(3), 430–444.

Hicks, J. L., Marsh, R. L., & Russell, E. J. (2000). The properties of retention intervals and their affect on retaining prospective memories. *Journal of Experimental Psychology: Learning, Memory, and Cognition, 26*(5), 1160.

Jacoby, L. L., & Dallas, M. (1981). On the relationship between autobiographical memory and perceptual learning. *Journal of Experimental Psychology: General, 110*(3), 306.

Janowsky, J. S., Shimamura, A. P., & Squire, L. R. (1989). Memory and metamemory: Comparisons between patients with frontal lobe lesions and amnesic patients. *Psychobiology, 17*(1), 3–11.

Kerr, N. L., & Tindale, R. S. (2004). Group performance and decision making. *Annu. Rev. Psychol., 55*, 623–655.

Kim, P. Y., & Mayhorn, C. B. (2008). Exploring students' prospective memory inside and outside the lab. *The American Journal of Psychology*, 241–254.

Kolers, P. A., & Palef, S. R. (1976). Knowing not. *Memory and Cognition, 4*(5), 553–558.

Koriat, A. (1993). How do we know that we know? The accessibility model of the feeling of knowing. *Psychological Review, 100*(4), 609.

Koriat, A. (1995). Dissociating knowing and the feeling of knowing: Further evidence for the accessibility model. *Journal of Experimental Psychology: General, 124*(3), 311.

Koriat, A., & Levy-Sadot, R. (2001). The combined contributions of the cue-familiarity and accessibility heuristics to feelings of knowing. *Journal of Experimental Psychology: Learning, Memory, and Cognition, 27*(1), 34.

Krinsky, R., & Nelson, T. O. (1985). The feeling of knowing for different types of retrieval failure. *Acta Psychologica, 58*(2), 141–158.

Latané, B., Williams, K., & Harkins, S. (1979). Many hands make light the work: The causes and consequences of social loafing. *Journal of Personality and Social Psychology, 37*(6), 822–832. https://doi.org/10.1037/0022-3514.37.6.822

Lee, J. L. (2008). Memory reconsolidation mediates the strengthening of memories by additional learning. *Nature Neuroscience, 11*(11), 1264.

Lee, J. L., Di Ciano, P., Thomas, K. L., & Everitt, B. J. (2005). Disrupting reconsolidation of drug memories reduces cocaine-seeking behavior. *Neuron, 47*(6), 795–801.

Lee, J. L., Milton, A. L., & Everitt, B. J. (2006). Cue-induced cocaine seeking and relapse are reduced by disruption of drug memory reconsolidation. *Journal of Neuroscience, 26*(22), 5881–5887.

Lewis, D. J. (1979). Psychobiology of active and inactive memory. *Psychological Bulletin, 86*(5), 1054.

Lindsay, D. S. (2008). *Source monitoring*. Retrieved from https://www.mysciencework.com/publication/show/e59283323e6e34e684ecf465ac5afad1

Marsh, E. J., & Tversky, B. (2004). Spinning the stories of our lives. *Applied Cognitive Psychology, 18*(5), 491–503.

Marsh, R. L., Hicks, J. L., & Landau, J. D. (1998). An investigation of everyday prospective memory. *Memory and Cognition, 26*(4), 633–643.

McDaniel, M. A., & Masson, M. E. (1985). Altering memory representations through retrieval. *Journal of Experimental Psychology: Learning, Memory, and Cognition, 11*(2), 371.

McDaniel, M. A., Roediger, H. L., & Mcdermott, K. B. (2007). Generalizing test-enhanced learning from the laboratory to the classroom. *Psychonomic Bulletin and Review, 14*(2), 200–206. https://doi.org/10.3758/BF03194052

McKenzie, S., & Eichenbaum, H. (2011). Consolidation and reconsolidation: Two lives of memories? *Neuron, 71*(2), 224–233.

Metcalfe, J., Schwartz, B. L., & Joaquim, S. G. (1993). The cue-familiarity heuristic in metacognition. *Journal of Experimental Psychology: Learning, Memory, and Cognition, 19*(4), 851.

Misanin, J. R., Miller, R. R., & Lewis, D. J. (1968). Retrograde amnesia produced by electroconvulsive shock after reactivation of a consolidated memory trace. *Science, 160*(3827), 554–555.

Nadel, L., Hupbach, A., Gomez, R., & Newman-Smith, K. (2012). Memory formation, consolidation and transformation. *Neuroscience and Biobehavioral Reviews, 36*(7), 1640–1645.

Nader, K. (2003). Memory traces unbound. *Trends in Neurosciences, 26*(2), 65–72.

Nader, K., Schafe, G. E., & LeDoux, J. E. (2000). Reply—Reconsolidation: The labile nature of consolidation theory. *Nature Reviews Neuroscience, 1*(3), 216–219.

Nelson, T. O., Gerler, D., & Narens, L. (1984). Accuracy of feeling-of-knowing judgments for predicting perceptual identification and relearning. *Journal of Experimental Psychology: General, 113*(2), 282.

Paulus, P. B., & Dzindolet, M. T. (1993). Social influence processes in group brainstorming. *Journal of Personality and Social Psychology, 64*(4), 575.

Payne, D. G. (1986). Hypermnesia for pictures and words: Testing the recall level hypothesis. *Journal of Experimental Psychology: Learning, Memory, and Cognition, 12*(1), 16.

Przybyslawski, J., & Sara, S. J. (1997). Reconsolidation of memory after its reactivation. *Behavioural Brain Research, 84*(1), 241–246.

Rajaram, S., & Barber, S. J. (2008). *Retrieval processes in memory.* Retrieved from https://www.mysciencework.com/publication/show/3c7f50b9dcd1826bdfe0ea18e68164d9

Rajaram, S., & Pereira-Pasarin, L. P. (2010). Collaborative memory: Cognitive research and theory. *Perspectives on Psychological Science, 5*(6), 649–663.

Reder, L. M. (1987). Strategy selection in question answering. *Cognitive Psychology, 19*(1), 90–138.

Reder, L. M. (1988). Strategic control of retrieval strategies. *Psychology of Learning and Motivation, 22*, 227–259.

Roediger, H. L. (2000). Why retrieval is the key process in understanding human memory. In E. Tulving (Ed.), *Memory, consciousness, and the brain: The Tallinn Conference* (pp. 52–75). Philadelphia, PA: Psychology Press.

Roediger, H. L., & Blaxton, T. A. (1987). Effects of varying modality, surface features, and retention interval on priming in word-fragment completion. *Memory & Cognition, 15*(5), 379–388.

Roediger, H. L., & Guynn, M. J. (1996). Retrieval processes. In E. L. Bjork & R. A. Bjork (Eds.), *Memory, 10,* 197–236. Retrieved from https://books.google.com/books?hl=enandlr=andid=f7p_nb040IACandoi=fndandpg=PA197anddq=Roediger+and+Guynn+1996andots=kA00-92-cuandsig=3SEe-wSTjx6Se9xZCFSZfWhWA1M

Roediger, H. L., & Karpicke, J. D. (2006a). Test-enhanced learning: Taking memory tests improves long-term retention. *Psychological Science, 17*(3), 249–255. https://doi.org/10.1111/j.1467–9280.2006.01693.x

Roediger, H. L., & Karpicke, J. D. (2006b). The power of testing memory: Basic research and implications for educational practice. *Perspectives on Psychological Science, 1*(3), 181–210.

Roediger, H. L., Meade, M. L., & Bergman, E. T. (2001). Social contagion of memory. *Psychonomic Bulletin and Review, 8*(2), 365–371.

Roediger, H. L., & Payne, D. G. (1985). Recall criterion does not affect recall level or hypermnesia: A puzzle for generate/recognize theories. *Memory & Cognition, 13*(1), 1–7. https://doi.org/10.3758/BF03198437

Roediger, H. L., & Thorpe, L. A. (1978). The role of recall time in producing hypermnesia. *Memory and Cognition, 6*(3), 296–305.

Rowe, M. B. (1987). Wait time: Slowing down may be a way of speeding up. *American Educator: The Professional Journal of the American Federation of Teachers, 11*(1), 38.

Schneider, D. M., & Watkins, M. J. (1996). Response conformity in recognition testing. *Psychonomic Bulletin and Review, 3*(4), 481–485. https://doi.org/10.3758/BF03214550

Schnyer, D. M., Verfaellie, M., Alexander, M. P., LaFleche, G., Nicholls, L., & Kaszniak, A. W. (2004). A role for right medial prefrontal cortex in accurate feeling-of-knowing judgments: Evidence from patients with lesions to frontal cortex. *Neuropsychologia, 42*(7), 957–966.

Smith, S. M. (1979). Remembering in and out of context. *Journal of Experimental Psychology: Human Learning and Memory, 5*(5), 460.

Smith, S. M., & Vela, E. (2001). Environmental context-dependent memory: A review and meta-analysis. *Psychonomic Bulletin and Review, 8*(2), 203–220.

Sorg, B. A. (2012). Reconsolidation of drug memories. *Neuroscience and Biobehavioral Reviews, 36*(5), 1400–1417.

Spear, N. E. (1973). Retrieval of memory in animals. *Psychological Review, 80*(3), 163.

Steiner, I. D. (1972). *Group processes and productivity.* New York, NY: Academic Press.

Spitzer, H. F. (1939). Studies in retention. *Journal of Educational Psychology, 30*(9), 641.

Stephenson, G. M., Abrams, D., Wagner, W., & Wade, G. (1986). Partners in recall: Collaborative order in the recall of a police interrogation. *British Journal of Social Psychology, 25*(4), 341–343.

Thomas, A. K., & McDaniel, M. A. (2007). Metacomprehension for educationally relevant materials: Dramatic effects of encoding-retrieval interactions. *Psychonomic Bulletin and Review, 14*(2), 212–218. https://doi.org/10.3758/BF03194054

Thomson, D. M., & Tulving, E. (1970). Associative encoding and retrieval: Weak and strong cues. *Journal of Experimental Psychology, 86*(2), 255–262. https://doi.org/10.1037/h0029997

Tulving, E. (1985). *Elements of episodic memory.* Oxford, England: Oxford University Press.

Tulving, E., & Pearlstone, Z. (1966). Availability versus accessibility of information in memory for words. *Journal of Verbal Learning and Verbal Behavior, 5*(4), 381–391.

Vojdanoska, M., Cranney, J., & Newell, B. R. (2010). The testing effect: The role of feedback and collaboration in a tertiary classroom setting. *Applied Cognitive Psychology, 24*(8), 1183–1195.

Vollrath, D. A., Sheppard, B. H., Hinsz, V. B., & Davis, J. H. (1989). Memory performance by decision-making groups and individuals. *Organizational Behavior and Human Decision Processes, 43*(3), 289–300. https://doi.org/10.1016/0749-5978(89)90040-X

Walmart Selling Car Seat That Alerts Parents When a Child Is Left Behind. (2015, July 24). Retrieved from https://consumerist.com/2015/07/24/walmart-selling-car-seat-that-alerts-parents-when-a-child-is-left-behind/

Weldon, M. S. (2001). Remembering as a social process. *The Psychology of Learning and Motivation: Advances in Research and Theory, 40*, 67–120.

Weldon, M. S., & Bellinger, K. D. (1997). Collective memory: Collaborative and individual processes in remembering. *Journal of Experimental Psychology: Learning, Memory, and Cognition, 23*(5), 1160.

Weldon, M. S., Blair, C., & Huebsch, P. D. (2000). Group remembering: Does social loafing underlie collaborative inhibition? *Journal of Experimental Psychology: Learning, Memory, and Cognition, 26*(6), 1568.

Woods, S. P., Dawson, M. S., Weber, E., Gibson, S., Grant, I., & Atkinson, J. H. (2009). Timing is everything: Antiretroviral nonadherence is associated with impairment in time-based prospective memory. *Journal of the International Neuropsychological Society, 15*(01), 42–52.

Zaromb, F. M., & Roediger, H. L. (2010). The testing effect in free recall is associated with enhanced organizational processes. *Memory and Cognition, 38*(8), 995–1008.

Zogg, J. B., Woods, S. P., Sauceda, J. A., Wiebe, J. S., & Simoni, J. M. (2012). The role of prospective memory in medication adherence: A review of an emerging literature. *Journal of Behavioral Medicine, 35*(1), 47–62.

©iStock.com/BrunS

Episodic and Autobiographical Memories

Chapter Outline

Overview

Central to how we see ourselves appears to be: what we remember and know of ourselves, what we have experienced, who we are now, and what we would like for the future. I have a hard time imagining myself without children who are now teenage boys, or without the experience of moving to a rural area after living in major cities for my entire life.

To illustrate the importance of memories for personal events, let's compare two dramatic real-life stories that parallel each other, but that had different impacts on the lives of the people who lived them because of the presence of personal memories. Vesna Vulovic was entered into the Guinness Book of Records in 1985 for having experienced "the highest fall survived without a parachute." She was a stewardess on a Serbian airline that exploded in mid-air in January of 1972 at 33,000 feet. Vulovic was the only survivor, and was trapped inside the tail cone of the plane, which landed near a village. Possibly the cone landed on a slope, and the snow and pine trees cushioned the impact. She suffered a number of fractures, fell into a coma, and was rescued. Vulovic never regained memory of either the accident or her rescue; but she nearly fully recovered with time and returned to work at the airline in a desk job. Vulovic once said, "I'm not lucky. Everybody thinks I am lucky, but they are mistaken. If I were lucky, I would never have had this accident."

Contrast this with what happened to Juliane Koepcke. On Christmas Eve, 1971, she and her mother boarded a plane headed to Lima, Peru, to visit her father. (Her parents were zoologists who worked in the rainforest.) Mid-flight, a lightning bolt hit one of the fuel tanks, and the plane lost its right wing. Koepcke remembers the plane dropping straight down. The plane fell apart around her in mid-air, and left Koepcke flying in the air strapped to her row of seats, spinning. She blacked out as she watched the jungle spinning toward her.

Koepcke woke up the next morning on the ground, strapped to the seats. Maybe the spin of the seats slowed her fall or perhaps the foliage in the canopy helped slow the impact; but she had only minor injuries: a concussion and some gashes. However, rescue teams couldn't locate the crash, so Koepcke spent ten days trying to find her way out of the jungle on her own. As she followed a stream, she came across some of the other passengers, all of whom had died in the fall. Koepcke remembers checking them to see if any was her mother. After passing crocodiles and wading past piranhas, she came to a small hut, where lumberjacks found her the next day.

In Koepcke's case, the memory of the crash and the aftermath haunted her for a long time. She described spending days just crying. No one offered her therapy, which wasn't that widespread in those days, after a disaster. Mixed in with this was experiencing her mother's death and being hounded by the press. It was ten years before Koepcke could openly talk about the experience. She recently published a memoir of her experience (Koepcke & Benjamin, 2011).

Both experiences were wildly traumatic and unusual, although similar. While both women had to deal with the accident and recovery, the memory of the accident seems to have made Koepcke's experience all the worse. In this chapter, we'll examine what we know about memories we have for events we experienced, and tie those to the sense of who we are as individuals.

Episodic Memories

Episodic memories are the memories of the events from everyday life that we have not forgotten (Cohen & Conway, 2008). A classic approach to episodic memories is to see them as memories of personal events. Episodic memories are often what people are referring to when they talk about memory in general. As we will see later, some memory researchers see episodic memories as a basic building block in our understanding of ourselves.

A successful ability to remember specific events has several cognitive implications (Baddeley, 2007). We have to be able to encode the many daily experiences we have so that we can distinguish them from each other later on. Much of what we do is routine or habitual, and the need to be able to distinguish different-but-similar events is a mental challenge. Then, the episodic memories have to be stored in a fashion that allows for search and retrieval later on. This is like trying to complete a puzzle that has many shapes that have been cut similarly and have a matching color palette with a lot of the other pieces. To elaborate, what processing of new events helps to delineate what happened at work on Tuesday from what happens on other Tuesdays, or on any other days? What happens to memories of events that we repeat frequently?

What appears to make an event more memorable is how the event relates to our goals. Where our interests and needs are now can color the depth of processing and attention we pay to an event, such as landing a first job interview after searching for work for a while. If we process the event more deeply, as the levels of processing theory would claim, then we may be able to recall it better later.

Some researchers have explored this idea by investigating those self-defining moments in life that we decide are particularly relevant and important. Blagov and Singer (2004) found that landmark personal events remind us about our identities. If the event was seen as particularly important, it affects several traits of the memory of it, including the emotional strength, vividness, links to other memories, and how often we rehearse the memory.

Reexperiencing Past Events

Music and smells are common retrieval cues for episodic memories. Janata, Tomic, and Rakowski (2007) culled the most popular songs from the "top 100" playlists over several years, and found that playing them for participants tended to trigger memories of personal events. Often they were nostalgic in nature.

Smells may be a potent source of retrieval cues, both because there are so many and because there is a neurological connection between the olfactory bulb and the limbic system. Willander and Larsson (2007) presented scents to their participants, with several conditions as their independent variable. Participants were asked to report any personal memories after smelling an odor, or after naming an odor only, or after both naming and smelling an odor. The smells by themselves, without a label, produced more personal memories that were older and often more emotional in nature than did the other two conditions. Having to provide a name for the scent seemed to suppress the memory retrieval process. An easy way to test this episodic memory and smell connection is to pick out some spices from your kitchen and smell them without looking at the label.

Involuntary Episodic Memories

Episodic memories can present themselves without a conscious search, involuntarily, such as getting a song stuck in your head. Berntsen, Staugaard, and Sørenson (2013) used both common and unusual sounds to try to provoke involuntary memories. They found that sounds that were novel tended to produce more involuntary memories, possibly because odd sounds require more attention to make sense of. Finnbogadóttir and Berntsen (2013) found that most of the involuntary memories sparked by this method are positive in nature.

Visual Perspectives in Episodic Memories

People report one of two perspectives when describing episodic memories. An observer perspective of an episodic memory is when an individual experiences the memory with a perspective outside of themselves, watching themselves. They themselves are seen as actors in the memory. This perspective is fairly common in childhood memories (Nigro & Neisser, 1983) and makes it difficult to judge whether the memory corresponds to real events or was something mentally created from a family video, photo, or story. In contrast, a field perspective is when people experience the event through their own eyes. The memory is immersive.

Often the observer perspective is less emotional, possibly because the event has a more detached view. Mimicking this, filmmakers often make conscious choices about whether to show a scene from the perspective of a character or merely to observe as a way to alter the emotionality of the scene. Someone remembering an episodic memory can alter these two perspectives consciously (Robinson & Swanson, 1993).

Characteristics of Episodic Memories

Memories of events include information from a variety of experiences of the moment, including what we sensed at the time, how we interpreted or perceived what went on, and our emotional reactions (Conway, 2005). Much of the sensory information is visual. People report they can remember their thoughts during an event as well, although these are likely to be difficult to confirm empirically. Usually the remembered events are short in duration. They begin and end based on the goals we had at the time, rather than on an endless video that recounts our day. Episodic memories seem to be spliced by what we found to be meaningful. Usually we can recall events in chronological order, at least approximately. The act of remembering and reexperiencing the event has been referred to as a kind of mental time travel (Tulving, 2002).

Rubin and Kozin (1984) asked college students to rate their three clearest memories, and to rate them for traits such as how important the memory was nationally, how important the memory was personally, the element of surprise in the memory, how vivid and emotional it was, and how often the event was discussed with others. The most commonly reported memories were of injuries and accidents, sports, and interactions with the opposite sex. There was overlap in some of the traits. Ratings of vividness, importance, surprise, and emotionality were all associated with each other.

There is evidence that the amount of time spent rehearsing the memory by reading and writing about an event and sharing it with others impacts how long we remember the event. Sehulster (1998) tested his memory for the details of 284 opera performances that he had attended over twenty-five years. He tried to recall the dates and casts of performances, and was able to assess his accuracy by checking his recall against the performance programs. He assessed "rehearsal" by correlating his accuracy for details with the amount of media surrounding each performance. He found that his memory for the content and casts of the performances were positively correlated with media present during the performances as expert ratings of the performances, but not for his recall of performance dates.

To elaborate on these two dimensions of the vividness of experience and rehearsal on remembering, Cohen and Faulkner (1988) confirmed that the vividness of a memory correlated with emotion, importance, and the amount of rehearsal; but these variables changed with the age of the participant. Vividness was better predicted by the emotionality and importance of an event for younger participants; but for older participants, the amount of rehearsal mattered most. Generally, births, marriages, and deaths were the most remembered and were remembered better if the participant was personally involved. It also helped if an event was a first-time or a unique situation.

How often an event is repeated seems to alter our memory of those events as well. When patients must see a doctor repeatedly for a chronic condition, all those visits tend to blend over time into one general memory (Means & Loftus, 1991). This was not the case for doctor visits that were one-time health checkups. Memories for the visits were stronger if the illness was more severe, however. Age also moderates this effect. Patients over the age of seventy tend to remember their doctor visits better than younger patients, probably because they are seen as being of greater importance.

Episodic Memory in Contrast With Other Kinds of Memories

Memory researchers believe that we tend to recall those events that we find personally relevant and important; that is, we retain those events that we associate with who we are. Our episodic memories act as a logbook of our progress on our current goals, not unlike a video highlight reel of a sports game. But the situation is not so simple.

The term "episodic memory" is usually reserved specifically for a memory of a past event and the ability to relive it. However, it takes general knowledge to be able to realize why a particular memory is important to us—why a certain email or phone call was so important—and then to explain our thoughts at the time. In other words, what we know of ourselves is not simply a collection of personal video clips. We seem to retain memories that we tie to who we are best, yet it takes an understanding of who we are in order to decide what is most relevant. It is likely that our "autobiographical memory system," the collection of memories about ourselves, is a mix of both kinds of memories. We'll take a closer look at the autobiographical memory system later in this chapter.

General knowledge and memory for episodes may be related by repetition. When we first encounter a situation, the memory will show signs of being episodic in nature; but with repeated encounters, the memory becomes more generalized (Conway, Cohen, & Stanhope, 1992).

Before the 1970s, memory was primarily viewed as a store for individual experiences and actions, like a mental bucket of events (Neisser & Hyman, 1999, p. 356). Tulving (1972) saw that a distinction could be made between both the form of memories as well as how they are retrieved (Gardiner, 2008). Remembering, according to Tulving (1985), describes what happens when we retrieve vivid, detailed memories and can relive them. Images, feelings, and other details tend to be recalled with them. We are usually consciously aware of the act of remembering (Tulving, 1999).

Knowing, however, describes retrieving general knowledge, or what we will call "semantic memory" in the next chapter. "Knowing" involves retrieving facts and concepts that are associated with past learning, but understanding when and where they were learned may not be possible. There is a less personal connection and a more generic experience to the retrieval. Retrieving general knowledge doesn't necessarily produce feelings or sensory experiences.

The line between episodic memory and general knowledge is not clearly defined, and we often retrieve elements of each when we recall something. We may remember what we had for breakfast; but, to understand the concept of "breakfast" will involve knowledge. We use general knowledge to interpret and classify episodic memories (H. L. Williams, Conway, & Cohen, 2008).

Do we have two memory systems, one for personal events and the other for knowledge? It's possible that these forms of memory are not stored in the same places in the brain, but the level of distinction is still not clear (Shanks & St. John, 1994). Some research has found different levels of responding for each type of memory. In laboratory-based memory tasks, the responses that participants claim they remembered tend to decline over time while the responses that feel known stay constant (Parkin & Walker, 1992). At the moment, the distinction is primarily to help classify and clarify the tasks and modes of retrieval that memory researchers are investigating.

Brain Processing of Episodic Memories

The frontal lobes and hippocampus have been identified as key areas for remembering episodic memories, although the specific hemisphere involved has not been consistent across studies. In one study, forty-eight photos were presented to participants in an fMRI machine, who had to decide whether the view shown was an indoor scene or not (J. B. Brewer, Zhao, Desmond, Glover, & Badrieli, 1998). The participants were surprised with a memory test involving photos they had seen, plus new ones. If they could recall the old scenes, they were asked whether they could remember observing the photo the first time. The researchers monitored areas of brain activation when participants reported remembering the photo. They found that remembering activated both right and left hippocampi and the right frontal lobe. Wagner and colleagues (1998) used the same approach, but they included words for stimuli. When participants were confident that they could remember seeing a word, the areas around the hippocampus and left frontal region were activated.

Schacter, Addis, and Buckner (2007) asked participants to recall specific episodes while brain activity was monitored by fMRI. They were asked to combine some episodes to generate an idea of something that might happen in the future. The researchers' assumption was that episodic memory is useful, in part, for basing predictions of future events. They found that the same areas around the hippocampus were active both in the recollection of episodic events as well as in generating a future scenario.

Flashbulb Memories

Flashbulb memories are particularly vivid episodic memories (Brown & Kulik, 1977; McCloskey, Wible, & Cohen, 1988). They are believed not to be a unique form of episodic memory in their own right—but a heightened example of them. Flashbulb memories are exceptionally vivid, often emotional, and feel very clear. In the study that coined the term, Brown and Kulik surveyed 80 adults, asking about memories of specific events that had made national news in the 1960s and 1970s. These events were mostly assassinations, such as of President John F. Kennedy, Malcolm X, Robert F. Kennedy, Martin Luther King, and others. These were chosen partially because all of them were considered important; but some of the events seemed to be more consequential than others, and some of the events were thought to be more consequential to one segment of society than another. What Brown and Kulik found was that all of their participants reported having as least some strong memories of hearing about these events. Those episodic memories included where they were when they heard the news, what they were doing at the time, and who told them the news. Some of the memories were very detailed, down to what clothing they were wearing and what their thoughts were at the time. These memories are usually very emotional, and people are quite confident in their ability to recall specific details of the time. Most of the participants could also recall a flashbulb memory from their own personal life.

Brown and Kulik saw these memories as having a special status due to the events' being culturally significant or personally important. More recent events that many people report having flashbulb memories of are the 9/11 attacks in New York City, Washington, D.C., and Pennsylvania and the elections of Barack Obama and Donald Trump. The role cultural significance in flashbulb memories can be seen in other situations as well, such as Colegrove's (1899) descriptions of interviews of 179 people about their memories of hearing about Lincoln's death, thirty-three years after his assassination. Most could recall where they were, the time of day, and who had informed them. In contrast, not as many could provide details about President Garfield's death. Because both the duration of her term as well as the controversies from her term as leader, many people in the UK report having flashbulb memories of hearing about Margret Thatcher's decision to resign as Prime Minister. This event seems to have caused fewer flashbulb memories in the United States (Conway et al., 1994).

Accuracy of Flashbulb Memories

What Brown and Kulik (1977) did not do, however, was to verify the accuracy of the reports of flashbulb memories that people provided. While participants provided vivid, detailed accounts, it was not clear to all researchers that the presence of many details meant that what had been recalled was necessarily accurate. To what extent do flashbulb memories correspond to true events? To find out, researchers had to collect data longitudinally, meaning that participants might complete a memory questionnaire about an event several times—months, or even years apart.

Longitudinal research on the recall of flashbulb memories has found that the memories feel accurate, but can contain a lot of inaccuracies. Two factors appear to predict the accuracy of flashbulb memories: the passage of time and physical proximity to the original event. In contrast, the vividness and confidence do not appear to be strongly correlated with the accuracy of the memory. Talarico and Rubin (2003) asked college students in North Carolina about finding out about the attacks on September 11, 2001. They were then reinterviewed three times: one week later, six weeks later, and thirty-two weeks later. Statements that were consistent with their initial interview dropped in time, and statements that were inconsistent increased over time.

Neisser and colleagues (1996) had questioned whether being more personally involved in an event would improve accuracy. A strong earthquake shook central California in 1989. This quake occurred during a broadcast of the pregame activities of a

Major League Baseball World Series game, and a line video of the event in Candlestick Park shows the park rocking. A portion of a double-decker freeway collapsed, and cars heading one direction fell onto cars headed in the other. Rescue efforts lasted for days. To get a sense of whether physical proximity to an event plays a role in creating strong episodic memories, questionnaires asking about memories of hearing about or experiencing the quake were quickly developed and given out to three groups of students: students in Ithaca, New York; students in Berkeley, California; and students attending UC Santa Cruz (nearest to the epicenter), California. The differences in geography resulted in differences in how students had experienced the quake. Students in Ithaca had, by and large, only heard about the quake, but they didn't necessarily have any personal connection to the people involved. Students in Berkeley hadn't necessarily had their immediate safety threatened, but they might have known people or have known of people who had been affected. Students attending UC Santa Cruz had their lives disrupted more severely, as their university and other offices closed for several weeks while emergency crews worked on rescue and repair.

Neisser et al. (1996) found from follow-up interviews that the original memory stayed more intact for those who had had higher personal involvement because of their proximity to the event. If students were not directly involved, then accuracy dropped. Neisser promoted a social explanation for the decrease in episodic memory accuracy over time that he called the narrative hypothesis. With an event we hear about, we rehearse the narrative by talking to others and absorbing media reports about it. Over time, the memory becomes altered as we incorporate all of the additional information we hear from other sources. In a way, this view can be seen as a problem of low source monitoring combined with trace updating theory.

While lacking a control group, Yuille and Cutshall (1986) present additional evidence that direct involvement in an event can mean fairly resilient memories of the event. A person attempted to rob a gun store in the daytime in Canada. The gun store owner gave chase after the individual, and gun fire was exchanged. About forth-five people were witnesses to the event that spilled out of the store and onto the street. The robber was killed. Police then took statements from all the witnesses, including the gun store owner and his wife. Because the robber was killed, the statements the police collected were available for memory researchers to use as the initial report of the memory of an event. Yuille and Cutshall (1986) contacted as many of the witnesses as possible for interviews three months later. They asked open-ended questions about what could be remembered. The researchers also tried to include a few false items to see whether the witnesses might be susceptible to suggestion. Comparing the answers of the follow-up interview to the police reports, Yuille and Cutshall (1986) found that the witnesses were, overall, fairly consistent and resistant to false information. One possible implication from this line of research is that the accuracy of a memory tends to relate to the depth of processing that the original event required. If something was simply a matter of hearsay, then it becomes easy to manipulate with more hearsay.

Autobiographical Memory System

Autobiographical memories are the memories that make up who we are. Autobiographical memories include episodic memories of personal events that define us, but will also include general knowledge about who we are. The "self" as we see ourselves is always the focus of autobiographical memories (Baddeley, 2012, p. 77). Autobiographical memories are not always one fixed slice of time. They include moments from our lives, activities we did repeatedly, as well as general time periods. We do not always consciously store those events that turn out to be important parts of who we are. Because of the diversity in types of memory, autobiographical memories are best thought of as a system, rather than just a subset of episodic memories.

One memory researcher has compared autobiographical memories to the experience of riding a merry-go-round (Rubin, 2012). Autobiographical memories include many different functions of the brain, such as sensations, perceptions, metacognitive judgments, emotions, and actions; and all of these functions interact with each other. There's knowledge of why those events occurred and what they meant for us, and those times we talked about these events with other people. These memories constitute the "story of me" (Fivush, 2012, p. 228). In this sense, the episodic memories for ourselves can't be separated from general knowledge about the world, since we have to use the conceptual understanding to make sense of those past events and why they mattered.

Autobiographical memories include how we have seen ourselves in the past (e.g., back in high school, when I cared what others thought about my appearance more than I do now) as well as how the culture we live in encourages us to interpret our lives (e.g., some cultures approach marriage as an arrangement, rather than a pronouncement of mutual love). So, autobiographical memories are not just about the event that took place, such as where and when; but they are also the subjective perspective or interpretation of the event. This subjectivity is the interpretation for why the event mattered. We can reflect on ourselves through these memories, and our perception of these events can change over time. These subjective perceptions can take time to develop, at least through adolescence. This is why, for autobiographical researchers, the "remember/know" dichotomy is more about recollection and belief.

Development into early adulthood may be important for autobiographical memories to form, since we need a sense both of the passage of time as well as of how the culture we live in teaches us to commonly interpret what happens to us. Culture and society inform us about what is expected, what behaviors at what ages are appropriate, and what behaviors to model (Fivush, 2011; Fivush, Habermas, Waters, & Zaman, 2011; Nelson & Fivush, 2004).

Dimensions and Functions of Autobiographical Memories

The precise nature of "autobiographical memories" is not completely clear. They represent biographical facts (e.g., "I went to parochial school in Nebraska until my family relocated in 1985"), but will also include copies of events (W. F. Brewer, 1986). While they feel like copies of the original event, they can be reinterpreted in light of later events. So, my confusion as a child over how my father behaved for a few years might change when I'm older and I better understand the work stress he was going through at a particular period of his life. Recent autobiographical memories feel like copies because we typically take a field perspective in them and they feel fairly vivid (Robinson & Swanson, 1993), but later ones may shift to an observer view, which can't be a copy (Cohen & Faulkner, 1988). Some autobiographical memories are fairly specific (e.g., "passing my driver's license test on the second try") while others are fairly general (e.g., "family dinners").

The importance and emotionality of an event changes over time. For example, a fairly minor encounter may turn into something more meaningful later, or what seemed very consequential in the moment turns out to be nothing days later. The effectiveness of salience and emotions as cues can decline over time. As an example of how difficult it is in the moment to determine, consider Michael Palin, a member of the British comedy group

Monty Python. He kept a diary during the most active time period of the group's rise and popularity in England and the United States and published those diaries (Palin, 2008). In rereading them, he was shocked to find that he had thought no fewer than six times that the group had disbanded—only for them to regroup later. In those moments, when his livelihood and the cause of his celebrity status appeared to be over, he wrote it down—and forgot about those bad days later on ("Chronicling Comedy in 'The Python Years,'" n.d.). These issues illuminate the "psychological context" of autobiographical memories. As we change what we think of an event, it alters the memorability of the event itself. We can reinterpret events in light of later events.

Autobiographical memories are believed to serve three overlapping functions (H. L. Williams et al., 2008). First, autobiographical memories serve a directive function, in that they can be accessed for information on how to resolve a problem based on what we tried the last time we encountered a situation (Baddeley, 1988). The directive role of autobiographical memories is present in the advice we get from our parents and give to our children. Parents explain what happened to them and use it to (hopefully) guide future actions of their children (Goldsmith & Pillemer, 1988). This role is also present in the choice many Americans made in avoiding air travel after the September 11, 2001 terrorist attacks (Pillemer, 2003).

According to Neisser and Hyman (1999), autobiographical memories support a social function as well. When something we see as important for ourselves has happened, we share it with others. They share their memories and thoughts about it as well. Autobiographical memories help us to make sense of who we are in the larger social context (Conway, 2012). The interaction of pooling our experiences with others helps us to understand the lives of other people and develop feelings of empathy for them (Fivush, Haden, & Reese, 1996). Conversation is more believable when we share personal memories as well (Pillemer, 1992). When episodic memory has been impaired through brain damage, social relationships have been found to suffer (Robinson & Swanson, 1990). The relating of and listening to personal stories may be the social glue that bonds people in society.

Finally, autobiographical memories are believed to serve a self function. The events that make up who we are become a "database of the self" (Conway, 2005). These memories contain who we are, what we have been, and what we think we will be. Conway and other researchers believe we strive to achieve a sense of coherence or consistency in our sense of self. One outcome from wanting coherence is that we experience an incentive to distort and possibly fabricate memories in a way that confirms our values for ourselves. This can be positive and enhancing in some ways, like a mentally healthy optimism for oneself and the future; or can be extremely negative or narcissistic.

Conway (1990) found evidence for autobiographical memories acting to preserve one's sense of self by using exam scores. Students who were about to take an exam were asked to predict what grade they expected on the exam and how important their performance on the exam was to them. Two weeks after taking the exam, he asked students to report again how important the exam score was in their minds. If students had done better on the exam than they had expected, the importance of the exam increased on the second report. If the results were worse than expected, then the score decreased in importance. In this way, autobiographical memories could be part of a cognitive system of self-justification, shifting our expectations and values after we see the outcome of an event.

One striking example of this role for autobiographical memory was Neisser's analysis (1981) of the accuracy of John Dean's testimony to the U.S. Congress about his involvement in Watergate. John Dean supplied a 245-page report that recalled dozens of meetings with a number of people over a period of several years. His apparent ability to accurately recall what was said, when, and by whom was impressive. Later, tape recordings of many of those meetings became public record, and people could check John Dean's memory with transcripts of the recordings. Neisser compared the two records and what he found was two-fold. First, John Dean was not as perfectly accurate as he had seemed, although the *gist* of what he recalled did tend to be accurate. John Dean himself partially credited using news reports to help him remember the various meetings that took place. Second, his personal role in the events tended to be overstated—the memories were more self-centered than the actual events. To some extent, the context of the retrieval (a major report to Congress about a personal role in a Presidential scandal) in some ways encouraged an exaggerated role.

People who have been diagnosed with depression tend to have autobiographical memories that are less detailed and vivid, and more emotionally negative (Healy & Williams, 1999). The rumination on negative thoughts and memories becomes self-perpetuating, as mood-congruent recall elicits autobiographical memories that match the current sense of oneself. What may permit more emotionally negative recall in depression is an altered criterion for how specific a response to a cue needs to be. J. M. G. Williams, Watts, MacLeod, and Mathews (1997) found that clinically depressed patients give very general responses to cue words for retrieval, whereas non-depressed participants prefer to give specific examples. With therapy, the depressed patients stopped giving overly general responses.

What is believed to drive the use of autobiographical memories as a part of how we see ourselves, our self-concept, is a desire to be consistent. The consistency bias is the motivation to see our current actions as consistent with our sense of self by bringing past feelings and beliefs more in-line with current views (D. Davis & Loftus, 2007; Schacter, 2001).

These proposed functions of autobiographical memories have been validated, to some extent. Hyman and Faries (1992) asked participants to provide autobiographical memories and the situations in which they used them. Their participants were aware primarily of using autobiographical memories to share their experiences and describe themselves to others, citing the social function over the directive and self functions. The functions are probably not completely independent of each other, either. Bluck, Alea, Habermas, and Rubin (2005) created a questionnaire about personal experiences that included direct questions about each function and found overlap between them in the participants' answers. The directive function was broadly applied and including thinking about the past instead of just the future. The social function seemed to include new relationships that were developing. Pasupathi (2003) provides a possible emotional function for autobiographical memories—retelling events allows us to gain some emotional control over what has happened to us and to elicit emotional responses from others.

Autobiographical memories do not all possess the same traits. We usually experience them voluntarily, but some are involuntary and will present themselves unintentionally. These are usually very vivid and emotional. One researcher found that people reported having an average of three to four of these involuntary autobiographical memories a day (Berntsen, 1996). To find out what usually triggered involuntary autobiographical memories, Mace (2004) asked participants to keep a diary for two weeks. Of the over 800 involuntary memories the participants reported, the majority of the involuntary autobiographical memories were cued by abstract thoughts or words. The abstract thoughts or words may have been internal, such as an idle thought, or external, overheard from a conversation or television. Involuntary memories have been found to impact the mood of the rememberer more than voluntary ones (Berntsen & Hall, 2004).

Contextual Complexities

While it is easier to think about autobiographical memories as pure events, in reality, they will always be some mix of personal event and general knowledge (Baddeley, 2012). The general knowledge is necessary to interpret the importance and meaning of the personal event. In some cases, an autobiographical event may include very little episodic memory. Movie actor Harrison Ford, famous for his roles in the Star Wars and Indiana Jones series, read a biography about himself in preparation for being interviewed for the television series "Inside the Actor's Studio." He claimed he simply no longer remembered some of the events that he was sharing about his own life with the audience. His retelling of them was more of a factual recounting from memory rather than a relived event.

These overlapping functions highlight the complex nature of autobiographical memories. Memories of personal events will be always be embedded in a particular context and tied to some set of personal goals of the time. Rubin (2012) points out how the situation may drive the quality of the encoding of the event. For an event that is ordinary and routine, the memory of the event will probably include less visual and emotional information. If an event was imagined, like a daydream, then the memory will include general knowledge, creative elements, and emotional reactions that could be tied to one's life story. A life-threatening event can produce vivid, emotional memories that may return as flashbacks. The context of retrieval may alter the memory as well. An event may be true but in the course of retelling it, the storyteller may enhance his or her role in it and take some freedoms with the details for the purpose of the story itself. Describing an event mechanically, just the basic events as they unfolded, may not seem very episodic at all.

In each situation, the activity level of the parts of the brain that support the creation and retrieval of autobiographical memories will change. The relationship between the episodic memory of the event and the general knowledge surrounding the meaning of the event will change as well. The dynamic nature of autobiographical memories is likely due to the fact that memories, whether episodic or general knowledge, are products—not the processes underlying them (Rubin, 2012).

The Structure of Autobiographical Memories

Autobiographical memories include grouped information around personal events, and they can be retrieved on demand. How are they organized and structured? Memory researchers have focused on two particular aspects of autobiographical memories: how they are organized by time or theme, and their emotionality. We will end this section with a theory that attempts to explain the overall structure of autobiographical memories.

Organization by Time or Theme

Autobiographical memories appear to be organized by time, chronologically or by periods of one's life, or by theme, such as "holidays," "parties," or "illnesses." Conway and Bekerian (1987) found that retrieval benefits when an individual is cued by a lifetime period, such as "time at college." Retrieval is faster when the order of recall is chronological (Anderson & Conway, 1993).

Autobiographical memories are not necessarily indexed by activities, but by themes and periods of one's life. In a good example of a diary study, Wagenaar (1986) recorded 2,400 events of his daily life over six years—writing down who was present at each event, what happened, where and when it was; and he added a critical detail. He was interested in finding out which facts would be likely to be retained and which were the best cues for retrieval. He also rated the pleasantness, emotionality, and saliency of each event. Wagenaar had a colleague quiz him. He would be questioned with one cue at a time, starting with any one of them, and then another and another, ending on the critical detail if he wasn't able to remember the event by then. Wagenaar found that more cues usually helped, which supports other research. His rate of forgetting went from 70 percent for recent memories down to 35 percent over the four years' worth of memories. The cues were not all equally effective. What the event involved was typically best, followed by where it occurred. The date of the event was nearly useless. Wagenaar concluded that most personal event memories are not marked by a precise date. Instead, we probably mentally organize events by themes and lifetime periods.

Barsalou (1988) used a variety of cues to see what affected remembering autobiographical memories, such as activities, traits about other participants, location, and time. He found that cues about who was involved elicited the most memories, particularly those that involved personal goals like "learning to drive." Only 21 percent of the memories were specific episodes; most were extended events or events that were repeated. Barsalou used a statistical technique known as a "cluster analysis" to see the pattern of groupings in the memories. Chronology appeared to be the broadest form of organization of the memories, and general time periods (e.g., "before I was married") after that. The time periods could overlap, as well.

Some evidence indicates that we do not group personal events along only one dimension. Lancaster and Barsalou (1997) asked participants to imagine different stories, each with a person, location, activity, and time. The participants were given a surprise test using the same four cues used in Barsalou (1988). Participants used each of the cues to categorize the stories, but the participants preferred activity and person cues. In fact, participants would often shift from one to the other while remembering. Each cue seems to act as a new perspective once a cue has been exhausted. Lancaster and Barsalou concluded that we organize events in memory fairly dynamically, and an event might be in more than one category. Possibly different memories are "tagged" or flagged by multiple cues, so retrieval can take on several pathways, depending on the needs of the person at the time of recall.

Emotions and Their Role

To see if emotions are used for organization, memory researchers will provide emotional words as cues and time how long it takes someone to report a memory. Robinson (1976) used a variety of cues for memory recall, and recall was the slowest with emotional cue words. However, Wagenaar (1986) found that ability to remember personal events was colored by how pleasant the event was: More pleasant events were better remembered, an effect referred to as the Pollyanna principle. (The name comes from a 1913 novel about a child who tries to see the positive in every situation. To say someone is "Pollyannaish" implies an optimistic naïveté about a situation and is usually meant to be condescending.) Schulkind and Woldorf (2005) presented musical excerpts to participants and asked what memories the music provoked. At a second session, participants were asked to date the memories they had reported at the initial session and rate them for valence, or emotional strength. Upbeat, positive music elicited memories with higher valence ratings, which indicated to the authors that perhaps emotions can be used as an organizational element.

Conway's Self-Memory System

Martin Conway has proposed a system to describe the organization and structure of autobiographical memories (Cohen & Conway, 2008; M. Conway, 2012; M. A. Conway, 2005; M. A. Conway & Pleydell-Pearce, 2000). This approach is more framework than theory (Conway, 2012). He sees autobiographical memories as belonging to a self-memory system that has two major components: a "working self" and an autobiographical knowledge base (see Fig. 9.1).

The working self is the perspective we have on ourselves today, our sense of who we are and what we want to become. In other words, it includes our conceptual sense of ourselves and a goal system. It is organized in and accessed in working memory. The purpose of the working self component is to limit what we spend time thinking about so that we can focus on what matters most to us. We can then make decisions about what we want to do, using our time effectively.

The information that the working self needs in order to make those decisions resides in the autobiographical memory knowledge base, and includes information grouped by lifetime periods, the most broad category (e.g., "since having children"), and general events (e.g., "grocery shopping"). Specific events reside underneath these, hierarchically. The lifetime periods and general events are information that is accessed by the working memory in relation to currently active goals.

At the most abstract level, the autobiographical knowledge base acts as a "life story." It includes factual knowledge about ourselves as well as evaluations about who we are. The information will refer to the different social roles we have, such as parent, sibling, child, and coworker. We can see ourselves in each role, a "self-image," that we use to access different parts of the knowledge base, so thinking about different roles will elicit different knowledge, general events, and specific memories. Our current working self houses recent experiences within the current lifetime period along with our current goals. When our goals change, we adjust how we see ourselves and form new goals that will alter how we organize our working self and related memories. The older version of the working self, the self we once were, is stored in memory as a general event with its related memories.

FIGURE 9.1   Overview of Conway's model of the autobiographical memory system

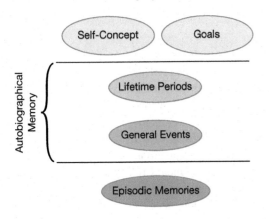

Developmental Changes in Autobiographical Memories

Our ability to form and retain autobiographical memories appears to change over the course of our lives (Fivush, 2011). Researchers who investigate the autobiographical memories people form over their lives focus on two kinds of changes: changes to the average properties of the memories one stores, and changes in how autobiographical memories are used over time (Fitzgerald & Broadbridge, 2013).

A popular technique for tracking changes in autobiographical memories by age is memory probes. Memory probes are cue words that are used to trigger a recollection. This approach has a long history. Sir Francis Galton (1879) would quiz himself with random words to see what memories they would provoke and was surprised to find a lot of the memories they sparked came from childhood. Sigmund Freud was aware of Galton's finding about his memories, and this became one basis for Freud's focus on early childhood as a special period in personality development, as well as Freud's use of "free-association" as a therapy technique. Crovitz and Schiffman (1974) revived this technique, and most recently, memory probes have been used to get a better sense of the distribution of memories across the human lifespan, a topic we will explore later in this section.

Research studies across the lifespan can have some special features. Since the variable "age" cannot be directly manipulated, researchers will usually take one of three approaches in order to capture differences by age. In a cross-sectional design, the performance of several groups of people of different ages are compared. A strength of this approach is that it is relatively practical and might not take a lot of time, relatively speaking. Of course, a major issue is that by comparing different groups of people who are in different stages of their lives, it's never completely clear to what extent differences in performance are due just to age. If you were to compare who you are today, and say, your political beliefs, to those of your parents, it's hard to say that any differences are solely due to age. The times we live in during major stages of life (adolescence, young adulthood, middle adulthood, and so on) will probably also have an effect on us and can't be completely ignored. Also, we can never be too certain just how similar the people are in the different groups. Are the differences in performance due to age, or differences in personality, intelligence, or emotional awareness?

The gold standard is the longitudinal design. In this approach, one set of individuals is tracked for many years and the participants are sought out repeatedly and retested. The strength of this approach is that changes to an individual over time are clearly tracked and act as something of a buffer from differences in time periods between groups. Of course, this design has its own issues. First, they can take a long time—decades, sometimes—which makes them costly to run. Second, longitudinal studies can suffer from what is called a mortality rate, meaning that some of the participants will not survive the study, drop out, become unreachable, or decline to participate later on. And, ultimately, this design doesn't completely negate the issue of different cultural time periods, since the entire sample will have experienced the same ones. To what extent, for example, did all young adults have their political beliefs shaped by the Vietnam War and the Watergate scandal?

One design incorporates features from both cross-sectional and longitudinal designs in order to gain the advantages of both and minimize some of the disadvantages. In a sequential design, several groups of participants of different ages will be assessed, and then assessed again some time later (see Fig. 9.2). For example, groups of participants at ages 5, 10, 15, and 20 can be evaluated once and then again five years later. At the second assessment, the groups' ages are now 10, 15, 20, and 25. What this approach allows for is tracking of genuine change over time plus comparison between different age groups. So, the age span included runs from 5 to 25 years, but it only took 5 years to complete. Additionally, the average performance of the groups at the end of the five-year period can be compared to the other group at the beginning, verifying that the differences are age-related and are not based on innate differences of each group. Loss of participants is kept to a minimum as well (Schaie, 1965).

FIGURE 9.2   Flowchart of the three designs unique to developmental research. Longitudinal approaches capture developmental change with one group, but take a long time and can produce missing data from participants who drop out. Cross-sectional approaches are quicker but lose any authentic developmental change over time. Sequential designs combine the best features of both to track developmental change in a shorter period of time than longitudinal studies.

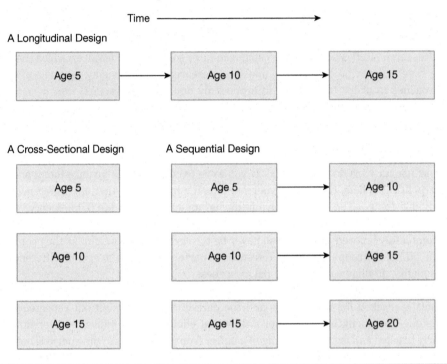

Using these designs, researchers have found that while autobiographical memories tend to be rich in details, the amount that any one person usually provides varies (this phenomenon is called intraindividual variability, as in variability *within* the individual). Fleeson and Jolley (2006) found the intraindividual variability often exceeded the variance across different groups for amount of details in autobiographical memories.

One of the difficulties with analyzing autobiographical memories is that they do not exist separately from one another. As time passes, memories can get reinterpreted based on later events. Memories of older events are used to filter and understand new events, so it's difficult to consider them completely separately. As autobiographical memory theorists have noted, remembering one's own wedding may be colored by the birth of a child from that union later, and then the wedding of that child. Each event colors the next, and the interpretation of each change.

Developing a Narrative

By adulthood, autobiographical memories include information on who was present, what happened, where and when it was, why and how people reacted to the event, both then

FIGURE 9.3 The use of story elements in recalled autobiographical memories increases with age (Bauer, Larkina, & Deocampo, 2011).

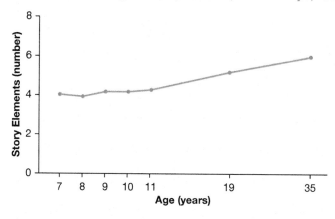

Source: Adapted from Berntsen, D., & Rubin, D. C. (2012).

Note: Hypothetical values; are approximates.

and now (Bauer, 2012). It has a story-like quality to it. Very young children, however, may confirm or deny that an event happened but that may be all to the recollection. By age 3, they can add a story element to it (Fivush, 2012; Nelson & Fivush, 2004). Adult participants gave children's recollections a modal rating of 1 out of 4 for the coherence.

Another method for studying the development of autobiographical memories is to use the cue-word method to provoke memories with different age sets (e.g., Bauer, Burch, Scholin, & Guler, 2007). In this cross-sectional study, Bauer, Larkina, and Deocampo (2011) used twenty cue words with seven- to eleven-year-olds, college students, and middle-aged participants (see Fig. 9.3). They then analyzed the memories for a number of features. They found a gradual increase in the scope of the story elements with older participants. Seven- and eight-year-olds were in their own category for story-telling ability. Adult-like story ability arrived by about age nine. Thirty-five-year-olds had much more in-depth narrative ability.

Fivush (2012) believes that when we are younger, we do not have the ability to create a narrative story of our memories, so we work with just the personal event memories alone. As we get older, we get better at connecting events into a story. This may not be a matter of developing an autobiographical memory system but learning the social and cognitive skills needed to understand context and ourselves in it. Autobiographical memories involve knowing ourselves and being able to link events over time.

The autobiographical memories in our preschool years have a highly subjective perspective. According to Fivush, autobiographical memories need three developments: children need to form a representation of themselves (sometimes called a "concept of self"); they need to understand their own internal states as tied to their actions; and they need to understand that others can have internal states that may or may not be the same.

To have a concept of oneself and be able to connect mental states to behaviors, a number of underlying developments are necessary and take time to develop. First, development of language is important, in order to be able to form the story narrative of the memory. With spoken references at about sixteen months of age, parents begin to elaborate on what language children can provide (Vygotsky, 1987). This process provides practice at framing ways to understand and think about some event. Fivush and colleagues found that with four-year olds, parents use more emotion words than the children do, as if they are modeling how to mentally represent the internal states (Fivush, 2011; Fivush,

Haden, & Reese, 2006). By age ten, children use more emotion and cognitive words (such as "think" and "believe").

Second, a theory of mind is necessary; that is, the understanding that others have a unique perspective of their own and that may not represent one's own perspective (broadly speaking; see Tomasello, 1999). It's only by age two that children recognize themselves in a mirror; the perspective they take on events tends to be simple perspectives of the immediate—just what is happening "here-and-now." Without a fuller self-concept, there is no life narrative yet.

Third, the ability to build the perspectives of others and make links between them over time is necessary, too. Tying mental states together across periods of time doesn't appear to happen until the end of the preschool years (Lagattuta, 2007, 2014). When children of different ages hear a short story about being approached by a friendly dog or seeing a friend, all preschoolers think the child in the story will be happy about the event, even if they were given a background story about a scary encounter with a dog a week before or a fight with friend. Hence, most preschoolers do not use a prior event to describe the current one. Only 39 percent of five-year-olds treat mental states (like fear, anger) as persisting over time. Of adults, 89 percent will use persistent thoughts to describe a later situation. It's not until after preschool that a subjective perspective that involves events that are associated with each other over time becomes possible.

Beyond having a concept of self and being able to link events, autobiographical memories require a personal timeline. This means having both an understanding of calendar time and important events in one's own culture. Understanding calendar time (days of the week, months) develops after the preschool years (W. J. Friedman, 2004). Infants can follow a fixed sequence of events. By the end of the first year, they can put a sequence in order. For preschoolers, putting events on specific days of the week will not be possible yet. When preschoolers use words like "yesterday" and "tomorrow," they usually mean to indicate any time in the past or any time in the future. By the end of preschool, a child can judge which of two events happened more recently. If the events were several months apart though, they are only guessing at the age of eight (W. J. Friedman, 1992; W. J. Friedman & Kemp 1998). In middle childhood and adolescence, a personal timeline forms.

While an understanding of calendar time arrives around the preteen years, adults still prefer to use lifetime periods over months and days of the week (Belli, Smith, Andreski, & Agrawal, 2007). Adults will use culturally defined time periods to delineate broad time periods to help date events. Developmental psychologists refer to these time periods using terms such as "puberty," "tweeners," and "emerging adulthood," for example. These cultural time periods can be broad (e.g., "Generation X," "Millennials") or more subcultural (e.g., Thorne & McLean, 2002).

Between childhood and adolescence, a number of advances take place (Bauer, 2012). The breadth of the memory stories grows. Separate events become more integrated, and the ability to link the meaning between those events grows, so the narratives around personal memories become more coherent. Most likely the underlying memory is better integrated as well. Between ages seven and eleven, the length and complexity of the narratives increase (Van Abbema & Bauer, 2005). The amount of information in the memory story almost doubles, and the chronological information improves (Morris, Baker-Ward, & Bauer, 2010). Between ages ten and twelve, children get better at explaining to the listener when and where the event occurred (Reese et al., 2011). By adolescence, the memory stories include an extended life narrative (Bohn & Berntsen, 2008; Habermas & Bluck, 2000).

Ultimately, autobiographical memory might not be just a memory system, but be more like your personal legend (Fivush, 2012).

Autobiographical Memory and Older Adults

Research into changes in autobiographical memory for older adults has focused on the accuracy of autobiographical memory as we age, and whether details of the remembered events are more readily forgotten. Accuracy is often hard to verify, since there is rarely an original recollection of the event. From the perspective of forming a life narrative, the accuracy of a personal memory may not necessarily be the most important factor. The usefulness may be more in terms of forming a coherent self-concept.

To find out what kinds of cues are most effective at retrieving autobiographical memories of older adults, Catal and Fitzgerald (2004) used the diaries of a seventy-eight-year-old woman and her seventy-nine-year-old husband to verify the memories they reported from a cue-word method. The diaries mostly included repetitive events, and she was usually the only participant. The researchers found that cues about what event occurred were the most helpful for retrieval, and cues about the date of the event were the least helpful. Mixing the activity and date of the event were often the best combination.

To what extent do we lose details as we age? There is evidence that details about episodes are lost as we get older. However, older adults are known to communicate fewer details by choice as a matter of trying to gauge the listener's interest. Levine, Svoboda, Hay, Winocur, and Moscovitch (2002) evaluated whether the change in reported details was due to differences in communication goals as we age or to changes to the prefrontal cortex over time. The number of recalled details in episodic and semantic memories of healthy older adults (aged sixty-six to eighty-nine) were compared to those of younger adults; and Levine and colleagues found a difference in the average number of episodic details that were presented. Older adults shared about twenty fewer. Details for semantic memories were the same for each age group, indicating that the difference was not due to a loss of brain functioning. Levine and colleagues then asked the participants for more details, simulating an interested listening. Younger adults added an average of thirty-five episodic details, and the older adults added twenty-five. So, some of the detail loss that older adults present stems from including information that seems pertinent to the listener.

Brain Processing Underlying Autobiographical Memories

Observing the brain functioning during autobiographical memory retrieval can help to explain the different processes involved, and which components of the brain support the general process of autobiographical memory recollection.

The challenge of researching autobiographies from a brain functioning perspective is maintaining a high level of experimental control while having participants engage in tasks that are lifelike, or have ecological validity, as discussed in Chapter 2. The generic cues method involves presenting participants with unique words that are meant to elicit memories unexpectedly (e.g., Cabeza & St. Jacques, 2007; St. Jacques, Kragel, & Rubin, 2011). The idea is to create memory retrieval that is more like everyday experiences than a memorized list of words would. Once participants have a memory, they are asked to spend time thinking about it and may rate the experience for the amount of "reliving" they experienced. This helps to distinguish truly relived memories and help researchers observe the process of an autobiographical memory being constructed.

A second method, the prospective method, involves asking participants to record personal events in a video diary using a small recorder. Images from these entries are used to cue memories (e.g., Daselaar, Fleck, Dobbins, Madden, & Cabeza, 2006; St. Jacques, Rubin, LaBar, & Cabeza, 2008). Sometimes the recorders are equipped with a fisheye lens, so the video will have a field-perspective look to them.

The Autobiographical Memory Retrieval Network

Generally speaking, retrieval of autobiographical memories usually begins with activity in the left hemisphere, although not always (Maguire, 2001). Several studies have found the lateral prefrontal cortex to be key (Petrides, 2005). The prefrontal cortex appears to be necessary for the sense of the memory being in relation to ourselves, or self-reference, an important part of autobiographical memories. Controlled attention to an autobiographical memory appears to engage the dorsal parietal cortex (Cabeza, 2008; Cabeza, Ciaramelli, Olson, & Moscovitch, 2008; see Fig. 9.4).

When looking at our own personal photos in contrast to someone else's, the activity in the prefrontal cortex is the same as looking at a fixation point on a screen (St. Jacques,

FIGURE 9.4   Areas of the brain associated with retrieval of autobiographical memories

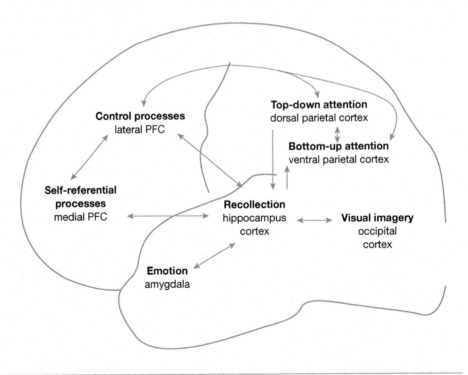

Source: Garrett (2015, Figure 9.20, p. 282).

Conway, Lowder, & Cabeza, 2011). Researchers generally see self-reference as a default mental state (Gusnard & Raichle, 2001; Raichle & Snyder, 2007), so this default mode of viewing the world overlaps well with autobiographical memory retrieval.

Retrieval for autobiographical memories is viewed by researchers as fairly complex, and a broad set of brain regions are responsible (Cabeza & St. Jacques, 2007). Besides the left prefrontal cortex, other areas of the brain that have been noted to support autobiographical memories include the hippocampus and retrosplenial cortex for their role in retrieval (Diana, Yonelinas, & Ranganath, 200), the amygdala for emotional processing (LaBar & Cabeza, 2006), and the occipital lobe and visual cortex for visual imagery (Daselaar et al., 2008). An analysis of 24 studies found the presence of emotion in an autobiographical memory tends to be what shifts the balance in brain activity from the left hemisphere to the right (Svoboda, McKinnon, & Levine, 2006).

Conway, Pleydell-Pearce, Whitecross, and Sharpe (2003) activation spread in the cerebral cortex using an EEG machine while participants read cue words. If a word triggered an autobiographical memory, they were to hold onto it, and then report it. Conway and colleagues found that the initial experience of the memory involved the prefrontal cortex, an area known for verbal and executive processing. Within moments, activation moved to the occipital and temporal lobes, a common pattern for experiencing visual imagery.

Relatedly, Daselaar and colleagues (2008) used a cue-word technique also, asking participants to press a button when they thought of an autobiographical memory. Meanwhile, brain activity was monitored using an fMRI machine. Twenty-four seconds after a button press, participants were asked to rate the emotion of the memory and whether they felt like they had relived it. When participants had autobiographical memory experiences, three areas were activated within one and a half seconds of seeing the cue word: the right prefrontal cortex, medial temporal lobe, and hippocampus. The right prefrontal cortex seemed to engage in a search to retrieve the memory and then used the other two areas of the brain for support. All three areas ended their involvement within three seconds of the presentation of the word. After three seconds, the visual cortex and left prefrontal cortex were activated and continued to increase in activation for twelve seconds before fading. If emotion was present, the hippocampus and amygdala were active. Interestingly, they were active before the individual had pressed the button, so the feeling of an autobiographical memory may arrive before an individual can consciously report on experiencing the memory.

Neurobiology techniques have also been used to try to understand a documented gender difference in autobiographical memories. Women tend to have longer and more detailed autobiographical memories than men (A. Friedman & Pines, 1991). They are more accurate at dating them (Skowronski & Thompson, 1990) and faster at recalling them (P. J. Davis, 1999). One possibility is that many autobiographical memory studies use words as prompts, which could lend themselves to a difference in retrieval, since gender differences with regards to language are well known (Andreano & Cahill, 2009). To balance this out, St. Jacques, Conway, and Cabeza (2011) used retrieval cues that were words or photographs, and found no gender differences for ratings of the memories for a sense of reliving, importance, vividness, emotion, or uniqueness. However, male participants showed a difference in brain activity for reliving autobiographical memories from visual cues than verbal, a difference not seen for the female participants.

CHAPTER SUMMARY

In this chapter, we took a closer look at one type of long-term memory, episodic memories. These are memories that are primarily viewed as personal events, and are contrasted to general knowledge, which is discussed in the next chapter. They take on the nature of "mental time travel," meaning that there is a sense of reexperiencing the event when episodic memories are recalled. Episodic memories can be viewed externally, an observer perspective, or from a first-person perspective, known as a field perspective. The observer perspective tends to make the memory less emotionally vivid.

Episodic memories include many characteristics of the event, including sensory information, emotions and thoughts during the event including goals at the time. Part of the retention of episodic memories is rehearsal that comes from socially sharing the event with others. Recalled personal events can vary by age, with episodic memories reflecting the general interests and goals of each age period. Whether episodic memories are stored as part of a system that is separate from general knowledge is not clear at this time. The frontal lobes and hippocampus appear to be key areas for episodic memory processing.

Particularly vivid episodic memories are sometimes referred to as flashbulb memories. The experience of flashbulb memories is a hyperawareness of the situation an individual was in when the event happened, usually of high personal consequence or national importance. Flashbulb memories have been found to lose accuracy over time as much as normal episodic memories, but the confidence in the accuracy of the memory remains high, nonetheless. This decrease in accuracy is mitigated at least somewhat if the individual is physically near or part of the event as it happens.

Some researchers have approached episodic memories as a part of a larger system for autobiographical memories. Autobiographical memories are believed to provide us with the conceptual understanding of who we are by providing us with access to the events that we believe define ourselves. Who we see ourselves as tends then to determine the course of action we take in many situations. Autobiographical memories are believed to inform us on how to solve problems, for sharing ourselves and what matters to us with others, and to help us better understand ourselves. We appear to have a need to take actions that we feel are consistent with who we are, a consistency bias.

Autobiographical memories are usually studied using diary studies and memory probes. Research using diary studies has found that trying to remember an event based on the date alone was almost never useful. Autobiographical memories are probably not organized by calendar dates then, but organized by themes in our lives or major events. Research using memory probes has found support for theme-based organization to autobiographical memories. Some themes are broad time periods, and others are shorter events that lasted for days. Conway has proposed a framework for thinking about autobiographical memories. He sees autobiographical memories as part of a self-memory system, with two major components: the working self, an understanding of who we are today, and a knowledge base comprised of autobiographical memories. The knowledge base acts as a collection of the stories of our lives.

Using one of three common research designs (cross-sectional, longitudinal, or sequential), researchers have found that autobiographical memories tend not to have a strong personal narrative when we are young. Three developments must occur in order for an autobiographical system to form. Initially, the child needs a representation of himself or herself as an individual. Second, the child needs a theory of mind. Finally, the child has to understand that others have internal mental states that may not match their own. Older adults report fewer details to their episodic memories, but this is likely due to self-censuring in order to not bore others rather than a decline brain functioning.

Research into the brain processes underlying the autobiographical memory system has been difficult to do, since autobiographical memories can be fairly complex. The left hemisphere tends to be activated more at the beginning of retrieval of autobiographical memories, with activation shifting to the right hemisphere subsequently. Other studies have found the prefrontal cortex to be active at the beginning of retrieval, with the occipital and temporal lobes becoming more active over time. If the memory is emotional, the activation within the hippocampus and the amygdala have been noted before the person can even report experiencing the memory.

REVIEW QUESTIONS

1. While the distinction between personal events and general knowledge has been useful for research on memory, can you think of a personal memory for which you need no knowledge to understand or think about?

2. What flashbulb memories do you have? What would it require to verify how accurate those memories are?

3. Diary studies have sparked a lot of theories and research about autobiographical memories, but they aren't used for all episodic memory research. What kinds of limitations do diary study memories have for explaining memories?

4. Does the idea of your autobiographical memory system as your personal legend resonate with you? What has been your personal legend, so far?

KEY TERMS

Autobiographical memories   224
Autobiographical memory
    knowledge base   230
Belief   225
Consistency bias   227
Cross-sectional design   231
Directive   226
Episodic memories   219
Field perspective   220
Flashbulb memories   222
Generic cues   235

Intraindividual variability   232
Knowing   222
Longitudinal design   231
Memory probes   231
Mental time travel   220
Mortality rate   231
Narrative hypothesis   224
Observer perspective   220
Pollyanna principle   229
Prospective method   236
Recollection   225

Remembering   222
Self   226
Self-defining moments   219
Self-justification   226
Self-memory system   230
Self-reference   236
Sequential design   231
Social   226
Theory of mind   234
Working self   230

FURTHER RESOURCES

1. Weblink: Speculation over a possible connection between weaker autobiographical memories and autism:
   - http://theconversation.com/memory-and-sense-of-self-may-play-more-of-a-role-in-autism-than-we-thought-63210

2. Weblink: Parts of the brain that are activated when autobiographical memories are triggered by smell:
   - https://www.youtube.com/watch?v=vY-HbcPInXw

REFERENCES

Anderson, S. J., & Conway, M. A. (1993). Investigating the structure of autobiographical memories. *Journal of Experimental Psychology: Learning, Memory, and Cognition, 19*(5), 1178.

Andreano, J. M., & Cahill, L. (2009). Sex influences on the neurobiology of learning and memory. *Learning & Memory, 16*(4), 248–266.

Baddeley, A. (2007). *Working memory, thought, and action.* Oxford, England: Oxford University Press.

Baddeley, A. (2012). Reflections on autobiographical memory. In D. Rubin (Ed.), *Understanding autobiographical memory: Theories and Approaches* (pp. 70–88). Cambridge, England: Cambridge University Press.

Baddeley, A. D. (1988). But what the hell is it for? In *Practical aspects of memory: Current research and issues. Vol. 1: Memory in everyday life* (pp. 3–18). Chichester, England: Wiley.

Barsalou, L. W., U. Neisser, & E. Winograd (Eds.). (1988). The content and organization of autobiographical memories. In *Remembering reconsidered: Ecological and traditional approaches to the study of memory* (pp. 193–243). Cambridge, England: Cambridge University Press.

Bauer, P. J. (2012). The life I once remembered: The waxing and waning of early memories. In *Understanding autobiographical memory: Theories and approaches* (p. 226). Retrieved from https://books.google.com/books?hl=en&lr=&id=JGAhAwAAQBAJ&oi=fnd&pg=PA226&dq=fivush+2012+understanding+autobiographical+memories&ots=7aaiZMM-WS&sig=j-SAKluUwX-qtETb-NK98KdWnq4

Bauer, P. J., Burch, M. M., Scholin, S. E., & Güler, O. E. (2007). Using cue words to investigate the distribution of autobiographical memories in childhood. *Psychological Science, 18*(10), 910–916.

Bauer, P. J., Larkina, M., & Deocampo, J. (2011). Early memory development. In *The Wiley-Blackwell handbook of childhood cognitive development* (vol. 2; pp. 153–179). Chichester, England.

Belli, R. F., Smith, L. M., Andreski, P. M., & Agrawal, S. (2007). Methodological comparisons between CATI event history calendar and standardized conventional questionnaire instruments. *Public Opinion Quarterly, 71*(4), 603–622.

Berntsen, D. (1996). Involuntary autobiographical memories. *Applied Cognitive Psychology, 10*(5), 435–454.

Berntsen, D., & Hall, N. M. (2004). The episodic nature of involuntary autobiographical memories. *Memory & Cognition, 32*(5), 789–803.

Berntsen, D., Staugaard, S. R., & Sørensen, L. M. T. (2013). Why am I remembering this now? Predicting the occurrence of involuntary (spontaneous) episodic memories. *Journal of Experimental Psychology: General, 142*(2), 426.

Blagov, P. S., & Singer, J. A. (2004). Four dimensions of self-defining memories (specificity, meaning, content, and affect) and their relationships to self-restraint, distress, and repressive defensiveness. *Journal of Personality, 72*(3), 481–511.

Bluck, S., Alea, N., Habermas, T., & Rubin, D. C. (2005). A tale of three functions: The self-reported uses of autobiographical memory. *Social Cognition, 23*(1), 91–117.

Bohn, A., & Berntsen, D. (2008). Life story development in childhood: The development of life story abilities and the acquisition of cultural life scripts from late middle childhood to adolescence. *Developmental Psychology, 44*(4), 1135.

Brewer, J. B., Zhao, Z., Desmond, J. E., Glover, G. H., & Gabrieli, J. D. (1998). Making memories: Brain activity that predicts how well visual experience will be remembered. *Science, 281*(5380), 1185–1187.

Brewer, W. F. (1986). What is autobiographical memory? In *Autobiographical memory* (pp. 25–49). New York, NY: Cambridge University Press. https://doi.org/10.1017/CB09780511558313.006

Brown, R., & Kulik, J. (1977). Flashbulb memories. *Cognition, 5*(1), 73–99.

Cabeza, R. (2008). Role of parietal regions in episodic memory retrieval: The dual attentional processes hypothesis. *Neuropsychologia, 46*(7), 1813–1827.

Cabeza, R., Ciaramelli, E., Olson, I. R., & Moscovitch, M. (2008). The parietal cortex and episodic memory: An attentional account. *Nature Reviews Neuroscience, 9*(8), 613–625.

Cabeza, R., & St. Jacques, P. (2007). Functional neuroimaging of autobiographical memory. *Trends in Cognitive Sciences, 11*(5), 219–227.

Catal, L. L., & Fitzgerald, J. M. (2004). Autobiographical memory in two older adults over a twenty-year retention interval. *Memory & Cognition, 32*(2), 311–323.

Chronicling comedy in "The Python Years." (n.d.). Retrieved from npr.org/templates/story/story.php?storyId=1415774.

Cohen, G., & Conway, M. A. (Eds.). (2008). *Memory in the real world* (3rd ed.). Psychology Press.

Cohen, G., & Faulkner, D. (1988). *Life span changes in autobiographical memory.* Retrieved from http://psycnet.apa.org/psycinfo/1988-97682-043

Colegrove, F. W. (1899). Individual memories. *The American Journal of Psychology, 10*(2), 228–255.

Conway, M. (2012). On the nature of autobiographical memories. *Understanding autobiographical memory: Theories and approaches.* Retrieved from https://books.google.com/books?hl=en&lr=&id=JGAhAwAAQBAJ&oi=fnd&pg=PA11&dq=rubin+basic+systems+model&ots=7aaiZMM-QL&sig=RS8HND1Mi_wimiPE8HicTqWtCsU

Conway, M. A. (1990). Associations between autobiographical memories and concepts. *Journal of Experimental Psychology: Learning, Memory, and Cognition, 16*(5), 799.

Conway, M. A. (2005). Memory and the self. *Journal of Memory and Language, 53*(4), 594–628.

Conway, M. A., Anderson, S. J., Larsen, S. F., Donnelly, C. M., McDaniel, M. A., McClelland, A. G., . . . Logie, R. H. (1994). The formation of flashbulb memories. *Memory & Cognition, 22*(3), 326–343.

Conway, M. A., & Bekerian, D. A. (1987). Organization in autobiographical memory. *Memory & Cognition, 15*(2), 119–132.

Conway, M. A., Cohen, G., & Stanhope, N. (1992). Very long-term memory for knowledge acquired at school and university. *Applied Cognitive Psychology, 6*(6), 467–482.

Conway, M. A., & Pleydell-Pearce, C. W. (2000). The construction of autobiographical memories in the self-memory system. *Psychological Review, 107*(2), 261.

Conway, M. A., Pleydell-Pearce, C. W., Whitecross, S. E., & Sharpe, H. (2003). Neurophysiological correlates of memory for experienced and imagined events. *Neuropsychologia, 41*(3), 334–340.

Crovitz, H. F., & Schiffman, H. (1974). Frequency of episodic memories as a function of their age. *Bulletin of the Psychonomic Society, 4*(5), 517–518. https://doi.org/10.3758/BF03334277

Daselaar, S. M., Fleck, M. S., Dobbins, I. G., Madden, D. J., & Cabeza, R. (2006). Effects of healthy aging on hippocampal and rhinal memory functions: An event-related fMRI study. *Cerebral Cortex, 16*(12), 1771–1782.

Daselaar, S. M., Rice, H. J., Greenberg, D. L., Cabeza, R., LaBar, K. S., & Rubin, D. C. (2008). The spatiotemporal dynamics of autobiographical memory: Neural correlates of recall, emotional intensity, and reliving. *Cerebral Cortex, 18*(1), 217–229.

Davis, D., & Loftus, E. F. (2007). *Internal and external sources of misinformation in adult witness memory.* Retrieved from http://psycnet.apa.org/psycinfo/2006-22582-007

Davis, P. J. (1999). Gender differences in autobiographical memory for childhood emotional experiences. *Journal of Personality and Social Psychology, 76*(3), 498.

Diana, R. A., Yonelinas, A. P., & Ranganath, C. (2007). Imaging recollection and familiarity in the medial temporal lobe: A three-component model. *Trends in Cognitive Sciences, 11*(9), 379–386.

Finnbogadóttir, H., & Berntsen, D. (2013). Involuntary future projections are as frequent as involuntary memories, but more positive. *Consciousness and Cognition, 22*(1), 272–280.

Fitzgerald, J. M., & Broadbridge, C. L. (2013). Latent constructs of the Autobiographical Memory Questionnaire: A recollection-belief model of autobiographical experience. *Memory, 21*(2), 230–248.

Fivush, R. (2011). The development of autobiographical memory. *Annual Review of Psychology, 62*, 559–582.

Fivush, R. (2012). Subjective perspective and personal timeline in the development of autobiographical. *Understanding Autobiographical Memory: Theories and Approaches*, 226.

Fivush, R., Habermas, T., Waters, T. E., & Zaman, W. (2011). The making of autobiographical memory: Intersections of culture, narratives and identity. *International Journal of Psychology, 46*(5), 321–345.

Fivush, R., Haden, C., & Reese, E. (1996). Remembering, recounting, and reminiscing: The development of autobiographical memory in social context. In D. Rubin (Ed.), *Remembering our past: Studies in autobiographical memory* (pp. 341–359). Cambridge, England: Cambridge University Press.

Fivush, R., Haden, C. A., & Reese, E. (2006). Elaborating on elaborations: Role of maternal reminiscing style in cognitive and socioemotional development. *Child Development, 77*(6), 1568–1588.

Fleeson, W., & Jolley, S. (2006). *A proposed theory of the adult development of intraindividual variability in trait-manifesting behavior.* Routledge Handbooks Online. Retrieved from https://www.routledgehandbooks.com/doi/10.4324/9781315805610.ch3

Friedman, A., & Pines, A. (1991). Sex differences in gender-related childhood memories. *Sex Roles, 25*(1), 25–32.

Friedman, W. J. (1992). Children's time memory: The development of a differentiated past. *Cognitive Development, 7*(2), 171–187.

Friedman, W. J. (2004). Time in autobiographical memory. *Social Cognition, 22*(5: Special issue), 591–605.

Friedman, W. J., & Kemp, S. (1998). The effects of elapsed time and retrieval on young children's judgments of the temporal distances of past events. *Cognitive Development, 13*(3), 335–367.

Galton, F. (1879). Psychometric experiments. *Brain, 2*(2), 149–162.

Gardiner, J. M. (2008). Remembering and knowing. In J. H. Byrne (Ed.), *Learning and memory: A comprehensive reference* (pp. 285–305). Oxford, England: Academic Press. https://doi.org/10.1016/B978-012370509-9.00167-4

Gluck, J., & Bluck, S. (2007). Looking back across the life span: A life story account of the reminiscence bump. *Memory and Cognition, 35*, 1928–1939.

Goldsmith, L. R., & Pillemer, D. B. (1988). Memories of statements spoken in everyday contexts. *Applied Cognitive Psychology, 2*(4), 273–286.

Gusnard, D. A., & Raichle, M. E. (2001). Searching for a baseline: Functional imaging and the resting human brain. *Nature Reviews Neuroscience, 2*(10), 685–694.

Habermas, T., & Bluck, S. (2000). Getting a life: The emergence of the life story in adolescence. *Psychological Bulletin, 126*(5), 748.

Healy, H., & Williams, J. M. G. (1999). Autobiographical memory. *Handbook of Cognition and Emotion,* 229–242.

Hyman Jr, I. E., & Faries, J. M. (1992). The functions of autobiographical memory. In *Theoretical perspectives on autobiographical memory* (pp. 207–221). Springer. Retrieved from http://link.springer.com/chapter/10.1007/978-94-015-7967-4_12

Janata, P., Tomic, S. T., & Rakowski, S. K. (2007). Characterisation of music-evoked autobiographical memories. *Memory, 15*(8), 845–860.

Koepcke, J. (2011). *When I fell from the sky: The true story of one woman's miraculous survival.* (R. Benjamin, Trans.). Nicholas Brealey.

LaBar, K. S., & Cabeza, R. (2006). Cognitive neuroscience of emotional memory. Nature Reviews. *Neuroscience, 7*(1), 54–64.

Lagattuta, K. H. (2007). Thinking about the future because of the past: Young children's knowledge about the causes of worry and preventative decisions. *Child Development, 78*(5), 1492–1509.

Lagattuta, K. H. (2014). Linking past, present, and future: Children's ability to connect mental states and emotions across time. *Child Development Perspectives, 8*(2), 90–95.

Lancaster, J. S., & Barsalou, L. W. (1997). Multiple organisations of events in memory. *Memory, 5*(5), 569–599.

Levine, B., Svoboda, E., Hay, J. F., Winocur, G., & Moscovitch, M. (2002). Aging and autobiographical memory: Dissociating episodic from semantic retrieval. *Psychology and Aging, 17*(4), 677.

Mace, J. H. (2004). Involuntary autobiographical memories are highly dependent on abstract cuing: The Proustian view is incorrect. *Applied Cognitive Psychology, 18*(7), 893–899.

Maguire, E. A. (2001). Neuroimaging studies of autobiographical event memory. *Philosophical Transactions of the Royal Society of London B: Biological Sciences, 356*(1413), 1441–1451.

McCloskey, M., Wible, C. G., & Cohen, N. J. (1988). Is there a special flashbulb-memory mechanism? *Journal of Experimental Psychology: General, 117*(2), 171.

Means, B., & Loftus, E. F. (1991). When personal history repeats itself: Decomposing memories for recurring events. *Applied Cognitive Psychology, 5*(4), 297–318.

Morris, G., Baker-Ward, L., & Bauer, P. J. (2010). What remains of that day: The survival of children's autobiographical memories across time. *Applied Cognitive Psychology, 24*(4), 527–544.

Neisser, U. (1981). John Dean's memory: A case study. *Cognition, 9*(1), 1–22.

Neisser, U., & Hyman, I. (1999). Memory observed: Remembering in natural contexts. Worth Publishers. Retrieved from http://books.google.com/books?hl=en&lr=&id=yf1F1c80AB4C&oi=fnd&pg=PR11&dq=neisser+memory+observed&ots=LLJt7e38Wo&sig=Z8YT06y7jZ0IxevRHMMNXZrP2xY

Neisser, U., Winograd, E., Bergman, E. T., Schreiber, C. A., Palmer, S. E., & Weldon, M. S. (1996). Remembering the earthquake: Direct experience vs. hearing the news. *Memory, 4*(4), 337–358. https://doi.org/10.1080/096582196388898

Nelson, K., & Fivush, R. (2004). The emergence of autobiographical memory: A social cultural developmental theory. *Psychological Review, 111*(2), 486.

Nigro, G., & Neisser, U. (1983). Point of view in personal memories. *Cognitive Psychology, 15*(4), 467–482.

Palin, M. (2008). *Diaries 1969–1979: The Python years* (Reprint edition). New York: St. Martin's Griffin.

Parkin, A. J., & Walter, B. M. (1992). Recollective experience, normal aging, and frontal dysfunction. *Psychology and Aging, 7*(2), 290.

Pasupathi, M. (2003). Emotion regulation during social remembering: Differences between emotions elicited during an event and emotions elicited when talking about it. *Memory, 11*(2), 151–163.

Petrides, M. (2005). Lateral prefrontal cortex: Architectonic and functional organization. *Philosophical Transactions of the Royal Society B: Biological Sciences, 360*(1456), 781–795.

Pillemer, D. (2003). Directive functions of autobiographical memory: The guiding power of the specific episode. *Memory, 11*(2), 193–202.

Pillemer, D. B. (1992). *Remembering personal circumstances: A functional analysis.* Retrieved from http://psycnet.apa.org/psycinfo/1993-97049-011

Raichle, M. E., & Snyder, A. Z. (2007). A default mode of brain function: A brief history of an evolving idea. *Neuroimage, 37*(4), 1083–1090.

Reese, E., Haden, C. A., Baker-Ward, L., Bauer, P., Fivush, R., & Ornstein, P. A. (2011). Coherence of personal narratives across the lifespan: A multidimensional model and coding method. *Journal of Cognition and Development, 12*(4), 424–462.

Robinson, J. A. (1976). Sampling autobiographical memory. *Cognitive Psychology, 8*(4), 578–595.

Robinson, J. A., & Swanson, K. L. (1990). Autobiographical memory: The next phase. *Applied Cognitive Psychology, 4*(4), 321–335.

Robinson, J. A., & Swanson, K. L. (1993). Field and observer modes of remembering. *Memory, 1*(3), 169–184.

Rubin, D. C. (2012). The basic systems model of autobiographical memory. In D. Rubin (Ed.), *Understanding autobiographical memory: Theories and approaches,* (pp. 11–32). Cambridge, England: Cambridge University Press.

Rubin, D. C., & Kozin, M. (1984). Vivid memories. *Cognition, 16*(1), 81–95.

Schacter, D. L. (2001). *The seven sins of memory.* Boston, MA: Houghton Mifflin. Retrieved from https://www.researchgate.net/profile/Daniel_Schacter/publication/13099436_The_seven_sins_of_memory_-_Insights_from_psychology_and_cognitive_neuroscience/links/0c96052f3f81c5ece0000000/The-seven-sins-of-memory-Insights-from-psychology-and-cognitive-neuroscience.pdf

Schacter, D. L., Addis, D. R., & Buckner, R. L. (2007). Remembering the past to imagine the future: The prospective brain. *Nature Reviews Neuroscience, 8*(9), 657–661.

Schaie, K. W. (1965). A general model for the study of developmental problems. *Psychological Bulletin, 64*, 92–107.

Schulkind, M. D., & Woldorf, G. M. (2005). Emotional organization of autobiographical memory. *Memory & Cognition, 33*(6), 1025–1035.

Sehulster, J. R. (1989). Content and temporal structure of autobiographical knowledge: Remembering twenty-five seasons at the Metropolitan Opera. *Memory & Cognition, 17*(5), 590–606.

Shanks, D. R., & John, M. F. S. (1994). Characteristics of dissociable human learning systems. *Behavioral and Brain Sciences, 17*(03), 367–395.

Skowronski, J. J., & Thompson, C. P. (1990). Reconstructing the dates of personal events: Gender differences in accuracy. *Applied Cognitive Psychology, 4*(5), 371–381.

St. Jacques, P. L., Conway, M. A., & Cabeza, R. (2011). Gender differences in autobiographical memory for everyday events: retrieval elicited by SenseCam images versus verbal cues. *Memory, 19*(7), 723–732.

St. Jacques, P. L. S., Conway, M. A., Lowder, M. W., & Cabeza, R. (2011). Watching my mind unfold versus yours: An fMRI study using a novel camera technology to examine neural differences in self-projection of self versus other perspectives. *Journal of Cognitive Neuroscience, 23*(6), 1275–1284.

St. Jacques, P. L. S., Kragel, P. A., & Rubin, D. C. (2011). Dynamic neural networks supporting memory retrieval. *Neuroimage, 57*(2), 608–616.

St. Jacques, P. S., Rubin, D. C., LaBar, K. S., & Cabeza, R. (2008). The short and long of it: Neural correlates of temporal-order memory for autobiographical events. *Journal of Cognitive Neuroscience, 20*(7), 1327–1341.

Svoboda, E., McKinnon, M. C., & Levine, B. (2006). The functional neuroanatomy of autobiographical memory: A meta-analysis. *Neuropsychologia, 44*(12), 2189–2208.

Talarico, J. M., & Rubin, D. C. (2003). Confidence, not consistency, characterizes flashbulb memories. *Psychological Science, 14*(5), 455–461.

Thorne, A., & McLean, K. C. (2002). Gendered reminiscence practices and self-definition in late adolescence. *Sex Roles, 46*(9), 267–277.

Tomasello, M. (1999). The cultural origins of human cognition. Cambridge, MA: Harvard University Press.

Tulving, E. (1972). Episodic and semantic memory. In E. Tulving & W. Donaldson (Eds.) *Organization of memory* (pp. 381–403). New York. Academic Press.

Tulving, E. (1985). *Elements of episodic memory.* Oxford, England: Oxford University Press.

Tulving, E. (1999). On the uniqueness of episodic memory. Retrieved from http://psycnet.apa.org/psycinfo/1999-04462-001

Tulving, E. (2002). Episodic memory: From mind to brain. *Annual Review of Psychology, 53*(1), 1–25.

Van Abbema, D. L., & Bauer, P. J. (2005). Autobiographical memory in middle childhood: Recollections of the recent and distant past. *Memory, 13*(8), 829–845. https://doi.org/10.1080/09658210444000430

Vygotsky, L. S. (1987). *The collected works of L. S. Vygotsky: Problems of general psychology, including the volume thinking and speech.* (R. W. Rieber & A. S. Carton, Eds.) (1988 edition). New York, NY: Plenum.

Wagenaar, W. A. (1986). My memory: A study of autobiographical memory over six years. *Cognitive Psychology, 18*(2), 225–252.

Wagner, A. D., Schacter, D. L., Rotte, M., Koutstaal, W., Maril, A., Dale, A. M., . . . Buckner, R. L. (1998). Building memories: Remembering and forgetting of verbal experiences as predicted by brain activity. *Science, 281*(5380), 1188–1191.

Willander, J., & Larsson, M. (2007). Olfaction and emotion: The case of autobiographical memory. *Memory & Cognition, 35*(7), 1659–1663.

Williams, H. L., Conway, M. A., & Cohen, G. (2008). Autobiographical memory. *Memory in the Real World, 3,* 21–90.

Williams, J. M. G., Watts, F. N., MacLeod, C., & Mathews, A. (1997). *Cognitive Psychology and Emotional Disorders.* 2nd Ed. Chichester: John Wiley.

Yuille, J. C., & Cutshall, J. L. (1986). A case study of eyewitness memory of a crime. *Journal of Applied Psychology, 71*(2), 291.

©iStock.com/vgajic

Semantic Memory

Chapter Outline

Learning Objectives

1. Summarize the evidence for Tulving's remember/know distinction.

2. Explain the connection between semantic meaning and retrieval prompts (recall versus recognition).

3. Define the issue of "knowledge representation" and the two general approaches theorists have taken to describe how knowledge representation happens.

4. Explain how associationistic theories explain the structure of knowledge in long-term memory.

5. Explain holistic approaches to the structure of knowledge.

6. Summarize the assumptions of constructivism.

Overview

Knowledge is the lens through which we view the world. We constantly interpret what we are experiencing with what we already know, and it happens so quickly we usually take it for granted. In other cases, we use our knowledge to try to reason through a problem (aiding working memory) or to make a prediction. Here's a brief example about what knowledge can do to our understanding of a situation.

Relatively few people successfully predicted the Great Recession that began in the mid-2000s; in his book about the years leading to the recession, Michael Lewis explains that there were about six individuals or teams in the financial industry who predicted that the strong economy was about to sputter and could collapse (Lewis, 2011). Why weren't more people aware that it might occur? The basic mechanism, credit default swaps, were a relatively new financial product, and were not necessarily easy to understand. These financial arrangements had the appearance of being sure-fire money-makers in which to invest, because they involved bundling together home loans of various qualities (high-risk to low-risk). Because there was (supposed to be) a mix of home loans packaged together, buying and insuring credit default swaps was seen as fairly low-risk. Rating agencies agreed.

Of course, those few people who took the time to find out what was inside the bundled packages of loans were surprised at how many of them were high-risk bad loans. No one else seemed to have noticed. To confirm their suspicions, some of the inquisitive few flew to rapidly growing housing developments to see what was going on. What they found were people who were unemployed being handed loans for homes they could never pay, exotic dancers owning a half-dozen properties they didn't earn enough to ever pay on, and home loan sellers who didn't necessarily complete the paperwork to even approve home buyers fully. The amounts due on the loans were scheduled to balloon in time, so loan signers thought they would be fine (if they were even aware of what they were signing). Loan sellers were paid based on the number of signers, not on the likelihood the loan applicant who had signed would be able to pay on the loan.

Those investors, now informed with a lot of knowledge, bet that the housing market would collapse—and it did, quickly. They made money from the collapse, and some of them were quite upset about profiting from the harm caused to others. Knowledge about a situation can deeply change what we think about what is going on. (In addition to his book, Lewis's writing about these people also became a movie; McKay, 2015.)

As we saw in the prior chapter, more than just personal event memories are needed in order to understand ourselves or the world around us. We need the general knowledge that we acquire about the world to help us interpret what those events mean and why they are important to us. This can involve memory about social conventions, family history, diverse academic domains, hobbies and interests, local and world geography, one or more languages, political and religious beliefs, and the arts and entertainment. The vast amount of information that we acquire over time is somehow seamlessly stored away and retrieved in an instant, often without much effort. In this chapter, we'll focus just on this kind of long-term memory—general knowledge, which is usually called "semantic memory."

Tulving's Episodic/Semantic Memory Distinction

In 1972, Endel Tulving proposed that memory for life events and memory for general information might operate as two separate memory systems. It might seem odd now, since any contemporary textbook on memory and cognition will implicitly assume that this is the case; but, up until that point, most researchers had assumed long-term memory was something of a large repository for all kinds of information, like a receptacle for any kind of information regardless of the type.

Tulving noted that knowledge and memory for events seemed to have some properties that were not the same. Episodic memories have a time factor that is usually central to the memory itself. There is a scene of some sort in an episodic memory that isn't there when we remember the capital of the state of Oregon or a math fact, like the answer to 2 times 3. Episodic memories include spatial and sensory information, at least to an extent. They often include some information about ourselves as well—what it was like to live through the event. Information about objects and basic concepts, like "chair" and "furniture" are also a matter of simply knowing them and are not typically tied to us as individuals.

He had realized (Tulving, 2002) that we are capable of a subjective experience of time; that is, we are capable of mentally reversing the flow and revising some other part of time. Second, our conscious awareness changes when we do this. We are aware that we are visiting some other time that is not in front of us, or daydreaming, an experience of "recollecting." Finally, there has to be a sense of oneself in order for our remembering of past events to occur. We have to have a sense of who we are to understand our past.

Remember/Know Judgments

Essentially, Tulving (1985) believed it was possible to separate episodic and semantic memories by whether we "remember" them or "know" them. So, I may remember a particular event, like the time my oldest son got his head stuck in some playground equipment in kindergarten. I spent about twenty minutes carefully trying to pull his head out, while he screamed. I remember where we were, about what month and year it was, and who was present. Other memories are facts and items of information that we simply possess. I know that Microsoft is located near Seattle, and where Seattle is located, but I haven't been there and I don't remember when or where I learned this. I have no memory for this knowledge other than the generic mental images of the Space Needle, Starbucks Cafe's, and an association with rainy, overcast weather.

Tulving claimed that people are cognizant of this distinction and can be asked whether they remember a stimulus or know they saw it. The remember/know judgment is used in research to demonstrate this distinction. Participants will be asked to study words in one of two conditions: for their color (the word "BOOK" might be shown in green ink) or for their meaning. Afterward, the participants will be shown the same words mixed in with many distractor words that were not part of the learning phase. For each word they identify, they will be asked whether they "know" the word was one they studied, or one that they "remember" having studied. While judgments about words that were studied for their color are usually split half-and-half with remember and know judgments, the recognized words studied for meaning are more likely to receive "remember" judgments (Gardiner, Ramponi, & Richardson-Klavehn, 2002). Other studies have found participants are more likely to have details about the event of learning, like time and place, with remember judgments (Rimmele, Davachi, & Phelps, 2012).

Neuroscience Evidence for a Distinction

The remember/know judgment, as a research task, generated behavioral evidence that people treated their own memories as being one of the two types. However, neuroimaging support for this distinction has been found as well. The areas of the brain that are activated during semantic memories are not the same as the areas that are activated during episodic memories. Habib, Nyberg, and Tulving (2003) used PET scans to demonstrate that retrieval of semantic memories tends to rely on the left hemisphere of the brain, and the retrieval of episodic memories tends to rely on the right hemisphere. Tulving (2002) believes that episodic memories are not just a kind of memory, but a memory system that is uniquely tied to the passage of time.

As we have seen with autobiographical memories, the two systems do have to interact to make sense of and process our memories. Both are also active during learning. Much knowledge may start as an event, say in a classroom, and over time become more generic and less episodic. At some point I must have realized that the earth is a sphere, but I no longer remember when and where this occurred. Later on, we use semantic memory to help us understand what is going on around us.

Of course, not everyone is in agreement about Tulving's episodic/semantic separation of systems, although it is very popular today. Some researchers use a processing model to claim that all memory exists in a single "store," just like a computer. But, different processes are used by the brain to interact with the store, so differences in events and knowledge are just the byproducts of these operations (Anderson, 1993; Crowder, 1976). This approach claims that instead of different storage systems, there are different memory processes that access specific kinds of memories.

Declarative Versus Nondeclarative Distinction

While not as ubiquitous as the episodic and semantic distinction, a popular distinction was made by Squire (1992) between declarative memory and nondeclarative memory. Declarative memory included any memory that could be made by conscious awareness, that is, be retrieved with awareness. Declarative memory includes semantic and episodic memories. Nondeclarative memory included only those memories that are implicit and could not be retrieved into conscious awareness.

Meaning and Context

When someone memorizes a word, the information stored in long-term memory is not a visual copy of the word (Craik & Lockhart, 1972). For example, when someone memorizes the word BOOK from a list, the memory will not be just the letters B-O-O-K. What is stored is the meaning of the word, altered by the context of the moment. The person will be able to distinguish memorizing the word BOOK in contrast to other times that he or she has encountered the word. Essentially, Tulving saw the memorized word as creating a new set of information in long-term memory. This information is not the entire conceptual understanding of the word "book," but a subset of it that is unique to this encounter. It will include information about the physical context as well (the encoding specificity principle, Chapter 7). As a result, retrieval cues that trigger this particular learning event will be useful for retrieving the memory of the word. However, not everything related to "books" more generally would retrieve this specific memory.

According to Tulving, a concept will include many possible features, and a new memory will include only a subset of those features. Which features are included in the memory depends on the physical context and thoughts that were present while forming the memory. To illustrate, Tulving and Thomson (1973) presented paired-associate words to participants in which the associations between the words were fairly weak such as blue-PLUM and spider-BIRD (rather than pen-INK, which has a stronger association). After completing the paired-associate word task, participants were given words strongly associated with the target words they had studied, such as EAGLE for "bird." The researchers then asked the participants to think of words they associated with these. Someone might say "wings, talons, soars, majestic, bird, cliffs." Participants were then asked if any of the words they generated were ones that had been learned earlier, like a self-generated recognition test. Participants recognized about 24 percent of the words they generated that were also on their original paired-associate word list. Then, participants were given the cue words from the paired-associate word list they had learned first, and they had to retrieve the target words. Participants were correct 63 percent of the time.

Essentially, participants were more successful at recalling the target words with a cue than they had been at recognizing those same target words. This finding is counterintuitive on its surface, since recognition tasks are usually much easier than recall tasks. Tulving and Thomson (1973) explained this as a matter of physical and cognitive context driving the creation of a new memory with only a subset of features. So, seeing "bird" in the context of "spider," the entire concept of "bird" is not instantiated or activated mentally—just those that reflect an association. Perhaps this would mean a medium-sized bird that would prey on insects and spiders. This subset of knowledge about "bird" becomes a new memory. So, when given the word "eagle" and participants generate "bird," this is not the same set of "bird" features that were generated in relation to small insects, but likely large, majestic animals. So, when looking for target words that were learned in the paired-associate word task, the same target word ("bird") may not have been recognizable. Other studies have found situations when participants can recall information without being able to recognize it (Fisher & Craik, 1977; Roediger & Adelson, 1980).

What a successful recall without recognition means is that items in memory are not likely (or are not required) to have a single, unified representation in long-term memory. So, "bird" will not be defined or coded the same way for all memories involving birds.

Recall in Semantic Memory

Memory researchers have proposed both single-stage and two-stage models of how recall of conceptual knowledge functions. The single-stage model proposes that recall depends on finding a match between the retrieval cues and the content of the memory for successful recall. If there is a large degree of overlap and the match is unique, making it distinctive from other knowledge, then the recall is much more likely to be successful. Recognition works similarly, according to this model.

According to two-stage models of retrieval, possible answers are generated in a first stage using the retrieval cues, and then the answers are examined to see whether any fit the criteria for a correct answer (Anderson & Bower, 1972; Bahrick, 1970, 1979; Jacoby, Bishara, Hessels, & Toth, 2005; Kintsch, 1974). So, attempting to think of words that have "n" as the second-to-last letter will generate a number of words, like "skins," "jumping," and "meant." Possibly, the time and place of learning can be used as cues as well to help generate and constrain possible answers. This kind of model explains why recall can be more difficult than recognition. In recall, people are completing two processes (generation, then recognition) rather than just recognition alone. Failure can happen at either stage (Anderson & Bower, 1972; Bahrick, 1970, 1979; Jacoby et al., 2005; Kintsch, 1974).

Recognition in Semantic Memory

Recalling and recognizing information are similar in many ways and are affected by some of the same variables—for example, whether information presented in an organized fashion for learning affects both kinds of retrieval (Mandler, Pearlstone, & Koopmans, 1969), and whether repetition helps both kinds of memory. But, some variables affect the two methods of retrieval differently. One variable on which recall and recognition differ is word frequency. A word's frequency is defined as the percent chance a word is likely to be encountered in daily life (through books, newspapers, and online) per million words. Words that are high-frequency, that is, more commonly experienced, are recalled more easily than low-frequency words. Oddly, low-frequency words are easier to recognize than high-frequency words (Deese, 1961; Gregg, 1976).

A second difference between recall and recognition involves the intention at the time of learning. Typically, recognition tasks are easier than recall tasks, but this appears to be limited to incidental learning conditions. That is, when learning is unintentional—perhaps the participants are reading an essay and are not aware that they will be quizzed about the words in the essay afterward—then recognition attempts beat recall attempts. However, under intentional learning conditions, recall is higher than recognition. With conscious effort, the participants appear to apply learning strategies that make the recall more effective later on (see Fig. 10.1).

Knowledge Representation

Beyond the basic phenomena of using and retrieving semantic memories, theorists have tried to make sense of the how long-term memory works. How does it function to store and make available to us such a broad amount of information incredibly rapidly? The general issue of knowledge representation is the issue of how semantic memory, or knowledge, is represented in the mind. There are two general approaches that theorists have taken in trying to explain how knowledge lives in the mind. The first approach is associationistic

FIGURE 10.1   Visualization of the interaction between intentional and incidental learning and recall or recognition retrieval. Recall is always more difficult than recognition, but tends to benefit from intentional learning, whereas recognition benefits from incidental learning.

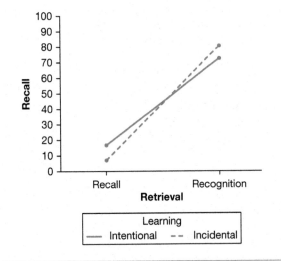

Note: Graph data are hypothetical.

in nature, meaning that it includes models of semantic memory as the accumulation of pieces of knowledge strung together in a web of connections. What are the basic elements of semantic memory, and do we process information at this level? This approach is similar to explaining human functioning at the level of neurons.

The second approach, which we will encounter later in this chapter, is more holistic in its approach, looking more at units of knowledge in large theoretical structures, such as "concepts," "models," and "schemas" of knowledge. Like understanding the brain at levels of neurological or brain structure, both can be seen as somewhat complementary even if not developed in tandem with each other.

Associationistic Models of Knowledge Representation

Many models that approach knowledge at an atomistic level propose that semantic memory is a sprawling network of associations. Units of knowledge, perhaps isolated cues like "bird" and "house," are stored as nodes. The term "node" is used because it is meant to be relatively neutral term for information. Associations, or links, between the nodes constitute the web of knowledge.

Related knowledge is activated or instantiated through existing links. So, assuming "bird" and "eagle" are nodes that are strongly associated, then thinking about eagles will quickly activated "bird" node. This hypothesis is known as spreading activation: Thinking about one concept will lead to the activation of other previously connected knowledge. The activation spreads toward other nodes in long-term memory along unidirectional or bidirectional pathways. This activation is automatic and is not within consciousness. Information that has become activated is ready to be pulled into conscious awareness (see Fig. 10.2).

In theory, this is why people find it easier to discuss a topic in a conversation once they have spent some time talking about it. The related areas of knowledge become activated and retrieving relevant information becomes quite fluid. This can also explain the phenomenon of completely misunderstanding a conversation we are overhearing.

FIGURE 10.2   A basic semantic network of a few linked nodes

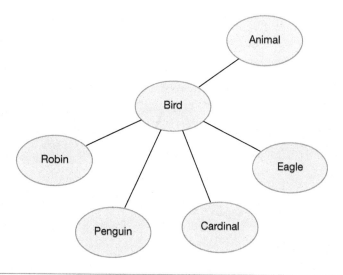

If two people are discussing an eagle they saw while traveling, someone overhearing the conversation could mistakenly activate sports information related to the Philadelphia Eagles and experience a lot of disorientation with trying to make sense of the conversation for a bit. Can you recall something like this happening to you? It happens to everyone now and then.

Semantic Networks of Associations

Collins and Quillian (1969, 1972) and later, Collins and Loftus (1975) proposed and refined a spreading-activation model that became the basis of later models. They proposed that links between nodes can vary in kind, containing information about similarity and identity. The nodes and links between them operate as a network and allow for making inferences. Modern semantic network models assume that **link strength** is the factor that leads to how strongly the activation is between nodes. When one node ("eagle") is activated, it will strongly activate any related nodes ("bird"; see Fig. 10.3). The activation does not happen more quickly—the activation level is simply stronger, making it easier to retrieve as a memory.

This model of semantic memory can explain how inferences are made. Information would be stored in a web of interconnected information. Genuses, for example, might be stored separate from specific animal families in the semantic network about the animal kingdom. So, asking, "Is a canary a bird?" can be answered by a semantic network model, since the nodes for canary and bird can become activated and are connected (associated). Consequently, someone can answer in the affirmative. Further, this model made the prediction that some questions would be easier to answer. For example, "Is a canary a bird?" should be easier to answer than "Is a canary an animal?" because the nodes for "canary" and "bird" would be more closely related than "canary" and "animal." Again, the model assumed that the more closely related information was, the closer it would be stored in the semantic network.

FIGURE 10.3   A semantic network with varying link strengths

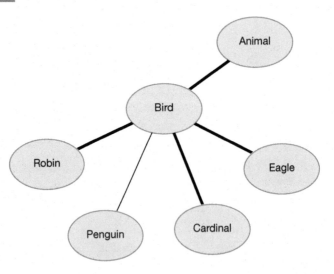

Some researchers have tried to time spreading activation. Most early semantic models assumed that activation took about 50 to 100 milliseconds per link, so the more associations that are required to resolve an inference, the longer it would take. Theorists also suspected that the spreading activation would fade over distance. That is, as the activation rolls out over each link, its strength would fade, like a wave encroaching on shore. But, research on spreading activation clouded the issue. One study found that the time taken to travel across nodes might be closer to one millisecond for each link (Wickelgren, 1976). Another study found that the time taken to reach a weakly associated or "remote" target word was no slower than the time taken to reach a strongly associated or "close" target word from the initial priming word (Ratcliff & McKoon, 1981). The strength of the priming effect was stronger for more strongly associated words, but the priming effect took time. It's possible that spreading activation occurs so quickly that there is no practical difference in the time it takes to connect nodes of information whether they are closely related or not.

Connectivity in Semantic Networks

It is not assumed that the amount of nodes and the number of links between those nodes are identical across all areas of long-term memory. According to the property of connectivity, the number of links between nodes will vary across nodes. For example, "dog" will have many connections but "gurney" is likely to have many fewer. Even for a similar node ("bird"), two different people may have different numbers of links leading to or from it. I suspect someone who works in ambulatory care might have many more connections to "gurney" than I might. Instead, it's expected that areas of expertise, for example, will greatly alter the number of nodes and the amount and strength of associated links between those nodes. The more connected a word is, the more easily it can be recognized or recalled (e.g., Nelson, Zhang, & McKinney, 2001).

The presence of intermediary nodes between other nodes can also be used, and they are influential. That is, a third item can share connections with nodes that are not typically brought up together. Thinking about the color "blue," for example, has been found to make identifying the word "cloud" faster (Balota & Lorch, 1986; McNamara, 1992). What appears to be happening is an intermediary word, SKY, bridges BLUE and CLOUD in such a way that the two concepts become interrelated even though we would not usually connect them directly by saying clouds are blue.

Nodes that are not directly cued in a search can also become activated as well, a phenomenon known as activation at a distance. Nelson, McEvoy, and Pointer (2003) used cue-target word lists to study connectivity, cue-target strength, and resonant links in long-term memory. Resonant links are those associations that are bidirectional. For example, "blue" can activate "sky," and likewise "sky" activates "blue." Essentially, the nodes mutually activate each other. Varying the amount of all three of these independent variables, the researchers found that increases in each one improved the chances of correct recall. But, improvements from connectivity—the number of links to and from a node—were unrelated to the number of resonant links. If a node has many links to other nodes, it may be irrelevant if any of those links are bidirectional and lead back from the target to the cue. The pattern of activation across all nodes may matter more than the precise direction of spreading activation. The idea that the pattern of activation matters more than the particular direction of activation is an idea present in connectionist models, as we will see in the following section.

Connectionist Models

An approach related to semantic networks is connectionist models (within the field of computer science, connectionist models are more commonly referred to as parallel-distributed models and neural network models). Instead of the more abstract approach in semantic networks, connectionist models to semantic memory are based on the operation of neurons. Basing models on neurons was not done necessarily because it was expected that there would be a perfect analogue to how connectionist models function in the brain, so much as neural functioning presented itself as an alternative to the standard computer metaphor common in information-processing.

Connectionist models are often developed with computer scientists to simulate knowledge to test predictions. Like semantic networks, the connectionist models include nodes of information that are linked together as a network, and the nodes activate by "firing." These models share many assumptions of the classic semantic network models (Hinton, 1989; McClelland, McNaughton, & O'Reilly, 1995; Rumelhart, 1990; Rumelhart & Todd, 1993), but individual nodes would not necessarily represent individual concepts.

Here's what this means. Instead of a node that represents "eagle," there might be an activated pattern of nodes that, together, represent "eagle." A different pattern of node activation might indicate "canary." The pattern of activation would not in any way visually appear like the object, although it's tempting to imagine it this way. More likely it would involve the series of features and traits that the person had learned help to distinguish one object from other ones that are related. Presumably, similar objects would have more overlap in which nodes are activated than ones that are dissimilar. "Meaning" in a connectionist model is the pattern of nodes that are activated to give rise to understanding.

One of the interesting aspects of connectionist models is that connectionist theorists see their models as providing an explanation for how people can generate new knowledge. When some idea is introduced to us, we incorporate it into our connectionist network of associations and can, from that, generate conclusions that we weren't explicitly exposed to or taught. For example, a child may know a little about fish—that they swim in water, have fins, and can lay eggs. When told, "Dennis is a guppy," and "A guppy is a fish," the child will probably be able to finish the statement "Dennis can ____" with "swim" correctly. From the perspective of the researcher, this means the child has successfully incorporated new material into his or her network and now can use it to create new content.

Given the ability to generate new connections with new input, you can see why computer scientists are interested in modeling knowledge for computers and robots. Trying to find ways to make machines intelligent has been a long-term pursuit of computer scientists beginning in the late nineteenth century (see Fig. 10.4).

Holistic Approaches of Knowledge Representation

Holistic or higher-order approaches to knowledge try to account for the functions of knowledge by examining how it may be structured and organized on a larger scale. Researchers look to not just the individual units of knowledge, but to whole groups of them working together about a single topic, for instance. Understanding any memory of a past event requires not only the event itself but also your understanding of why the event was happening and why it was important. It's one thing to remember a dinner with family, but another to interpret the dinner as part of the reception for my sister's wedding. Presumably, related concepts may have some form of internal organization beyond nodes and links.

FIGURE 10.4   A sample connectionist model

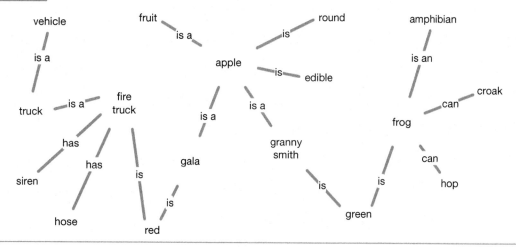

Source: Adapted from Rumelhart, D. E. & Todd, P. M., (1993).

Concepts

For most higher-order theories of knowledge representation, the smallest piece of knowledge is a **concept**, the basic unit of information. A concept cannot be reduced any further than what it is and retain meaning. The primary purpose of a concept is to accurately categorize different instances (examples) in the real world or thought. Any one object or situation can be categorized as being an example of a concept, or not. People form concepts of a broad variety of classes of instances, including things we find in nature such as gold and cats, nonexistent kinds of objects such as zombies and ghosts, objects that people make (e.g., furniture), social roles such as uncles and bus drivers, psychological constructs such as jealousy and intelligence, and abstract constructs such as trapezoids and truth (Brewer, 1993). An object or idea does not have to be real for us to be able to form a concept for it.

Generally, concepts are meant to represent or parallel the real world in some way. Usually a concept represents some situation or state fairly directly and is not propositional: that is, some instance or situation is either an example of a concept, or it is not. Often the mental structure of the concept mirrors the real-world situation (Johnson-Laird, 1980). Research on concepts tends to focus on concepts for physical objects, which is a known limitation of existing research, since not all concepts are meant to describe physical objects (Brewer, 1993). Concepts for non-physical objects could have properties that are not present in concepts for physical objects.

Some concepts are developed in a highly contextual manner as well. Barsalou (1993) noted that some conceptual categories are developed in the moment. There is a category for "things to take from one's home during a fire" (e.g., children and pets, blanket) that do not share any other similarities or traits.

Next, let's look at several theories that attempt to describe how an interrelated group of concepts could function together as a mental model, scripts, and schemas.

Mental Models

To understand a situation or a story, one proposal is that we make a "mental model" about it—an internal representation of the situation based on what we know (Johnson-Laird, 1980). This mental model is likely to be active in working memory using semantic memory from long-term memory (Brewer & Nakamura, 1984). This situational mental model can be used for a range of functions, including understanding the situation as a whole, establishing the spatial context of actors in a set of events, making inferences, and generating predictions about what might happen next. Mental models may be simply logical in nature, as we might use when trying to evaluate an argument, or story, or attempt to understand the physics of a situation, such as why a helicopter moves forward when its nose is aimed downward.

Here's an example of a study that examined the mental models that readers formed of a story. Bransford, Barclay, and Franks (1972) presented series of short stories such as these to participants. Each participant would receive either version A or version B, but not both.

Version A: A beaver hit a log that a turtle was sitting on and the log flipped over from the shock. The turtle was very surprised by the event.

Version B: A beaver hit a log that a turtle was sitting beside and the log flipped over from the shock. The turtle was very surprised by the event.

In a recognition test, participants who had read version A, above, tended to recognize the sentence:

A BEAVER HIT THE LOG AND KNOCKED THE TURTLE INTO THE WATER.

which was neither included in the story nor explicitly described. What this implies is that participants who read version A had mentally modeled the scene, which included the spatial context and a causal chain of events between the turtle, beaver, and log.

Mental models can include spatial contexts for information, and this modeling of the spatial environment means inferences can be made (Glenberg, Meyer, & Lindem, 1987; Haenggi, Kintsch, & Gernsbacher, 1995; O'Brien & Albrecht, 1992; Rinck, Williams, Bower, & Becker, 1996). Mental models have also been found to include causal relationships and the goals and emotions of the individuals in a story (Morrow, 1994; Zwaan & Radvansky, 1998; Zwaan, Radvansky, & Whitten, 2002). Mental models can also include temporal information for tracking what happens to the actors in the story as well. One study presented participants with versions of a story about a woman who went to the movies and that the movie was forgotten about later because the person was fast asleep. A projectionist was mentioned in the story. As an independent variable, the person who fell asleep was described using either a female pronoun, "she," or a male pronoun, "he" (referring to the projectionist). Participants reading the story did not hesitate when reading the female pronoun, since it fit the flow of the story overall, but participants reading the male pronoun slowed down, as a sign of having to recalibrate their mental model of the events. Studies have repeatedly shown that when information about time is presented in a story and later information is presented that is incompatible with the original timeline, participants read more slowly and do not recall the story as well (Bestgen & Vonk, 1995; Ohtsuka & Brewer, 1992; Rinck, Hahnel, & Becker, 2001; Zwaan, 1996).

Children have been found to develop their own mental models of the shape of the earth at early ages (Vosniadou & Brewer, 1992). Children between six and ten years of age were interviewed about their beliefs about the shape of the Earth, using drawings and props as well. The children showed a number of mental models of Earth, some of which showed signs of trying to incorporate elements of what they had learned in class, but not always successfully. The youngest children tended to rely on flat models of the

FIGURE 10.5   Common models of the earth (Vosniadou & Brewer, 1992)

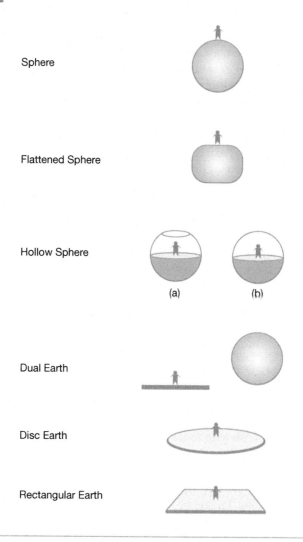

Sphere

Flattened Sphere

Hollow Sphere

(a)   (b)

Dual Earth

Disc Earth

Rectangular Earth

Source: Vosniadou, S., & Brewer, W. F. (1992).

earth, including a disc-shaped earth (like a pancake). Others used a hollow sphere shape, with us inside the sphere on a flat plane, to explain how the Earth seemed flat, while adults had tried to convince them that the earth was a sphere. Some of the older children in the study had a tendency to "flatten" the spherical shape of Earth in their mental model in order to accommodate the awkwardness of believing people had to reside on some side of a sphere and not fall off by failing to account for gravity. Whichever the model the children relied on, they would use them to consistently answer questions about whether one could walk to the "edge" of the Earth, and whether people would fall off if they did (see Fig. 10.5).

Schemas

Sir Francis Bartlett is known for having originated the idea of a schema, although it has been extended past what he described in 1932. A schema is a structure of generic knowledge about some object or event, "masses of organised past experiences" (Bartlett, 1932, p. 213). It is information that is well-learned and quickly retrievable from long-term memory, ready to apply to a relevant real-world situation. His primary assumption was that all new information we encounter interacts with the old information represented in the schema (Brewer & Nakamura, 1984). So, after years of experience with driving, you are likely to have a "driving" schema now, which enables you to work a vehicle with less attention than when you were learning. The act of learning will likely involve lots of focus and forming a mental model of how to operate a car on the road. A schema implies that the foundational skills and actions are routinized. A schema is thought to be like a "template" of knowledge with "slots" for the properties of the actual object that we encounter in daily life. This offers some flexibility. So, while you may have learned to drive primarily using your mother's car, if you try driving a friend's car, most of the "driving" schema will map onto that car as well. It's not like starting from scratch. Instead it's just a matter of locating the key pedals and levers for this particular vehicle.

Bartlett (1932) defined a schema as an organized mass of past reactions and experiences that operate to interpret current activities. His data primarily came from the use of stories and drawings that he would show to participants (e.g., Bartlett, 1916, 1920. 1921). A particularly famous example is his "War of the Ghosts" story, an adaptation of an American Indian folktale that was translated by Franz Boas:

"The War of the Ghosts"

One night two young men from Egulac went down the river to hunt for seals, and while they were there it became foggy and calm. Then they heard war cries, and they thought, "Maybe this is a war party." They escaped to the shore and hid behind a log. Now canoes came up and they heard the noise of paddles, and saw one canoe coming up to them. There were five men in the canoe, and they said, "What do you think? We wish to take you along. We are going up river to make war on the people."

One of the young men said, "I have no arrows." "Arrows are in the canoe," they said. "I will not go along. I might be killed. My relatives do not know where I have gone. But you," he said, turning to the other, "may go with them."

So one of the young men went, but the other returned home. And the warriors went on up the river to a town on the other side of Kalama. The people came down to the water and they began to fight, and many were killed. But presently the young man heard one of the warriors say, "Quick, let us go home; that Indian has been hit." Now he thought, "Oh, they are ghosts." He did not feel sick, but they said he had been shot.

So the canoes went back to Egulac, and the young man went ashore to his house, and made a fire. And he told everybody and said: "Behold, I accompanied the ghosts, and we went to fight. Many of our fellows were killed, and many of those who attacked us were killed. They said I was hit, and I did not feel sick." He told it all, and then he became quiet. When the sun rose he fell down. Something black came out of his mouth. His face became contorted. The people jumped up and cried.

He was dead.

Bartlett intentionally used a story that would require knowledge about Native American culture to fully understand, and most white Europeans were unlikely to have this schema knowledge. Bartlett, believing schema knowledge as key for understanding the world around us, believed people would be likely only weakly to remember points of the story that didn't make sense and to distort the story to fit their own cultural norms when recalling it later.

Bartlett found evidence for just this kind of distortion and omitting. One participant described the story as being about two men who went fishing (instead of hunting seals). Most likely, the original comment about hunting for seals seemed unusual given the Native American story, and fishing seemed more likely from the perspective of knowledge Europeans would have about Native Americans. The hiding place of a log was frequently changed to a boulder or a tree, a sensible reconstruction for the purpose of the story.

The battle scene presented more recall problems and was typically not well remembered. In great part, the battle doesn't make sense to someone unfamiliar with the related mythology. Who the ghosts are is unclear, and why many lives are lost but the warriors decide to leave when someone is hit. Bartlett believed that many listeners tried to follow the story using an "adventure" schema that doesn't fit the story well.

Bartlett saw schemas as something like lenses that we use to build an explanation of the events around us, like an interpreter. If there are elements that do not make sense, they are likely to be forgotten. If there are events that are implied, the schema supplies the missing material to make sense of the unstated background.

Bartlett proposed that schemas are what we use to interpret the world around us, at a general level. Schemas improve memory by helping us to remember the details that are consistent with the schema, while attempting to take what details do not fit and make them more consistent (explaining our ability to distort events during recall). Bartlett also saw schemas as helping to integrate content, helping the world to make sense. Schemas are the bodies of knowledge that we use to help the details around us to become coherent and "belong together." These schemas acted primarily unconsciously, according to Bartlett.

The errors people made when recalling the material he had provided to them convinced him that schemas were not like passive jigsaw puzzles that were partially complete and could accept new pieces if provided. The errors that people made were predictable, meaningful, and conventional. In Bartlett's mind, his participants were actively trying to make sense of the material he gave them by using schema information. He called this process "effort after meaning" (Brewer & Nakamura, 1984).

Structure of Schemas

Starting in the 1970s, schemas have been used in artificial intelligence, linguistics, cognitive psychology, and even explanations of motor skill performance. Schema theory takes a different approach than the atomistic theories that propose the mind can be understood using small basic elements. The belief is that small mental elements working in concert give rise to larger theoretical frameworks of knowledge having special properties that the individual pieces would not. Modern theories have described schemas as "frames" (Minsky, 1975) consisting of fixed or a constant set of nodes, with slots that are filled in by details from the environment. The slots will accept only certain classes of information. So the slot for the "brake" in the "driving" schema is not likely to be open to something highly unusual, like a button on the dashboard. These slots will have "default assignments" of what is expected to be most typical. Some theorists have suggested that there are a range of possible options that the slots will accept (Rumelhart & Ortony, 1977).

Schema theory is said to explain how people can form expectations about some activity that allow them to rapidly assimilate the environment and smoothly interact with it, while retaining some flexibility about what they will eventually encounter. Like a computer program, they are active in how they process the information provided to them (Rumelhart, 1980).

In modern schema theory, schemas are viewed as the unconscious mental structures and processes that underlie human knowledge on a large scale. They contain generic knowledge, and will be structurally different depending on the domain and environment for which they are going to be used. Incoming information from the environment interacts with the schema in a way that can modify the information in the appropriate schema and create a specific memory of that moment in time. This theorized system of knowledge can then allow for a range of responses that is appropriate for a given situation and for many new situations. According to Brewer and Nakamura (1984), schema knowledge can be used to explain why people who walk into a room without a ceiling will be surprised. However, at the same time, most people who claim that a room they were just in had a ceiling didn't look up high enough to check—as eye movement recordings will indicate. When asked, people will be more likely to guess that the ceiling is made of plaster, rather than glass (due to learned default assignments); and when recalling a room that had an unusual ceiling (acoustic tile), they will remember plaster for the ceiling instead (Brewer & Treyens, 1981).

Evidence for large-scale knowledge structures is robust (Alba & Hasher, 1983). When people read about common events such as going to the doctor's office, people will recall events that were not mentioned in the original story (Bower, Black, & Turner, 1979). If people read a story in which events in a common activity were rearranged and put in some unusual order (e.g., paying for a meal before receiving it at a restaurant), people tend to rearrange the events and put them into a more conventional order.

In a classic schema study, Brewer and Treyens (1981) asked participants who had signed up for a psychology experiment to wait in a graduate student office (pictured in Fig. 10.6). They waited for about half a minute. In the testing room, they were asked to write down as much as they could about the room they were just in, including all of the contents they could recall. What they found was that people tended to recall objects that were common to an "office" schema, such as a desk, but were less likely to remember unusual objects such as a skull. They would list objects that were not actually there, such as books, if they fit the schema. Books, in fact, were the fourth most recalled item, but they had been removed from the room.

Functions of Schemas

Schemas have been proposed to support a variety of functions, and all of the functions rely primarily on the idea that schema knowledge provides us with the background to understand what is going on around us.

Providing meaning helps with memory (Welborn & English, 1937). Ebbinghaus himself found that recall for poetry was about ten times better than recall for nonsense syllables (which is, ironically, what led him to abandon meaningful material, a position that Bartlett later rejected).

Participants who know more about, or have more schema knowledge of, some domain will show higher recall for new information related to that domain. Consider an avid sports fan who is watching a televised event, in contrast to someone who follows the sport more casually. Typically the one with the greater knowledge base retains more information. Research has found the same by examining expert chess players (Chase & Simon, 1973),

FIGURE 10.6   Photo of the office from Brewer and Treyens (1981)

Source: Brewer, W. F., & Treyens, J. C. (1981).

baseball (Chiesi, Spilich, & Voss, 1979), and Western and Aboriginal medicine using Western and Australian Aboriginal subjects (Steffensen & Colker, 1982). This is particularly true when the new information fits the existing schema (Brewer & Treyens, 1981; Kintsch & van Dijk, 1978; Lichtenstein & Brewer, 1980; Mandler & Johnson, 1977; Meyer & McConkie, 1973; Thorndyke, 1977).

There are several theorized ways that schemas could provide these benefits (Brewer & Nakamura, 1984). Schemas may influence the amount of attention given to some information in our environment. The schemas themselves could operate as a general framework for creating episodic memories. The generic schema information is likely to interact with new episodic information in order to create a new memory that is a combination of the generic information and specific episodic details. Schemas may be involved in deciding what information should be retained from an event. Schemas could help with retrieval, by helping to locate information in episodic memory.

In the next section, we'll look at one particular form of schemas: scripts.

Scripts

Today, *scripts* are generally seen as a type of schema knowledge based around an expected sequence of events. The slots in a schema have been proposed to specify default values, which could include the typical order of events for a doctor's visit, paying for groceries, or ordering at a drive-thru (e.g., Schank & Abelson, 1977). Many stories require use of our existing script knowledge, so the author doesn't necessarily have to include every possible event or detail, since he or she can rely on the reader's having some amount of pertinent background knowledge to make sense of what is happening in the story.

A script includes fairly standardized information about stereotyped events (Schank & Abelson, 1977). Scripts develop after repeated experience with a particular event. Scripts help with understanding the event, inferring the relevant information, and guiding next actions.

Scripts develop beginning in childhood, as we observe how to order in restaurants versus fast-food places, how to wait in line and take turns, and how to operate a phone. Because the event is repeated over time, we gradually learn what parts of the event will remain more-or-less constant. Those become the template form of the script. The script may include the typical surrounding, sequence of events, objects, and people. The people are often involved as roles. In a restaurant script, there may be "actors," who would act as servers, host, and cashier; and a set of props just as the menu, chairs, and tables.

Living through an experience for which we have a script means matching the script to the events as they unfold. As long as they match, the event seems to make sense. Besides making sense of the situation, the script also helps us to infer information that we can't recall later. For example, if someone asks me what was on the menu, and I can't recall actually having seen a menu, I will infer that (most likely) there was one. Overall, I don't have to remember each minor detail about the restaurant since I have a restaurant script that encapsulates most of the necessary information.

So, scripts help us to recall chairs and a menu from dining at a restaurant—not because the event had such as strong effect on our memory, necessarily—but we can infer that chairs and a menu were likely to have been present. Scripts also help us to identify objects quickly, without much demand on attention. Recognizing a table as such in a restaurant happens without much effort. Hence, recalling a table as being present might be quite easy, even though the details may be difficult to recall (Friedman, 1979; Graesser, Gordon, & Sawyer, 1979; Mandler & Goodman, 1982). The exception to this is highly unusual or odd details that do not fit the normal script. I remember very clearly a food server at one restaurant who was remarkably clumsy. The server stood out because, after spilling drinks, bumping the table, and dropping a tray of food, I realized just how much coordination and balance the job typically entails.

Schank and Abelson (1977) claimed that scripts are what help us to determine what is happening in a story. A remarkable amount of information can be supplied by using script knowledge from long-term memory about these short snippets:

- John ordered food and a drink, and eventually they arrived. The food went unfinished, and he left a small tip.

- Mary heard the bell ringing outside and went into her room to check her piggy bank. Then she ran outside to get an ice cream.

- Ted saw the deflated tire on his bike and headed into the garage.

- Michelle went outside with her pool toys but came back in when she saw the dark clouds approaching.

For these, we can determine a lot of additional information about the situation, including emotional states, time of year, and possibly the age of the characters. Schank and Abelson (1977) claimed we use these higher-order structures to make sense of what is going around us. One of the functions of scripts is to map out causal chains of events for meaning. The basis of causality can be physical, like how rain clouds bring rain and lightning; or the basis in causality can be psychological, such as John's disappointment in how long the food took to arrive.

Schank and Abelson (1977) believe that when it comes to people, our scripts help to determine the goals and motivations of others. The choices people make (which scripts they put to use) say something about what their apparent intentions are. If I hear that a friend of mine picked up a weekend job on top of his full-time job during the week, I would guess that he needs money. Most actions are committed with intent of some sort, and many scripts appear to signal a kind of intent to observers. People reading a story, for example, have been found to infer the character's mental state and goals from the character's actions and will remember them later on, as well (O'Brien & Albrecht, 1992; Rinck et al., 2001; Seifert, Robertson, & Black, 1985).

A theoretical challenge to the schema and script concepts is one of scope and scale. It is hard to know in advance what schemas and scripts people have, and how they interact. It has been proposed that some scripts operate as different scenes, independently from each other, so there may be a script for "waiting at the doctor's office" and "waiting at the dentist's office" that are mentally held separately. This would explain why a memory of waiting at an office could confuse the two. However, is there also a "waiting at the optometrist's office" script? How many scripts to see medical professionals are necessary before we are just describing episodic memories? With schemas and scripts, the boundaries between them and their number are unclear.

Constructivism

The empiricist tradition, established by John Locke and Ebbinghaus's primary approach, treated memories as images that were copies of the physical sensations at the time we experienced them (from Chapter 1). According to this tradition, we build a large mental database of images that are the building blocks of thought and knowledge. Constructivism, a more recent tradition beginning in the 1930s, assumes that episodic memories are interpreted by the semantic information we have at the time of the event. Another term for this semantic memory information is prior (or background) knowledge. This means that an event interacts with our existing prior knowledge. This is regardless of whether we are discussing semantic memory as stored in semantic networks, or concepts grouped as mental models, schemas, or scripts. New memories are the result of the interaction between prior knowledge and our experiences. Misconceptions can result if we have expectations that are violated—such as default assignments for "books" being in an office when none are there.

Due to the work and theories of Sir Frederick Bartlett and Jean Piaget, the primary code in long-term memory is not sensory information, but rather semantic codes, representations of meaning. Viewing the world by what the objects mean aids in interpretation of the events around us as well as memory.

A memory I have for a given event is, thus, my memory of my understanding for the particular event, more than a mental recording of the sensations I experienced at the time. Often this sense of meaning about the event is quite holistic—so "attending my sister's wedding" can be formed as a general event description beyond the many smaller episodes that made up the event. This tenet of constructivism dovetails with Conway's idea of "general events" in his theory of autobiographical memory (Conway & Pleydell-Pearce, 2000).

According to constructivism, the background knowledge we employ to understand a particular event becomes a part of the memory. The higher-level meaning of the event becomes more important than the specific events themselves. For people in the UK, Margaret Thatcher's decision to retire was a monumental event that capped years of controversy and employment upheaval. Many people living in England formed flashbulb memories of hearing the event (Conway et al., 1994). However, here in the United States, the news was generally viewed with more distance, less meaning, and as more of an announcement. Less meaning was applied, and few people formed flashbulb memories of the change.

The constructivist approach has one other tenet that distinguishes itself from the empirical approach to memory. Empiricists claim that the content stored previously can be recalled, intact, into conscious awareness. No other processing of the information occurs other than making the information conscious. But constructivism claims that at the time of recall, we reconstruct the memory. We use any information that can be retrieved from the original event as well as prior knowledge related to the event from long-term memory simultaneously. We work to interpret the event as the information is retrieved. This process affects the memory itself, since any weak areas in the recall of the content can shift to become more like the prior knowledge over time. Constructivism seems to have predicted some of what the neurobiologists had found with reconsolidation theory (see Chapter 8).

To review, constructivism assumes memory is fairly dynamic—at the act of both encoding as well as retrieving. Prior knowledge, in whatever theoretical form, helps guide attention to the important details during the event. Later, prior knowledge colors the retrieval of the memory, guiding interpretation and filling in missing areas with expected values.

Ebbinghaus had assumed that memory could be studied using reductionism, examining memory at its more basic "units." This way, memory could be assessed purely by the number of units retrieved across different situations. He used nonsense syllables as a way to try to ascertain "pure" learning and forgetting functions, devoid of content. His assumption was that more complex material would operate the same way as these basic functions. In contrast, Bartlett believed it was unrealistic to measure human memory in units at all. In human understanding, there is no "unit" that is devoid of interpretation or meaning. Even if we tried to isolate learning and retrieval of concepts, the entire event itself is still conceptualized by some framework ("participating in a psychology research study," "grocery shopping," or "attending a party"). Using only random, nonsense syllables for study would ignore some of the most important elements of human learning and recollection.

Jean Piaget (see Chapter 5), the Swiss developmentalist and biologist, extended Bartlett's ideas (most notably in Piaget & Inhelder, 1973). Piaget saw schemas as interpretive, as Bartlett did, but proposed that schemas themselves can be highly interrelated or loosely organized as well. A memory that is based on an interrelated set of schemas will tend to be a stronger memory, like one formed in a domain related to an area of expertise. If we have few integrated schemas for some event, the resulting memory will be weak.

Modern Constructivism

It's taken for granted today that memories do not simply move into conscious awareness with retrieval (Neisser, 1967). Neisser saw memories as using some of the original information, but we use higher-order memory structures to fill in gaps and interpret the event as we experience it. Events that do not fit any higher-order structure will not make sense. Sensory information is retained, but is not the primary memory code.

Today, constructivist ideas appear in neural network simulations of memory. Computer scientists model human memory using units of information that work in concert to give rise to higher-order structures that act like schemas (McClelland, Rumelhart, & Hinton, 1986). Another area of intense research has been the nature of interpreted memories and their errors: That is, what kinds of memory errors are people susceptible to when they retrieve information. How susceptible to error is the human memory system? How can we tell the difference between a recalled memory that is factually incorrect versus an intentional lie? We'll visit these issues in the next chapter on forgetting and other memory errors.

CHAPTER SUMMARY

We began the chapter by taking a look at Tulving's now-classic claim that memories in long-term memory could be split into at least two general forms. Some long-term memories appeared to be reexperienced episodic events (episodic memory). Others seem to be more like factual retrieval (semantic memory); there is little if any reliving of the original exposure to the learning event. He used the Remember/Know Judgment task to show that participants themselves seemed to be able to decide which they were experiencing. Neuroscience evidence indicates that there are some trends in brain activation that distinguish between the two.

Other distinctions between forms of long-term memory exist as well. **Declarative memory** has been used to indicate memories that can be made conscious, including episodic and semantic memories. Nondeclarative memories are those that are implicit in nature, like well-learned procedural skills, that cannot be readily brought into consciousness. Additionally, memory performance seems to vary based on whether a task involves recognition or recall, and the roles of meaning and context seem to interact in determining the relative success rates of either approach.

Since semantic memory does not appear to parallel experienced events, theorists have proposed possible structures that semantic memory might take, or knowledge representation. These approaches tend to be either associationistic at the level of basic units of information, or higher-order, holistic structures comprised of many bits of information. Popular atomistic models include Collins and Loftus's (1975) semantic networks model, which proposes that nodes of information are associated unidirectionally or bidirectionally by links, forming a hierarchical web of knowledge.

Bringing one node into conscious awareness will tend to activate other linked nodes in a spreading activation fashion.

Connectionist models are a more recent alternative to Collins and Loftus's models. They are based on neurological functioning, and do not require that information be stored hierarchically. Evidence supports the idea that nodes activate other nodes in terms of strength of activation, but not in terms of speed. Also, nodes that are not directly cued but are related to a number of other activated nodes can become activated indirectly, a phenomenon called activation from a distance. Connectionist models are sometimes evaluated in a computational way by being programmed into computers in an attempt to simulate human thought on computers. These computer-based connectionist models are called neural networks.

Proposed higher-order structures of knowledge include concepts, mental models, schemas, and scripts. **Concepts** are the basic conceptual units of thought that cannot be reduced any further without losing the meaning of the concept. The essential role of concepts is to allow for categorizing instances in the real world (whether experienced or imagined). Learning a concept can be thought of as learning how to accurately categorize instances as being a member of or not. Mental models are combinations of concepts used to mentally simulate a situation—whether a physical situation from a story, the intentions and goals of others, or logical reasoning needed to solve a problem. Mental models rely on semantic memory information but may be operated in working memory as the individual struggles to understand a situation, in order to make predictions or test different hypotheses. Schemas are large structures of general knowledge that are not consciously accessed but are quickly applied to guide attention, to make sense of events around us, to fill in missing information when we try to recall a memory, and to interpret our memories. Scripts are a form of schema that involve the temporal sequence of events. Both involve well-learned material that acts like a template for what usually happens and what is expected to occur, with "slots"

available for whatever pertinent details the current environment provides.

The chapter ended with an overview of a recent framework outlining what semantic memory means for how we understand the world. Constructivism claims that unlike earlier empirical approaches, prior knowledge exists to help us make meaning of world around us; and it can lead us to form misconceptions or false memories when events do not neatly fit into our preexisting understanding of the world.

REVIEW QUESTIONS

1. While Tulving's remember/know judgment has been applied in research to specific details that someone might remember about stimuli they were asked to memorize, in every day life, both forms of memory are accessible and work largely in concert. Think of any activity you have done recently, such as working out, watching a sporting event, or reading a novel. Can you separate out parts of what you recall about the experience that were episodic in nature, and parts that required knowledge to comprehend or understand?

2. Just for the experience of trying, diagram your knowledge of dogs on a scratch sheet of paper, following the guidelines that Collins and Quillan or any of the connectionist theorists propose. Use nodes for main concepts, link them for associations, and use thickness of the lines for the strength of the association. Some associations might be

unidirectional, some might be bidirectional. Features and traits (e.g., "has two eyes") can hang off of the nodes. Stop after about ten minutes. What does this exercise tell you about the nature of your knowledge for a "simple" concept, like dogs? Do you think you could ever draw out everything you know about dogs?

3. Contrast concepts, mental models, schemas, and scripts with each other. Think of an activity you enjoy doing. Can you think of examples of knowledge you apply when doing that activity that fit each of these theoretical constructs?

4. Consider Ebbinghaus's and Bartlett's philosophical differences of opinion about what kinds of stimuli should be used to study memory. Do you believe there is a clear winner in their disagreement, or can their views be reconciled in some way? How so?

KEY TERMS

Activated   251
Activation at a distance   253
Activation from a distance   265
Associationistic   265
Concept   255
Concepts   265
Connectionist models   254
Connectivity   253
Constructivism   263
Declarative memory   248
Encoding specificity principle   249
Episodic memory   265
Higher-order   265
High-frequency   250
Know   247

FURTHER RESOURCES

1. Weblink: Conceptually, what's the difference between a seed, a nut, a vegetable, and a fruit?:
   - http://www.straightdope.com/columns/read/1611/whats-the-difference-between-fruits-and-vegetables

2. Weblink: A graphical explanation of how neural networks operate:
   - https://www.youtube.com/watch?v=ILsA4nyG7I0

REFERENCES

Alba, J. W., & Hasher, L. (1983). Is memory schematic? *Psychological Bulletin, 93*(2), 203.

Anderson, J. R. (1993). Development of expertise. In B. G. Buchanan & D. C. Wilkins (Eds.), *Readings in knowledge acquisition and learning: Automating the construction and improvement of expert systems* (pp. 61–77). San Francisco, CA: Morgan Kaufmann.

Anderson, J. R., & Bower, G. H. (1972). Recognition and retrieval processes in free recall. *Psychological Review, 79*(2), 97.

Bahrick, H. P. (1970). Two-phase model for prompted recall. *Psychological Review, 77*(3), 215.

Bahrick, H. P. (1979). Maintenance of knowledge: Questions about memory we forgot to ask. *Journal of Experimental Psychology: General, 108*(3), 296.

Balota, D. A., & Lorch, R. F. (1986). Depth of automatic spreading activation: Mediated priming effects in pronunciation but not in lexical decision. *Journal of Experimental Psychology: Learning, Memory, and Cognition, 12*(3), 336.

Barsalou, L. W. (1993). Flexibility, structure, and linguistic vagary in concepts: Manifestations of a compositional system of perceptual symbols. In A. F. Collins, S. E. Gathercole, M. A. Conway, & P. E. Morris (Eds.), *Theories of memory* (pp. 29–101). Hillsdale, NJ: Erlbaum.

Bartlett, F. C. (1916). An experimental study of some problems of perceiving and imaging. *British Journal of Psychology, 1904–1920, 8*(2), 222–266.

Bartlett, F. C. (1920). Some experiments on the reproduction of folk-stories. *Folklore, 31*(1), 30–47.

Bartlett, F. C. (1921). The functions of images. *British Journal of Psychology. General Section, 11*(3), 320–337.

Bartlett, Frederic C. (1932). *Remembering: A study in experimental and social psychology.* (Cambridge, England: Cambridge University Press).

Bennett, D. J., & McEvoy, C. L. (1999). Mediated priming in younger and older adults. *Experimental Aging Research, 25*(2), 141–159.

Bestgen, Y., & Vonk, W. (1995). The role of temporal segmentation markers in discourse processing. *Discourse Processes, 19*(3), 385–406.

Bower, G. H., Black, J. B., & Turner, T. J. (1979). Scripts in memory for text. *Cognitive Psychology, 11*(2), 177–220.

Bransford, J. D., Barclay, J. R., & Franks, J. J. (1972). Sentence memory: A constructive versus interpretive approach. *Cognitive Psychology, 3*(2), 193–209.

Brewer, W. F. (1993). What are concepts? Issues of representation and ontology. In G. V. Nakamura, D. L. Medin, & R. Taraban (Eds.), *Categorization by humans and machines* (Vol. 29, pp. 495–533). San Diego, CA: Academic Press.

Brewer, W. F., & Nakamura, G. V. (1984). The nature and functions of schemas. In J. Robert S. Wyer & T. K. Srull (Eds.), *Handbook of social cognition* (Vol. 1, pp. 119–160). Hillsdale, NJ: Erlbaum.

Brewer, W. F., & Treyens, J. C. (1981). Role of schemata in memory for places. *Cognitive Psychology, 13*, 207–230.

Buchanan, B. G., & Wilkins, D. C. (1993). *Readings in knowledge acquisition and learning: Automating the construction and improvement of expert systems.* San Francisco, CA: Morgan Kaufmann. Retrieved from http://dl.acm.org/citation.cfm?id=170641

Chase, W. G., & Simon, H. A. (1973). The mind's eye in chess. In W. G. Chase (Ed.), *Visual information processing* (pp. 215–281). Oxford, England: Academic.

Chiesi, H. L., Spilich, G. J., & Voss, J. F. (1979). Acquisition of domain-related information in relation to high and low domain knowledge. *Journal of Verbal Learning & Verbal Behavior, 18*, 257–273.

Collins, A. M., & Loftus, E. F. (1975). A spreading-activation theory of semantic processing. *Psychological Review, 82*(6), 407.

Collins, A. M., & Quillian, M. R. (1969). Retrieval time from semantic memory. *Journal of Verbal Learning and Verbal Behavior, 8*(2), 240–247.

Collins, A. M., & Quillian, M. R. (1972). Experiments on semantic memory and language comprehension. In L. W. Gregg & G. H. Bower, *Cognition in learning and memory* (pp. 117–138). New York, NY: Wiley.

Conway, M. A., Anderson, S. J., Larsen, S. F., Donnelly, C. M., McDaniel, M. A., McClelland, A. G., . . . Logie, R. H. (1994). The formation of flashbulb memories. *Memory & Cognition, 22*(3), 326–343.

Conway, M. A., & Pleydell-Pearce, C. W. (2000). The construction of autobiographical memories in the self-memory system. *Psychological Review, 107*(2), 261.

Craik, F. I. M., & Lockhart, R. S. (1972). Levels of processing: A framework for memory research. *Journal of Verbal Learning and Verbal Behavior, 11*(6), 671–684. https://doi.org/10.1016/S0022-5371(72)80001-X

Crowder, R. G. (1976). *Principles of learning and memory.* Hillsdale, NJ: Erlbaum.

Deese, J. (1961). Associative structure and the serial reproduction experiment. *The Journal of Abnormal and Social Psychology, 63*(1), 95.

Fisher, R. P., & Craik, F. I. (1977). Interaction between encoding and retrieval operations in cued recall. *Journal of Experimental Psychology: Human Learning and Memory, 3*(6), 701.

Friedman, A. (1979). Framing pictures: The role of knowledge in automatized encoding and memory for gist. *Journal of Experimental Psychology: General, 108*(3), 316.

Gardiner, J. M., Ramponi, C., & Richardson-Klavehn, A. (2002). Recognition memory and decision processes: A meta-analysis of remember, know, and guess responses. *Memory, 10*(2), 83–98.

Glenberg, A. M., Meyer, M., & Lindem, K. (1987). Mental models contribute to foregrounding during text comprehension. *Journal of Memory and Language, 26*(1), 69–83.

Graesser, A. C., Gordon, S. E., & Sawyer, J. D. (1979). Recognition memory for typical and atypical actions in scripted activities: Tests of a script pointer + tag hypothesis. *Journal of Verbal Learning and Verbal Behavior, 18*(3), 319–332.

Gregg, V. (1976). *Word frequency, recognition and recall.* Retrieved from http://psycnet.apa.org/psycinfo/1977-11959-007

Habib, R., Nyberg, L., & Tulving, E. (2003). Hemispheric asymmetries of memory: The HERA model revisited. *Trends in Cognitive Sciences, 7*(6), 241–245.

Haenggi, D., Kintsch, W., & Gernsbacher, M. A. (1995). Spatial situation models and text comprehension. *Discourse Processes, 19*(2), 173–199.

Hinton, G. E. (1989). Connectionist learning procedures. *Artificial Intelligence, 40*(1–3), 185–234.

Jacoby, L. L., Bishara, A. J., Hessels, S., & Toth, J. P. (2005). Aging, subjective experience, and cognitive control: Dramatic false remembering by older adults. *Journal of Experimental Psychology: General, 134*(2), 131.

Johnson-Laird, P. N. (1980). Mental models in cognitive science. *Cognitive Science, 4,* 71–115.

Kintsch, W. (1974). *The representation of meaning in memory.* Retrieved from http://psycnet.apa.org/psycinfo/1975-20379-000

Kintsch, W., & van Dijk, T. A. (1978). Toward a model of text comprehension and production. *Psychological Review, 85*(5), 363.

Lewis, M. (2011). *The big short: Inside the doomsday machine* (Reprint ed.). New York, NY: W. W. Norton & Company.

Lichtenstein, E. H., & Brewer, W. F. (1980). Memory for goal-directed events. *Cognitive Psychology, 12*(3), 412–445.

Mandler, G., Pearlstone, Z., & Koopmans, H. S. (1969). Effects of organization and semantic similarity on recall and recognition. *Journal of Verbal Learning and Verbal Behavior, 8*(3), 410–423.

Mandler, J. M., & Goodman, M. S. (1982). On the psychological validity of story structure. *Journal of Verbal Learning and Verbal Behavior, 21*(5), 507–523.

Mandler, J. M., & Johnson, N. S. (1977). Remembrance of things parsed: Story structure and recall. *Cognitive Psychology, 9*(1), 111–151.

McClelland, J. L., McNaughton, B. L., & O'Reilly, R. C. (1995). Why there are complementary learning systems in the hippocampus and neocortex: Insights from the successes and failures of connectionist models of learning and memory. *Psychological Review, 102*(3), 419–457.

McClelland, J. L., Rumelhart, D. E., & Hinton, G. E. (1986). The appeal of parallel distributed processing. In D. Rumelhart, R. McClelland, & DPD Research Group (Eds.), *Parallel distributed processing* (pp. 3–44). Cambridge, MA: MIT Press.

McKay, A. (Producer), & Director. (2015). *The big short* [motion picture].

McNamara, T. P. (1992). Theories of priming: I. Associative distance and lag. *Journal of Experimental Psychology Learning Memory and Cognition, 18,* 1173–1173.

Meyer, B. J., & McConkie, G. W. (1973). What is recalled after hearing a passage? *Journal of Educational Psychology, 65*(1), 109.

Minsky, M. (1975). Minsky's frame system theory. In TINLAP (Vol. 75, pp. 104–116). Cambridge, MA.

Morrow, J. D. (1994). *Game theory for political scientists.* Princeton, NJ: Princeton University Press. Retrieved from https://pup.princeton.edu/titles/5590.html

Neisser, U. (1967). *Cognitive psychology.* East Norwalk, CT: Appleton-Century-Crofts.

Nelson, D. L., McEvoy, C. L., & Pointer, L. (2003). Spreading activation or spooky action at a distance? *Journal of Experimental Psychology: Learning, Memory, and Cognition, 29*(1), 42.

Nelson, D. L., Zhang, N., & McKinney, V. M. (2001). The ties that bind what is known to the recognition of what is new. *Journal of Experimental Psychology: Learning, Memory, and Cognition, 27*(5), 1147.

O'Brien, E. J., & Albrecht, J. E. (1992). Comprehension strategies in the development of a mental model. *Journal of Experimental Psychology: Learning, Memory, and Cognition, 18*(4), 777–784.

Ohtsuka, K., & Brewer, W. F. (1992). Discourse organization in the comprehension of temporal order in narrative texts. *Discourse Processes, 15*(3), 317–336.

Piaget, J., & Inhelder, B. (1973). *Memory and intelligence.* Basic Books (AZ).

Ratcliff, R., & McKoon, G. (1981). Does activation really spread? *Psychological Review, 88*(5), 454.

Rimmele, U., Davachi, L., & Phelps, E. A. (2012). Memory for time and place contributes to enhanced confidence in memories for emotional events. *Emotion, 12*(4), 834–846.

Rinck, M., Hähnel, A., & Becker, G. (2001). Using temporal information to construct, update, and retrieve situation models of narratives. *Journal of Experimental Psychology: Learning, Memory, and Cognition, 27*(1), 67–80.

Rinck, M., Williams, P., Bower, G. H., & Becker, E. S. (1996). Spatial situation models and narrative understanding: Some generalizations and extensions. *Discourse Processes, 21*(1), 23–55.

Roediger, H. L., & Adelson, B. (1980). Semantic specificity in cued recall. *Memory & Cognition, 8*(1), 65–74.

Rumelhart, D. E. (1980). Schemata: The building blocks of cognition. In R. J. Spiro, B. C. Bruce, & W. F. Brewer (Eds.), *Theoretical issues in reading comprehension* (pp. 33–58). Hillsdale, NJ: Erlbaum.

Rumelhart, D. E. (1990). Brain style computation: Learning and generalization. In *An introduction to neural and electronic networks* (pp. 405–420). Cambridge, MA: Academic Press.

Rumelhart, D. E., & Ortony, A. (1977). The representation of knowledge in memory. In R. C. Anderson, R. J. Spiro, & W. E. Montague (Eds.), *Schooling and the acquisition of knowledge* (pp. 99–135). Hillsdale, NJ: Erlbaum.

Rumelhart, D. E., & Todd, P. M. (1993). Learning and connectionist representations. In D. E. Meyer & S. Kornblum (Eds.), *Attention and performance XIV: Synergies in experimental psychology, artificial intelligence, and cognitive neuroscience* (pp. 3–30). Cambridge, MA: MIT Press.

Schank, R. C., & Abelson, R. (1977). *Scripts, goals, plans, and understanding.* Hillsdale, NJ: Erlbaum.

Seifert, C. M., Robertson, S. P., & Black, J. B. (1985). Types of inferences generated during reading. *Journal of Memory and Language, 24*(4), 405–422.

Squire, L. R. (1992). Declarative and nondeclarative memory: Multiple brain systems supporting learning and memory. *Journal of Cognitive Neuroscience, 4*(3), 232–243.

Steffensen, M. S., & Colker, L. (1982). *The effect of cultural knowledge on memory and language.* Center for the Study of Reading Technical Report; No. 248. Retrieved from https://www.ideals.illinois.edu/bitstream/handle/2142/17769/ctrstreadtechrepv01982i00248_opt.pdf?sequence=1

Thorndyke, P. W. (1977). Cognitive structures in comprehension and memory of narrative discourse. *Cognitive Psychology, 9*(1), 77–110.

Tulving, E. (1972). Episodic and semantic memory. From E. Tulving & W. Donaldson, (Eds.) *Organization of memory* (pp. 381–403). New York, NY. Academic Press.

Tulving, E. (1985). *Elements of episodic memory.* Oxford, England: Oxford University Press.

Tulving, E. (2002). Episodic memory: From mind to brain. *Annual Review of Psychology, 53*(1), 1–25.

Tulving, E., & Thomson, D. M. (1973). Encoding specificity and retrieval processes in episodic memory. *Psychological Review, 80*(5), 352.

Vosniadou, S., & Brewer, W. F. (1992). Mental models of the earth: A study of conceptual change in childhood. *Cognitive Psychology, 24,* 535–585.

Welborn, E. L., & English, H. (1937). Logical learning and retention: A general review of experiments with meaningful verbal materials. *Psychological Bulletin, 34*(1), 1.

Wickelgren, W. A. (1976). Network strength theory of storage and retrieval dynamics. *Psychological Review, 83*(6), 466.

Zwaan, R. A. (1996). Processing narrative time shifts. *Journal of Experimental Psychology: Learning, Memory, and Cognition, 22*(5), 1196.

Zwaan, R. A., & Radvansky, G. A. (1998). Situation models in language comprehension and memory. *Psychological Bulletin, 123*(2), 162.

Zwaan, R. A., Radvansky, G. A., & Whitten, S. (2002). Situation models and themes. In M. Louwerse, & W. van Peer, (Eds.), *Thematics: Interdisciplinary studies* (pp. 35–53). Philadelphia, PA: John Benjamins.

©iStock.com/maaram

Forgetting

Chapter Outline

Overview

Forgetting happens. Usually an inability to retrieve is pretty minor. A while ago, a friend of mine refilled her coffee mug at work, put the cup on a shelf inside a cabinet next to the microwave, waited a bit, opened the cabinet, and took a sip of (still) cold coffee.

This chapter brings to a close much of what we started exploring with the chapter on retrieval. In this chapter, we review and enhance what we have encountered so far by taking a look at what happens when the memory system doesn't work as we would've desired. Let's look at why we forget, how fast we forget, and how rates of forgetting change over the lifespan.

Forgetting Is Normal

Forgetting is a normal, everyday part of living, but most of the time it feels like a failure of our normal functioning. Sometimes the inability to recall information is temporary; other times it is more permanent. What is easy to overlook is that forgetting is adaptive. How and why we forget is a natural result of our memory system working as well as it does. Knowing why we forget can inform us about the how human memory works like it does.

It may seem like the purpose of memory is to enable us to capture past experiences so that we can relive them. However, having a memory that worked like a video recorder would not be much use. The past does not occur again exactly as it did before, so being able to replay from a mental set of "video archives"—if you will—would not have much adaptive value to our changing environments (Nairne & Pandeirada, 2008). Occasionally specific information is necessary, such as remembering the lot where we parked, which foods we have an intolerance for, or retelling an event in a courtroom under oath. Generally, we do not need this level of specificity, but rather a more abstract sense of what we need to know to make a decision now. What memory does is to let us use information from the past to help us with our present (Suddendorf & Corballis, 1997; Tulving, 2002). We use memory to help understand the present as well as to anticipate what will happen in the future.

Much of this abstracting seems to be the result of the semantic coding that is the basis of much of long-term memory. As we have seen in prior chapters, semantic memory helps us to interpret our environment as well as our autobiographical past. We tend to process the meaning of an event and store connections to existing knowledge over vivid memories that can replicate an event perfectly (Bartlett, 1932; Schacter & Addis, 2007). Given the emphasis on meaning in our memory system, it makes sense that we have will have some trouble reproducing information. This is particularly true if the event seemed unimportant at the time we experienced it. Even when we can recall details of an event, we don't usually take it for granted that details of an event will be able to be recalled forever, either.

So, another way to look at forgetting is to see it as being adaptive (e.g., Altmann & Gray, 2002; Bjork & Bjork, 1996). For instance, since our recall will not have perfect fidelity with reality, we are forced to make inferences and use strategies to navigate situations, making us think in the moment (Schooler & Hertwig, 2005). Our imperfect recall means we work to detect causal relationships as well (Kareev, 2000). Luria (1968) proposes that as our environment changes constantly, so having a flexible memory and cognition system helps us to stay sane.

Also, there is a remarkable amount of information that is simply no longer needed in time. Our memories are gauged somewhat by how likely we think information will be needed well into the future, partially so that we do not carry totally unnecessary information any longer, like where we parked at a ball game several years ago, which socks we wore a few weeks ago, and passwords and PIN numbers that are obsolete.

Statistically, the common arc of forgetting seems to mirror the likelihood that we will need to remember an encounter later on. The memory system likely evolved as an aid for remembering encounters with predators—there would be a need to remember where an encounter took place, but the likelihood of meeting the predator again in the same spot will drop over time. The statistical function of a recurring event has a slope that is negatively accelerated (Anderson & Schooler, 1991). Essentially, the statistical likelihood of an event's recurring is relatively high, but it drops quickly. Forgetting tends to take on a very similar function. Many details are remembered for a little while, but then forgetting sets in very quickly. One perspective on forgetting, then, is to see it as the memory system's sensitivity to the statistical likelihood of events recurring. As an event becomes less likely to repeat, we forget details that have little long-term value (Nairne & Pandeirada, 2008).

Normal Rate of Forgetting

If forgetting is normal, and conceivably adaptive, what is the normal rate of forgetting? The overall arc of forgetting a set of material, such as a word list, is fairly well established: We retain well initially, but we forget a lot of information very rapidly. Eventually forgetting levels off and we retain pertinent details for quite some time. This curve of forgetting has held up for different kinds of information, as well as for the amount of information. It has held up using different measures of retrieval as well (see Fig. 11.1). Another perspective of the same phenomena is Jost's Law, which states, "Given two associations of the same strength, but of different ages, the older falls off less rapidly in a given length of time" (Britt, 1935; Jost, 1897; Simon, 1966; Wixted, 2004). If two memories are equally strong, then the older will be

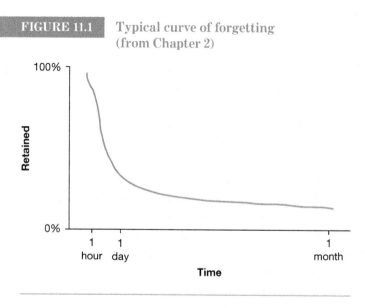

FIGURE 11.1   Typical curve of forgetting (from Chapter 2)

more durable and less likely to be forgotten. As time passes, what memories remain tend to become more resilient.

Ebbinghaus is well known for his demonstration of the curve of forgetting, although Galton had beaten him to it (Galton, 1879). Ebbinghaus used what he called his savings method as a way to track how much was saved from one study session to the next. For example, he would memorize lists of nonsense syllables until he could recite them twice without a mistake. Then he would restudy the same lists later. The interval between study sessions was intentionally varied: It could be anywhere from one hour to a month. He calculated the percent savings as the amount of time needed to relearn, subtracted from the original amount of learning time, and expressed as a percentage of the original learning time. The greatest savings was, of course, when relearning was carried out within about an hour of the original learning session. After that, the decline in savings was large until a plateau where retention took hold; the effect of forgetting lessened over time (Ebbinghaus, 1885/1964). What remains stays so well that he was unsure if it would ever be forgotten at all. Researchers today are still unsure if what is retained is ever lost (Wixted, 2004).

Some researchers have attempted to describe the rate of forgetting mathematically. Linear functions are clearly unworkable; Ebbinghaus suggested a logarithmic function. For example, Rubin and Wenzel (1996) use a power-logarithmic function to capture the rate of normal forgetting. Their power law of forgetting states that memory strength = f log (time). Other mathematical functions are possible, but most researchers rely on power functions.

Despite clear evidence about the shape of the curve of forgetting, there is no one law of forgetting (e.g., Wixted, 2004; Wixted & Carpenter, 2007). Part of the problem is that different researchers have proposed different mathematical models, and to pick a best model means having consensus over what criteria is necessary for choosing the best model. Most researchers prefer a goodness-of-fit measure, which means picking a formula that captures the most data the best (e.g., Anderson & Schooler, 1991; Rubin & Wenzel, 1996; Wixted & Ebbesen, 1991). There are multiple ways of calculating goodness-of-fit, and their differences are beyond the scope of this text. Basically, they operate by summing up the differences between what a formula would predict and the actual data that have been collected. Using the same goodness-of-fit measure of several formulas on the same set of data can indicate which mathematical model "fits" the data best. However, goodness-of-fit calculations do not take into account how complex a formula is; so someone could simply make a formula needlessly complex in order to fit a set of data perfectly (Pitt, Myung, & Zhang, 2002; Roberts & Pashler, 2000). The more complex model isn't contributing much to our understanding about forgetting so much as artificially matching the data perfectly. Another conceptual issue is whether or not forgetting at different levels of retention is equal. It's not clear that a 10 percent drop in forgetting from 90 percent down to 80 percent has the same psychological weight as the same 10 percent drop from 20 percent to 10 percent (Nairne & Pandeirada, 2008).

Some researchers have attempted to measure forgetting over the lifespan. This creates new issues for describing a normal rate of forgetting. Measuring forgetting means requiring repeated testing of the same participants at different times, which means both that (a) people can drop out of the study over time, leaving incomplete data, and (b) repeated testing of the same material can improve retention over time. Testing different groups of people at different ages in a cross-sectional design doesn't guarantee the pattern of changes in forgetting that will occur for any one individual (Chechile, 2006; Rubin & Wenzel, 1996). Also, memories can last a lifetime, which means not all mathematical functions can be applied to real data (Chechile, 2006; Wixted, 2004). Additionally, there is no way to evaluate long-term retention at or near point zero (immediately), since sensory memory and working memory will complicate retention at that point.

Finally, not everyone agrees on the measurement of retention that is most important. Ebbinghaus used a savings function, but other options include the proportion correct recall, a discriminability-index of being recognized (percent change of an item's being recognized), or other implicit measurement tasks. It's not clear that these dependent measures are all measuring retention in the same manner. Complicating the issue of measurement is the presence of retrieval cues that may help retention or divided attention tasks that worsen performance. Another related question is how the delay between different retests should be calculated: the passage of time, time on some relative index (Bjork & Whitten, 1974), or the presence of intervening events (Waugh & Norman, 1965)? Of course, the longer the time, the more intervening events will have likely occurred, since they are correlated and thus confounded (Chechile, 1987).

In any case, forgetting is initially very rapid, which slows off in time. In fact, the rate of forgetting gradually declines.

Forgetting Motor Skills

Motor skills can be remarkably resistant to forgetting. If you learned to ride a bike, swim, or skateboard in childhood, then it's likely you can get engaged in those activities again without much trouble, even after an absence of years. Do we ever forget motor skills? One study tested participants who were training to fly planes on a flight simulator (Fleischman & Parker, 1962). When retested nine to twenty-four months later, the participants showed the same level of performance—no forgetting was noted.

Most likely this is not true for all skills. As we saw in Chapter 3, some skills are closed-loop (or continuous) skills: each action cues the next action. Biking and swimming, for example, are closed-loop skills. Remembering a few actions is enough to set the chain of behaviors into action. Handwriting and typing are open-loop skills: each action is in response to different stimuli. Closed-loop skills are more resistant to forgetting, compared to open-loop skills (e.g., Adams, 1971).

Of course, many real-world skills are not one or the either but a mix. In a study of cardiac resuscitation skills, 215 participants were trained on CPR and evaluated on a life-size mannequin (McKenna & Glendon, 1985). Feedback was given. Participants were brought back anytime from three months to three years after training. Forgetting was dramatic: The predicted survival rate of a patient receiving the CPR skills that had been retained dropped from 100 percent to 15 percent within a year. Some skills, particularly complex ones, need practice.

Forgetting Events Over Time

Many memory studies track retention for only a month or so, and often the material is rather inconsequential to the participant (such as random lists of words). Often we attempt to recall events from months or years ago, however. The challenge with this kind of work is a matter of verification—it's not enough to ask people if they can remember what they were doing ten or twenty years ago, but we must be able to check the accuracy. One approach is to use news-making national events that most, if not all, of the participants in the study will have been exposed to. Warrington and Sanders (1971) used headline news from the prior year to more than thirty years ago and tested their participants' memory for these events. Warrington and Sanders found that forgetting does occur, and that the younger participants had a better memory for both recent and older events than did the more elderly participants.

A different approach was taken by researchers who tested 392 high school alumni for their ability to recognize classmates and recall their names using their high school yearbooks (Bahrick, Bahrick, & Wittlinger, 1975; Bahrick, Hall, & Berger, 1996). They found the rate of forgetting for this content was relatively slow: The ability to recognize a face or a name remained at 90 percent for at least fifteen years and stayed high for over thirty years. The authors attributed this to lots of practice and "overlearning"—the process of studying more than is necessary. Recalling a classmate's name, however, showed a more typical pattern of forgetting by about 60 percent up to forty-eight years later. After fifty years, the performance declines appeared to be confounded with memory decline associated with aging, rather than with normal forgetting.

Ohio Wesleyan University hosts alumni reunions for its graduates annually, and Harry Bahrick (now a Professor Emeritus at Ohio Wesleyan) made use of this tradition by approaching attendees of the reunions and quizzing them about their college grades. He and his colleagues would then (with permission) verify the accuracy of the grades (for a review, see Bahrick, Hall, & Da Costa, 2008). Comparing alumni from as few as one to as many as fifty-four years after graduating, his studies have tracked 276 alumni recalling 3,967 grades. Of those, 3,025 were accurate, a rate of more than 76 percent correct. Bahrick, in earlier writings, had called this kind of memory store that is resistant to change a permastore, similar to the permafrost around the poles of Earth. Some information seems to become frozen in time. Better students made fewer mistakes, possibly because there would be a smaller range of grades to remember. When someone gave a wrong grade, the grade they reported was better than the actual grade 81 percent of the time. Distorting grades happened quickly after graduation, and remained over time. Confidence stayed stable regardless of accuracy. Bahrick believes that forgetting and distortion are separate processes, and that once something has been forgotten, we fill the memory gap by using autobiographical information that is more emotionally gratifying.

Forgetting Over the Lifespan

Some researchers have attempted to monitor our ability to recall life events over the entire lifespan. The focus of this line of research is exclusively autobiographical memories. Remarkably, the classic curve of forgetting does not cleanly apply to the entire lifespan. There are two exceptions to it: a kind of amnesia that takes place in early childhood, and a "bump" of episodic memories from the early twenties. Let's take a look at these in turn.

Childhood Amnesia

Childhood amnesia is a label for the lack of clear and integrated memories that we all experience from the first few years of our lives. While an exact age is difficult to pin down, most research finds that people can reliably produce a clear first memory only at around ages three to three-and-a-half years. That memory itself tends to be disconnected from other events, is often short, and may be relatively shallow-feeling—like a moment in time. Any earlier memories are like snapshots, if at all. The term "childhood amnesia" means a deficiency in our ability to recall events from early childhood, but it does not necessarily mean early memories are completely lost. Whether there are no memories from the first years of life is an issue that hasn't been clearly resolved at this time. Sigmund Freud originally named this phenomenon in 1905.

Developmental researchers see this as an important development in growing up. The loss of early childhood memories means that the memories we form and the autobiographical system is becoming more adult-like (Bauer et al., 2012). Childhood amnesia seems to involve a lack of memories from the first years, and the distribution of memories—given the normal rate of forgetting—is unusual.

First, different studies using different research methods have all found similar results. Whether using a questionnaire; free recall; or a known, verifiable fixed event like the birth of a sibling or a family move, the first memory is usually placed at about thirty-eight months of age with a range of from twenty-eight to forty-five months. This estimate hasn't changed for over 100 years (Bauer et al., 2012). Long-lasting memories tend to start between thirty and thirty-six months of age.

Second, when researchers monitor how many memories are remembered by children, the number that they remember is fewer than would be expected, given the normal rate of forgetting. Bauer, Burch, Scholin, and Güler (2007) used a cue-word technique with 20 seven- to ten-year-olds, asking them to think of a memory that each word reminded them of. These memories were then dated and verified by the children's parents. The forgetting of memories followed an exponential pattern rather than the power function—the children were losing half of their memories for each year, as they grew more distant. The researchers interpreted this to mean that the memories were not well consolidated yet and were more vulnerable to disruption than when we are older.

In a larger study, Bauer Larkina, and Deocampo (2011) presented twenty cue words to spark memories to 100 children between seven and eleven years of age, and to college students and parents who were thirty-five years of age. This produced almost 3,000 memories. The power function for recall fit the adults, but not the children. Children lost about half of their memories each year; so if there were 100 memories at age four, by a year later, they would have only 50, then 25, then 12.5 at age eight. If a power function was determining the forgetting rate, then at age eight, 73 memories should still have been available. Bauer and colleagues state that children experience "an accelerated rate of forgetting for memories from their childhoods" (2011, p. 216).

In effect, childhood amnesia is like a "memory wall" at around age three. After age three, autobiographical memories become richer over time, and fewer of them are forgotten. The two primary approaches in trying to isolate the age of the earliest memory are prospective and retrospective studies.

In prospective studies, children are asked to recollect some memories and then are tested on those memories at a later time. These studies, like longitudinal research, can take a long time and are difficult to conduct. Here's representative prospective study on childhood amnesia. Van Abbema and Bauer (2005) recorded three-and-a-half-year-old children and their mothers discussing events from the recent past. All were brought back in for testing, but at 3.5, 4.5, or 5.5 years later, making the children now seven, eight, or nine years old. The seven-year-olds remembered 60 percent of the now-older events from age three; the eight- and nine-year-olds remembered only 35 percent of them (see Fig. 11.2). As children age, they begin to forget the earlier memories, which seems to start between five-and-a-half and seven-and-a-half years of age. What memories are retained were just as detailed as at age three.

FIGURE 11.2   Memories we remembered at age three start to fade by age seven (Van Abbema & Bauer, 2005).

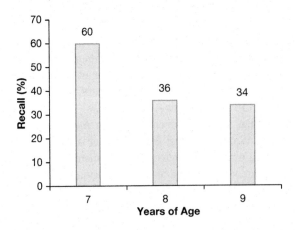

In retrospective studies, direct comparisons between children and adults are made using identical research methods. Sometimes both the children and the adults will report on the earliest childhood memory, or both will generate memories in response to cue words so the shape of the distribution of memories can be graphed (for a review, see Bauer et al., 2007).

Cohen and Faulkner (1988) documented the "trivia-like" knowledge of early memories —children do appear to organize their memories, but what adults say about these early memories does not appear to be organized. About one-fifth of the memories adults recall from early childhood they see as trivia. The memories are pointless, have no context, aren't emotional, or even important. Why the early memory was preserved may not be clear. Bruce and colleagues (2005) call the earliest memories "fragment memories," since they didn't seem to even encapsulate an event.

Peterson and Whalen (2001) tracked emergency room visits that were made by participants between the ages of two and thirteen. The benefit of using medical visits is that they can be verified. The participants were asked about the visits anywhere from one week to five years later (so the participants were between seven and eighteen years of age at the 5-year checkpoint). They found that if the emergency visit happened at the age of two, the central event details and peripheral details are recalled equally. If the visit occurred at later ages, the central event details are more often recalled, instead.

Perhaps what is memorable to a child is not memorable to an adult. With time, what was stored does not make sense any longer. One of the functions of autobiographical memories is sharing them with others, and what a child found understandable may not be something that can be shared easily as they get older (Hudson, 1990).

The very young do appear to have memories. McDonough and Mandler (1994) found infants between nine and twenty-one months of age can watch someone playing with a toy and imitate those actions. The amount of time between observation and imitation can get longer the older they become. At this age, the infant is preverbal, so the learning is probably implicit. Myers, Perris, and Speaker (1994) found a pair of five-year-olds who could verbally describe an activity they did in the lab at ten to fourteen months of age.

At these young ages, the learning and recall is likely to be implicit. As children develop verbal skills, explicit recall is possible. More scripts (semantic memories) are available to help with detail and elaboration. The scripts children have help with goals and intentions (Nelson, 1986).

Possible Causes of Childhood Amnesia

Numerous causes for childhood amnesia have been suggested. First, it could be that those early memories are lost due to a lack of linguistic ability (Schachtel, 1947). Language may be a very common form of retrieval cue, and without language skills at encoding, we lose a particularly useful kind of retrieval cue. Simcock and Hayne (2002) demonstrated this possibility by having children interact with a rigged box they called the "incredible shrinking machine." It was a simple magic trick—whatever object was placed into the top of the box seemed to turn into a smaller version of itself on the other side of the box (see Fig. 11.3). This trick was repeated for a number of objects. When the children were brought back two years later, they all remembered the machine; but they remembered only those objects that they had a word for at the initial encounter with the machine.

A second possibility is that young children do not have good strategies for encoding the information, using cues at the time of learning that are not helpful for later retrieval (Winograd & Killinger, 1983). Children between the ages of three and five may show little recall for something routine (such as dinner), instead showing more recall for the details of a novel event, like a trip to a museum or a zoo (Hudson & Nelson, 1986). Between the ages of five and seven, the child forms more general knowledge of classes of events, with fewer details. Hudson and Nelson (1986) based these ideas on evidence from a field trip that children took to a Jewish museum. Asking about this trip as a "trip to a museum" didn't trigger many memories, but asking about the "archeology trip" did. They suspect that information was being associated with cues for retrieval that were not necessarily optimal (archeology instead of museum). Possibly, early memories are lost because the child associates retrieval cues that are not helpful later on, so the memories are lost. As children get older, they will also begin to use better strategies

FIGURE 11.3   The "incredible shrinking machine," from Simcock and Hayne (2002)

Source: Simcock, G., & Hayne, H. (2002, p. 227).

for remembering information and can associate events with a broader base of general knowledge, understanding the event more clearly. All of this helps with memory retrieval. At a young age, the mismatch between encoding and retrieval cues means that memories appear lost.

A third option is that the brain has not developed to a point that allows for processing and storage of personal memories for a long duration. Brain development could also change what children are capable of attending to and associating (Fivush & Hamond, 1990), and the additional knowledge they have accumulated and can access as they get older changes how they understand events (Usher & Neisser, 1993).

A fourth possibility is that young children lack a theory of mind (Perner & Lang, 1999). The development of a theory of mind means that children can understand that other people can have mental states that are not shared with themselves; other people can have different emotional reactions to the same event, or understand the event differently. In order to have a theory of mind, children have to have a concept of themselves, and be able to connect what is going on around them to that self-concept. With a self-concept, they can understand that remembering some event will involve having a personal experience with it (Welch-Ross, 1995). This would certainly parallel Tulving's (2002) belief that episodic memory requires a sense of self in order to be effective. Perner and Lang found that three- and four-year-olds could say what the object was that they saw being put into a box. But only the four-year-olds could explain how they knew.

Finally, social interaction seems to matter (Fivush, 1994; Haden, Haine & Fivush, 1997). When mothers use an elaborative rehearsal style of discussion (connecting information to other events, building on what is said in conversation), their children develop much more detailed memories of events than the children of mothers who do less elaboration. It's as if the mothers who take the more elaborative method of conversation are rehearsing good mental strategies for the children as part of the social interaction.

Of course, there may be more than one factor (Harley & Reese, 1999). The social interaction, development of self-concept, and the biological advances that help language develop all might be behind the dramatic change in memory recall after age three.

Reminiscence Bump

Childhood amnesia is not the only deviation from a power-function type forgetting over the lifespan. The other change in how much we remember of personal events is the reminiscence bump, which is an increase in memories between the ages of ten and thirty, before dropping off again (Rubin & Schulkind, 1997; see Fig. 11.4). What a power law would predict is that the number of memories people can provide from any period in their lives should decrease as they age, with more that are recent and fewer that are older.

Instead, for participants over the age of thirty-five, there is a period of stronger recall. This can be found using words, phrases, or pictures as cues (Conway, Wang, Hanyu, & Haque, 2005; Fitzgerald, 1996). Even free associating (open recall) memories without cues can produce this effect. Oddly, memories cued by smell do not usually show this effect: smell-based memories peak between six to ten years and are often more emotional in nature (Chu & Downes, 2002; Willander & Larsson, 2006).

Rubin, Rahhal, and Poon (1998) found that this period of higher recall is not as high as for recent memories. It can include autobiographical memories as well as memories about the culture of the time, such as popular movies, music, and national news events. This phenomenon is cross-cultural as well (Conway et al., 2005).

FIGURE 11.4   A greater percentage of memories are reported between ages 10 and 30 than at any other time period except recent memories (Jansari & Parkin, 1996).

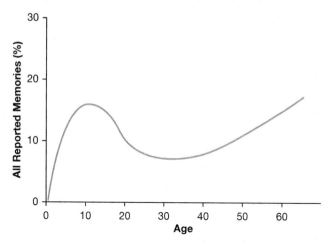

Source: Adapted from Jansari, A., & Parkin, A. J. (1996).

Note: Hypothetical values; are approximates.

Rubin and Berntsen (2003) found evidence for the Pollyanna principle in the memories from the reminiscence bump as well (more of the memories were positive than negative). Examining 3,541 memories from 659 people between fifty and ninety years of age, Gluck and Bluck (2007) found only the positive events stood out. Sad memories tend to be recalled evenly across the lifespan (Berntsen & Rubin, 2002).

What causes the reminiscence bump? One early explanation has been discarded. It was thought that, perhaps, this time period in peoples' lives involved a lot of novel, first-time events (entering the job market, college, marriage, and kids, for example). However, Fitzgerald (1988) found that only 20 percent of the memories from the bump were first-time events.

There are three general theories about this unusual period (Fitzgerald & Broadbridge, 2012). The first is that this period of time is called the self-narrative hypothesis (Fitzgerald, 1988, 1992). The person develops a sense of his or her identity in a narrative or story form and has compiled the memories to support it. This could explain why only positive events tend to be reflected in the bump, since it would be maintaining self-esteem (Baddeley, 2012). Holmes and Conway (1999) found the memories between ages ten and twenty tend to be about the cultural events of the day (spirit of the times), whereas between twenty and thirty, the memories were more about personal relationships.

Another possibility, according to the life-script hypothesis, is that the bump is due to forming a script about our lives, instead of separate narratives (Conway & Pleydell-Pearce, 2000). This idea is tied to Erikson's famous theory of psychosocial development, and proposes that we make some memories "central" about ourselves over those that are self-defining.

The final proposal is that the reminiscence bump is the result of the three-part Conway's *self-memory system* (Conway et al., 2005; Conway & Pleydell-Pearce, 2000). The bump in memories, according to this view, is that these memories are self-defining in a way that other personally important memories are not. These memories point to long-term personal concepts we hold about ourselves and unresolved conflicts. These memories tend to be linked to other similar concepts and memories, so they are highly interrelated as a group.

Whatever the cause, the reason for the bump is due to enhanced encoding (Rubin & Shulkind, 1997). We encode some personally relevant events during this time period in a way that beats out the usual factors like novelty, vividness, and effort.

Causes of Forgetting

As we have seen, it's not easy to completely describe the process of forgetting. Forgetting can be thought of as adaptive; and in many ways, it mimics how events tend to repeat themselves only relatively quickly and not as often over time. No one rule seems to apply, although forgetting typically happens quickly and then more slowly. The importance and context of the information can slow forgetting down. In early life, several years of memory appear to be forgotten; then meanwhile, in early adulthood, many personally relevant memories (some cultural and some relationship-based, many positive) seem to be more resistant to forgetting.

Given the rate of change in forgetting that tends to occur—very quickly, then more slowly over time—it's not enough to say that forgetting is just a matter of not having the right retrieval cue present. The process of weaning out information that may no longer be needed appears to be more complex than that.

There are four popular explanations for forgetting today (as described in an overview by Nairne & Pandeirada, 2008). These are decay, interference from other information, changes in the presence of a necessary cue, and inhibition, an "active" or desired forgetting (Anderson, 2003; Bjork & Bjork, 1992; Bower & Forgas, 2000; McGeoch, 1932). Let's consider each in turn.

Decay

Of the four common explanations for forgetting, decay may be the most intuitive. Decay is the automatic and spontaneous process of losing information over time. It's not controlled or effortful, and it is expected that there is a neurological reason for it. Essentially, the memory deteriorates.

Deciding when decay has been the reason for a lost memory is not always easy. Learning new information can interfere with retrieving similar information, like having different four-digit PINs for a debit card, a phone extension, and pass code on your phone. Having trouble remembering something because learned material is too similar is a matter of "blocking," which we will look at in the next section on interference. Also, rehearsal should fight decay, so to determine that a memory is lost due to decay, the individual should not have spent time thinking about the memory. These other factors make pinpointing decay as a culprit difficult to do. For research purposes, the optimal situation would be to create an isolated memory that isn't accessible or connected to other learned information so the process of decay by itself could be monitored.

Researchers attempt to detect decay by giving participants divided-attention tasks, such as trying to remember words while listening for a tone in the background (Reitman, 1974). Listening for the tone was meant to discourage rehearsal, while a tone should be different enough from words that interference shouldn't be a problem. So, the loss of the words should be primarily a matter of decay. With delayed recall, participants could not remember as much, indicating that decay happens over time.

It's important to note that decay in laboratory settings is usually measured over short periods of time. Forgetting over longer periods of time is not commonly thought to be due to decay. First, long-term memories can stay available and improve over time (McGeoch, 1932), which makes discussion of decay over the long term problematic. Furthermore, people often relearn information they had "forgotten" earlier at a rate that was much faster than they had learned originally—indicating that the information was not truly forgotten (de Jonge & Tabbers, 2013).

Perhaps forgetting over the long term is not due to time delays at all (McGeoch, 1932). The activities that go on during the delay can be what truly affects forgetting, not time itself. If two groups of participants study a word list and one group is allowed to rest while the other group has to memorize a second list of words, then forgetting is more likely to happen with the second group. This is particularly true if both word lists are similar to each other. The intervening events over time are more important than just elapsed time.

Delay may only apply definitively to short-term memory systems, such as Baddeley and Hitch's (1974) working memory model (see Chapter 7). When memory traces are being processed and temporarily stored in different subsystems, not rehearsing will cause traces to decay (Page & Norris, 1998). Even within short time intervals, the intervening activities can have an effect on the rate of forgetting. Memory traces may not fully exist apart from the conditions of learning (Tulving, 1983).

Overall, decay over time may be a cause of forgetting, but how to pinpoint it precisely is difficult, particularly when other competing events may be just as challenging for retaining or interfering with information. The finding that people can recall new information with repeated attempts without study means that at the second attempt to recall, the environment is better for cuing the material. Hence, the process of decay can't be fully divorced from the context of retrieval. Some of what is lost during learning as part of "decay" may be useful if the information is not going to be used for retrieval cueing later. This makes for difficulty in theorizing about decay.

Interference

Interference is the claim that we forget because other events interfere either with the storage or the retrieval of memories. Interference does not assume that a memory trace would fade in time—the assumption is that forgetting happens because other mental events disrupt the normal storing and retrieving processes. In a classic study of interference, Baddeley and Hitch (1977) asked rugby football players to recall the names of teams that they had played earlier in the season. Players would miss some games for one reason or another, so Baddeley and Hitch could monitor the weeks elapsed from one game to the next as well as the number of intervening games somewhat separately. With this approach, time did not appear to be nearly as important as the number of intervening games (see Fig. 11.5).

Interference predicts that forgetting is the result of a similar event blocking storage and retrieval; so without an intervening event, forgetting should stop. There have been attempts to try this, by restricting the abilities of a person or animal after learning. Minami and Dallenbach (1946) taught cockroaches in a maze to avoid turning into a dead end by providing them with an electric shock whenever they did so. They retested them after learning for a variety of times—anywhere from ten minutes to twenty-four hours. The set of cockroaches that were kept immobilized forgot about avoiding the dead end only 25 percent of the time, but other cockroaches who had been allowed to continue moving forgot 70 percent of the time.

FIGURE 11.5   Recent events tend to interfere with our ability to remember older, similar events (Baddeley & Hitch, 1977).

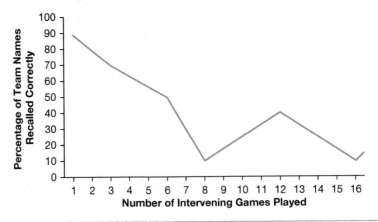

Source: Adapted from Baddeley, A. D. (2007).

Note: Hypothetical values; are approximates.

Trying to reduce interference with human participants has been tried in a variety of ways. One simple way is to encourage people to study immediately before going to sleep at night, which does show better retention a day later than studying in the morning (Jenkins & Dallenbach, 1924), but this could be due to the physiological systems that consolidate memories at night.

Usually when we talk about interference, we are defaulting to new learning that seems to replace or hide old memories. Retroactive interference is the term used to describe when old information cannot be retrieved due to learning new information. So, having made good friends with the new hire at Payroll, in time it might become harder to remember the person who formerly worked in that position with whom we were only somewhat acquainted with. Being in a calculus class now can make older algebraic information harder to recall. Perhaps taking a French class will make remembering Spanish from last term harder to do. It's not clear that the new information weakens the old information, or if the new information simply supersedes it in some way, perhaps through a stronger association.

Retroactive interference is not the only kind of interference, though. Another sign of interference is when old information—information we might have thought forgotten—suddenly presents itself again. Proactive inhibition is when we remember old information more strongly than the more recent learning, such as recalling the postal code of our old home rather than the current one, or the name of someone who used to work in Payroll but now is working in Marketing. This is a particular problem when we have memorized the incorrect information (the wrong locker combination, for example), and then find ourselves remembering the wrong number more readily than the correct one!

The idea that older information can interfere with newer information was introduced by Underwood (1957). Participants in his research spent time memorizing lists of nonsense syllables to study learning and memory; and presumably, some of them may have spent many hours in laboratory studies like his own. While most students forgot many of the nonsense syllables they had learned within twenty-four hours, Underwood thought perhaps what was happening was that prior learning was interfering with new learning. He diagrammed the amount of forgetting that occurred in a 24-hour period as a result of prior experience. As you can see in Figure 11.6, the more lists of

FIGURE 11.6 The number of word lists studied prior dampens recall performance (Underwood, 1957).

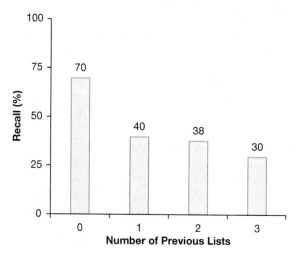

Source: Adapted from Underwood, B. J. (1957).

nonsense syllables a person is asked to learn, the more likely the most recent list is going to be forgotten. While the social context to the individual may indicate that an old list is no longer useful information, the memory processes in the brain do not necessarily stop processing the information and form a "blank slate" for the next list of words.

A clear point to be learned from the existence of proactive and retroactive interference is that our memories are not completely separated from each other. Similar memories may interact particularly strongly. Expecting people to be able to recall related or similar events as separate, whether in a courtroom or on a survey, is not necessarily a realistic expectation.

Trace Degradation

Is it possible to be more specific about how two memories can interfere with each other? There are two general ways that interference is believed to work. First, in the case of retroactive inhibition, new memories degrade the existing memory, a hypothesis called trace degradation. The older memory might be thought of as erased or overwritten. This would explain why sleeping would keep learned material from being erased by other activities (e.g., Jenkins & Dallenbach, 1924).

Trace degradation makes a prediction that is nearly the opposite of the idea of decay: the expectation is that a memory trace will become more resistant to interference because of trace consolidation (see Chapter 8). As time passes, the memory traces become "consolidated" or strengthened, and become less likely to be lost. This would explain why head trauma usually disrupts very recent memories rather than ones formed in the past. However, the evidence for this proposal has been mixed. Retroactive interference can occur with events that happened long after the original learning, well past the time period of consolidation. The amount of forgetting due to interference, whether the intervening event was days ago or immediate, is about the same (Wickelgren, 1977). On its face, this doesn't support the idea that disruption to consolidation might be the primary cause for interference. But then, consolidation may take longer than is generally acknowledged (Dudai, 2004). It could also be that the trace doesn't degrade so much as the retrieval cues that access a memory are degraded—a different cause that would produce a similar effect.

Cue Impairment

Interference has been hypothesized to be the result of impairment to the memory trace. A second possibility is that the memory is held relatively constant but the effectiveness of the retrieval cue is altered. The assumption is that we query what we know using a retrieval cue, similar to entering a keyword into a search engine website. The belief that we use cues to elicit memories is the basis of the paired-associate tests, studying cue words to retrieve target words. If a cue word used to retrieve a target word, but no longer does, we might say the target word has been forgotten.

In the previous sections, we looked at ways the target memory might have been degraded. However, it could be that the target memory hasn't been altered at all—the association between the cue word and the target word was altered. It could be that the link between the cue and the word has been forgotten and become extinct (e.g., McGeoch & Irion, 1952; Melton & Irwin, 1940). The retrieval cue no longer links to the same target memory, but could now be associated with other memories. The association could have been lost through extinction, unlearned through Pavlovian conditioning (see Chapter 3). In contemporary terms, this might be similar to the experience you have when trying out different keywords as search terms when looking for articles or other resources for a class assignment. There is a certain amount of "trying out" different terms, like retrieval cues, to see what kind of material it connects with.

Another option for cue impairment is cue overload (sometimes called "response competition," "cue distinctiveness," or the "fan effect"). Over time, the retrieval cue becomes associated with different target memories. As this happens, its strength to any one target will weaken. In an experiment, a cue word on the first list (e.g., "bird") might be associated with "nest;" but on the second list, "bird" becomes associated with "dinner"; and then on the third list, with "finger." As this happens, the likelihood of "bird" retrieving "nest" will decrease. You can see how this might happen—the more you learn about something, the more any one retrieval cue might become associated with many other concepts. What might have been a relatively easy cue when we were younger, say "birthday party," becomes more convoluted as we get older and we have attended many birthday parties, had a few ourselves, and hosted some for our own children, possibly.

Studies have found that as there are more items within a category to memorize, the name of the category (e.g., "vehicles," "furniture") becomes less effective as a retrieval cue (Roediger, 1973; Tulving & Pearlstone, 1966). As any list becomes longer, recalling any one item from that list becomes more difficult. Many seniors find that keeping track of their children's, grandchildren's, and great-grandchildren's birthdays becomes nearly impossible solely by memory, without a personal calendar of some kind. A "cue overloading" explanation of this could be the category ("family birthdays") becomes overloaded as a cue (Watkins & Watkins, 1975). Additionally, as there are more possible responses to any one cue, it becomes harder to mentally verify that a target is correct (Anderson & Reder, 1999).

A cue overload explanation of retroactive interference is that a retrieval cue becomes associated to new learning; the old information remains, but the cue has been updated and fanned out to new information. For proactive interference, the association between the cue and the original material is strong enough that it presents itself more readily than the association to newly learned material.

Cue Availability

If retrieving a memory is cue-driven, then if the cue isn't available, the memory becomes unavailable. The memory is dependent on the cue, and forgetting involves not having the cue present (Tulving, 1974). The target memory is not impaired and the association still exists, but we can't access the right retrieval cue.

Forgetting due to lacking the right retrieval cue explains why some memories that have been forgotten can be recalled later. Instead of being obscured by other information, the right cue isn't accessible (Tulving & Pearlstone, 1966). The context of a second attempt might provide the right retrieval cue that allows for recall. The retrieval cue might be external, such as the right place as the encoding specificity principle would expect, or internal, such as a mood or a particularly meaningful hint.

So, remembering is a matter of retrieval cues being present at the moment of recall, and presumably some retrieval cues are better than others. Research into which retrieval cues were best is what produced the encoding specificity principle (Tulving & Thomson, 1973; see Chapter 8), which proposes that retrieval cues are effective only if the information that connects them to the target information is stored at the time of encoding. This is why the context at the time of encoding can have an influence on our ability to remember. Part of conscious, focused study should include time spent asking questions like, "How will I remember this later? What about this is most important for when I need it?" Tulving and Thomson found that the existing semantic knowledge between a pair of words did not matter as much as the interpretation that a learner places on a cue and target word at the time of study, and whether the learner will remember that interpretation at the time of retrieval.

What is less clear about retrieval cues is whether it's a matter of finding the right one so much as a retrieval cue that is relatively better than others provided by the context. In any particular moment, numerous cues are present for recalling information, and some might be particularly strong but are associated with a variety of memories. Most likely there isn't a perfect index of "matching strength" between retrieval cues and memories, so much as the value of a cue among other (distracting) cues to help indicate what we are searching for (Nairne, 2002).

For focused learning and study time, probably an emphasis on creating multiple cues for retrieval will help ease the problem of cue availability as well. Having more cues to be dependent on should make for a higher likelihood of retrieving what we need at the time we need it.

Retrieval-Induced Inhibition

Of the three proposed processes discussed so far, all of them work fairly automatically or passively. This final possible form of forgetting is more active: retrieval-induced inhibition is the action of making the memory trace inaccessible through the use of suppression, temporarily. Suppressing a memory from becoming conscious does not alter or damage the memory, but the access to the memory is blocked. This is not the same as cue overload, where several cues present themselves as options and one cue and target memory will be picked and the others are overlooked.

One example of inhibition on retrieval comes from a research technique that involves asking people to memorize lists of categories and sample members, such as "vehicle-car" and "vehicle-truck" (e.g., Anderson et al., 1994). Practice will involve rehearsing about a quarter of all of the possible associations (half of the items from half of the categories). Then participants are asked to recall all of the sample members from each category.

The sample members that were practiced are recalled better than unpracticed ones, but unpracticed members from categories that were practiced are recalled less than unpracticed members from categories that were not practiced. In other words, practicing only some of the members of a category put the other members at a relative disadvantage compared to categories (and members) that were not practiced at all. This research technique, known as the retrieval practice paradigm, seems to create suppression of the ignored members of the practiced categories.

As Nairne and Pandeirada (2008) note, it could be to our benefit that we actively suppress information. There are an ever-present, large number of retrieval cues, so inhibition is one way of trying to minimize the irrelevant distractions. Deciding to drive to the grocery store should produce many possible roads and routes to take, but we can focus on the route that is most relevant. Entering a PIN to use a debit card could produce all kinds of number combinations we could use, but only one is desired (Levy & Anderson, 2002). The sheer number of names we can recall becomes unhelpful when we are approached by a person that we know and we need to recall his or her name.

Whether Memories Can Be Inhibited Unconsciously

As you may be aware, Sigmund Freud proposed that some memories can be inhibited through a process he called repression (Freud, 1915), and it is sometimes referred to as "motivated forgetting" today. Repression is one of Freud's "defense mechanisms," coping strategies that the ego uses to handle the anxiety, shame, and guilt that stem from unconscious conflicts. The goal of the defense mechanisms is to temporarily delay the negative feelings that result from some past or present situation. Freud did not consider them healthy: the individual does not directly deal with the issue at hand. In modern terms, we would think of these as maladaptive coping strategies. For Freud, these get enacted with little or no conscious awareness. Freud theorized that repression was a mechanism for keeping anxiety-producing memories, usually due to a traumatic event, from entering conscious awareness (Boag, 2006).

What makes Freud's proposal for repressed memories unique is that it is the opposite of what is typically expected. Usually, emotional personal events create powerful memories that we remember well, vividly. While we prefer autobiographical memories that are positive in nature when we are engaged in free recall, we can readily recount negative events from our lives when pressed: time spent serving in combat, being mugged or assaulted, experiencing a car accident, being fired, days spent hungry or homeless, or being incarcerated for a time. Freud's proposal is that some situations are severe enough that we mentally hide the event from ourselves, a remarkably fascinating idea, although not what is normally expected or experienced.

Of course, Freud made his theories well before psychology established many of its modern approaches to data collection and analysis. From a modern scientific perspective, where does his theory of repressed memories stand? One challenge to verifying Freud's defense mechanisms in general is that we cannot ethically test forgetting of traumatic memories in controlled experimental conditions. In terms of a controlled experiment, this would mean exposing people to environments that we expect would produce traumatic responses. (To fully follow Freud's thinking, these events should focus on early childhood experiences, so we would need to conduct them with young children who were five years old or younger.) Obviously this is a huge ethical issue.

Experiments are the gold standard in psychology, but they cannot be used in this case to verify Freud's idea of repression. What other forms of evidence are there? The evidence for repression of traumatic memories is largely based on reports of amnesia that was trauma-induced and on recovery of memories in therapy. Surveys have been conducted on individuals who were sexually abused and reported forgetting the abuse for a period of time (e.g., Williams, 1994; Schooler et al., 1997). As you might guess, this form of evidence has not completely persuaded researchers (e.g., Kihlstrom, 2004, 2005, 2006a, 2006b). To be clear: it's not that repression does not necessarily exist or never happens. It's simply not well established empirically.

What are the issues with the evidence for repressed memories? As Nairne and Pandeirada (2008) describe, there are three main issues with the evidence for repression. First, when a client "recovers" a memory during therapy, it has not always been possible to verify that the original traumatic event occurred. This is a subtle issue that may not be immediately clear: there may be very good reasons for a therapist not to challenge the statements of a client during therapy. Investigating a client's claims independently is not necessarily ethical (Shobe & Kihlstrom, 2002). However, that doesn't necessarily make the statements made during therapy good for scientific evidence. The standard for scientific research is higher than what is merely anecdotal, from an outsider's perspective.

A second issue is that clients have been known to produce memories that could be established later as false. The client may produce a memory in order to gain sympathy, or might unintentionally have come to believe that an event happened that did not. This situation has been referred to as "therapy-induced" false memories. In recent years, therapeutic concerns have been primarily focused on recovered memories of sexual abuse; but in the less-distant past, some therapeutic focus was on recovered memories of alien abductions (Sagan, 2011), prenatal experiences, and recovered memories from past lives. In other words, there is a history of unverifiable and unscientific pronouncements about recovered memories. Over time, this creates a general air of skepticism around the topic.

The third issue is a theoretical one. There are many ways to forget, as we have seen. Should forgetting of a traumatic event occur, a memory researcher would want to establish that repression was the cause of the forgetting, rather than other forms of forgetting. Even memories of traumatic events should be prone to decay, interference, and cue unavailability. While this does mean that the current attitude of the field is skeptical, it doesn't mean that repression may not ever occur—it simply means we have not been able to test and verify it empirically, particularly in contrast to other forms of forgetting.

Other Retrieval Errors

As we have seen so far, there are a number of ways that information can become inaccessible to us, whether through decay, interference, a lack of helpful cues, or inhibition. What other kinds of memory errors are there?

Output Monitoring Failures

If we stretch the definition of an "error" a little, one kind of error is inattention. If we focus only on effortful, controlled learning, it is clear that we cannot recall some information simply from a lack of paying enough attention to some event or detail at the time. This is not strictly a problem with encoding, storage, or retrieval, but a by-product of naturally focusing on what appears to be the most important, pertinent information at any one time. Perhaps in that moment, we were preoccupied, fatigued, or believed the important substance of the moment was elsewhere.

The consequences of inattention assert themselves particularly strongly on errors of prospective memory. Prospective memory, if you recall, is remembering to take some action in the future. Errors of prospective memory, often called failures of output monitoring, result from not paying enough attention to what we are doing it while we are doing it. Eyeglasses get misplaced, car keys are left in odd places, and important papers we meant to bring with us get left behind. In some cases, we can't remember whether we truly did something or not.

A number of kinds of output monitoring failures have been proposed. Koriat, Ben-Zur, and Sheffer (1988) describe two kinds of output monitoring errors: omissions, where we think we performed some action but did not; and repetitions, when we forget that we did some action, so we repeat it. Norman (1981) credits absentmindedness as the reason behind making the wrong action or forgetting to do something at all.

In a systematic study of monitoring failures, Reason (1979) asked thirty-five participants to keep diary records of their "slips of action" for two weeks and compiled about 400 mistakes. Categorizing them, he found about 40 percent of the slips of action were repetition errors, repeating something that had already been done. Repetition errors were the most commonly reported type of error. An example of this would be starting up the dish washing machine, and later, starting it up again without unloading it. Goal switches, moving from one goal to another during an activity without realizing it, made up 20 percent of the slips. It's not terribly uncommon for me to begin driving my kids to my place of work in the morning, instead of taking them to school first. They usually allow the drive to continue just long enough for it to be a source of embarrassment for me, which they enjoy. Omissions and reversals, forgetting a key step in a chain of actions, were described in about 18 percent of the slips. I receive a fair number of emails where the sender forgot to attach a file! Confusions and blends, or mixing up the objects needed for an action from another action at the same time, was reported in 16 percent of the slips. An example of this would be grabbing a tape dispenser to staple a page and then realizing something was seriously wrong.

Generally, output monitoring errors are the result of automatic, well-rehearsed actions that people take on while multitasking. Often anxiety or fatigue plays a role as well.

Source Monitoring Failures

Another kind of error is when we retrieve a particular memory, but it is in some way incorrect—perhaps we thought it happened to us but it didn't, or we can no longer recall where we read a specific news story. The source of the memory has been lost or misconstrued. It is possible to recall a memory generally correctly while forgetting the origin of the memory. These are errors of misattribution or, as they are known, failures of source monitoring.

Source monitoring is the metacognitive act of judging the source of a memory, such as whether we read a particular bit of information, or where we read it. Was the memory something that happened to us personally, or was it something a friend told us about, or something we saw in a movie?

A particularly famous example of this was a story former U.S. President Ronald Reagan told while campaigning, about a WWII gunner who could not eject from a falling plane. The commander, who could have parachuted, refused, saying, "Never mind, son, we'll ride it down together." He allegedly was posthumously awarded the Congressional Medal of Honor. Someone wondered how it would have been clear what the commander would have said (since he and the other witness would have died) and investigated the story, only to find it was the plot of a 1944 movie, *Wing and a Prayer*. Reagan's retelling of the story is generally seen as an error of source monitoring, rather than the intentional presentation of a lie for votes. His past as a movie actor makes an unintended mix-up more plausible.

How do we determine the origin of a memory in source monitoring? Details of the circumstance of the event can be used in deciding (Lindsay, 2008). These details include the physical environment at the event, when the event occurred, what sensations were evoked at the time, and other people who were present.

The source of a memory is not necessarily stored with the memory itself. A memory is often retrieved for its own sake, but when and where it occurred may not be retrieved as well. In some cases, the source of a memory is embedded into the memory itself, such as catching a fly ball in the stands at the baseball stadium; but frequently the source information is secondary to the focus of a memory. Storing the information, "The exam has been pushed back to next week" doesn't necessarily present itself with information on the time of day, the day of the week, the setting, or the speaker. It is possible that the source information is grasped nearly automatically, and as such, little attention is paid to what at the time seemed like a secondary detail. For those of us who are fluent readers, the act of reading means very little cognitive processing goes into storing details of the reading process itself. Usually the event surrounding learning something is of less importance than the message itself; however, it can become more important later, when friends debate who exactly made a claim about when they were supposed to meet up, or when someone is testifying in court over what was overheard during an office meeting.

Information about specific time periods tends to be lost as well, and what is retained is relatively coarse (Dodson & Hege, 2005). While I might be able to recall a particular day something happened, and whether it was morning or evening, I may struggle to pinpoint an exact hourly time. This phenomenon is often violated in police crime dramas on television. For example, a witness is unexpectedly interviewed on the job by detectives about something that happened a week ago. They ask the witness to provide specific time and place information: "When did you see the man leave the restaurant?" The witness can spontaneously remember the date and time, down to the minute.

Recalling the source event information of a memory becomes more difficult when different sources are highly similar (Ferguson, Hashtroudi, & Johnson, 1992; Lindsay & Johnson, 1991). This includes family members with similar voices, or news websites with a similar appearance to them. Possibly the physical location might be very similar between two memories, such as encountering someone at one of several possible chain restaurants, gymnasiums, or convention halls. Every so often, students share with me something they learned about operant conditioning that they attribute to me; but I don't find it familiar, and might even sound incorrect! When I ask if they might have heard it from someone else, they find they can't recall where they heard it because they are taking several psychology classes at the same time, and operant conditioning theory was mentioned in more than one of them.

One explanation for how we judge the sources of our memories is that we monitor the details of the memories we retrieve and see if the details match our expectations about which source we think it came from (Johnson & Raye, 1981). We consider the qualities of the memory and compare those qualities to what we expect we would remember if we had encountered the event the way we think we did (e.g., overheard it, read it online, saw it on a billboard; Dodson & Schacter, 2002). This might include the emotions, the situation, and even other thoughts at the time.

As familiarity with a source increases, our ability to use source information about the source seems to decrease. To demonstrate, researchers showed participants a list of names of people who were not famous (Jacoby, Woloshyn, & Kelley, 1989). Participants were then asked to identify truly famous people from a list of names either immediately after or a day later. This list included non-famous names, some of which had been on the earlier non-famous list (such as "Sebastian Weisdorf"). The group of participants who had reviewed the non-famous list of names a day earlier tended to recognize the names from the non-famous list as being famous!

High emotional arousal also tends to blur the memory of the source (Johnson, Nolde, & De Leonardis, 1996). Mitchell, Mather, Johnson, Raye, and Greene (2006), for example, found emotional pictures were easier to recognize compared to neutral ones from an earlier exposure. However, participants did a better job of matching the neutral photos to a particular spatial location, where they had viewed them, than the emotional ones.

It appears then that source memory information is not necessarily stored in a packaged or whole memory in the brain, since recall tends to favor the memory itself over the how, when, and where information of the event. So retrieving the source information along with a memory is likely to require retrieving both kinds of information and relating them together. The medial temporal lobes appear to be responsible for binding or connecting these parts of memories together (Kroll, Knight, Metcalfe, Wolf, & Tulving, 1996). Since sensations and movements can be a part of source monitoring judgments too, the sensory and motor cortices will also be involved (Gonsalves et al., 2004). Vividly imagined scenes have a tendency to be remembered as real, later.

Forms of Source Monitoring Failures

Source memory failures have been known to take on a variety of forms. The knew-it-all-along (KIA) effect, also called hindsight bias, is the term for when people report they had information before they truly did (Lindsay, 2008). The research technique for studying this effect is to ask people for answers to a set of questions, then to provide them with answers to some of those questions, and then to ask them to give their original answers to the same questions. What researchers find is people will gravitate toward giving the correct answers as if they were their own. Are they just reporting themselves as more correct than they truly were, or are the participants having false recollections of their answers? Arnold and Lindsay (2002, 2005) found that participants appear to question themselves and their understanding when presented with the right information, and in the process muddy their recall for their original answers.

Another failure of source monitoring is cryptomnesia. Cryptomnesia is the act of unintentionally presenting an idea as one's own when it was not. It's a form of plagiarism but without any intent to defraud others, since the individual believes the idea originated with him or her. It is a source monitoring problem or a reality monitoring problem, more specifically, since the individual incorrectly believes he or she internally generated the idea.

George Harrison, as a former member of The Beatles, published a single "My Sweet Lord" that resulted in a lawsuit because it was similar to "He's So Fine" by The Chiffons. The judge believed it was unintentional and "subconscious" (*Bright Tunes Music Corp v. Harrison's Music Ltd,* 1976; Self, 1993), and this started a concern in the music industry over unintentional plagiarism. Other examples abound: Freud's idea that everyone begins life as a bisexual was an idea from a colleague who had suggested it two years earlier. Freud denied it, before remembering it later (Macrae, Bodenhausen, & Calvini, 1999; Perfect & Stark, 2008; Taylor, 1965).

Bower and Murphy (1989) attempted to pin down the rate of unconscious plagiarism, and found plagiarized errors occurred for all forms of items. Determining a specific rate at which people reproduce an item they believe is original is difficult because some items are more likely to occur by chance. Some items simply come to mind readily and are easier to generate. In group situations, a person may generate an answer to a question, but another person gives the answer first. So the individual is left with the memory of recalling it, but wasn't actually credited with producing it.

Marsh and Bower (1993) gave participants sixteen letters to produce as many words as possible against a computer. Later, all participants were asked to write down those words they had produced, but not the computer. About 10 percent of the words the participants listed were computer-generated.

Cryptomnesia for someone else's idea is not the only form this kind of retrieval error takes. Sometimes people even attribute new ideas to themselves from earlier parts of their lives, plagiarizing themselves, or attributing their own ideas to someone else! (Bink, Marsh, Hicks, & Howard, 1999; Hoffman, 1997). B. F. Skinner himself found he rediscovered his own ideas in old age (Skinner, 1983).

One particularly intriguing form of source monitoring is reality monitoring, the judgment of whether a memory was something we truly experienced or if it was something we imagined ourselves, such as a dream. The "source" in reality monitoring judgments is whether the source is external or internal. Since we do not explicitly seem to add source information to memories, people appear to judge a memory itself by characteristics that make a memory seem more likely to have been "real" or "imagined" (Johnson, Hashtroudi, & Lindsay, 1993).

To find out what cues people use to decide whether the memory of an event was actually experienced, Johnson, Bush, and Mitchell (1998) found people take a two-stage approach. First, they question whether the memory has features of a typical real event. This includes perceptual, contextual, semantic, cognitive, and emotional cues (Sluzenski, Newcombe, & Ottinger, 2004). If a memory has many contextual details, people are more likely to judge the memory as being of a real event. Second, people expect different kinds of cognitive processing to have gone on during internal events.

While reality monitoring may appear to be a rather innocuous issue, errors in reality monitoring present themselves in more serious situations: unconscious acts of plagiarism and hallucinations in schizophrenia, and imaginary memories in other memory disorders.

While cryptomnesia could either be simply embarrassing or cause a lawsuit, the hallucinations that people diagnosed with schizophrenia experience are a reality monitoring problem that can be very distressful. The experience of auditory hallucinations (speech) is the most common feature of schizophrenia, followed by tactile hallucinations. The individual with schizophrenia may have trouble separating the internally generated or imagined speech from speech that is externally produced (Bentall, Baker, & Havers, 1991).

Schizophrenia can also include a hallucination known as "thought insertion": the individuals, unable to control their own thoughts, will come to believe that other people are inserting disagreeable thoughts into their own minds, forcing them to think about disturbing ideas or images. Here, again, is the inability to understand the true source of the thoughts.

One researcher believes there may be a biological component to any process that involves comparing internal versus external events, like reality monitoring (Blakemore, 2003; Jones & Fernyhough, 2007). To pursue a goal, we have to make actions that will try to turn some outcome into a reality. So, we spend a certain amount of time comparing the outcomes of our actions with our expectations, similar to the test-operate-test-exit or TOTE model (see Chapter 1). Ordinarily, believes Blakemore, this "comparator" function operates automatically, quickly allowing us to compare our situation with what we wanted to achieve. In schizophrenia, this comparator function is disrupted, so internal events seem external. The lack of a match between what people were intending to do and the result gives individuals the impression that they are not in control of their own actions, such as hearing a voice unexpectedly. One unexpected bit of evidence for such a biological function is that most individuals can't tickle themselves (since they know they are the ones doing the tickling). However, people diagnosed with schizophrenia can, possibly because they can experience the sensation as external to themselves (Blakemore, Wolpert, & Frith, 2000).

A confabulation is a fully imagined memory that seems real, and is usually made to cover up the loss of a memory. Most people, whether amnesiac or not, do not do this; but people with Korsakoff's amnesia do (Alba & Hasher, 1983). Korsakoff's amnesia is a disease that includes memory loss after long-term overuse of alcohol, which deteriorates parts of the brain. Patients with Korsakoff's will combine bits of information that they know are likely to have occurred at some event in order to create a realistic-sounding memory to share with others. Some researchers think confabulation is a disruption of reality monitoring that is caused by brain damage to the frontal lobes.

Suggestibility and Bias

Besides the act of forgetting, we have seen errors of inattention and failures to properly track the source of a memory, or to identify if in the fact the memory was real. Another potential problem our memory system has is with suggestibility and bias. As we saw in the semantic memory chapter, we use script and schema information to form patterns of expectations as our prior knowledge. This information generally helps memory, because we do not have to retain every bit of information from what we experience repeatedly. Of course, the problem is that when we do not precisely remember something, we tend to infer what went on. This biases us toward what typically happens, and it works fine unless something unusual or unexpected happened.

The social situation can present us with pressure to conform our memories as well. Broadly speaking, embellishment denotes the changes and additions we make to a memory as part of retrieval, and it may be quite common. Sir Fredrick Bartlett (1932) found that when people were shown a line drawing (of a Native American tribal shield, or an owl) and asked to redraw what they remembered each day for about a month, the line drawing they produced would change over time. Generally the embellishments came from simplifying the original line drawing or adapting the object in the line drawing into something more common. The owl might turn into a cat without the participant's awareness, or the shield would gradually turn into a face. Once the memory for the object shifted into something more common or easier for the rememberer, it tended to stick, despite some changes. Bergman and Roediger (1999) replicated Bartlett's classic work and were able to show that the modification occurs as part of the replication process.

The social situation can create pressure to impress or to entertain, so we may embellish a memory to please our audience. The act of enhancing a story changes the later retrieval as well. Dudukovic, Marsh, and Tversky (2004) asked people to retell a story in accurate or entertaining ways. They found retrieval was affected by embellishment on a later test, if the test was a recall test (recognition stayed the same).

False Memories

While embellishment may seem relatively minor, the constructive nature of our memory retrieval system, along with problems of reality monitoring, can lead to having entirely false memories, memories that are simply not true but feel as if they are.

One source of evidence for false memories is the Deese-Roediger-McDermott (DRM) procedure. Underwood (1965) and Deese (1959) had found that if a list of words to be memorized all had a theme (e.g., "sand," "water," "waves"), then participants would often mistakenly recall an associated word (e.g., "beach"). The words on the list seemed to activate the missing word strongly enough that it would be recalled, too. The missing word is like a lure that can trick participants into believing it was on the list. Roediger and McDermott (1995) found that participants were confident that the lures were originally on the list, even when they told the participants not to guess. The recall of the lure is viewed as a kind of false memory. Later research found that the "recall" of the lure happened about 45 percent of the time, when real items on the list were recalled from 52 percent to 60 percent of the time, making the false memory rate not significantly different from the target recall rate (Payne, Elie, Blackwell, & Neuschatz, 1996). After a delay, participants were more likely to forget the target items than the lures. Solving some math problems reduced recall for the target items more than recall for the lures. Strangely, the false-item recall is fairly resistant to change relative to the recall of true items.

Roediger, Balota, and Watson (2001) proposed that the recall of false items could be due to spreading activation. That is, studying interrelated words could prime related words. Spreading activation could act in concert across links (Roediger et al., 2001). As interrelated concepts are activated, the overall strength of the activation to a lure should increase. Some evidence for this idea was found in Robinson and Roediger (1997). Lists of associated words of varying length (three, six, nine, twelve, or fifteen) were given to participants to memorize. The researchers found that participants remembered fewer words for the longer lists, but the likelihood of the lure being "recalled" increased with the length of the lists.

Unfortunately, it's not yet possible to reliably determine whether a memory is veridical (that is, matches reality) or false (Bernstein & Loftus, 2009). One study used scripts to generate false memories; and if so, whether there might be a way to distinguish between the veridical and false memories (Lampinen, Faries, Neuschatz, & Toglia, 2000). Participants read stories based on familiar scripts, and afterward they were tested for their knowledge of the stories. Some of the facts they were asked about were not present in the original stories. As the participants evaluated their memory for the stories, they were asked to make remember/know judgments about their answers. That is, they were asked if they had semantic memories for their responses, or episodic memories for them. The assumption was that a false memory for some detail would receive a "know" judgment if it was inferred from script knowledge, and perhaps a "remember" judgment if it was more of an episodic false memory. There were more remember judgments for the original items from the readings and fewer remember judgments for items falsely remembered. However, this was not a perfect association; about 50 percent of the incorrect items were judged as "remembered." The researchers also found no difference in the amount of perceptual, emotional, verbal, or cognitive details. The researchers concluded that prior knowledge can produce false memories that can't be distinguished from accurate content.

CHAPTER SUMMARY

Forgetting seems like a problem, something we have to struggle to overcome. We need the process, though. It's no use to remember every book we have ever read when entering the library, or to remember every place we ever parked in a parking garage, or every dinner we ever had at home at the kitchen table. If we cannot forget, we would be bombarded with old information that would overwhelm any ability we had to concentrate. (Luria, 1968, describes a journalist to whom this happened.) Forgetting is a matter of cleaning up the mind—taking out the mental trash.

We can forget in many ways—we may lose information through a lack of use (decay), which seems most likely to happen with short-term memories. We can lose ability to access information because of difficulty accessing just one memory over others (interference). Or perhaps the best retrieval cue isn't present when we need it, internally or externally. Finally, remembering just some information can make other related information weaker. These factors make the study of forgetting difficult, since what seems forgotten may be recovered under a different situation.

Forgetting is not random, but it has a fairly regular rate—typically we lose quite a bit quickly, and what is left is retained for a long time. There are some exceptions or alterations to this rule, however. Motor skills resist forgetting for a long time. Memories that we find more meaningful seem to hold better as well. All of us have trouble remembering the first years of life as we get older, and it's not completely clear why. Language development appears to play a key role. Another deviation from the normal forgetting curve is the reminiscence bump: a period of more accessible memories between the ages of from ten to thirty years of life.

To review, we have seen a variety of other forms of retrieval errors besides finding a memory inaccessible or producing a wrong answer. Prospective memories can produce their own errors as well, or "slips of action" when we do something that we didn't intend to, or at the wrong time. Adding information to a memory, or embellishment, is another kind of retrieval error. Information on the source of a memory, such as who told us some information, can be lost. In some cases, it becomes unclear whether it was real or imagined. Some people will encounter unintended acts of plagiarism by assuming an experience as their own idea, or may experience internal sensations as external, or generate whole memories to fill in the gaps of what should be available.

REVIEW QUESTIONS

1. Why might the normal rate of forgetting mirror the statistical likelihood of a repeated event over time?

2. Thinking across different chapters of the textbook, what might be some reasons for why motor skills may be more resistant to forgetting?

3. What is your earliest memory? Is it fragmentary, as research suggests it might be? Can you put a date on the memory?

4. Among laypersons, decay is probably the most commonly believed cause of forgetting. Why is the research on decay not very supportive of this idea?

5. If you major in a subject area, you'll take more and more classes within the same domain of knowledge. What learning strategies might counter the very real possibility of experiencing more interference with study?

6. What implications does retrieval-induced inhibition have for your personal study habits?

7. Which retrieval errors are you consciously aware of having made before?

KEY TERMS

FURTHER RESOURCES

1. Dunlosky, J., Rawson, K. A., Marsh, E. J., Nathan, M. J., & Willingham, D. T. (2013). Improving students' learning with effective learning techniques: Promising directions from cognitive and educational psychology. *Psychological Science in the Public Interest, 14*(1), 4–58.

   o https://doi.org/10.1177/1529100612453266

2. The benefits of forgetting (n.d.):

   o http://www.apa.org/pubs/highlights/peeps/issue-26.aspx

3. Juskalian, R. (2009, July 6). Is unconscious plagiarism a real phenomenon? *Newsweek*. Retrieved from http://www.newsweek.com/unconscious-plagiarism-real-phenomenon-81861

4. Compare for yourself:

   a. Audio: George Harrison, "My Sweet Lord":

      o https://www.youtube.com/watch?v=0kNGnIKUdMI

   b. Audio: The Chiffons, "He's So Fine":

      o https://www.youtube.com/watch?v=rinz9Avvq6A

REFERENCES

Adams, J. A. (1971). A closed-loop theory of motor learning. *Journal of Motor Behavior, 3*(2), 111–150.

Alba, J. W., & Hasher, L. (1983). Is memory schematic? *Psychological Bulletin, 93*(2), 203.

Altmann, E. M., & Gray, W. D. (2002). Forgetting to remember: The functional relationship of decay and interference. *Psychological Science, 13*(1), 27–33.

Amazon.com: Elements of Episodic Memory (Oxford Psychology Series) (9780198521259): Endel Tulving: Books. (n.d.). Retrieved April 9, 2017, from https://www.amazon.com/Elements-Episodic-Memory-Oxford-Psychology/dp/0198521251/ref=sr_1_1?ie=UTF8&qid=1491750664&sr=8-1&keywords=Elements+of+episodic+memory.

Anderson, J. R., & Reder, L. M. (1999). The fan effect: New results and new theories. *Journal of Experimental Psychology General, 128*, 186–197.

Anderson, J. R., & Schooler, L. J. (1991). Reflections of the environment in memory. *Psychological Science, 2*(6), 396–408.

Anderson, M. C. (2003). Rethinking interference theory: Executive control and the mechanisms of forgetting. *Journal of Memory and Language, 49*(4), 415–445.

Anderson, M. C., Bjork, R. A., & Bjork, E. L. (1994). Remembering can cause forgetting: retrieval dynamics in long-term memory. *Journal of Experimental Psychology: Learning, Memory, and Cognition, 20*(5), 1063.

Arnold, M., & Lindsay, D. S. (2005). Remembrance of remembrance past. *Memory, 13*(5), 533–549.

Arnold, M. M., & Lindsay, D. S. (2002). Remembering remembering. *Journal of Experimental Psychology: Learning, Memory, and Cognition, 28*(3), 521.

Baddeley, A. (2012). Reflections on autobiographical memory. In D. Rubin (Ed.), *Understanding autobiographical memory: Theories and approaches* (pp. 70–88). Cambridge, England: Cambridge University Press.

Baddeley, A. D., & Hitch, G. (1974). Working memory. *Psychology of Learning and Motivation, 8*, 47–89.

Baddeley, A. D., & Hitch, G. J. (1977). Recency re-examined. *Attention and Performance VI*, 647–667.

Bahrick, H. P., Bahrick, P. O., & Wittlinger, R. P. (1975). Fifty years of memory for names and faces: A cross-sectional approach. *Journal of Experimental Psychology: General, 104*(1), 54.

Bahrick, H. P., Hall, L. K., & Berger, S. A. (1996). Accuracy and distortion in memory for high school grades. *Psychological Science, 7*(5), 265–271.

Bahrick, H. P., Hall, L. K., & Da Costa, L. A. (2008). Fifty years of memory of college grades: Accuracy and distortions. *Emotion, 8*(1), 13.

Bartlett, F. C. (1932). Experiments on remembering: The method of serial reproduction. In F. C. Bartlett (Ed.), *Remembering: A study in experimental and social psychology* (Vol. II Picture Material, pp. 177–185). Cambridge, England: Cambridge University Press.

Bauer, P. J., Burch, M. M., Scholin, S. E., & Güler, O. E. (2007). Using cue words to investigate the distribution of autobiographical memories in childhood. *Psychological Science, 18*(10), 910–916.

Bauer, P. J., Doydum, A. O., Pathman, T., Larkina, M., Güler, O. E., & Burch, M. (2012). It's all about location, location, location: Children's memory for the "where" of personally experienced events. *Journal of Experimental Child Psychology, 113*(4), 510–522.

Bauer, P. J., Larkina, M., & Deocampo, J. (2011). Early memory development. *The Wiley-Blackwell Handbook of Childhood Cognitive Development, 2*, 153–179.

Bentall, R. P., Baker, G. A., & Havers, S. (1991). Reality monitoring and psychotic hallucinations. *British Journal of Clinical Psychology, 30*(3), 213–222.

Bergman, E. T., & Roediger, H. L. (1999). Can Bartlett's repeated reproduction experiments be replicated? *Memory & Cognition, 27*(6), 937–947.

Bernstein, D. M., & Loftus, E. F. (2009). How to tell if a particular memory is true or false. *Perspectives on Psychological Science, 4*(4), 370–374. https://doi.org/10.1111/j.1745-6924.2009.01140.x

Berntsen, D., & Rubin, D. C. (2002). Emotionally charged autobiographical memories across the life span: The recall of happy, sad, traumatic, and involuntary memories. *Psychology and Aging, 17*(4), 636–652.

Berntsen, D., & Rubin, D. C. (n.d.). *Understanding autobiographical memory: Theories and approaches*. Amazon.com: Books. Retrieved March 26, 2017, from https://www.amazon.com/Understanding-Autobiographical-Memory-Theories-Approaches/dp/0521189330/ref=sr_1_1?ie=UTF8&qid=1490556756&sr=8-1&keywords=understanding+autobiographical+memory

Bink, M. L., Marsh, R. L., Hicks, J. L., & Howard, J. D. (1999). The credibility of a source influences the rate of unconscious plagiarism. *Memory, 7*(3), 293–308.

Bjork, E. L., & Bjork, R. A. (1996). Continuing influences of to-be-forgotten information. *Consciousness and Cognition, 5*(1–2), 176–196.

Bjork, R. A., & Whitten, W. B. (1974). Recency-sensitive retrieval processes in long-term free recall. *Cognitive Psychology, 6*(2), 173–189.

Blakemore, S.-J. (2003). Deluding the motor system. *Consciousness and Cognition, 12*(4), 647–655.

Blakemore, S.-J., Wolpert, D., & Frith, C. (2000). Why can't you tickle yourself? *Neuroreport, 11*(11), R11–R16.

Boag, S. (2006). Freudian repression, the common view, and pathological science. *Review of General Psychology, 10*(1), 74.

Bower, G. H., & Forgas, J. P. (2000). Affect, memory, and social cognition. In *Cognition and emotion* (pp. 87–168). New York, NY: Oxford University Press.

Britt, S. H. (1935). Retroactive inhibition: A review of the literature. *Psychological Bulletin, 32*(6), 381.

Brown, A. S., & Murphy, D. R. (1989). Cryptomnesia: Delineating inadvertent plagiarism. *Journal of Experimental Psychology: Learning, Memory, and Cognition, 15*(3), 432.

Bruce, D., Wilcox-O'Hearn, L. A., Robinson, J. A., Phillips-Grant, K., Francis, L., & Smith, M. C. (2005). Fragment memories mark the end of childhood amnesia. *Memory & Cognition, 33*(4), 567–576.

Chechile, R. A. (1987). Trace susceptibility theory. *Journal of Experimental Psychology: General, 116*(3), 203.

Chechile, R. A. (2006). Memory hazard functions: A vehicle for theory development and test. *Psychological Review, 113*(1), 31–56.

Chu, S., & Downes, J. J. (2002). Proust nose best: Odors are better cues of autobiographical memory. *Memory & Cognition, 30*(4), 511–518.

Cohen, G., & Faulkner, D. (1988). *Life span changes in autobiographical memory*. Retrieved from http://psycnet.apa.org/psycinfo/1988-97682-043

Conway, M. A., & Pleydell-Pearce, C. W. (2000). The construction of autobiographical memories in the self-memory system. *Psychological Review, 107*(2), 261.

Conway, M. A., Wang, Q., Hanyu, K., & Haque, S. (2005). A cross-cultural investigation of autobiographical memory on the universality and cultural variation of the reminiscence bump. *Journal of Cross-Cultural Psychology, 36*(6), 739–749.

de Jonge, M., & Tabbers, H. K. (2013). Repeated testing, item selection, and relearning. *Experimental Psychology*. Retrieved from http://econtent.hogrefe.com/doi/full/10.1027/1618-3169/a000189

Deese, J. (1959). On the prediction of occurrence of particular verbal intrusions in immediate recall. *Journal of Experimental Psychology, 58*(1), 17.

Dodson, C. S., & Hege, A. C. (2005). Speeded retrieval abolishes the false-memory suppression effect: Evidence for the distinctiveness heuristic. *Psychonomic Bulletin & Review, 12*(4), 726–731.

Dodson, C. S., & Schacter, D. L. (2002). Aging and strategic retrieval processes: Reducing false memories with a distinctiveness heuristic. *Psychology and Aging, 17*(3), 405.

Dudai, Y. (2004). *Memory from A to Z: Keywords, concepts, and beyond*. Retrieved from https://philpapers.org/rec/DUDMFA-2

Dudukovic, N. M., Marsh, E. J., & Tversky, B. (2004). Telling a story or telling it straight: The effects of entertaining versus accurate retellings on memory. *Applied Cognitive Psychology, 18*(2), 125–143.

Ebbinghaus, H. (1964). *On memory* H. A. Ruger & C. E. Bussenius, Trans.). New York: Teachers' College, 1913. Paperback edition. New York: Dover. (Originally published in 1885)

Ferguson, S. A., Hashtroudi, S., & Johnson, M. K. (1992). Age differences in using source-relevant cues. *Psychology and Aging, 7*(3), 443.

Fitzgerald, J. M. (1988). Vivid memories and the reminiscence phenomenon: The role of a self narrative. *Human Development, 31*(5), 261–273.

Fitzgerald, J. M. (1992). Autobiographical memory and conceptualizations of the self. In *Theoretical perspectives on autobiographical memory* (pp. 99–114). Springer. Retrieved from http://link.springer.com/chapter/10.1007/978-94-015-7967-4_6

Fitzgerald, J. M. (1996). The distribution of self-narrative memories in younger and older adults: Elaborating the self-narrative hypothesis. *Aging, Neuropsychology, and Cognition, 3*(3), 229–236.

Fitzgerald, J. M., & Broadbridge, C. L. (2013). Latent constructs of the Autobiographical Memory Questionnaire: A recollection-belief model of autobiographical experience. *Memory, 21*(2), 230–248.

Fivush, R. (1994). Young children's event recall: Are memories constructed through discourse? *Consciousness and Cognition, 3*(3–4), 356–373.

Fivush, R., & Hamond, N. R. (1990). *Autobiographical memory across the preschool years: Toward reconceptualizing childhood amnesia*. Retrieved from http://psycnet.apa.org/psycinfo/1991-97187-008

Fleischman, E. A., & Parker, J. F. (1962). Factors in the retention and relearning of perceptual-motor skills. *Journal of Experimental Psychology, 64*(3), 215–226.

Freud, S. (1915). The unconscious. *Standard Edition, 14*(1957), 159–215.

Galton, F. (1879). Psychometric experiments. *Brain, 2*(2), 149–162.

Gonsalves, B., Reber, P. J., Gitelman, D. R., Parrish, T. B., Mesulam, M.-M., & Paller, K. A. (2004). Neural evidence that vivid imagining can lead to false remembering. *Psychological Science, 15*(10), 655–660.

Haden, C. A., Haine, R. A., & Fivush, R. (1997). Developing narrative structure in parent-child reminiscing across the preschool years. *Developmental Psychology, 33*(2), 295–307.

Harley, K., & Reese, E. (1999). Origins of autobiographical memory. *Developmental Psychology, 35*(5), 1338.

Hoffman, H. G. (1997). Role of memory strength in reality monitoring decisions: Evidence from source attribution biases. *Journal of Experimental Psychology: Learning, Memory, and Cognition, 23*(2), 371.

Holmes, A., & Conway, M. A. (1999). Generation identity and the reminiscence bump: Memory for public and private events. *Journal of Adult Development, 6*(1), 21–34.

Hudson, J. A. (1990). The emergence of autobiographical memory in mother-child conversation. In R. Fivush & J. A. Hudson (Eds.), *Emory symposia in cognition, Vol. 3. Knowing and remembering in young children* (pp. 166–196). New York: Cambridge University Press.

Hudson, J., & Nelson, K. (1986). Repeated encounters of a similar kind: Effects of familiarity on children's autobiographic memory. *Cognitive Development, 1*(3), 253–271.

Jacoby, L. L., Woloshyn, V., & Kelley, C. (1989). Becoming famous without being recognized: Unconscious influences of memory produced by dividing attention. *Journal of Experimental Psychology: General, 118*(2), 115.

Jansari, A., & Parkin, A. J. (1996). Things that go bump in your life: Explaining the reminiscence bump in autobiographical memory. *Psychology and Aging, 11*(1), 85–91. https://doi.org/10.1037/0882-7974.11.1.85

Jenkins, J. G., & Dallenbach, K. M. (1924). Obliviscence during sleep and waking. *The American Journal of Psychology, 35*(4), 605–612.

Johnson, M. K., Bush, J. G., & Mitchell, K. J. (1998). Interpersonal reality monitoring: Judging the sources of other people's memories. *Social Cognition, 16*(2), 199–224.

Johnson, M. K., Hashtroudi, S., & Lindsay, D. S. (1993). Source monitoring. *Psychological Bulletin, 114*(1), 3.

Johnson, M. K., Nolde, S. F., & De Leonardis, D. M. (1996). Emotional focus and source monitoring. *Journal of Memory and Language, 35*(2), 135–156.

Johnson, M. K., & Raye, C. L. (1981). Reality monitoring. *Psychological Review, 88*(1), 67.

Jones, S. R., & Fernyhough, C. (2007). Thought as action: Inner speech, self-monitoring, and auditory verbal hallucinations. *Consciousness and Cognition, 16*(2), 391–399.

Jost, A. (1897). Die Assoziationsfestigkeit in ihrer Abhängigkeit von der Verteilung der Wiederholungen. Leopold Voss. Retrieved from https://books.google.com/books?hl=en&lr=&id=ZZo-AAAAYAAJ&oi=fnd&pg=PA5&dq=Jost,+1897&ots=cuLMoe-1q3&sig=I13uggoQLOX9PTk0-5LYEi9fqII

Kareev, Y. (2000). Seven (indeed, plus or minus two) and the detection of correlations. *Psychological Review, 107*(2), 397.

Kihlstrom, J. F. (2004). An unbalanced balancing act: Blocked, recovered, and false memories in the laboratory and clinic. *Clinical Psychology: Science and Practice, 11*(1), 34–41.

Kihlstrom, J. F. (2005). Dissociative disorders. *Annual Review of Clinical Psychology, 1*, 227–253.

Kihlstrom, J. F. (2006a). Repression: A unified theory of a will-o'-the-wisp. *Behavioral and Brain Sciences, 29*(05), 523–523.

Kihlstrom, J. F. (2006b). Trauma and memory revisited. *Memory and Emotions: Interdisciplinary Perspectives*, 259–293.

Koriat, A., Ben-Zur, H., & Sheffer, D. (1988). Telling the same story twice: Output monitoring and age. *Journal of Memory and Language, 27*(1), 23–39.

Kroll, N. E., Knight, R. T., Metcalfe, J., Wolf, E. S., & Tulving, E. (1996). Cohesion failure as a source of memory illusions. *Journal of Memory and Language, 35*(2), 176–196.

Lampinen, J. M., Faries, J. M., Neuschatz, J. S., & Toglia, M. P. (2000). Recollections of things schematic: The influence of scripts on recollective experience. *Applied Cognitive Psychology, 14*(6), 543–554.

Levy, B. J., & Anderson, M. C. (2002). Inhibitory processes and the control of memory retrieval. *Trends in Cognitive Sciences, 6*(7), 299–305.

Lindsay, D. S. (2008). *Source monitoring*. Retrieved from https://www.mysciencework.com/publication/show/e592833 23e6e34e684ecf465ac5afad1

Lindsay, D. S., & Johnson, M. K. (1991). Recognition memory and source monitoring. *Bulletin of the Psychonomic Society, 29*(2), 203–205.

Luria, A. R. (1968). *The mind of a mnemonist: A little book about a vast memory*. Cambridge, MA: Harvard University Press.

Macrae, C. N., Bodenhausen, G. V., & Calvini, G. (1999). Contexts of cryptomnesia: May the source be with you. *Social Cognition, 17*(3), 273–297.

Marsh, R. L., & Bower, G. H. (1993). Eliciting cryptomnesia: Unconscious plagiarism in a puzzle task. *Journal of Experimental Psychology: Learning, Memory, and Cognition, 19*(3), 673.

McDonough, L., & Mandler, J. M. (1994). Very long-term recall in infants: Infantile amnesia reconsidered. *Memory, 2*(4), 339–352.

McGeoch, J. A. (1932). Forgetting and the law of disuse. *Psychological Review, 39*(4), 352.

McGeoch, J. A., & Irion, A. L. (1952). *The psychology of human learning*. Retrieved from http://psycnet.apa.org/psycinfo/1952-05377-000

McKenna, S. P., & Glendon, A. L. (1985). Occupational first aid training: Decay in cardiopulmonary resuscitation (CPR) skills. *Journal of Occupational Psychology, 58*(2), 109–117.

Melton, A. W., & Irwin, J. M. (1940). The influence of degree of interpolated learning on retroactive inhibition and the overt transfer of specific responses. *The American Journal of Psychology, 53*(2), 173–203.

Minami, H., & Dallenbach, K. M. (1946). The effect of activity upon learning and retention in the cockroach, Periplaneta americana. *The American Journal of Psychology, 59*(1), 1–58.

Mitchell, K. J., Mather, M., Johnson, M. K., Raye, C. L., & Greene, E. J. (2006). A functional magnetic resonance imaging investigation of short-term source and item memory for negative pictures. *Neuroreport, 17*(14), 1543–1547.

Myers, N. A., Perris, E. E., & Speaker, C. J. (1994). Fifty months of memory: A longitudinal study in early childhood. *Memory, 2*(4), 383–415.

Nairne, J. S. (2002). The myth of the encoding-retrieval match. *Memory, 10*(5–6), 389–395.

Nairne, J. S., & Pandeirada, J. N. S. (2008). Forgetting. In Byrne J. (Ed.), *learning and memory: A comprehensive reference*, (Vol 2., 179–194). Cambridge, MA: Academic Press.

Nelson, K. (1986). Event knowledge: Structure and function in development. Hillsdale, NJ: Erlbaum.

Norman, D. A. (1981). Categorization of action slips. *Psychological Review, 88*(1), 1.

Page, M. P. A., & Norris, D. (1998). The primacy model: A new model of immediate serial recall. *Psychological Review, 105*(4), 761–781. https://doi.org/10.1037//0033-295X.105.4.761-781

Payne, D. G., Elie, C. J., Blackwell, J. M., & Neuschatz, J. S. (1996). Memory illusions: Recalling, recognizing, and recollecting events that never occurred. *Journal of Memory and Language, 35*(2), 261–285.

Perfect, T. J., & Stark, L. J. (2008). Tales from the Crypt . . . omnesia. *A Handbook of Metamemory and Memory*, 285–314.

Perner, J., & Lang, B. (1999). Development of theory of mind and executive control. *Trends in Cognitive Sciences, 3*(9), 337–344.

Peterson, C., & Whalen, N. (2001). Five years later: Children's memory for medical emergencies. *Applied Cognitive Psychology, 15*(7), S7–S24.

Pitt, M. A., Myung, I. J., & Zhang, S. (2002). Toward a method of selecting among computational models of cognition. *Psychological Review, 109*(3), 472.

Reason, J. T. (1979). *Actions not as planned: The price of automatization*. Retrieved from https://philpapers.org/rec/REAANA-2

Reitman, J. S. (1974). Without surreptitious rehearsal, information in short-term memory decays. *Journal of Verbal Learning & Verbal Behavior, 13*, 365–377.

Roberts, S., & Pashler, H. (2000). How persuasive is a good fit? A comment on theory testing. *Psychological Review, 107*(2), 358.

Robinson, K. J., & Roediger III, H. L. (1997). Associative processes in false recall and false recognition. *Psychological Science, 8*(3), 231–237.

Roediger, H. L. (1973). Inhibition in recall from cueing with recall targets. *Journal of Verbal Learning and Verbal Behavior, 12*(6), 644–657.

Roediger, H. L., & McDermott, K. B. (1995). Creating false memories: Remembering words not presented in lists. *Journal of Experimental Psychology: Learning, Memory, and Cognition, 21*(4), 803.

Roediger III, H. L., Balota, D. A., & Watson, J. M. (2001). Spreading activation and arousal of false memories. *The Nature of Remembering: Essays in Honor of Robert G. Crowder*, 95–115.

Rubin, D. C., & Berntsen, D. (2003). Life scripts help to maintain autobiographical memories of highly positive, but not highly negative, events. *Memory & Cognition, 31*(1), 1–14.

Rubin, D. C., Rahhal, T. A., & Poon, L. W. (1998). Things learned in early adulthood are remembered best. *Memory & Cognition, 26*(1), 3–19.

Rubin, D. C., & Schulkind, M. D. (1997). The distribution of autobiographical memories across the lifespan. *Memory & Cognition, 25*(6), 859–866. https://doi.org/10.3758/BF03211330

Rubin, D. C., & Wenzel, A. E. (1996). One hundred years of forgetting: A quantitative description of retention. *Psychological Review, 103*(4), 734.

Sagan, C. (2011). *Demon-haunted world: Science as a candle in the dark*. Random House Publishing Group.

Schachtel, E. G. (1947). On memory and childhood amnesia. *Psychiatry, 10*(1), 1–26.

Schacter, D. L., & Addis, D. R. (2007). Constructive memory: The ghosts of past and future. *Nature, 445*(7123), 27–27.

Schooler, L. J., & Hertwig, R. (2005). How forgetting aids heuristic inference. *Psychological Review, 112*(3), 610.

Shobe, K. K., & Kihlstrom, J. F. (2002). Interrogative suggestibility and "memory work." *Memory and Suggestibility in the Forensic Interview, 309–327.*

Self, C. J. (1993). The "My Sweet Lord"/"He's So Fine" plagiarism suit. Retrieved from https://web.archive.org/web/20081221135306/http://abbeyrd.best.vwh.net/mysweet.htm

Simcock, G., & Hayne, H. (2002). Breaking the barrier? Children fail to translate their preverbal memories into language. *Psychological Science, 13*(3), 225–231. https://doi.org/10.1111/1467-9280.00442

Simon, H. A. (1966). A note on Jost's law and exponential forgetting. *Psychometrika, 31*(4), 505–506.

Skinner, B. F. (1983). Intellectual self-management in old age. *American Psychologist, 38*(3), 239–244.

Sluzenski, J., Newcombe, N., & Ottinger, W. (2004). Changes in reality monitoring and episodic memory in early childhood. *Developmental Science, 7*(2), 225–245.

Suddendorf, T., & Corballis, M. C. (1997). Mental time travel and the evolution of the human mind. *Genetic, Social, and General Psychology Monographs, 123*(2), 133–167.

Taylor, F. K. (1965). Cryptomnesia and plagiarism. *The British Journal of Psychiatry, 111*(480), 1111–1118.

Tulving, E. (1983). *Elements of episodic memory.* New York, NY: Oxford University Press.

Tulving, E. (2002). Episodic memory: From mind to brain. *Annual Review of Psychology, 53*(1), 1–25.

Tulving, E., & Pearlstone, Z. (1966). Availability versus accessibility of information in memory for words. *Journal of Verbal Learning and Verbal Behavior, 5*(4), 381–391.

Tulving, E., & Thomson, D. M. (1973). Encoding specificity and retrieval processes in episodic memory. *Psychological Review, 80*(5), 352.

Underwood, B. J. (1957). Interference and forgetting. *Psychological Review, 64*(1), 49–60. https://doi.org/10.1037/h0044616

Underwood, B. J. (1965). False recognition produced by implicit verbal responses. *Journal of Experimental Psychology, 70*(1), 122–129.

Usher, J. A., & Neisser, U. (1993). Childhood amnesia and the beginnings of memory for four early life events. *Journal of Experimental Psychology: General, 122*(2), 155.

Van Abbema, D. L., & Bauer, P. J. (2005). Autobiographical memory in middle childhood: Recollections of the recent and distant past. *Memory, 13*(8), 829–845. https://doi.org/10.1080/09658210444000430

Warrington, E. K., & Sanders, H. I. (1971). The fate of old memories. *The Quarterly Journal of Experimental Psychology, 23*(4), 432–442.

Watkins, O. C., & Watkins, M. J. (1975). Buildup of proactive inhibition as a cue-overload effect. *Journal of Experimental Psychology: Human Learning and Memory, 1*(4), 442.

Waugh, N. C., & Norman, D. A. (1965). Primary memory. *Psychological Review, 72*(2), 89–104.

Welch-Ross, M. K. (1995). An integrative model of the development of autobiographical memory. *Developmental Review, 15*(3), 338–365.

Wickelgren, W. A. (1977). *Learning and memory.* Prentice Hall. Retrieved from http://psycnet.apa.org/psycinfo/1978-30981-000

Willander, J., & Larsson, M. (2006). Smell your way back to childhood: Autobiographical odor memory. *Psychonomic Bulletin & Review, 13*(2), 240–244.

Winograd, E., & Killinger, W. A. (1983). Relating age at encoding in early childhood to adult recall: Development of flashbulb memories. *Journal of Experimental Psychology: General, 112*(3), 413.

Wixted, J. T. (2004). On common ground: Jost's (1897) law of forgetting and Ribot's (1881) law of retrograde amnesia. *Psychological Review, 111*(4), 864.

Wixted, J. T., & Carpenter, S. K. (2007). The Wickelgren power law and the Ebbinghaus savings function. *Psychological Science, 18*(2), 133–134.

Wixted, J. T., & Ebbesen, E. B. (1991). On the form of forgetting. *Psychological Science, 2*(6), 409–415.

©iStock.com/4x6

Learning and Memory in the Real World

Chapter Outline

Overview

This chapter takes a more phenomenological approach than the other chapters by examining learning and memory in a variety of contexts and subfields. First, we'll look at the study of how consumers form attitudes about different brands and how the sensory experiences shape shopping and eating experiences. Then, we'll look at the suggestions from operant conditioning theory about setting up a classroom environment and how to handle misbehavior. Next is a section describing popular methods for training employees as well as managers. Following that is an examination of research on violent acts from exposure to violent media, numbness to violence, and connections to social learning theory. We end with a section that examines the most well-documented limitations to eyewitness memory.

Learning and Advertising: Consumer Research

Consumer research is a broad area of study of consumer behavior, thoughts, and feelings, with the express goal of understanding how to market and sell to people effectively. Of interest to us is how theories of learning have been studied in this pursuit. Consumer research has been primarily focused on attitude formation: how advertising and shopping conditions can successfully form positive attitudes in potential customers. Social psychologists have described attitudes as having three components: a cognitive component, an affective or emotional component, and a behavioral component (Aronson, Wilson, & Akert, 2012). Consumer psychologists, who study consumer behavior, see the attitude a consumer forms about an advertisement as having cognitive and affective components with a behavioral component of the likelihood to make the desired behavior, such as purchasing a product (Madden, Allen, & Twible, 1988) or evaluating one brand against others (e.g., with professional football teams; Sierra, Taute, & Heiser, 2012). So, a marketing campaign might want to inform consumers about a product, which means influencing the cognitive part of an attitude, by means of an advertisement that uses humor, celebrities, or peppy music for an emotional connection, in order to influence their behavior. Not all advertisements are aimed at altering attitudes about a product, but rather might be intended to influence healthy behavior, such as public service announcements, or PSAs (Taute, McQuitty, & Sautter, 2011), or to sway potential voters. Consumer research also involves the shopping experience, in-store and online: how to encourage customers to spend more time and make purchases through the store atmosphere? First, we'll examine research on advertising, then on attitudes about brands, and last on creating retail store atmosphere to improve sales.

Advertising

What makes for an effective advertisement has been heavily researched, including how emotions are evoked in advertising, how background music and celebrities should be used in ads, and what the textual versus pictorial components of an ad contribute to an ad's overall effectiveness. Classical conditioning theory (see Chapter 3) is generally viewed as the basis for consumers' forming attitudes about products through advertising.

Evoking Emotions Using Advertising

The emotional reactions consumers have to advertisements are important, both in terms of the reaction to the brand that the advertiser is promoting as well as to the ad itself (Batra & Ray, 1986a). The interest in understanding how emotions can moderate the effectiveness of an advertisement is fairly recent, starting in the late 1980s (Holbrook & Batra, 1987). Holbrook and Batra used seventy-two television commercials and participants' emotional ratings of them to create a model of emotional dimensions for products. They used a statistical technique called an exploratory factor analysis to reduce the large data set into a smaller set of core factors based on trends in the ratings. They found three core emotional dimensions (pleasure, arousal, domination) and six content variables (emotional, threatening, mundane, sexy, cerebral, and personally-relevant) related to television ads for products.

But, what is the role emotions produced by an advertisement play (Gardner, 1985)? Generally, people will make behaviors that are mood-congruent, that is, engaging in behaviors that they see as matching their own mood. So, positive moods are likely to encourage performance of desired behaviors (e.g., buying a wanted product, spending time in a favorite store), but negative mood states may not have as clear an impact on behavior. Some actions, like alleviating a bad mood by helping someone else, are strategies that older children possess but younger ones may not. Gardner's review found support for controlling the temperature inside stores and making sure the service isn't frustrating and confusing. And nice weather helps, of course. Ultimately, being in a good mood should help to retrieve positive behaviors associated with being in a good mood. Stores that produce negative moods in all customers may not be able to survive (p. 293).

Pham, Geuens, and De Pelsmacker (2013) compiled survey results from 1,576 participants and their reactions to 1,076 television commercials. The researchers found that the emotions a TV ad evoked played a major role in the evaluation of the brand being advertised, as well as the advertisements themselves. These associations didn't matter if the product was personally relevant for an individual consumer, but the type of product advertised did matter. The emotional response was a greater indicator of the success of the ad if the product was more hedonic or was for pleasure, such as a movie, rather than utilitarian, like laundry detergent.

Galvanic skin response (GSR) has been used to evaluate emotional reaction to advertisements. GSR readings are believed to show physiological arousal by tracking the sweat glands on the skin: With more arousal, skin becomes more conducive to electricity. Aaker, Stayman, and Hagerty (1986) found the "warmth" of an ad could be monitored using GSR, and that how warm an advertisement was appeared within fifteen seconds of the start of a commercial. They were not able to show that the presence of warmth improved memory of the commercial, however.

Theoretical Basis for Emotional Conditioning Through Advertisements

The emotional component of an attitude toward a product probably acts as a source of information for consumers, an idea Pham (2004) calls the feelings-as-information hypothesis. The individual experiencing the emotional response uses it as a guide for thinking about the product in the advertisement beyond facts about the product. This is similar to Petty and Cacioppo's (1986) classic model of persuasion, which suggests that behavioral change can come from two sources: specific knowledge about an action, the central route for persuasion, or peripheral details about the behavior like endorsements, feelings, and catchy theme songs, the peripheral route for persuasion. Processing central route information requires attention and focus on the part of the listener to process the arguments being made. Peripheral route processing is more superficial and is easy to do when preoccupied.

The most popular explanation for how attitudes are formed using advertisements is classically conditioning (e.g., Gresham & Shimp, 1985; Grossman & Till, 1998). It could be argued that classical conditioning is the foundational learning theory used by the entire marketing industry. Most researchers appear to implicitly use classical conditioning approaches to explain the emotional component of product attitudes (Argyriou & Melewar, 2011). Classically-conditioned attitudes toward a product appear to be long-lasting (Grossman & Till, 1998). Kim, Lim, & Bhargava (1998) pointed out that the connection between the emotions produced in the advertisement and the product do not have to be meaningful. A good example of this is a Pepsi commercial aired during a Super Bowl game that featured bears dancing to a disco song to sell Pepsi (https://youtu.be/DR_vdikpKZA).

As classical conditioning theory would predict, repetition or repeated pairings of the product with the unconditional stimulus, or UCS (as discussed in Chapter 3), help solidify the association (Batra and Ray, 1986b). Repeatedly pairing a product with humorous cartoons created an implicit attitude change for a brand (Strick, van Baaren, Holland, & van Knippenberg, 2009). Can you think of any brands that advertise car insurance a lot, always using humor?

While researchers have generally used classical conditioning as the mechanism to explain the learning that advertisers hope to create with an ad, whether the pure classical conditioning theory as posited by Pavlov is accurate enough is debated by consumer researchers. Some prefer to talk about evaluative conditioning as an explanation that is related to classical Pavlovian conditioning but may have some differences in predicted outcomes (De Houwer, Thomas, & Baeyens, 2001; Hofman, De Houwer, Perugini, Baeyens, & Crombez, 2010). De Houwer and colleagues compared evaluative conditioning to classical conditioning and didn't find many conceptual differences. Stuart, Shimp, and Engle (1987) conducted four experiments that used evaluative conditioning techniques to confirm that forming emotional attitudes toward brands in advertising seemed to follow normal classical conditioning principles. For example, forward conditioning (the neutral stimulus is presented before the UCS during learning trials) is more effective than backward conditioning (the UCS is presented before the neutral stimulus). Hofman and colleagues presented a comprehensive of a modern meta-analysis of how evaluative conditioning works in contrast to classical conditioning. Their general conclusions from the merging of 253 different studies were that evaluative conditioning works better (1) if the learner is consciously aware of the unconditioned stimulus and the relationship between the unconditioned stimulus and the neutral stimulus and (2) tends to be measured better using self-report (a conscious measure) than using implicit measures. The authors believe that evaluative conditioning works propositionally; that is, learners form a conscious connection between the stimuli presented (e.g., happy music, smiling people, food from a restaurant must mean people enjoy eating at this restaurant).

Not all consumer behaviorists agree. Social psychologists have believed attitude formation can happen implicitly through classical conditioning for some time (Olson &

Fazio, 2001). Maison, Greenwald, and Bruin (2004) used the Implicit Association Test and a survey of consumer attitudes toward fast food restaurants and soda pop brands and found that the implicit associations were a better predictor of behavior than stated attitudes. Using an extremely rigorous classical conditioning paradigm, Pine, Mendelsohn, and Dudai (2014) found preferences resist extinction; and they point out that the unconscious learning of preferences can last up to a lifetime. The only adjustment to implicit preferences they found was through reconsolidation—fully retrieving memory of an attitude in order to add new information to it. Essentially, existing attitudes may be more amenable to tweaking than to extinction. Some theorists have proposed theories that try to bridge the explicit and implicit aspects of attitudes (see, e.g., Gawronski & Bodenhausen, 2006).

One major question for advertisers (but having received relatively little study) is whether attitudes can change toward brands on which consumers have already formed attitudes toward. Given how inundated we are with advertisements, there are relatively few major brands that we have never been exposed to. Machleit and Wilson (1988) found that the attitude formation process for brands that were familiar versus those that were unfamiliar were different: Advertisements worked to change feelings toward a brand if the brand was unfamiliar. Advertisements were unable to change feelings toward a familiar brand. Possibly, more exposures to the ad would be needed. Gibson (2008) found that attitudes toward a brand could be changed in an experiment, but not if the preexisting preference toward a well-known brand (e.g., Coke or Pepsi) is strong. Implicit attitude change was more likely, but only when the participants were under a higher cognitive load (that is, busy with another task).

What features make for a better advertisement? Let's take a look at the use of background music, celebrities, visuals in advertising, and ad placement.

Background Music in Advertising

A sample of 3,456 advertisements found 94 percent use music (Allan, 2006). Most involved popular music, particularly if the product was automotive, audio/video equipment, or food. Usually the music was "needledrop music," meaning that it is generic, conventional music without a specific purpose. Often it's licensed to be used each time it is played with an advertisement. So, while music in ads is almost ubiquitous, can we show that it is useful empirically?

The first studies on music in advertising might have been by Wintle (1978), showing that music can influence the emotions an advertisement creates. Gorn (1982) documented that music played in the advertisement affected the attitudes toward the product. While this conclusion is generally accepted, one study was unable to replicate Gorn's original study (Kellaris & Cox, 1989), which pointed out that participants could have figured out what the hypothesis was of the study. Participants may then intentionally play along with the study, heightening the effect. This is one reason why participants are sometimes misled as to the nature of a psychological study. If there is any misleading, they must be debriefed as to the true nature of the study afterward. All research has to meet the ethical standards and review of the institution hosting the research and of any institution awarding money for the work.

In a review of what research had been published early on, Bruner (1990) examined what was known about the use of music in advertisements and pointed out some issues that make study of the topic challenging. For instance, Bruner points out that few researchers studying the use of music in advertisements take participants' preexisting preferences for music itself into account. Additionally, "music" isn't a constant, fixed entity, but a complex stimulus that can be highly unstructured, has many elements, and is variable. Generally speaking, research up to that point had found that fast music was viewed by participants as happier or more pleasant than slower music. Slow music evoked more sentimental, calm moods. Music with a higher pitch often felt happier than lower pitched tunes. Bruner found research that tried to parcel out the effects of different instruments (e.g., brass instruments sound more triumphant, woodwinds tend to be mournful). In stores, loud music was seen to produce more sales. Also, in some cases slower music, rather than faster, prompted people to spend more time in a store. One study found the effect of store music on the perception of time varied by the age of the shopper.

In a more recent meta-analysis of the use of background music, Kämpfe, Sedlmeier, and Renkewitz (2010) found that there was no one overall main effect to explain background music. If anything, the presence of music may disrupt the reading process and could dampen recall for details, but it does appear to improve emotional reactions. The authors conclude that there are so many kinds of background music that treating "music" as a monolithic variable may be impossible at best and unwise at worst.

What has more recent research found? Kellaris and Kent (1993) manipulated three musical features: tempo, tonality (major/minor keys), and texture (classical vs. pop music). They found fast-tempo classical music in a major key was the most pleasurable, but fast pop music was more arousing. These results make a good argument that the elements of the music may be more important than simply "music" itself as a variable.

But what about the use of the music for creating an attitude toward a product that is memorable? Guido and colleagues (2016) found that music that suddenly cuts off at the end of an ad reduced memory for the brand due to distraction. They suggest advertisers use music that fades out or ends on a tone. In radio ads, faster music has been found to reduce recall of the message (Oakes & North, 2006). The authors interpreted this finding as indicating that faster music creates a higher cognitive workload, which lessens storage capacity in working memory, hence worse encoding and later retrieval.

Musical Congruence With Brand

Another tack some researchers have taken is to examine the congruity between the music and the message of the ad, instead of the individual elements of music. Besides the musical genre itself acting as a retrieval cue for the product (Yeoh & North, 2010), music can be a functional part of the advertisement (e.g., Scott, 1990). Music can be used as a kind of language; or used to create moments of dissonance, or motion, or repetition. Its inclusion in an advertisement can be used as a narrative for the events shown, or for establishing the passage of time, and even for identification with the message of the ad (e.g., patriotic anthems).

For example, radio ads that are heavily fact-oriented perform better with listeners when the background music appears to them to be congruent with the brand (Lavack, Thakor, & Bottausci, 2008), such as classical music played with jewelry advertisements. Noting that most advertisements do not require a lot of cognitive processing, Alpert, Alpert, and Maltz (2005) found participants' intent to buy a product was higher if sad music matched the message of the advertisement (see Fig. 12.1). North, Mackenzie, Law, and Hargreaves (2004) found the perceived match between the music and the speaker to matter for both likability and recall. In this study, the "fit" of the voice was altered based on gender, accent, and the speed of delivery. It's important to point out that there isn't a measure of musical "congruity" in some objective sense—the researchers are testing participants' preferences for attending to a message that has elements that may or may not be stereotypical. North and colleagues (2004) found that the perceived fit of the music and the voice mattered for product likability regardless of the complexity of the ad.

FIGURE 12.1 Alpert, Alpert, and Maltz (2005) found a congruent effect for sad music and a sad message in an advertisement with participants' intent to purchase.

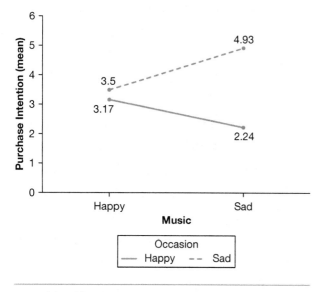

Source: Adapted from Alpert, M. I., Alpert, J. I., & Maltz, E. N. (2005).

Ultimately, the use of background music is probably dual-purpose: The music acts to gain attention while seeking to boost the message of the advertisement in a congruous way (Kellaris, Cox, & Cox, 1993). Incongruent music will undercut the message. Kellaris and colleagues matched a range of musical selections to ads, creating some very off-beat combinations, including a Franz Liszt classical piece (with soft gentle moments interspersed with loud, triumphal sections) with a public service announcement about drugs. Attention-getting traits and musical congruity interacted with each other, such that music that was attention-getting and congruent with the message of the ad produced the highest mean brand recall score and recall of the ad's message (see Fig. 12.2).

Celebrities in Advertising

Of course, it's not just music that is paired with a message in advertisements, hoping to create an emotional association with a product or, say, a travel destination (Van der Veen & Song, 2014). Celebrities are also paid to appear in ads. Similar to research on background music, researchers usually take a classical conditioning approach to explain the effectiveness of celebrity endorsements and have tested the perceived fit between the product sold and the celebrity (Till, Stanley, & Priluck, 2008). Till and colleagues found that better matches between the product and celebrity mattered (e.g., Jennifer Aniston paired with a hair styling gel vs. a sports drink, or Michael Jordan and hair styling gel vs. a sports drink). The association from a celebrity endorsement lasted at least two weeks, from a follow-up study. The association persisted despite attempts to sever the connection.

Attempts to validate the classical conditioning properties of celebrity endorsements have not been many. Miller and Allen (2012) documented that forward conditioning (a brand is shown being endorsed by a celebrity) works as expected, but little else has been tested. Many brands that are endorsed are well-known, familiar brands, so endorsements may not work the same way as with unfamiliar brands. Also, celebrity endorsements can come with a cost if the celebrity is a controversial figure or becomes embroiled in a scandal. The reality television show "Jersey Shore" was popular for a time, but somewhat through infamy. Fashion accessory designers mailed free samples of their *competitor's* purses to Nicole "Snooki" Polizzi so that she would be photographed in public with their competitor's wares, apparently anticipating an emotionally negative association (How Snooki Got Her Gucci: The Dirt on Purses; observer.com/2010/08/how-snooki-got-her-gucci-the-dirt-on-purses/). The term for this competitive form of marketing is sometimes called counter-branding.

FIGURE 12.2   Brand recall was greatly helped by a match between the music and the message of the ad, if the music and message were upbeat and energetic.

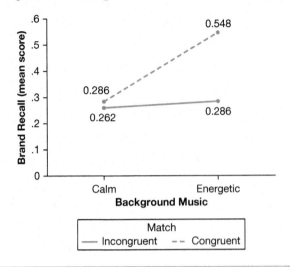

Source: Adapted from Kellaris, J. J., Cox, A. D., & Cox, D. (1993).

A missing variable in much of the research on existing brands is the reputation a company can have. According to Goldsmith, Lafferty, and Newell (2000), the credibility of the corporation matters more than that of the celebrity in the advertisement. The reputation of the corporation behind the ad, they note, is a broad construct that includes trustworthiness and expertise. The corporation's reputation influences how consumers perceive a product, their advertisement, and the brand. Imagine the change of attitude after BP Global, which had advertised itself as an environmentally sensitive company for years, was involved in the massive oil spill in the Gulf of Mexico due to the explosion of Deepwater Horizon (BP Goes for Public Relations Makeover to Get Beyond Gulf Spill; www.forbes.com/sites/greatspeculations/2012/02/07/bp-goes-for-public-relations-makeover-to-get-beyond-gulf-spill/). Or Apple Inc., which has a reputation for devices that are "innovative" and are meant for creative professionals, released an updated laptop design after four years that didn't appear to be powerful enough (Apple Inc. (AAPL) Angers New MacBook Pro Fans yet Again; http://investorplace.com/2016/11/apple-inc-aapl-new-macbook-pro-iplace/#.WV1U9rjXuSo). In a survey of 152 consumers for a fictional advertisement, Goldsmith and colleagues (2000) found that the celebrity endorsement had the stronger impact on the attitude toward the ad itself, whereas the credibility of the corporation had the greater impact on attitudes toward the brand.

Finally, people do have preexisting attitudes toward advertising itself, or a *global attitude toward advertising* (Muehling, 1987). As ads have crept into all areas of life, consumers have responded by shutting off cable TV service ("cutting the cord") and by installing ad-blocking software on their computers. In a way, advertisers have to create advertising experiences to an audience that is fairly used to advertising (and generally dislikes it). In a relatively small survey of 88 people, Muehling found that his participants distinguished between the purpose of advertising (its function to sell products and keep prices low) and the practices of advertisers (methods for advertising) and didn't treat the two exactly the same. The purpose of advertising was viewed more positively than the practices advertisers take. While stating that advertising was essential, respondents didn't believe advertising helped keep prices low, and they blamed advertising for encouraging people to buy products they didn't really need.

Text Versus Visual Components in an Advertisement

Mitchell (1986) and Childers, Heckler, and Houston (1986) tried to parcel out processing of the text of an ad (or "ad copy") and any visual information that is included with the text. Childers and colleagues showed fifty-six participants ads that contained text and visuals that were sometimes consistent or sometimes inconsistent. After rating the ads, participants were tested on their recognition of the ads two days later. In some cases, the ads they were asked to recall were varied from what they had actually seen. Childers and colleagues found that it was likely that the two elements of an ad are not processed in the same way: The visual information was encoded more elaborately and distinctly than was the ad copy, creating a picture superiority effect.

Weaker processing of ad copy might be a matter of the quality of the text itself. Debevec and Romeo (1992) found that ad copy that asked people to consider themselves in relation to the product in the ad, using a second person voice (such as "When you work hard and play hard, drink Twist"), produced the highest attitudinal ratings for the product. These ratings were higher than for ad copy touting benefits from using the product or describing the product for "people," instead of the reader. This effect was greatest when a photo of the product by itself was shown, rather than a photo of several people using the product.

Ad Placement

Does it matter where an observer encounters an ad? Researchers have documented attitude formation of products from advertisements that are displayed in online videogames (Redondo, 2012) and smartphone apps (Kim & Han, 2014). Wilson and Till (2011) examined whether the message of billboard advertisements could be countered by or interact with the outdoor environment around the billboard, its fixed location. They found no negative effects from the environment around the billboard on the message of the ad, which might explain why billboards are everywhere.

Product Perception

Consumer behaviorists and psychologists studying "cross-modal perception" have examined the process of evaluating a product by how it feels, looks, and tastes. Cross-modal perception (or "multisensory perception") is the study of how information from one sense can cross over and influence another. The role of attention and bottom-up versus top-down processing (piecing together an object from sensory input versus using prior knowledge) factor into how consumers perceive the actual products with which they interact with. See Chapter 3 to review these topics.

Dr. Charles Spence (Oxford University) has spearheaded much of the cross-modal research examining how the presentation of products can influence how consumers experience them. For instance, Shankar, Levitan, and Spence (2010) proposed that tasting the flavor of grape in juice is somewhat dependent on the color of the liquid and one's culture. Twenty Britons and fifteen Taiwanese drank dyed water from six clear cups. Each drink was one of six colors. Seventy percent of the British participants reported a cola flavor when they drank the brown-dyed water, but half of the Taiwanese participants reported a grape flavor for the brown-dyed water. Top-down processing appears to have been influencing the taste buds. Color seems to influence the perception of food flavor, but it's not clear if the color of food influences the intensity of flavor (Spence, Levitan, Shankar, & Zampini, 2010).

The color of the plate holding food (in this case, a strawberry mousse dessert) can alter the perception of the food it holds (Piqueras-Fiszman, Alcaide, Roura, & Spence, 2012). Participants rated the dessert to be sweeter and more likeable when served on a white rather than black identical plate. The shape of the plates did not affect the perception of flavor, although a different study found heavier plates to improve the taste of yogurt (Piqueras-Fiszman, Harrar, Alcaide, & Spence, 2011). Relatedly, a particular color of a cup improved participants' ratings of hot chocolate over other cup colors (Piqueras-Fiszman & Spence, 2012).

Along the same lines, research has found cross-modal perception effects for labels on food and the sounds we make while eating. Participants found brown M&Ms taste more chocolaty than green M&Ms, particularly when they were labeled as "dark chocolate" instead of "milk chocolate" (Shankar, Levitan, Prescott, & Spence, 2009). The sounds we make when eating food seem to be a cue for the intensity of the food as well: People were found to rate potato chips as crisper and less stale when the sound of eating them was manipulated (Zampini & Spence, 2004). Chips taste fresher when the act of eating them sounds louder and uses a higher frequency pitch. (The role of sound for altering the experience of eating is explored more fully in a review by Spence and Shankar, 2010.)

Store Atmospherics

Besides handling products directly, there is the experience of looking for something to buy in a retail establishment. Simply placing different products next to each other, for instance, can produce "spillover" from one product to the other, particularly if one of the products produces an emotional response. The spread of an emotional response from one product to another is called "emotional contagion" (Hasford, Hardesty, & Kidwell, 2015). If we grant that we are conditioned to have an emotional response to products, what happens when we encounter several products next to each other on a store aisle? Hasford and colleagues found that this can be the case, particularly for books and magazines that tend to use provocative images and headlines. When people use emotions as information, having a controversial celebrity on a magazine cover can emotionally spill over to other unrelated products.

Emotional contagion doesn't have to be negative; the use of visual art has been found to increase consumers' perceptions of products (Hagtvedt & Patrick, 2008). Art appears to cue "luxury," which may explain why marketers incorporate artistic elements in packaging and product design as well.

Research has extended to the use of background music inside retail stores and the aromas that may be present, too (even in online shopping: Ding & Lin, 2012). Morin, Dubé, and Chebat (2007) and Spence, Puccinelli, Grewal and Roggeveen (2014) view spending time in a store as a multisensory experience. If customers in a store like the music that is played, it should associate positively with the shopping experience, leading to higher purchase rates. Yalch and Spangenberg (2000) found that store music altered customers' perception of time: Customers thought they had spent a longer amount of time in a store when the store played music that was familiar to them. But in reality, they had stayed longer in stores that played unfamiliar music. In a field experiment, Ferreira and Oliveira-Castro (2011) varied music inside a mall and found that the music played, in fact, tied to customer attitudes and sales. Yalch and Spangenberg (1990) note, though, that the age of

FIGURE 12.3 Shoppers found the presence of a scent to be more pleasing when loud music was present in the store.

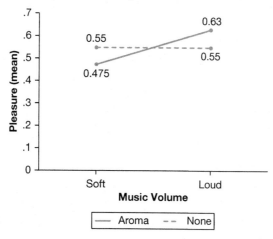

Source: Adapted from Debevec, K., & Romeo, J. B. (1992).

Note: Hypothetical values are approximates.

customers and their likely preferences for music vary across the open hours of a store or mall, but rarely does the music change to accommodate different customers.

The use of aromas to alter the retail experience has been around for a long time. To this day, the Walt Disney Theme Parks use a host of hidden scent emitters to create a fuller experience (e.g., popcorn, baking scents on Main Street). Deploying a scent in a store has been found to cause shoppers to rate the store more highly (Spangenberg, Crowley, & Henderson, 1996). Shoppers in stores that were asked to use scents believed they had spent less time shopping than people who had been in stores that were not scented. One study found an interaction between scent and sound: Managers of a group of fashion stores were asked to play music at either a high or low volume and to deploy either a vanilla scent or no scent (Morrison, Gan, Dubelaar, & Oppenwal, 2011). The shoppers (young adults, mostly) stayed longer and spent more in stores with loud music and a vanilla scent (see Fig. 12.3).

Learning and Education: Classroom Management

Managing behavior in a school classroom can be particularly challenging. It's easy to forget the number of uncontrolled variables that encroach on the formal learning environment in K–12 education. By definition the learners are immature. They have virtually no choice in the curriculum (for important reasons). The children have issues with behavior, controlling attention, lack of much real-world experience, and qualitatively different thinking styles. Within one classroom, the children can vary by motivation, interest, and ability. Most schools do not group children by ability or interest level. Family backgrounds and expectations on respect for authority vary widely. One can't assume every child will respond to the same expectations and consequences identically. And, most teaching is not individualized, but whole-group.

The modern classroom is a child's place of work, as is developmentally appropriate. They are working at learning. So, some forms of play are "work," if they are educationally pertinent. Ultimately, proper behavior in the classroom, as in a workplace, is doing the assigned work without interfering with others' ability to do their own work (Ormrod, 2011). How do teachers encourage and maintain a productive learning environment?

The learning theories that generally provide the strongest recommendations for classroom management behavior are operant conditioning, classical conditioning, and motivational theory.

The approach that modern motivational theories encourage teachers to take involves facilitating existing interest and treating everyone fairly. Ultimately, a child who is engaged in the learning activity will rarely exhibit problem behavior. If they find the work enjoyable or interesting, most other problems resolve themselves. This means trying to facilitate intrinsic motivation when possible. Teachers can take concrete steps to make this kind of engagement more likely.

First, classroom rules have to be clear or age-appropriate for the students, informational, and aimed at getting work done. They are not about control but facilitating everyone's learning. This puts the classroom manager, the teacher, in the role of facilitating rather than being an authoritarian (e.g., Baumrind, 1991). Ideally the rules should be available and discussed starting the first day of the year and consistently enforced thereafter. That's what equity theory would expect—most students to see the classroom environment as fair. Equity theory would also predict that opportunities for roles in the classroom (e.g., "line leader," feeding the fish) have to be dispersed fairly and rotated every so often. Any opportunities for extra credit or special events (parties for good behavior) have to be provided to everyone, provided they exhibit the behavior that allows them to earn the privilege. No favoritism allowed.

The physical setup of a classroom also communicates to the class. Cues from room decor and the arrangement of tables and chairs signal some kinds of behavior over others. For instance, tables and chairs arranged into "pods" that face each other will encourage social interaction—which is excellent, if that is part of the lesson. The younger age-sets cannot focus on the teacher and ignore the classmates who are facing them directly in their line of sight. Incidentally, it's popular to heavily decorate the walls of classrooms for students in the primary grades, yet their working memory spans are smaller and they have less self-control over their thoughts. By overdecorating, it could be creating a highly overstimulating environment that can create cognitive focus problems for younger students. Ironically, high school students, with better inhibitory control and attentional focus, are treated to classroom walls that are as plain and boring as prison walls.

Maslow's hierarchy and Alderfer's ERG (existence, relatedness, and growth, as presented in Chapter 6) theory see social needs as a strong motivational need. This means that a teacher should work to create a sense of community and belongingness among students. Activities that include everyone form bonds across the class. The class can have pride in its own collective identify, whether doing community work together, planting flowers outside the building, or writing letters to kids in the lower grades from Santa.

Part of feeling like belonging to a group means forming a teacher-student relationship based on respect. As the teacher, we can learn our students' names, learn the basics about their lives, ask about them, and notice changes about them. Everyone can be asked for their input on class decisions and their answers handled respectfully. In many ways, the teacher is also modeling civil behavior to students who are learning how to become adults and may not receive the best role models at home.

Some educational activities can be made to include a social component as well. Short periods of group work or open discussion enable a chance for social interaction that at some age periods (early adolescence) are remarkably powerful. Instead of fighting the natural desire they have to interact, incorporating social elements is wiser, if possible. This does mean modeling proper behavior for social interaction and setting up boundaries for the work.

Expectancy theory would predict that students will be encouraged when they see the work as being achievable and worthwhile. This can be a hard sell at times, but if we can't defend why we are asking students to do the work, then maybe we should ask why we are requiring them to do it. Work design theory predicts that student motivation is higher if they can incorporate some personal preferences into their work. For projects, for example, letting the students have some autonomy over the choice of topics can help.

Both Vygotsky and Piaget would expect that the work should not be too simple, which is not challenging but at a level that is just ahead of what the child can do now. Those tasks that are achievable with some guidance and oversight are optimal for interest and growth.

Of course, children do not enter education like blank slates with no prior learning about acceptable behaviors. What is tolerated at home might not be in a formal educational environment, and behaviors that were acceptable to last year's grade teacher may not be now. How to reduce those undesirable behaviors that interfere with the work of learning?

Here, operant conditioning tends to lead the way at providing possible mechanisms for reducing behavior. Behaviorsts would expect that all behavior happens for a reason—anticipation of a reinforcement or avoidance of punishment. While the behavior might strike us as obviously wrongheaded or even dangerous, the child engaged in it is looking for something that reinforces it, whatever that might be. Often, it's attention, even if it is an angry rebuke from a teacher and mockery from other students. Or, being kicked out of the classroom is exactly what was desired, once the shame has ended. Punishment is often our first go-to in these situations, largely out of an emotional desire to retaliate; but punishment is problematic. As we saw in Chapter 4, it produces a lot of unintended by-products, such as the message that the teacher is controlling, that the child is "bad," and the punishment can readily escalate. Physical punishment in the school environment, as you may or may not be aware, is not legal in most states; and where it is legal, it tends to be used very unevenly and without evidence of effectiveness.

So, other techniques and mild punishers should be employed first. Assuming the responsibility for the behavior doesn't exist within faults of the lesson plan (it can happen—the best plans can go awry) or the context, such the day before a holiday, and if the behavior must be dealt with, then a number of options exist. An initial option is not to reinforce the behavior by ignoring it. If the behavior is attention-seeking, then the teacher can choose to let it slide. Extinction as a behavior modification technique can work, but keep some caveats in mind. First, if it works, the child will become more upset initially, and may try harder. This means that the attention was in fact reinforcing the child, but the rules have changed. So, the child will get louder or bigger for a while, or resort to more childish behavior. This is called an *extinction burst*. Unfortunately, the teacher has to stay the course during this period. To reinforce the increased misbehavior now will solidify the behavior at this new level. Second, extinction takes some time. The emotional value of any one reinforcement is greater than the emotional loss of value from extinction. It can be a while before it is effective, which takes patience.

Some mild forms of punishment might be enough. Making direct eye contact with a frown or providing a sharp scold can stop behavior and remind the child to get back on task. Occasionally all that is needed is a direct acknowledgement that the current behavior is not what is expected, and hopefully the child will refocus. Scolds should be brief, sharp, and firm, without much anger. They are meant to be jarring.

If extinction and reprimands haven't worked, another option is to develop self-regulation strategies after directly communicating to the child about the problem. If a child understands the problem, and both the teacher and the child can agree to a self-imposed improvement program, then the child may be able to learn some autonomy skills. This might involve keeping a log on her desk for when she properly raises her hand to answer a question, or for keeping track of how long he remained seated successfully. Small incentives can be used as reinforcers at the end of the week if behavioral goals have been met.

If a child doesn't have the desire to engage in change, then longer forms of punishment might be necessary. This includes the use of time-outs and loss of privileges. Time-outs are short periods of removal from the activity, a form of negative punishment. Usually most appropriate if the behavior seems to be done for attention, it involves being placed for no more than about ten minutes in a boring, isolated spot. It is usually best to discuss the reasons for the time-out afterward, because many children will have forgotten what behavior was specifically a concern during that time. Loss of privileges means losing the opportunity for something, such as attendance at a class party. It's popular to lose recess privileges; but unfortunately, some children who frequently get in trouble need recess to improve, and without it, their day gets worse.

With any kind of punishment, it's important to monitor for damages to the child's sense of self-worth. The behavior is being punished, not the child. This nuance is easy to forget; and, if ignored, then the child can lose a sense of belongingness to the classroom environment and possibly the school.

Learning and the Workplace: Employee Training

While people are hired based on the match between their existing skills and abilities with the expectations of a particular job, the needs of any organization will change over time. Organizational change can result from technological change, fluctuations in the economy, and changing buying patterns from customers. In manufacturing, employers perceive a "skills gap" between what they need and the applicants they can quickly find (The Manufacturing Institute," n.d.). In addition, firing someone whose skills have become outdated and replacing them with someone new is expensive and takes time. A better answer is to provide employee training and development so as to enhance the skills and abilities of existing employees as times and needs change. The study of training and development is in the subfield of industrial/organizational psychology (I/O), the study of the psychology of workplace. The name refers both to the research on factory-line efficiency that started during the Industrial Revolution as well as to the more recent holistic "systems" approach to companies. I/O psychology involves personnel selection (hiring), employee performance appraisal, employee motivation, leadership, and employee training—that is, learning. Hiring employees is time-consuming, and it benefits companies if they can train and retrain employees for current needs instead of firing them and hiring others.

Employees might have to be trained on a new sets of procedures, such as changes to the law governing health care for employees, new computing procedures as companies move more of their data to the "cloud," or adapting to new software for getting their jobs done. In 2008, Starbucks shut down all of its stores for three hours to retrain every barista on how to make their drinks (Grynbaum, 2008). Second, training may be necessary simply to get employees to become more automatic at their existing skills, that is, faster at recognizing when to make some action and taking it. Finally, employees may be trained on how to better identify situations and scenarios that need intervention, a common goal of managerial training.

If it's not immediately clear what the training needs are, a company may conduct a training needs assessment, a self-study of what training needs there are. This can be at the level of employees or the entire organization, and may be conducted internally or contracted out to specialists. In I/O psychology, a common dichotomy of learning objectives are knowledge, skills, and abilities, or KSAs. So, the trainers, sometimes employed at the organization and sometimes contracted for training, will evaluate who at the company needs training (the trainees) and what kinds of KSAs the training should involve before selecting specific training techniques. The assessment will usually include information on the organization's existing training resources and where it is lacking, the tasks that need to be taught, and identifying which employees would benefit from training (Muchinsky, 2011). What follows is a summary of workplace-training techniques that differ from traditional classroom formats, following Blanchard and Thacker (2013).

Approaches to training can be divided into two general categories: traditional and computer-based. Traditional approaches include lectures and discussions, demonstrations, games and stimulations, and on-the-job training (OJT). Computer-based approaches include virtual reality simulations and "intelligent tutoring systems," among others. We'll look at the strengths and weaknesses of these as we consider them in turn.

You're probably familiar with lectures (or "direct instruction"). Lectures are direct instruction, usually by simply telling someone something they need to know. Virtually all training will include some amount of lecture. Lectures and lecture/discussions are generally best for developing knowledge around some topic; and they are techniques that use elaborative processing to try to create meaning that hopefully will be stored for the long term in the trainees' minds. The popularity of lectures is probably based on two factors: They are efficient in that they do not use up a lot of resources, and can be reproduced readily in a variety of situations and formats, whether print, oral, or online. The audience can be small or fairly large, so it's suitable to a range of environments. The lecturer retains a high level of control over the situation. By now, you've had a lot of experience with sitting through them as well.

The list of limitations of lectures is pretty long, however. Listener fatigue can set in quickly if the trainer is not engaging. There are no ways within the lecture to correct misunderstandings; and in some cases, questions can't be solicited. Trainers are encouraged to use shorter lectures intermixed with other techniques. Other problems include poor presentation skills—like talking in a monotone voice, using lots of unfamiliar jargon, and reading from prepared slides.

In today's computer-based world, employers can migrate from strictly lecture-based training to computers. Computer-based training (CBT) is the use of instruction to trainees by computer and may use a variety of multimedia in order to accomplish this. In some cases, the training can be modestly interactive, where employees will receive practice quizzes and a full evaluation that has to be passed at a certain level at the end of the training module. Many institutions deliver sexual-harassment in the workplace training this way now, since CBT permits a certain amount of privacy in tackling the sensitive nature of the topic, and the organization can keep a record of which employees have completed the training.

Lectures can include elements of discussion, which can expand the quality of the lecture. The trainer or trainees can ask questions. The questions can be more open-ended ("How might this apply to where you work in the company?") or closed-ended for review ("So what were the three steps to remember when . . . ?"). The trainer can gather audience reactions to help gain insights on what the trainees are learning, which itself acts as feedback on the lecture for the trainer. Incorporating discussion means the trainer can strive for more complex learning objectives as well. When trainees ask questions, they are having to generate ideas based on what they have learned, which helps retention. Being able to effectively ask questions in a group situation is a skill that takes time and effort to develop.

Demonstrations make use of social learning theory to teach knowledge and skills. Usually combined with lecture and discussion, demonstrations will show how something works while providing an explanation of the principles at the same time. As we saw in Chapter 5, the model has to engage the attention of the trainees, be clear and organized so the trainees can retain the information, and give the trainees the chance to produce or try out the behaviors being modeled. Finally, the trainees have to be motivated to learn what the model is demonstrating.

Lectures, discussions, and demonstrations are common in classroom and workplace learning environments, but the following techniques seem nearly entirely to occur only in the workplace environment. Simulations are the use of equipment (real or virtual) to reproduce the working environment. Simulations are often used when practice time on the actual equipment in the working environment (e.g., aircraft career, spacecraft, military combat) is highly unsafe or impractical. Usually a trainer will provide tasks that need to be accomplished on the simulator, and feedback is provided after attempts are made. A major focus with simulators is trying to recreate an environment that is as similar to the real experience as possible, so the practiced skills and abilities transfer to the real environment well. Business games are another form of simulation: Trainees will be given a set of rules and principles that may reflect research or actual operating procedures with a company and will be asked to make decisions about what to do. Feedback is given, and the trainees continue making decisions for a certain amount of time or until some result is achieved. Business games are often used in management training, with the goal of helping to develop leadership skills and to improve decision-making skills in a safe environment. These games can simulate a single department or a range of departments across a company, and they can take a few hours or a few weeks to complete.

A version of a simulation and role-play, the in-basket technique is used for both training as well as evaluating applicants for a job. Trainees are given a packet of documents, like an "in-basket," that represents what someone in a particular position—manager, engineer, supervisor—might receive on a given day. It could include reports, requests for signatures, messages about phone calls that need to be returned, documents needing to be proofed, and emails. Possibly a scenario is presented as well, to provide a focus or urgency for handling the requests. The trainee then has to process all the information, prioritize the needs, and then make decisions about how he or she would respond to the requests. Often not enough time is given to handle all of the information, so the trainee has to make decisions about what will matter most and what has to be left for later. Sometimes the trainee has to actually place phone calls to issue orders, allowing for interpersonal skill assessment; but generally the orders are written down for feedback. Often the trainee will have to explain his or her rationale to a group of evaluators after the activity. This approach is sometimes done as an evaluation for promotion.

Another variant of simulations are case studies. A case study typically involves the history of an incident or event in a related business, current employer or past, with issues faced by the organization. Key artifacts such as news articles, letters, or parts of reports might be included. Typically the better case studies are real, rather than hypothetical. Case studies can be only a few pages long or much longer. The trainee or trainees will read the case study and discuss possible options and solutions, weighing different alternatives and possible consequences. Some case studies are used to highlight processes that were successful, and others will be chosen to encourage understanding of what went into organizational failures. Relatedly, much legal training involves the use of case studies to understand the law.

For interpersonal skill development, role-play might be used. After some background is given, trainees will assume roles and attempt to resolve the scenario. This approach is often used for working on managing conflict, such as dealing with upset customers or resolving issues between supervisors and subordinates. Some role-play situations are scripted, with trainees reading off prewritten dialog that they can discuss and analyze later, and other roles are more spontaneous and impromptu.

On-the-job training (OJT) is the use of more experienced employees to train less-skilled employees. It is generally an informal process that is used as the need arises, although some formal OJT programs exist. The learning principles involved are similar to modeling, but come in a variety of forms. The job instruction technique (JIT) is a form of OJT that focuses on skill development. The trainer is first required to prepare the trainee for the task: What is necessary? Why is this task important? Then the trainer explains and demonstrates the task, and the trainee is then asked to do the job. Finally, progress checks are made later on to make sure the trainee is performing adequately.

Other OJT approaches include apprenticeship, coaching, and mentoring. Apprenticeship training, usually seen in skilled trade and professional unions such as pipe fitters and electrical workers, will require up to two years of training and classroom instruction. Coaching is one-on-one instruction and tutoring for improving KSAs. In business, coaching usually means a consultant is contracted to help high-level managers in a company improve performance. As you might have guessed, there are training programs for coaches! While supervisors may be spend up to 50 percent of their time coaching (Brown & Karagozoglu, 1993), they have not necessarily received training in how to give feedback, or they might delay on giving negative feedback. Many supervisors find themselves too busy to adequately coach and monitor for progress. Finally, mentoring is a version of coaching in which a senior employee in management will develop a continuing relationship with a junior employee to help guide the junior employee through the organizational structure. Usually mentoring is not focused on specific skills but on attitude development and an understanding of the institution's history, so that the junior employee comes to fit the organization better over time.

Learning and Aggression: Violence and Media

Violence in the media, whether in television shows, movies, or video games, is more common and more graphic than it was decades ago. With the advent of content ratings, a greater range of graphic acts could be depicted as long as an appropriate rating was placed on the product. While we may not want violence in our daily lives, we enjoy it in art and in sports. Watching conflict and a physical means to resolution is more dramatic than watching the Avengers hash out their differences over wine and cheese.

For students of psychology, this presents a quandary. It is harder to innocently enjoy popular entertainment while asking some serious questions about the effects it may be having on us. Advertising and marketing rely on classical conditioning to teach us to make associations about what to buy: Would this not apply to violent entertainment as well? Operant conditioning and social learning theory claim we can learn by vicariously watching how others are reinforced in school and at work: Would this not apply to violent entertainment as well? This is why some psychologists see the racks of video games in a store as a wall of carnage. While some store chains make a policy of not selling the most violent games directly to children (GameStop Playground—For Parents; http://www.gamestop.com/stores/playground/parents.aspx), parents can override this policy. Children can be exposed rather easily to television shows that were not made with them in mind.

This is a topic that can be controversial, since it runs into issues of what we find personally entertaining and fears of attempts to censure—so a few points are worth mentioning in advance. First, most research in this area comes from a place of concern over what kinds of long-term effects exposure to media violence can create in a special population, namely children. Children of young ages cannot always distinguish reality from fantasy, and they cannot control their environment or their impulses the way adults can. While normal, healthy adults may gain violent ideas from media, they are clearly consciously able to reason about those ideas and the harm that may come to others. Children may lack empathy or the social skills to understand the consequences of their actions. Nor can they necessarily leave a movie theater if they don't like what they are seeing, as an adult can. Second, despite the rise in media violence, some researchers claim that the evidence suggests that violence worldwide had decreased (Pinker, 2011), so it's not clear that rising media violence is co-occurring with higher levels of daily violence. Finally, we can also learn to be prosocial from watching others, so the mechanisms behind learning to be aggressive mean that unlearning can happen as well.

Experiments on Aggressive Imitation

Research on learning to be aggressive from media exposure usually examines the learning on one of two levels: likelihood to commit an aggressive act after exposure to violence, and changes in acceptance of violence after exposure. The former is a behavioral measure, whereas the later is a more cognitive measure.

In their classic studies, Bandura, Ross, and Ross (1961, 1963) had an adult interact with an inflatable Bobo doll, the kind that acts as a punching bag that stands back up once it's been hit. Children in another room watched an adult interact with the Bobo doll, either seeing the adult slapping it around and yelling at it, or seeing the adult merely talking to it. When given time to play in the same room as the doll, children who had been exposed to the aggressive adult acts would (as you probably guessed) imitate the aggressive acts, and devise new ways of beating up on the doll. Children who had not been exposed to the aggressive behavior exhibited almost no aggressive behaviors toward the doll. (Bandura's Bobo doll now tours the country at psychology conferences; see Bandura and Bobo, n.d.).

Researchers have used experimental techniques for a few decades to try to evaluate to what extent exposure to violent media increases aggressive acts. For example, Liebert and Baron (1972) had one group of children watch a violent police drama and another, the control group, watch an exciting sport game (that was nonviolent). Each group of children was then allowed to play in another room with a different group of children while observers looked for aggressive acts. As Bandura might have expected, those who watched the violent police drama were more aggressive than those who watched the sporting event. In general, research has found that thoughts, behaviors, and emotions become more aggressive when exposed to violence, but the research has not always found an effect, and sometimes the effect is small (Aronson, Wilson, & Akert, 2012). Carnagey & Anderson (2005) found a notable exception: video games that reward the player for killing. Games that give points or access to new levels for aggressive acts seem to directly increase aggressive feelings, thoughts and actions. Anderson and Huesmann

(2003) found that increased hostility is the result of increased physiological arousal, an automatic desire to imitate, and unconscious priming of aggressive impulses.

Numbing Effect

While an increased likelihood to commit aggressive acts after media exposure is a concern, subtler effects are also. Research has found that repeated exposure to televised violence appears to have a numbing effect: we become desensitized to the events. An older study found physiological responses by viewers of a particularly bloody boxing match varied by the amount of television watching each viewer reported (Cline, Croft, & Courier, 1973). Viewers who watched a lot of television had little physiological arousal and showed no additional excitement, but viewers who watched less TV showed major arousal. Prior exposure to media violence tends to numb us to violence. Imagine what this kind of numbing could do to, say, jurors who are heavy television watchers sitting on a domestic violence case.

But does the numbing from watching televised violence extend to real-life situations? Participants in the study by Thomas, Horton, Lippincott, and Drabman (1977) watched either a violent police drama or an exciting but nonviolent sporting event (as a control). Later, participants observed a fight between preschoolers. As you might have guessed, those participants who had watched the police drama responded less emotionally to the preschoolers fighting than did the control group. This could have real consequences for having empathy for victims of violence. In one study, violent video game players were more likely to dehumanize immigrants in contrast to players of other kinds of games (Greitemeyer & McLatchie, 2011).

Some Perspective

So what does this mean? So much of modern entertainment (and news) contains violence, yet it is not clear that people are more violent. In fact, violence seems to be down worldwide. While exposure to violence is clearly a problem for young children who may not be able to separate reality from fantasy, it's not completely clear that violence in the media creates violent adults. In fact, social learning theory would claim it is something of a two-way street: "Reciprocal determinism" (Chapter 5) claims that those individuals with violent tendencies will usually seek out violent entertainment, and that the entertainment does not necessarily create violent individuals. The numbing effect, however, could be a greater cause for social concern, as judges and jurors could be swayed toward leniency for actions that are harmful toward victims but seen as "not that big a deal." To what extent can being cognizant and aware of the numbing effect ameliorate dismissive attitudes toward victims? Perhaps, one day, that research will be done.

Memory and the Law: Eyewitness Memory

The testimony of eyewitnesses is a common form of evidence presented at trials. However, its use has been called into question since memory researchers began researching its accuracy in the 1980s and 1990s (Rattner, 1988; Wells, 1993). Earlier in the twentieth century, psychologists had expressed concerns about the reliability of eyewitness testimony (Munsterberg, 1908/1925). With the advent of DNA testing and investigations by the Innocence Project (http://www.innocenceproject.org), eyewitness testimony could be evaluated on the basis of biological evidence. Eyewitness testimony was the main form of evidence in 70 percent of the cases that have been overturned on the basis of biological testing.

The issue of accurately identifying a defendant can be viewed through the lens of *signal detection theory.* The goal of the court is to determine whether a particular person perpetrated a crime. The person either did or did not; the evidence from eyewitnesses will either agree or not agree. Can the correct situation be detected? This creates a set of four possible situations. First, the reality could be that the defendant did commit the crime, and the eyewitnesses testify to that—both match. Second, the person did not commit the crime, and the eyewitnesses do not identify the defendant. Both of these situations—when the testimony matches with reality—are not a major concern, since the identification system is working correctly. According to signal detection theory, correctly detecting the suspect is considered to be a hit; and correctly ruling out the defendant is a correct reject, another kind of hit. The other two situations are the problem: The reality is that the defendant did commit the crime but cannot be accurately identified, so the person goes free; or (perhaps worse), the defendant did not commit the crime but is incorrectly identified, and he or she will spend years incarcerated or put on death row. This last situation, when someone is incorrectly identified, is known as a *false alarm* in signal detection theory. The concern over false alarms has sparked a tremendous amount of research.

The amount of research available from the past few decades is more than can be included in a chapter, so this section will cover only some the major known variables that affect the accuracy of eyewitness memory. All of these variables are known as "estimator variables," meaning that these are variables of human memory that the police and court system cannot control (Wells, 1978). A second set of variables, called "system variables," are those variables that are controlled by the legal system, such as the line-up instructions given to eyewitnesses, whether the attending police do not know if the possible suspect is in a line-up, and whether feedback is given to the eyewitness after an identification. Research on system variables works to improve the quality of police procedures in order to minimize those uncontrollable problems with memory. If you are interested in the state of research on better police methods, I suggest Neuschatz and Cutler (2008) as a good place to start.

While DNA testing suggests that not all eyewitnesses are perfectly accurate, just how accurate are they? Is there a way to tell, empirically? Some jurors are encouraged to take the confidence of eyewitnesses into account when evaluating their claims (*Neil v. Biggers,* 1972). In experiments, participants will usually watch a videotaped, scripted crime and be asked to identify a suspect from a line-up. This approach allows researchers to get an approximate value for the level of agreement between eyewitness confidence and accuracy. In a meta-analysis, a merging of a range of similar types of studies, Sporer and colleagues (1995) combined data from thirty studies and over 4,000 witnesses to produce an average correlation of 0.29 between confidence and accuracy, which is awfully modest on a scale of from 0 to 1. If the eyewitness were believed to have recognized the suspect, the correlation was 0.41; but if not, then it was lower at 0.12.

The situation of a crime can be remarkably different from one that is conducive to learning and remembering. Unlike, say a normal classroom environment, the crime is likely to be unexpected, not take very long, and the suspect can use a disguise. None of this is well-suited for memorizing details of the situation. Additionally, there can be added stress because of a potential for violence. Let's look at each of these variables in term.

As you might expect, longer *exposure time* of a suspect leads to better memory and identification of a suspect (Ellis, Shepherd, & Davies, 1979; Shapiro & Penrod, 1986).

In a meta-analysis that included 128 studies, Shapiro and Penrod (1986) tracked the amount of exposure time different studies used as well as the effect size of improved memory. They found longer exposures improved correct recognition of a suspect by 12 percent, while lowering the rate of false alarms by 4 percent. However, most of these studies assume no change in the suspect's appearance.

Do changes in a suspect's appearance affect correct identification? In general, yes, in a manner that the encoding specificity principle would suggest. In a series of studies, participants watched videotaped crimes when the suspect wore a baseball cap or the suspect's head was uncovered (Cutler, Penrod, & Martens, 1987a, 1987b). Correct recognition was higher when the head was uncovered, in each study. The average improvement over all of the studies was 13 percent (Cutler, 2006). Simple changes such as removal of facial hair between exposure and test can impair recognition (Read, Hammerslex, Cross-Culvert & McFaden, 1989). Aging also degrades recognition performance. Read, Vokey, and Hummersley (1990) had participants look at high school yearbook photos of students in Grades 10 and 12 and try to match them up. Successful matches were highest for photos that were the most similar at 54.5 percent correct and lowest when aging had changed the individual more, at 32.6 percent correct.

We appear to be better at recognizing strangers who look similar to ourselves. As people became exonerated using DNA testing, a pattern emerged. Often a white eyewitness had inaccurately identified a black suspect (Meissner & Brigham, 2001). Named own-race bias, research has confirmed that people are better at recognizing others who are from their own race than others (called cross-race identifications). The typical research paradigm that is used to evaluate the own-race bias is to show participants photographs of the faces of a variety of people and then, after a delay, show them some of the same face photos mixed in with brand new, previously-unseen face photos. Correctly identifying a face from one's own race is about 40 percent higher than a face from another race (Meissner & Brigham, 2001). Conversely, incorrectly identifying someone from another race was 60 percent higher than one's own. Similarly, people have been found to show biases toward recognizing people of similar ages (own-age bias; Anastasi & Rhodes, 2006; Wright & Stroud, 2002) and the same gender (own-gender bias; Wright & Sladden, 2003). Why these biases exist is not completely clear. It could be that people tend to become experts at recognizing their own race (and age, and gender), or that people pay more attention to others of their own race, or that the identification of an individual's race is somehow a feature that determines what other facial features are "salient," or noticeable (Wright & Loftus, 2008).

The presence of a weapon appears to distract eyewitnesses from paying attention to the suspect, an effect called weapon focus (Loftus, Loftus, & Messo, 1987). If someone appears to have a weapon, the weapon exists as a kind of competition to the face of the suspect for the observer's attention. The first experiment of its kind had participants waiting in a room participate in an experiment (Johnson & Scott, 1976). While they waited, half of the participants overheard a conversation with the receptionist and someone else about an equipment problem. Then a "suspect" entered the room holding a pen, said a line, and left. In another condition, they overheard an argument, heard a crash, then saw the "suspect" enter the room with a bloody letter opener, say a line, and leave. Participants in the "no weapon" condition were more likely to identify the suspect in a photo array (49 percent) than participants in the "weapon" condition (33 percent). While dramatic, too many variables were altered between the two conditions for this study to represent a convincing test of weapon focus (Loftus, 1979). Even the line the suspect said differed in each condition.

A more convincing test of the weapon focus concept was done by Loftus et al. (1987). Loftus and her colleagues tracked the eye movements of participants as they looked at images of a person approaching a store counter with either a check or a weapon. People looked at the weapon longer and more often than the check, and they also remembered less of the person's image when a weapon was present.

It does not appear to be the presence of a weapon that draws focus necessarily; it appears to be the extent to which the object is unusual. Pickel (1998, 1999) showed that a weapon elicited a weapon focus effect when carried by a preacher, but not a police officer. Presumably, the more unusual the context for the weapon is what determines a change in attentional processing, not whether a weapon is present.

Our final topic for this section is whether experiencing stress helps with memory formation or not. Observing or being the victim of a crime can be highly stressful, and it's a long-standing assumption within the legal community that with the additional stress comes a greater focus and memory of the event. It's possible that the emotional duress gives an added emotional boost to the memory (Schmechel, O'Toole, Easterly, & Loftus), but not everyone agrees. Like the weapon focus effect, it could be that additional stress is a distraction or a sign of mental processing (e.g., for safety) that is not conducive to forming a detailed memory of the event.

As you might guess, researchers cannot ethically put people into life-threatening situations (or even the appearance of them) in order to study the relationship between stress and memory. So, researchers have had to be creative. Often researchers will use violent and scary movie clips versus exciting sports games, or have participants plunge one arm into a bucket of ice during a learning trial in order to simulate the physiological effects of shock.

One option is to interview witnesses to an actual crime. Yuille and Cutshall (1986) interviewed observers of a murder and were able to match up the accuracy of what they remembered several months after the murder to their police statements at the time of the shooting. Usually researchers are not able to get hold of police statements like this; but the criminal had attempted to rob a gun shop during the day, and the store owner had killed the robber in the street. Because the identity of the perpetrator was clear and the person was no longer alive, the police considered the case closed and the researchers were able to request their materials. In this case, they found that the observers who were closer to the gunfire gave more details and were more accurate, indicating that the additional stress was not a problem for the formation of a memory.

In another creative approach, Morgan et al. (2004) asked active-duty military personnel who had been interrogated in military survival school to try to identify their interrogators from photo line-ups. The interrogations required some personnel to be interrogated in a high-stress fashion with actual physical confrontation, or in a low-stress fashion without any physical confrontation. In contrast to Yuille and Cutshall's (1986) general finding, the military personnel who had experienced low-stress interrogation were much more likely to be able to identify their interrogators than personnel who had experienced high-stress interrogations (62 percent to 27 percent). A meta-analysis of stress and memory studies (Deffenbacher, Bornstein, Penrod, & McGorty, 2004) found this to be generally true: Stress usually inhibits both accuracy in identification and accuracy in details.

Is there a way to consolidate findings from studies like Yuille and Cutshall's (1986) that find stress aids memory and others that do not? Possibly. The relationship between stress and memory is not a linear one, meaning that more stress doesn't have the same effect on memory. Instead, it depends on how much stress. Some amount of stress, for example, for the people in Yuille and Cutshall's study who observed the shooting and were in some danger but were not the target of the gunfire, the aroused state helped form a strong memory. However, under high levels of stress, such as being the focus of a physically intense interrogation, the stress has a negative impact on the formation of an accurate memory. Deffenbacher et al. (2004) believe that the relationship between stress and memory is similar to the Yerkes-Dodson law (Yerkes & Dodson, 1908). The relationship has an inverted-U function, meaning that low levels of stress may help memory; but after a peak, the stress begins to worsen memory. Possibly, under high periods of stress, much mental processing is devoted to surviving the event itself, rather than to studying the details of the event (Christianson, 1992).

CHAPTER SUMMARY

Humans are constantly learning and storing information for later use. As you have seen, we appear to absorb information from a number of different "modalities," whether by pure associations, or through consequences, observation, and knowledge building. The information may be stored in a multitude of different systems (episodic or semantic, implicit, autobiographical) that we then hopefully retrieve at the right time. In this chapter, we saw examples of the wide range of environments where issues of learning and memory are brought to bear: forming attitudes of products and stores, managing schoolchildren, training employees and managers, being exposed to violence, and being witnesses in the courtroom. Altogether, human learning can be seen as a multifaceted, complex activity to build the base of knowledge that we carry with us to adapt to the events in our daily lives.

REVIEW QUESTIONS

1. What is consumer research?

2. What are the learning principles that consumer researchers believe underlie successful advertising, creating a positive perception of products, and an inviting store atmosphere?

3. If a teacher asked an operant conditioning behaviorist about how he or she should improve his or her classroom management, what advice would the behaviorist be likely to give?

4. What does memory research have to say about exposure to violence in the media and possible ties to aggression?

5. The strengths and limitations of our memory system become clear in situations in which someone is asked to testify about what he or she witnessed. What does memory research find about recall of events that involved a crime, could be stressful, and may involve a weapon?

KEY TERMS

Apprenticeship training 321
Attention 313
Attitudes 306
Bottom-up 313
Business games 320

Case studies 320
Central route 308
Classical conditioning theory 307
Classically conditioning 308
Closed-ended 319

Coaching 321
Computer-based training 319
Consumer psychologists 306
Consumer research 306
Correct reject 324

FURTHER RESOURCES

1. Video: Pepsi Bears BerryChains. (2008). Pepsi Bear commercial:

   o https://www.youtube.com/watch?v=DR_vdikpKZA

2. Video: Bandura's Bobo Doll studies:

   o https://www.youtube.com/watch?v=hHHdovKHDNU

3. Weblink: Bandura's Bobo Doll on display:

   o https://www.psychologicalscience.org/publications/observer/obsonline/bandura-and-bobo.html#.WOJY4061tcw

4. Despite the headlines, Steven Pinker says the world is becoming less violent:

   o http://www.npr.org/2016/07/16/486311030/despite-the-headlines-steven-pinker-says-the-world-is-becoming-less-violent

REFERENCES

Aaker, D. A., Stayman, D. M., & Hagerty, M. R. (1986). Warmth in advertising: Measurement, impact, and sequence effect. *Journal of Consumer Research, 12* (March), 365–381.

Allan, D. (2006). Effects of popular music in advertising on attention and memory. *Journal of Advertising Research, 46*(4), 434–444. https://doi.org/10.2501/S0021849906060491

Alpert, M. I., Alpert, J. I., & Maltz, E. N. (2005). Purchase occasion influence on the role of music in advertising. *Journal of Business Research, 58*(3), 369–376.

Anastasi, J. S., & Rhodes, M. G. (2006). Evidence for an own-age bias in face recognition. *North American Journal of Psychology, 8*(2). Retrieved from https://sites.google.com/site/rhodesmemorylab/Anastasi%20%26%20Rhodes%20(2006)-NJAP.pdf

Anderson, C. A., & Huesmann, L. R. (2003). Human aggression: A social-cognitive view. *Handbook of social psychology*, 296–323.

Argyriou, E., & Melewar, T. C. (2011). Consumer attitudes revisited: A review of attitude theory in marketing research. *International Journal of Management Reviews, 13*(4), 431–451. https://doi.org/10.1111/j.1468–2370.2011.00299.x

Aronson, E., Wilson, T. D., & Akert, R. M. (2012). *Social psychology* (8th ed.). Boston, MA: Pearson.

Bandura, A., Ross, D., & Ross, S. A. (1961). Transmission of aggression through imitation of aggressive models. *Journal of Abnormal and Social Psychology, 63*(3), 575–582.

Bandura, A., Ross, D., & Ross, S. A. (1963). Imitation of film-mediated aggressive models. *The Journal of Abnormal and Social Psychology, 66*(1), 3–11. https://doi.org/10.1037/h0048687

Bandura and Bobo. (n.d.). Retrieved December 7, 2016, from https://www.psychologicalscience.org/publications/observer/obsonline/bandura-and-bobo.html

Batra, R., & Ray, M. L. (1986a). Affective responses mediating acceptance of advertising. *Journal of Consumer Research, 13*(2), 234–249.

Batra, R., & Ray, M. L. (1986b). Situational effects of advertising repetition: The moderating influence of motivation, ability, and opportunity to respond. *Journal of Consumer Research, 12*(4), 432–445.

Baumrind, D. (1991). The influence of parenting style on adolescent competence and substance use. *The Journal of Early Adolescence, 11*(1), 56–95.

BerryChains. (2008). *Pepsi Bear commercial.* Retrieved from https://www.youtube.com/watch?v=DR_vdikpKZAand feature=youtu.be

Blanchard, P. N., & Thacker, J. W. (2013). Effective Training: Systems. *Strategies, And Practices* (5th Edition) New Jersey: Pearson Prentice Hall.

Brown, W. B., & Karagozoglu, N. (1993). Leading the way to faster new product development. *The Academy of Management Executive, 7*(1), 36–47.

Bruner, G. C., II (1990). Music, mood, and marketing. *Journal of Marketing, 54*(4), 94–104.

Carnagey, N. L., & Anderson, C. A. (2005). The effects of reward and punishment in violent video games on aggressive affect, cognition, and behavior. *Psychological Science, 16*(11), 882–889. https://doi.org/10.1111/j.1467-9280.2005.01632.x

Childers, T. L., Heckler, S. E., & Houston, M. J. (1986). Memory for the visual and verbal components of print advertisements. *Psychology and Marketing, 3*(3), 137–149.

Christianson, S.-A. (1992). Emotional stress and eyewitness memory: A critical review. *Psychological Bulletin, 112,* 284–309.

Cline, V. B., Croft, R. G., & Courrier, S. (1973). Desensitization of children to television violence. *Journal of Personality and Social Psychology, 27*(3), 360.

Cutler, B. L. (2006). A sample of witness, crime, and perpetrator characteristics affecting eyewitness identification accuracy. *Cardozo Public Law, Policy & Ethics Journal, 4,* 327.

Cutler, B. L., Penrod, S. D., & Martens, T. K. (1987a). Improving the reliability of eyewitness identification: Putting context into context. *Journal of Applied Psychology, 72*(4), 629.

Cutler, B. L., Penrod, S. D., & Martens, T. K. (1987b). The reliability of eyewitness identification: The role of system and estimator variables. *Law and Human Behavior, 11*(3), 233.

De Houwer, J., Thomas, S., & Baeyens, F. (2001). Associative learning of likes and dislikes. *Psychological Bulletin, 127*(6), 853–869. https://doi.org/10.1037//0033-2909.127.6.853

Debevec, K., & Romeo, J. B. (1992). Self-referent processing in perceptions of verbal and visual commercial information. *Journal of Consumer Psychology, 1*(1), 83–102.

Deffenbacher, K. A., Bornstein, B. H., Penrod, S. D., & McGorty, E. K. (2004). *A meta-analytic review of the effects of high stress on eyewitness memory.* Springer. Retrieved from http://psycnet.apa.org/journals/lhb/28/6/687/

Despite the headlines, Steven Pinker says the world is becoming less violent. (n.d.). Retrieved December 7, 2016, from http://www.npr.org/2016/07/16/486311030/despite-the-headlines-steven-pinker-says-the-world-is-becoming-less-violent

Ding, C. G., & Lin, C.-H. (2012). How does background music tempo work for online shopping. *Electronic Commerce Research and Applications, 11*(3), 299–307.

Ellis, H. D., Shepherd, J. W., & Davies, G. M. (1979). Identification of familiar and unfamiliar faces from internal and external features: Some implications for theories of face recognition. *Perception, 8*(4), 431–439.

Ferreira, D. C. S., & Oliveira-Castro, J. M. (2011). Effects of background music on consumer behaviour: Behavioural account of the consumer setting. *Service Industries Journal, 31*(15), 2571–2585. https://doi.org/10.1080/0264206 9.2011.531125

GameStop Playground—For Parents. (n.d.). Retrieved December 7, 2016, from http://www.gamestop.com/stores/playground/parents.aspx

Gardner, M. P. (1985). Mood states and consumer behavior: A critical review. *Journal of Consumer Research, 12*(3), 281–300.

Gawronski, B., & Bodenhausen, G. V. (2006). Associative and propositional processes in evaluation: An integrative review of implicit and explicit attitude change. *Psychological Bulletin, 132*(5), 692.

Gibson, B. (2008). Can evaluative conditioning change attitudes toward mature brands? New evidence from the Implicit Association Test. *Journal of Consumer Research, 35*(1), 178–188.

Goldsmith, R. E., Lafferty, B. A., & Newell, S. J. (2000). The impact of corporate credibility and celebrity credibility on consumer reaction to advertisements and brands. *Journal of Advertising, 29*(3), 43–54.

Gorn, G. J. (1982). The effects of music in advertising on choice behavior: A classical conditioning approach. *The Journal of Marketing*, 94–101.

Greitemeyer, T., & McLatchie, N. (2011). Denying humanness to others: A newly discovered mechanism by which violent video games increase aggressive behavior. *Psychological Science, 22*(5), 659–665.

Gresham, L. G., & Shimp, T. A. (1985). Attitude toward the advertisement and brand attitudes: A classical conditioning perspective. *Journal of Advertising, 14*(1), 10–49.

Grossman, R. P., & Till, B. D. (1998). The persistence of classically conditioned brand attitudes. *Journal of Advertising, 27*(1), 23–31.

Grynbaum, M. M. (2008, February 27). Starbucks takes a 3-hour coffee break. *The New York Times*. Retrieved from http://www.nytimes.com/2008/02/27/business/27sbux.html

Guido, G., Peluso, A. M., Mileti, A., Capestro, M., Cambò, L., & Pisanello, P. (2016). Effects of background music endings on consumer memory in advertising. *International Journal of Advertising, 35*(3), 504–518.

Hagtvedt, H., & Patrick, V. M. (2008). Art infusion: The influence of visual art on the perception and evaluation of consumer products. *Journal of Marketing Research (JMR), 45*(3), 379–389. https://doi.org/10.1509/jmkr.45.3.379

Hasford, J., Hardesty, D. M., & Kidwell, B. (2015). More than a feeling: Emotional contagion effects in persuasive communication. *Journal of Marketing Research, 52*(6), 836–847.

Hofmann, W., De Houwer, J., Perugini, M., Baeyens, F., & Crombez, G. (2010). Evaluative conditioning in humans. *Psychological Bulletin, 136*(3), 390–421. https://doi.org/10.1037/a0018916

Holbrook, M. B., & Batra, R. (1987). Assessing the role of emotions as mediators of consumer responses to advertising. *Journal of Consumer Research, 14*(3), 404–420.

Johnson, C., & Scott, B. (1976, September). *Eyewitness testimony and suspect identification as a function of arousal, sex of witness, and scheduling of interrogation.* Presented at the meeting of the American Psychological Association, Washington, DC.

Kämpfe, J., Sedlmeier, P., & Renkewitz, F. (2010). The impact of background music on adult listeners: A meta-analysis. *Psychology of Music*, 0305735610376261.

Kellaris, J. J., & Cox, A. D. (1989). The effects of background music in advertising: A reassessment. *Journal of Consumer Research, 16*(1), 113–118.

Kellaris, J. J., Cox, A. D., & Cox, D. (1993). The effect of background music on ad processing: A contingency explanation. *The Journal of Marketing*, 114–125.

Kellaris, J. J., & Kent, R. J. (1993). An exploratory investigation of responses elicited by music varying in tempo, tonality, and texture. *Journal of Consumer Psychology, 2*(4), 381.

Kim, J., Lim, J.-S., & Bhargava, M. (1998). The role of affect in attitude formation: A classical conditioning approach. *Journal of the Academy of Marketing Science, 26*(2), 143–152.

Kim, Y. J., & Han, J. (2014). Why smartphone advertising attracts customers: A model of Web advertising, flow, and personalization. *Computers in Human Behavior, 33*, 256–269. https://doi.org/10.1016/j.chb.2014.01.015

Lavack, A. M., Thakor, M. V., & Bottausci, I. (2008). Music-brand congruency in high- and low-cognition radio advertising. *International Journal of Advertising, 27*(4), 549–568.

Liebert, R. M., & Baron, R. A. (1972). Some immediate effects of televised violence on children's behavior. *Developmental Psychology, 6*(3), 469.

Loftus, E. F. (1979). *Eyewitness testimony.* Cambridge, MA: Harvard University Press.

Loftus, E. F., Loftus, G. R., & Messo, J. (1987). Some facts about "weapon focus." *Law and Human Behavior, 11*(1), 55.

Machleit, K. A., & Wilson, R. D. (1988). Emotional feelings and attitude toward the advertisement: The roles of brand familiarity and repetition. *Journal of Advertising, 17*(3), 27–35.

Madden, T. J., Allen, C. T., & Twible, J. L. (1988). Attitude toward the ad: An assessment of diverse measurement indices under different processing "sets." *Journal of Marketing Research, 25*(3), 242–252.

Maison, D., Greenwald, A. G., & Bruin, R. H. (2004). Predictive validity of the Implicit Association Test in studies of brands, consumer attitudes, and behavior. *Journal of Consumer Psychology, 14*(4), 405–415.

The Manufacturing Institute. (n.d.). *Skills gap in manufacturing.* Retrieved from http://www.themanufacturinginstitute.org/Research/Skills-Gap-in-Manufacturing/Skills-Gap-in-Manufacturing.aspx

Meissner, C. A., & Brigham, J. C. (2001). *Thirty years of investigating the own-race bias in memory for faces: A meta-analytic review.* American Psychological Association. Retrieved from http://psycnet.apa.org/journals/law/7/1/3/

Miller, F. M., & Allen, C. T. (2012). How does celebrity meaning transfer? Investigating the process of meaning transfer with celebrity affiliates and mature brands. *Journal of Consumer Psychology, 22*(3), 443–452. https://doi.org/10.1016/j.jcps.2011.11.001

Mitchell, A. A. (1986). The effect of verbal and visual components of advertisements on brand attitudes and attitude toward the advertisement. *Journal of Consumer Research, 13*(1), 12–24.

Morin, S., Dubé, L., & Chebat, J.-C. (2007). The role of pleasant music in servicescapes: A test of the dual model of environmental perception. *Journal of Retailing, 83*(1), 115–130.

Morgan, C. A., Hazlett, G., Doran, A., Garrett, S., Hoyt, G., Thomas, P., . . . & Southwick, S. M. (2004). Accuracy of eyewitness memory for persons encountered during exposure to highly intense stress. *International Journal of Law and Psychiatry, 27*(3), 265–279.

Morrison, M., Gan, S., Dubelaar, C., & Oppewal, H. (2011). In-store music and aroma influences on shopper behavior and satisfaction. *Journal of Business Research, 64*(6), 558–564. https://doi.org/10.1016/j.jbusres.2010.06.006

Muchinsky, P. M. (2011). *Psychology applied to work* (10th ed.). Summerfield, NC: Hypergraphic Press.

Muehling, D. D. (1987). An investigation of factors underlying attitude-toward-advertising-in-general. *Journal of Advertising, 16*(1), 32–40.

Munsterberg, H. (1925). *On the witness stand: Essays on psychology and crime.* New York, NY: Doubleday, Page. (Original work published 1908)

Neil v. Biggers, 409 U.S. 188 (1972).

Neuschatz, J. S., & Cutler, B. L. (2008). Eyewitness identification. *Learning and memory: A comprehensive reference.* Hillsdale, NJ: Erlbaum.

North, A. C., Mackenzie, L. C., Law, R. M., & Hargreaves, D. J. (2004). The effects of musical and voice "fit" on responses to advertisements. *Journal of Applied Social Psychology, 34*(8), 1675–1708.

Oakes, S., & North, A. C. (2006). The impact of background musical tempo and timbre congruity upon ad content recall and affective response. *Applied Cognitive Psychology, 20*(4), 505–520. https://doi.org/10.1002/acp.1199

Olson, M. A., & Fazio, R. H. (2007). Implicit attitude formation in classical conditioning. *Psychological Science, 12(5)*, 413–417.

Ormrod, J. (2011). *Educational psychology : Developing learners* (7th ed.). Boston, MA: Pearson/Allyn & Bacon.

Petty, R. E., & Cacioppo, J. T. (1986). The elaboration likelihood model of persuasion. In *Communication and persuasion* (pp. 1–24). New York, NY: Springer. Retrieved from http://link.springer.com/chapter/10.1007/978-1-4612-4964-1_1

Pham, M. T. (2004). The logic of feeling. *Journal of Consumer Psychology, 14*(4). Retrieved from http://papers.ssrn.com/s013/papers.cfm?abstract_id=508083

Pham, M. T., Geuens, M., & De Pelsmacker, P. (2013). The influence of ad-evoked feelings on brand evaluations: Empirical generalizations from consumer responses to more than 1000 TV commercials. *International Journal of Research in Marketing, 30*(4), 383–394.

Pickel, K. L. (1998). Unusualness and threat as possible causes of" weapon focus." *Memory, 6*(3), 277–295.

Pickel, K. L. (1999). The influence of context on the "weapon focus" effect. *Law and Human Behavior, 23*(3), 299.

Pine, A., Mendelsohn, A., & Dudai, Y. (2014). Unconscious learning of likes and dislikes is persistent, resilient, and reconsolidates. *Frontiers in Psychology, 5.* https://doi.org/10.3389/fpsyg.2014.01051

Pinker, S. (2011). The better angels of our nature: Why violence has declined. New York, NY: Viking.

Piqueras-Fiszman, B., Alcaide, J., Roura, E., & Spence, C. (2012). Is it the plate or is it the food? Assessing the influence of the color (black or white) and shape of the plate on the perception of the food placed on it. *Food Quality and Preference, 24*(1), 205–208. https://doi.org/10.1016/j.foodqual.2011.08.011

Piqueras-Fiszman, B., Harrar, V., Alcaide, J., and Spence, C. (2011). Does the weight of the dish influence our perception of food? *Food Quality and Preference, 22*(8), 753–756. https://doi.org/10.1016/j.foodqual.2011.05.009

Piqueras-Fiszman, B., & Spence, C. (2012). The influence of the color of the cup on consumers' perception of a hot beverage. *Journal of Sensory Studies, 27*(5), 324–331.

Rattner, A. (1988). Convicted but innocent: Wrongful conviction and the criminal justice system. *Law and Human Behavior, 12*(3), 283.

Read, J. D., Hammersley, R., Cross-Calvert, S., & McFadzen, E. (1989). Rehearsal of faces and details in action events. *Applied Cognitive Psychology, 3*(4), 295–311.

Read, J. D., Vokey, J. R., & Hammersley, R. (1990). Changing photos of faces: Effects of exposure duration and photo similarity on recognition and the accuracy-confidence relationship. *Journal of Experimental Psychology: Learning, Memory, and Cognition, 16*(5), 870.

Redondo, I. (2012). The effectiveness of casual advergames on adolescents' brand attitudes. *European Journal of Marketing, 46*(11–12), 1671–1688. https://doi.org/10.1108/03090561211260031

Schmechel, R. S., O'Toole, T. P., Easterly, C., & Loftus, E. F. (2006). Beyond the ken? Testing jurors' understanding of eyewitness reliability evidence. *Jurimetrics,* 177–214.

Scott, L. M. (1990). Understanding Jingles and Needledrop: A rhetorical approach to music in advertising. *Journal of Consumer Research, 17*(2), 223–236.

Shankar, M. U., Levitan, C. A., Prescott, J., & Spence, C. (2009). The influence of color and label information on flavor perception. *Chemosensory Perception, 2*(2), 53–58. https://doi.org/10.1007/s12078-009-9046-4

Shankar, M. U., Levitan, C. A., & Spence, C. (2010). Grape expectations: The role of cognitive influences in color–flavor interactions. *Consciousness and Cognition, 19*(1), 380–390. https://doi.org/10.1016/j.concog.2009.08.008

Shapiro, P. N., & Penrod, S. (1986). Meta-analysis of facial identification studies. *Psychological Bulletin, 100*(2), 139.

Sierra, J. J., Taute, H. A., & Heiser, R. S. (2012). Explaining NFL fans' purchase intentions for revered and reviled teams: A dual-process perspective. *Journal of Retailing and Consumer Services, 19*(3), 332–342. https://doi.org/10.1016/j.jretconser.2012.03.007

Spangenberg, E. R., Crowley, A. E., & Henderson, P. W. (1996). Improving the store environment: Do olfactory cues affect evaluations and behaviors? *The Journal of Marketing,* 67–80.

Spence, C., Levitan, C. A., Shankar, M. U., & Zampini, M. (2010). Does food color influence taste and flavor perception in humans? *Chemosensory Perception, 3*(1), 68–84. https://doi.org/10.1007/s12078-010-9067-z

Spence, C., Puccinelli, N. M., Grewal, D., & Roggeveen, A. L. (2014). Store atmospherics: A multisensory perspective. *Psychology and Marketing, 31*(7), 472–488. https://doi.org/10.1002/mar.20709

Spence, C., & Shankar, M. U. (2010). The influence of auditory cues on the perception of, and responses to, food and drink. *Journal of Sensory Studies, 25*(3), 406–430.

Sporer, S. L., Penrod, S., Read, D., & Cutler, B. (1995). Choosing, confidence, and accuracy: A meta-analysis of the confidence-accuracy relation in eyewitness identification studies. *Psychological Bulletin, 118*(3), 315.

Strick, M., van Baaren, R. B., Holland, R. W., & van Knippenberg, A. (2009). Humor in advertisements enhances product liking by mere association. *Journal of Experimental Psychology: Applied, 15*(1), 35–45. https://doi.org/10.1037/a0014812

Stuart, E. W., Shimp, T. A., & Engle, R. W. (1987). Classical conditioning of consumer attitudes: Four experiments in an advertising context. *Journal of Consumer Research, 14*(3), 334–349.

Taute, H. A., McQuitty, S., & Sautter, E. P. (2011). Emotional information management and responses to emotional appeals. *Journal of Advertising, 40*(3), 31–44.

Till, B. D., Stanley, S. M., & Priluck, R. (2008). Classical conditioning and celebrity endorsers: An examination of belongingness and resistance to extinction. *Psychology and Marketing, 25*(2), 179–196. https://doi.org/10.1002/mar.20205

Thomas, M. H., Horton, R. W., Lippincott, E. C., & Drabman, R. S. (1977). Desensitization to portrayals of real-life aggression as a function of television violence. *Journal of Personality and Social Psychology, 35*(6), 450.

Van der Veen, R., & Song, H. (2014). Impact of the perceived image of celebrity endorsers on tourists' intentions to visit. *Journal of Travel Research, 53*(2), 211–224.

Wells, G. L. (1978). Applied eyewitness-testimony research: System variables and estimator variables. *Journal of Personality and Social Psychology, 36*(12), 1546–1557.

Wells, G. L. (1993). What do we know about eyewitness identification? *American Psychologist, 48*(5), 553.

Wilson, R. T., & Till, B. D. (2011). Effects of outdoor advertising: Does location matter? *Psychology and Marketing, 28*(9), 909–933.

Wintle, R. R. (1978). *Emotional impact of music on television commercials.* Retrieved from http://digitalcommons.unl.edu/dissertations/AAI7901953/

Wright, D. B., & Loftus, E. F. (2008). Eyewitness memory. *Memory in the real world,* 91-105.

Wright, D. B., & Sladden, B. (2003). An own gender bias and the importance of hair in face recognition. *Acta psychologica, 114*(1), 101-114.

Wright, D. B., & Stroud, J. N. (2002). Age differences in lineup identification accuracy: People are better with their own age. *Law and Human Behavior, 26*(6), 641.

Yalch, R., & Spangenberg, E. (1990). Effects of store music on shopping behavior. *Journal of Consumer Marketing, 7*(2), 55–63.

Yalch, R. F., & Spangenberg, E. R. (2000). The effects of music in a retail setting on real and perceived shopping times. *Journal of business Research, 49*(2), 139–147.

Yeoh, J. P. S., & North, A. C. (2010). The effect of musical fit on consumers' memory. *Psychology of Music, 38*(3), 368–378. https://doi.org/10.1177/0305735609360262

Yerkes, R. M., & Dodson, J. D. (1908). The relation of strength of stimulus to rapidity of habit-formation. *Journal of Comparative Neurology, 18*(5), 459-482.

Yuille, J. C., & Cutshall, J. L. (1986). A case study of eyewitness memory of a crime. *Journal of Applied Psychology, 71*(2), 291.

Zampini, M., & Spence, C. (2004). The role of auditory cues in modulating the perceived crispness and staleness of potato chips. *Journal of Sensory Studies, 19*(5), 347–363.

Index